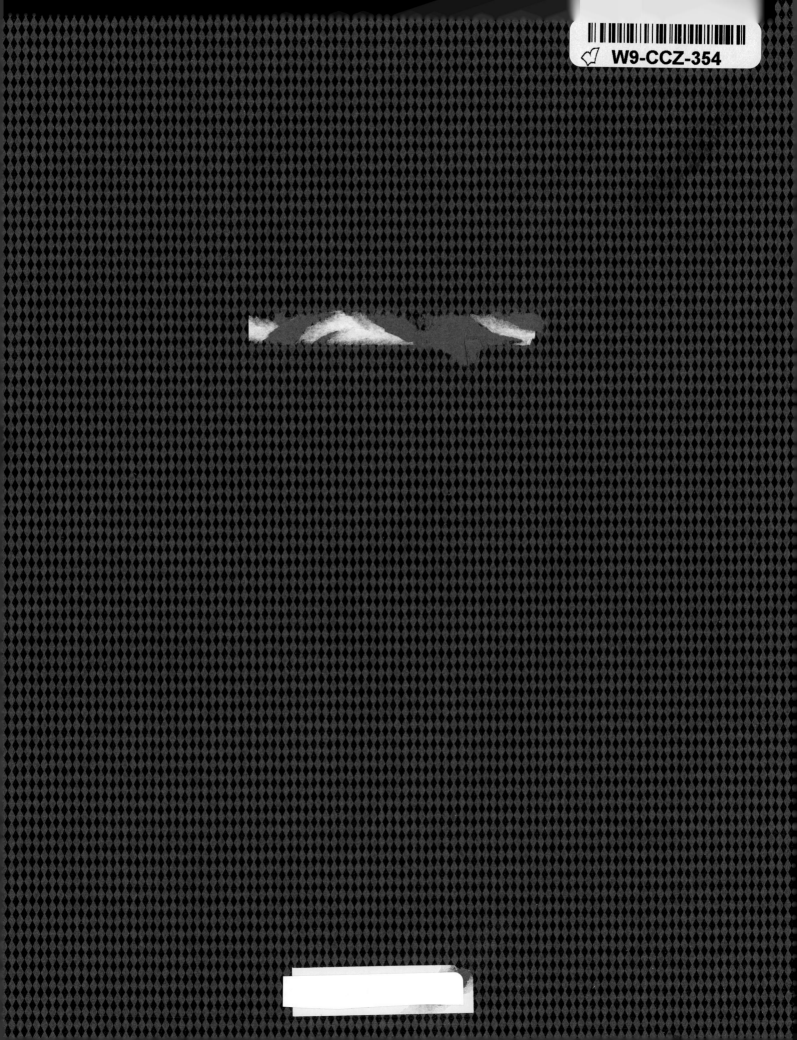

Nothing But the
BLUES

Nothing But the BLUES

◆

THE MUSIC AND THE MUSICIANS

LAWRENCE COHN

MARY KATHERINE ALDIN, BRUCE BASTIN,
SAMUEL CHARTERS, JOHN H. COWLEY,
DAVID EVANS, MARK A. HUMPHREY, JIM O'NEAL,
BARRY PEARSON, RICHARD K. SPOTTSWOOD,
AND CHARLES WOLFE

ABBEVILLE PRESS ◆ PUBLISHERS ◆ NEW YORK ◆ LONDON ◆ PARIS

Jacket front: Lonnie Johnson
Spine: Bessie Smith
Jacket back: Chippie Hill and Montana Taylor
Frontispiece: Leadbelly
Title page: Big Bill Broonzy
Contents spread: Durham, N.C.
Copyright/dedication spread: Unidentified singer in Atlanta

EDITOR: Alan Axelrod
DESIGNER: Molly Shields
PRODUCTION EDITOR: Paul Macirowski
PRODUCTION SUPERVISOR: Simone René

Library of Congress Cataloging-in-Publication Data
Nothing but the Blues / edited by Lawrence Cohn.
p. cm.
Discography: p.
Includes bibliographical references and index.
ISBN 1-55859-271-7
1. Blues (Music)—History and criticism. I. Cohn, Lawrence.
ML3521.N68 1993
781.643'09—dc20   93-2791

To (Lord) Rory McEwen—Thanks for the twelve-string, but I'd much rather you were still with us playing yours. Cheers, old friend.

To Simon Napier—a wonderful friend and gentleman, whose knowledge of blues was overwhelming and who was taken from us at an all-too-early age. Simon, I hope that this book pleases you.

To Piet Schellevis—Pete, I think that you would have liked this project. You certainly were an appreciative listener as well as a skillful producer.

JUN 28 190

CONTENTS

JUN 28 1995

FOREWORD

B. B. KING

◆◆◆

I first met Larry Cohn in 1969, after having read a most favorable article he wrote about me and my career as it was at that time. It wasn't too hard to see that not only was he interested in my music, he was interested in the blues, period. Well, lots of time has passed since that meeting. Many nights have been spent on the road touring. I've made lots and lots of records, had—like everyone else—high points and low points, but what has always stayed the same has been the blues. The thrill may be gone for other things, but not for the blues.

It has been a long haul. From Blind Lemon Jefferson and Charley Patton to Son House and Robert Johnson, from Lightnin' Hopkins and Muddy Waters to Eric Clapton and Johnny Winter, to Robert Cray and the many other blues players and singers. Some recorded, some never did. Some traveled and performed, some stayed at home. But whatever the way, the tradition has carried on. In many cases, it had to take a European detour before some Americans would recognize their own music, but I feel that it is now firmly entrenched in the consciousness not only of Americans, but of music lovers throughout the world.

This book will take the reader on an adventure—an adventure through the "houses of the blues," where many different individuals will be encountered. Some are colorful, some are mysterious, all are interesting.

So, read on, knowing full well that the blues is alive and well and will be so when you finish this lovingly presented portrait of the music and the musicians.

B.B. King

PREFACE

LAWRENCE COHN

◆◆◆

My earliest American vernacular music memories center around the radio when I was nine or ten years old. Saturday evenings—quite late, after my father had (without success) insisted that I go to sleep—I would pull the covers over my head and lovingly, if surreptitiously, take the radio with me.

What distant pleasures! Country music from WWVA, Wheeling, West Virginia, the "World's Original Jamboree," and if and when I could or would stay awake past midnight, the rocking, rousing, roof-shaking church services from Baltimore, Washington, and Philadelphia, which made the adrenalin pump so that sleep was an oh so distant concept. And then, during the week, a radio program devoted to boogie-woogie, hosted by (of all unlikely individuals) a classical pianist. Imagine, boogie-woogie for the masses presented by a "longhair." A wondrous wonder of wonders for a young boy, to be able to hear the likes of Albert Ammons, Pete Johnson, and Meade "Lux" Lewis—the vaunted Boogie-Woogie Trio—to hear solo performances by these artists as well as by others and, on occasion, to be blessed by blues vocals from such as Big Joe Turner, magnificently accompanied by Pete Johnson.

This, for me, was the beginning of a journey that has yet to end, and when I bought my very first 78-rpm disk, Freddie Slack's "Down the Road a Piece," at a used-record store, my indoctrination was completed, my addiction already established, and the die cast for the rest of my life.

Many years have passed, ever so quickly, as I look back, hoping as we all do on occasion, to retrieve my life. Needless to say, time is irretrievable, but the memories are there. I count myself extremely fortunate to have had an all-consuming passion for the blues since I was youngster. All of the missed lunches, movies, and other sacrifices in order to save enough to buy one or two 78s, and later on perhaps an LP or two, are assuredly things that I would most agreeably repeat if I were able to start all over again. Just the opportunity to have savored the varied and several emotional levels of the blues has been, I not immodestly propose, payment enough for my addiction and dedication.

The blues has helped me through troubled times, blessed me with meeting countless interesting and fascinating individuals associated with the genre, afforded lessons in American history that could not be gained through books, given me a rich insight into society—and societies—through music and poetry, and has thoroughly ingrained the concept that blues is not only a people's music, blues is the music of the people.

What we have tried to achieve in this volume is an expert overview of the major aspects of the blues. We do not delude ourselves for a moment into thinking that what is presented is either complete or the final word on the subject. For "complete," we would require a work the size of the *Encyclopedia Britannica*. However, the writers whom we have enlisted in this work have written their chapters with a view toward educating, entertaining, and engendering interest on the part of the reader, who will, we hope, be encouraged to further exploration, reading, and listening. As to the "final word," we are most thankful that, as John Lee Hooker said to me more than thirty years ago, "The blues will always be here; sometimes more popular than at other times, but it will always be here!"

From your lips to God's ears, John!

ACKNOWLEDGMENTS

This project started a few years ago with Ann Shields, the Abbeville editor to whom I first brought the project, a wonderful lady who has since become a friend. Ann never stopped believing in the value of the project, and, without her, I would never have continued with it.

Alan Axelrod, our editor, is a gentle, brilliant man who always displayed patience and understanding, and who contributed enormously to the entire undertaking, always making my life significantly easier and his infinitely more difficult.

Molly Shields is just about the best designer one could ask for and, thankfully for me, loves the subject matter. She has been an absolute joy to work with. She also has a great sister.

To my sister, Gloria Cohn: I apologize for having held you prisoner when you were a young girl, forcing you to listen endlessly to Leadbelly—and to my inane and indecipherable explanations of the same. Yes, there is life after Huddie Ledbetter!

To Frank Driggs, who provided an endless treasure trove of rare photographs for this undertaking. Here's to our next thirty-eight!

To my family: Lee and Laurie, my children, you have taught me as much as I (think) I have taught you. And to my ex-wife, Beverly Cohn, who predicted that we would win a Grammy for the Robert Johnson project before we had even begun it, and who loves Blind Willie McTell, Lonnie Johnson, and Jelly Roll Morton as I do. The woman does have taste!

Lawrence Cohn
Beverly Hills, California
January 1993

WORKIN' ON THE BUILDING

ROOTS AND INFLUENCES

SAMUEL CHARTERS

◆◆◆

*People keep asking me where the blues started and all I can say is that
when I was a boy we always was singing in the fields. Not real singing,
you know, just hollerin', but we made up our songs about things that was
happening to us at that time, and I think that's where the blues started.*

Son House, 1965

The singer was sitting on the faded linoleum that covered the uneven dirt floor of
the small hut close to the mouth of the Gambia River in West Africa. A handwoven
rug was spread under his dark robes to keep them out of the dust. A handful of people who had heard the music as they passed by were crowded into the small space.
Since there was no door, they only had to push aside the flowered cloth curtain that
hung in the door opening. He was half singing, half chanting in long, free, poetic
lines, reciting a story about a local king before the Europeans came, a king who was
fighting against another tribe coming into his territory. As he sang, the people clus-
tered in the room, most of them in shirtsleeves and rumpled cotton trousers, mur-
mured and nodded.

In his hands he was holding a small, homemade string instrument that he
played in a series of rhythmic figures, over and over, the soft, muted tone of the
strings a light, scurrying accompaniment to the deep resonance of his voice. There
was a gentle sound of bare feet tapping against the linoleum, following the movements of his fingers. In each of the West African languages there is a different word
for singer, but each of them also uses a more general word, griot. The singer in the
open hut was a griot of the Wolof tribe, and it is possible that someone like him first

began to shape the music we know today as the blues. In the many years that have passed since songs like the one he was singing made their long journey to the United States, much in the griots' music, in the instruments they play, and in the songs themselves have inevitably changed. Some of the changes can still be traced; other elements that shaped the modern blues have been lost, probably irretrievably, somewhere in the harsh years of African-American experience.

Early travelers along the west coast of Africa—the area from which almost all of the slaves who were brought to the United States were taken—described the griots and their songs, though they sometimes used the local word for "singer." In 1745 a compendium of travel writings published in London, Green's *Collection of Voyages*, included descriptions of the singers by an English voyager named Jobson:

> *Of the role of the musicians in the society there seems to be considerable agreement, although there are differences in the name. Those who play on the instruments are persons of a very singular character, and seem to be their poets as well as musicians, not unlike the Bards among the Irish and the ancient Britons. All the French authors who describe the countries of the Jalofs and the Fulis call them Guiriots, but Jobson gives the name of Juddies, which he interprets fiddlers. Perhaps the former is the Jalof and Fuli name, the latter the Mandindo.*
>
> *The traveler Bardot says the Guiriot in the language of the Negroes toward the Sanaga, signifies Buffoon, and that they are a sort of sycophant. The Kings and great men in the country keep each of them two or more of these Guiriots to divert them and entertain foreigners on occasion.*

The three tribes mentioned in the passage are known today as the Wolof, the Fula, and the Mandingo. Since the tribes had no written languages until recent years, the spelling of the names varies. In Senegal alone more than thirty spellings can be found of the name Wolof. The word Juddies, which Jobson interpreted as "fiddlers," is probably the Mandingo word Jali, the term for singer. Since the word is interpreted as fiddlers, however, it is possible that he was referring to Fula griots, who are known as Jelefo. The Fula singers accompany themselves on a small one-string fiddle called the riti.

The instrument the singer was playing for the informal cluster of listeners in the little house in Gambia in his compound was made from an elongated gourd that had dried to the hardness of thick plastic. It had five strings cut from a length of plastic fishing line tied to the rubbed wooden stick that worked as the instrument's neck. Four of the strings went to the end of the stick, and the fifth was tied close to the body of the instrument, shortening its length and raising its pitch. There was a hand-carved bridge holding the strings off the taut piece of goatskin that covered the opening cut into the side of the gourd. In the singer's own language, Wolof, the instrument was called the halam. In the language of the African musicians who brought it to the American South, it had a different name, the banjo.

Like everything else brought from Africa to the South, the banjo changed in the years that passed between the time it arrived and the moment, perhaps a century and a half later, when the first banjos were played into a cylinder recording machine. There is an eighteenth-century painting of a slave dance in Virginia that shows an instrument that still looked very similar to the African banjo, but by the 1830s and 1840s, as more and more entertainers on the crude stages of the nation's small cities

A young Mississippian plays the rural version of the one-string slide guitar. The instrument and this approach to it were common throughout the South during the 1920s and 1930s; many of our greatest blues artists started in this fashion. CHAPTER OPENER

Son House—one of the most
important blues artists of all time
and quite possibly the genre's
greatest singer.

began to blacken their faces and perform the songs and dances they appropriated from African-American musicians, the instrument began to change.

One of the most popular of the pre–Civil War performers of banjo specialties, "Picayune" Butler, still used an instrument made out of a gourd as late as the 1840s, but when the first band of blackface performers appeared on the stage of what was to become the first minstrel show in 1853, the banjo had been Americanized. The skin head was now stretched over a round frame, first made of wood, and later metal. The rounded stick had been replaced by a flat neck, and the short string was fixed to the side of the neck with a peg. The long strings were also attached to the neck with pegs, first wood, as on a violin, then metal screw pegs. The skin head was now like the head of a marching drum, and, as it changed, the clamps and the ring holding it tight also became metal screws.

The instrument was the same small five-stringed halam—or konting, as a larger version of the same instrument is called—but instead of the soft plucking sound, it was now louder, and since the strings could be drawn tighter, it was played at a higher pitch. It had become the banjo, its sound usually described as "ringing." It was the banjo, along with the ubiquitous fiddle, that became the most common instrument of the plantation South. The banjo was not, finally, the instrument that would shape the blues, but it was the instrument that helped develop the techniques that became part of the background of the blues. It could be thought of as the halfway step from the music of the griots to that of the first blues singers.

It is difficult to follow this development because, by the time southern vernacular music was being extensively recorded, the banjo had been largely taken over by white singers like Buell Kazee, Dock Boggs (also called Doc Boggs), and Clarence Ashley. Nearly all of them spoke freely about the influence of African-American neighbors who had taught them how to play. They learned not only all of the playing techniques, which had come directly from the finger styles of the griots, but also some of the songs and rhythm patterns. Many old banjo songs, performed as "old folk

This photograph of Papa Charlie Jackson, with its lovely filigree, is taken from a Paramount Records catalog of the 1920s.

melodies" by white banjo players, still have the shape of their original African melodies, and some of the "nonsense" verses of the songs contain African words and phrases. It is possible, in fact, to trace, without a break in continuity, the development of the banjo from the Bambara basin of West Africa, one of the areas from which many slaves were taken, to the "bluegrass" style of musicians like Earl Scruggs. What is sometimes thought of as a distinctly southern white cultural expression is actually one of the most vigorous survivals of the African cultural influence on American music.

By the 1920s, however, when record companies first began to document the blues, only a few singers were still using the banjo. One of them, Papa Charlie Jackson, who began recording for Paramount Records in 1924, was very popular, but he used the instrument in a band style, for, by this time, the banjo was usually thought of as a rhythm instrument in jazz and dance orchestras. Only one country banjo player, Gus Cannon, who led a jug band for Victor Records in the late 1920s, recorded extensively. In one of his recordings, "Jonestown Blues," it is possible to hear how the banjo style had developed to accommodate the specific qualities of the blues. In his accompaniment, Cannon uses the precise chords of the early blues to follow the vocal line, then he ends each line with a banjo flourish. The flourish could be a fragment of the earlier kind of embellishment that is more characteristic of halam playing, though it had to be fitted into the regular rhythm that is also one of the elements that distinguished the blues (see Example 1, p. 28).

It seems obvious that part of the reason the banjo lost its central role in rural African-American musical life was because much of its repertoire had been taken over by white performers and because it had become associated with the white minstrel shows and their pervasive racism. Also, the changes in the instrument—the higher pitch and the tension of the strings, which could not produce a sustained note—meant that the banjo wasn't as useful as an accompaniment instrument. It still served that function for white singers, however, since they used higher vocal pitches, often falsetto tones, and sang with a hard nasal quality that gave a sharp clarity to the their song texts. African-American singing style, in contrast, used lower vocal pitches and emphasized slower tempos, making the banjo's short, bright "plink" awkward to sing against.

The solution to the problems of the banjo was the guitar, which has a deeper bass sound and, especially if it is tuned below standard concert pitch, produces a tone that sustains long enough to fill in the pauses of a slowly sung vocal line. The guitar also has all the other characteristics necessary for a folk instrument to become widespread: it is cheap, easy to carry around, relatively durable, and can be played with a variety of other instruments. It was the guitar that became the instrument of the blues, but many of the early blues styles were built on the rhythmic and harmonic patterns that had been developed and sustained on the banjo. In the first blues recordings, one hears many accompaniment styles clearly derived from banjo techniques.

While it is possible to follow some of the developments in the instruments that became part of the blues background, the emergence of the blues itself is almost impossible to trace. This is in large part because the blues is defined as a specific musical form. Ragtime and jazz, styles that developed at about the same time, are easier to follow, since they were both considered a way of performing as much as they were a separate body of composition. Although there is a kind of vocal and instrumental style associated with the blues, it is the form of the blues itself, a unique verse form and harmonic structure, that defines it. And this is precisely what has been impossible to find: the moment when this unique pattern developed.

Late-nineteenth-century folk-song collectors documented much of the music of the newly freed African-American population, and although there are brief melodic patterns with some similarity to what we know of the early blues, as well as lines and phrases of textual material that became part of the blues vocabulary, there is nothing with the distinctive form of the blues.

As it developed and first appears in notated form, the blues was a strophic song built of three short musical phrases that accompanied a lyric verse as specific as the harmonic sequence of the phrases. The classic form of the blues is the well-known three-line verse, in twelve measures of 4/4 rhythm, with an A-A-B rhyme pattern and a line length usually measured by five stressed syllables. There was some early use of shorter—eight-measure—verses on blues themes and texts, but they were so quickly and completely superseded by the twelve-measure verse form that the later form came to be one of the definitions of the blues. Of course, there have been many variations on the basic twelve-bar verse, but it was survived as a distinct musical expression for most of this century. The meter of the three lines of text is accentual, since there is no effort to count the five stressed accents by syllables. It is the repetition of the first line and the use of the verses as thematic building blocks rather than narrative units that give the blues verse its unique character.

The term blues itself was a common American word long before the birth of the music. It can be traced back to Elizabethan English, and by the middle of the

Cannon's Jug Stompers, one of the classic jug band aggregations of all time, consisted of (left to right) Gus Cannon, Ashley Thompson, Noah Lewis. Cannon lived not quite to an age of one hundred, but Noah Lewis died prematurely in abject poverty.

1800s in the United States it was used in much the same way it is today. To say, "I've got the blues" in the 1830s and 1840s meant to be bored, but, by the 1860s, it connated unhappiness. When I talked to the New Orleans trombone player Harrison Barnes in the 1950s, he told me that the songs themselves had been around when he was young—the turn of the century—but they called them "ditties." The New Orleans musician who first developed what was considered a jazz style of playing, Buddy Bolden, was said to have played "blues," but the specific songs other musicians remember from his repertoire don't have any of the elements that define the blues, so ditties were probably short folk melodies.

The term blues was first used for a song title by a young white dance-orchestra musician from Oklahoma City named Hart Wand, who played the violin. When I met him in 1958 he was operating a small rubber stamp company in New Orleans. As I described in The Country Blues, he said that when he played a certain little melody on his violin in the back of his father's tent drugstore, an African-American porter, who had come up from Dallas and swept the store for them, would whistle the tune along with him. One afternoon the porter leaned on his broom while Wand was playing and said, "That gives me the blues to go back to Dallas."

Wand asked a friend, Annabelle Robbins, to arrange the music for him, and he published "The Dallas Blues" as an instrumental composition in March 1912. The sheet-music cover of Wand's piece was printed in gold on dark blue paper and sold for ten cents a copy. It sold so well in Oklahoma City and then in small cities outside it, that by the time he copyrighted it on September 12, 1912, it was already in its third printing.

W. C. Handy fronts one of his many big bands in 1936.

The first published blues by W. C. Handy, who was later to advertise himself as "The Father of the Blues," was an instrumental composition he named "Memphis

Blues," obviously reflecting Wand's piece, published a few months earlier. Unlike "The Dallas Blues," which in its twenty measures included a close approximation to the classic blues form, "Memphis Blues" was a new version of a song called "Mister Crump," which Handy had been playing for political rallies. A year later, in 1913, Handy's music company published a song called "Jogo Blues," which had been written, or at least performed, by a local piano player. The piece was not a commercial success, but a year later Handy added two more strains to it and published it as "St. Louis Blues." It was this composition that brought the blues its first large audience.

"St. Louis Blues" was significant not only because it was a major success, but because, as Handy published it, the first strain, the "Jogo Blues" melody, used the classic blues pattern, both in text and musical form. It employed the three-line verse with the A-A-B rhyme scheme, and the line length of five stressed accents. The harmony was the three-phrase pattern that became part of the definition of the blues:

I–IV–I–I7
IV–IV–I–I
V7–V7–I–I

To make certain he had a hit, Handy turned the second strain into a tango, since that was the latest dance novelty. The third strain went back to the three-line verse form, but the melody itself was closer to ragtime than it was to what would later be thought of as the blues. With the novelty "blues" first strain, followed by a tango and a little ragtime, Handy had managed to catch most of the latest styles, and

W.C. Handy's "Memphis Blues" was written in 1911 as a campaign song for Memphis mayor Edward H. "Boss" Crump and enjoyed more than local success. In 1914, Handy followed up this song with "The St. Louis Blues," which became an international sensation and is sometimes cited as the world's first published jazz composition.

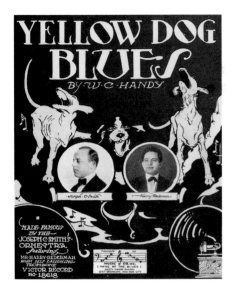

Less well known than "The Memphis Blues" and "The St. Louis Blues" is W. C. Handy's "Yellow Dog Blues."

Clifton Chenier, the undisputed King of Zydeco music, is to zydeco what Muddy Waters is to Chicago blues. Chenier gave new meaning to "accordion music."

the song had a major influence on the new directions of American popular music. The opening phrase of the second strain, in fact, was used by George Gershwin as the basis for his song "Summertime."

Although the blues was obviously a rural folk style, it is impossible to discuss the first country blues recordings without taking into consideration the success of the published blues. Commercial recording of country blues singers didn't begin until nine years after the publication of "St. Louis Blues," which, for a popular song style, is a very long time. When commercial recording directors selected artists and material, they were looking for "blues"—the musical form they were familiar with from the success of the first published blues pieces, and, what is more important, the form that the rural singers themselves were also familiar with, since records by singers like Bessie Smith sold everywhere in the South.

By the time the first country recordings were made, rural musical styles had been so influenced by commercial blues forms that it is very difficult to sift through the performances and discern more than an irregular outline of what might have been preblues styles.

A number of facts suggest that the blues may first have taken shape in Mississippi. The state had a large and isolated African-American population and was an area of pervasive poverty, which meant that people were forced to create their own entertainment. In the northwest counties of Mississippi, the famous Delta cotton country, the concentration of African-American communities was so dense that the musical life preserved elements of African melody and instrumental style that had all but died out elsewhere in the South. It was in Mississippi that fife and drum bands were found, with African pieces as part of their repertoire. W. C. Handy first heard what he called "primitive" music—an instrumental trio—in Cleveland, Mississippi, and one of the first blues songs, "Yellow Dog Blues," contains a reference to Moorehead, Mississippi, where the lines of the Southern Railroad crossed the "Yellow Dog," the local name for the Yazoo and Delta Railroad.

What would also suggest Mississippi as the birthplace of the blues is the number of singers from the Delta counties who were recorded and the amount of song material they used that can be traced to work-farm or gang-song sources. It is always important to emphasize, however, that there was no sociological or historical reason for the blues verse to take the form it did. Someone sang the first blues. There doesn't seem to be any way we will ever find out who the singer was who first developed the blues as we know it, but it is a specific song form, and somewhere, probably in a Delta cabin, a singer who knew the melodies and the improvised verses of Mississippi work songs decided to sing them in a new way, and that was the blues.

It is always difficult to resist the temptation to continue to look for social influences instead of the individual performer behind the development of the blues. In recent years, however, a number of new musical styles have emerged in the African-American community, and since we have recordings of how the music developed, we can see that in each case it was possible to single out an individual performer as the creative force behind the new style. The electric blues in postwar Chicago was given its first shape and definition by Muddy Waters and his early bands. Zydeco was shaped by Clifton Chenier. Even in something as decisive as the adaptation of Chicago blues to what was to become modern rock 'n' roll, the influence of one musician, Chuck Berry, is clearly evident. It seems certain that somewhere in northern Mississippi in the late 1890s or the early 1900s there was a musician who performed the same creative role in the development of the blues.

Sometimes in the South today you still can walk along a country road and, from across a sunlit field or from a yard close to a tar-paper house, you can hear somebody singing to himself. The songs are free and simply rhymed, with short verses of one or two melodic phrases. The name usually given to them is "hollers," and it is these melodies that became one of the two important sources from which the blues was derived.

The work song, with its steady rhythms and its short rhymed phrases, was the other major source of the blues. Twenty or thirty years ago it was still possible to pass segregated gangs of black workers scattered alongside the dirt roads in Mississippi, Louisiana, or Texas chopping weeds or dragging away stumps and trash. As they worked they followed a song leader who kept them together by singing short impro-

Prison road gangs were a common sight in the South of the 1930s and produced their share of work songs and blues shouts.

Charley Patton was quite possibly the blues' most talented all-around artist. A magnificent guitar player, songwriter, and singer, he exerted an influence that extended from Son House to Howlin' Wolf and Robert Johnson.

This image of Texas Alexander, taken from an old catalog, is the only known photograph of this artist.

vised phrases that they answered with a single repeated line as a refrain. These loose chants were the work songs, and until the 1950s it was possible to hear the rhythmic pattern of work-song styles in some of the blues recorded by Mississippi artists.

It could be that there was a predominance of "holler"-style blues from Texas and a rich variety of work-song-based blues from Mississippi because of the different work conditions in the two states—though such generalizations have to be taken with some skepticism. Texas had a smaller African-American population than Mississippi, and with its drier soil there was more isolated work on the small farms. The work songs collected in Texas have usually come from the prison farms along the shallow river bottoms in the south fringe of the state. Mississippi, more heavily populated, had large work gangs on the plantations of the Delta and on the prison farm at Parchman.

The elements of the holler style that became part of the blues were the high tone of the voice—since the singers were alone and they wanted their voices to carry, they usually sang at the top of their range—and the rhythmic looseness of their phrasing. Often the melodies had a characteristic high-to-low progression, beginning on a tone close to the top of the melody, then descending in intervals of a third. The vocal scale was usually what is known as a gapped pentatonic, a five-tone scale that probably reflects African scales, which are also usually pentatonic, rather than the eight-tone diatonic scale of European music. The melody for "Texas Easy Street Blues," recorded by Texas Alexander in 1928, is typical of these holler-style blues (see Example 2, p. 29).

The long, free rhythms of this kind of melodic line continued as part of the Texas style until the 1950s, particularly in the blues of Lightnin' Hopkins, who had learned part of his style from his cousin Alger "Texas" Alexander, who didn't play the guitar and was even freer than Hopkins in his vocal lines. One of the greatest Texas

singers, Blind Lemon Jefferson, found a way to accompany such vocal lines with freely strummed chords or pauses, filling in at the end of the vocal line, much as Gus Cannon did in his "Jonestown Blues." The only essential difference between a song like Jefferson's "That Crawlin' Baby Blues" and a holler was the repetition of the first line, which turned Jefferson's utterance into a blues (see Example 3, p. 29).

In contrast to holler-inspired blues, the early blues that show the influence of work songs employ shorter phrases, with more specific points of rhythmic emphasis. One way to mark these emphases was to play the rhythm on the guitar. A blues recorded by the Mississippi singer Son House in 1942, "Depot Blues," still exhibited vestigial traces of a recurring work-song pattern in the pauses in the vocal line, which were filled with a percussive note on the bass strings of the guitar. The tempo is close to the rhythm of wood chopping, or some other work where a song leader set the pace by singing rhythmic phrases to keep the movements of the men in the gang together (see Example 4, p. 30).

Lightnin' Hopkins, looking rather sophisticated here, became the darling of the folk blues world shortly after he was "discovered" in Texas.

Other Mississippi singers worked with longer work-song phrase lengths, and they retained the chant of the song leader almost without change except for the usual doubling of the first line, which transformed the work song into a blues. This involved adding an irregular rhythmic unit to accommodate the anticipatory notes of the singer's melodic line. The half measure that began each sung phrase continued into some of the first Chicago blues, since nearly all of the postwar Chicago singers were from northern Mississippi and still were close to older blues traditions. It was only when the form of the electric blues band became fixed that the irregular rhythm patterns disappeared. "Down the Dirt Road Blues," recorded by Charley Patton in 1929, is an example of the earlier kind of phrasing (see Example 5, p. 31).

As we consider blues roots, it is also useful to remember that the first blues recordings also included almost any kind of song—not just holler and work-song styles. Some of the pieces that were recorded as blues were folk ballads, children's songs, or country ragtime. It was only as the blues recording industry became more sophisticated that the material took on a deadening sameness. It is also important to remember that the recording done in the South was under the supervision of a handful of white A&R (artists and repertoire) men, who were working for white-owned record companies and who often used as scouts white owners of local music stores, like James Baxter Long in Durham, North Carolina, or H. C. Speir in Jackson, Mississippi. What we have of the rural blues is what they chose to record.

Unidentified revelers make music sometime early in the century.

Interviews with older blues singers make it clear that most of the performers had a large repertoire of other kinds of songs—and sometimes they did record religious material, but usually under pseudonyms. One of the most popular songs in the repertoire of the Mississippi singer Robert Johnson was his version of "My Blue Heaven."

The knowledge we have of the early blues will always be skewed by the commercial decisions of the men who directed the recording. Frank Walker of Columbia Records, who supervised much of the company's rural blues recording in the 1920s, described their approach to the music in an interview with Mike Seeger:

> *We recorded in a little hotel in Atlanta, and we used to put singers up and pay a dollar a day for their food and a place to sleep in another little hotel. And then we would spend all night going from one room to another, and they kept the place hopping all night in all the different rooms that they were in. You would have to go from one room to another and keep your pen working and decide we won't use this and pick out the different songs that they knew, because you couldn't bring songs to them because they couldn't learn them. Their repertoire would consist of eight or ten things that they did well, and that was all they knew.*
>
> *So, when you picked out the three or four that were best in a man's so-called repertoire you were through with that man as an artist. It was all. It was a culling job, taking the best that they had. You might come out with two selections or you might come out with six or eight, but you did it at that time. You said goodbye. They went back home. They had made a phonograph record and that was the next thing to being President of the United States in their mind.*

What we know of the early blues was filtered through the tastes and attitudes of the men like Frank Walker.

How is the music of the griots reflected in the blues? I think there are elements in the blues that can be traced to the African song styles—the vocal timbre, a certain harmonic ambiguity, and a series of what could be called rhythmic "modes"—although the influences are faint and tenuous. The blues form itself, the strophic verse with its repeated harmonic pattern, bears no relationship to the melodic styles of the West African griots, even today. A contemporary recording by the griot Ali Farka Toure from Mali includes a song, "Sidy Gouro," that has some similarities to a blues melody, and he accompanies himself on the guitar, which emphasizes the similarity. The descriptive notes to the collection, however, make it clear that when he was just beginning to sing, a friend in his village gave him an album by John Lee Hooker, which influenced the song. The melodies for the rest of the album are in the more freely extended griot style.

An example of the text of a griot performance shows the great differences between the two styles of song. This is the opening section of "Nege Sirimang," sung in 1974 by the Serrehule griot Alhaji Samara Sahone, who was living in a village outside of Banjul, the small capital of Gambia. He accompanied himself on the large version of the halam called the konting.

> *Nege Sirimang is a very brave man who is never afraid of any battle.*
> *Whoever fears a battle, Nege Sirimang would face it*

A man who had grown up who is never of any use to others is good for nothing—even a child is better than such a man. A man must be useful and always know his duty. This song is always played for men who are brave and of use to others, not for men who can be trifled with.

I am calling for men who can save the lives of other men whenever there is trouble, when there is hunger for those who can stand it and fight for their rights. This song is for those men.

Two characteristics of the blues, however, can perhaps be traced back to the griots. The rhythms of the griot songs, even with only a voice and instrument, are typical of the layering of rhythm of most West African musical styles. What this means is that there is a complex weave of beats, and there is a conscious avoidance of the kind of single stressed rhythm that is characteristic of European folk music. An easy generalization would be to say that African folk styles "float," while European folk styles "march." In technical terms, African music from the slave areas is polyrhythmic, and European music is monorhythmic.

One of the marked characteristics of the blues is this same kind of floating accent, despite the regularity of the accompaniment rhythm. The guitar usually follows the chord pattern with a regular beat, but it is almost impossible to find a blues where the vocal entrance of the new phrase comes at the same moment that the chord changes. The voice sometimes follows the change, but the usual shift is to

Two young men identified only as "Duffy and Sanders from Sneed's band" play homemade one-string slide guitars, a mainstay of down-home blues.

anticipate it. The voice begins at least a beat, and sometimes as many as three beats, before the chord change. This kind of anticipation can be traced throughout the rural blues areas, and it would be possible to do a study of these rhythmic shifts as an element of the different regional styles. The anticipation gives the blues a little of the "float" of the griots' performances.

The harmonic "feel" of the blues, and of almost all African-American music, perhaps also goes back to these same roots. There was, in the early years of research into blues and jazz, a considerable interest in what were called "blue notes." These were the tones of the European scale, usually the fourth of the seventh, that in the blues and jazz were often sung and played with a raising or lowering of pitch. What seems to have happened in this kind of melodic scale was that the two scale patterns, the African pentatonic and the European diatonic, came into conflict. When songs such as the holler and the work song were performed without accompaniment, the pentatonic scale was used, but the European instruments that were employed in the jazz orchestra or the blues accompaniment were constructed to play a diatonic scale. The "blue notes" were clearly an effort by African-American musicians to play what they sang.

With the early guitar accompaniments there was another way to solve the dilemma, and that was with the "slack key" guitar styles that were popular in the United States before World War I. This method of playing seems to have developed in Hawaii. Essentially, the guitar was tuned to an open chord, and the melody was played by sliding a metal bar up and down the strings. With this kind of tuning, the blues singer could play the melody using the altered tones of the vocal scale and work out a harmonic accompaniment on the lower strings. It was this solution to a specific problem of the blues that led to the various tunings and slide or bottleneck styles of the modern blues.

A final characteristic of the blues could come from this dimly glimpsed background of the African musical idiom. The blues almost never uses a true minor harmonic mode. There are only a handful of blues with specifically fingered minor chords in the accompaniment. At the same time, there is a continuous use of major/minor configurations that occur throughout most blues pieces. Likewise, the griots have only a small number of pieces in a true minor but the ambiguities of the pentatonic scale (in European terms) means there is not often a true major harmony either. The blues pianists found a number of ways to achieve a quick shift between minor and major that resembled the griots' "ambiguous" modality. The third of the chord was played both in major or minor modes—sometimes the major in the right hand followed the minor in the left, so there was some of the harmonic "feel" of the griots' music in the ambiguity (see Example 6, p. 31).

It is out of all these elements—the singing of the West African griots, the holler, the work song, the song traditions of the southern countryside, and even slack-key guitar—that the blues was formed. There probably always will be the one element we will never know—who it was that first sang a blues verse—but it is clear now that it is possible to trace much of the development of this vital musical style, which for almost a hundred years has continued to find ways to keep its unique identity even as it has continually changed and renewed itself.

EXAMPLE 1.

As I left Lu-la goin' to Jones - town,—

Man, I left Lu - la goin' to Jones–

town. Those —

Jones- town browns, boy, make you turn your dam-per down.—

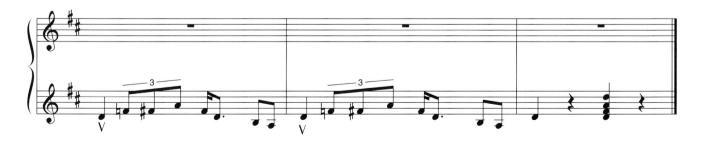

EXAMPLE 2.
(TEXAS EASY STREET BLUES)

Um- m—— what's the mat - ter now———— te - ll—

me ma - ma what's the mat - ter now.—— I'm

goin' back to Tex - as, live on Ea - sy Street.

EXAMPLE 3.

The wo - man rocks the cra - dle and I de - clare she rules the home.

Wo - man rocks the cra - dle

and I de - clare she rules the home.

Ma - ny man rocks some oth - er man's ba-by and the fool thinks he's rock - ing his own.

EXAMPLE 4.

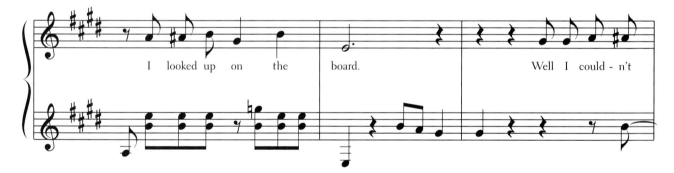

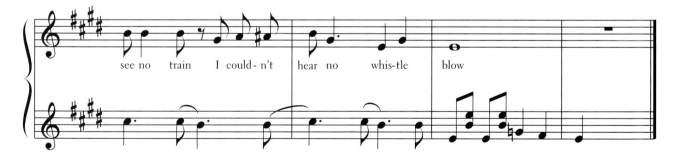

EXAMPLE 5.
(DOWN THE DIRT ROAD BLUES)

Some peo - ple'll _____ tell me o' seas blues ain't

(guitar)

bad _____ sp: (of course they are) Some peo - ple'll _____ tell you

(guitar)

o' seas blues ain't bad _____ It must

not have been them o' seas blues I had.

EXAMPLE 6.

GOIN' UP THE COUNTRY

BLUES IN TEXAS AND

THE DEEP SOUTH

DAVID EVANS

♦♦♦

No one can say precisely where the blues first came into being, but the evidence strongly suggests that it was somewhere in the vast area stretching from inland Georgia and north Florida across to Texas. This area spreads south and then west of the Appalachian Mountains, takes in the Mississippi Valley as far north as southern Illinois and the Missouri Bootheel, and runs westward, skipping over the Ozark Mountains, to include southeastern Oklahoma and east and central Texas. It is an area of cotton farms and plantations, intersected by patches of hardwood forests, piney woods, and cypress swamps that have been progressively cleared in the twentieth century. It is the newer part of the South. With the exception of the French and Spanish settled cities of the Gulf Coast and French-speaking southwest Louisiana, most of this territory was inhabited by Indians or was uninhabited until the first half of the nineteenth century. Cotton was king in this region, and large numbers of black workers toiled in the fields to plant, cultivate, and harvest it, first as slaves and later as sharecroppers and sometimes renters and owners of the land. In some of the plantation areas where cultivation was most intense, such as the Mississippi Delta and the Black Belt of Alabama, the black population could reach as high as 80 or 90 percent of the total.

Most of the blues innovators who carried forward the music's stylistic development lived in this area or started their musical careers here. Even today the area remains a stronghold of blues activity. The earliest reports of blues from this region come from shortly after the beginning of the twentieth century. If we can assume that these reports describe a type of folk music that had already had some time to spread from its place of origin, it is not unlikely that blues music began sometime in the 1890s. Later recollections by musicians and other observers, in fact, place the

This page from a Paramount Records catalog, ca.1925, features an intriguing mix of important female artists, Alberta Hunter, "Ma" Rainey, Ida Cox, and Trixie Smith, along with some marginal ones. They are anchored by the Norfolk Jazz Quartet, a group at home in both the secular and religious worlds. Sometimes called the Norfolk Jazz and Jubilee Quartet, the Norfolk Jubilee Quartet, and the Jubilee Gospel Singers, the group also recorded for Okeh and Decca. RIGHT

Frank Stokes, considered by many to have been the "King of Beale Street," recorded as part of the Beale Street Sheiks and as a solo artist. His influence was so widespread that he was, perhaps, the single most important bluesman to have come out of Memphis.
CHAPTER OPENER

blues in cities like New Orleans, St. Louis, and Shreveport before the turn of the century, the music probably having been brought there by migrants from the nearby countryside. Contemporary accounts of the blues begin to be published soon after 1900. In 1901 and 1902 Charles Peabody, excavating an archaeological site near the Delta community of Stovall, noted that his black workers often sang improvised songs to guitar accompaniment about everyday life, love, hard luck, and good times. His description of the context of these pieces and the tune and verse fragments that he prints suggest that blues was prominent among the songs of his workers. Around this same time folklorist Gates Thomas heard blues in south Texas, including variants of lines and tunes encountered by Charles Peabody in Mississippi and recalled by Jelly Roll Morton from New Orleans. Professional black musicians, too, were encountering and adopting this new folk music. "Ma" Rainey, a singer in traveling stage shows, recalled hearing blues for the first time in 1902 in a small Missouri town and incorporating this music into her act. A year later bandleader and composer W. C. Handy heard blues played on stringed instruments in the Mississippi Delta. He was so impressed with the power of this music and the favorable audience reaction that he arranged these tunes for his group of trained musicians.

The most detailed early account of blues in this region was given by sociologist and folklorist Howard W. Odum, who published a large field collection of black folksongs made in Lafayette County, Mississippi, and Newton County, Georgia, between 1905 and 1908. Odum printed many verses that would turn up in later blues recordings. He stated that many of the songs were accompanied by the guitar or other stringed instruments and that the performers were often semiprofessional traveling "songsters," "musicianers," or "music physicianers." Odum noted that these songs were performed after work or after church for dances and other social gatherings, for courtship, or even by a lonely singer sitting on his doorstep or by his fireside. He also

Cotton pickers labor deep in one of the rural blues' great venues, the Mississippi Delta, around 1920.

observed that these singers sometimes performed for white audiences. About this same time folklorist John Jacob Niles encountered an itinerant white guitarist in Kentucky who was recasting traditional mountain lyric folksongs into typical three-line blues stanzas. There are further reports of folk blues in the years before World War I from Mississippi, Tennessee, and Texas. By 1912 blues had been popularized on the black vaudeville stage and printed in sheet-music form. These popular productions drew from the growing folk blues tradition and in turn influenced it, being adopted into the repertoires of the songsters, musicianers, and music physicianers.

The early observers of folk blues in the Deep South and Texas during the first two decades of the twentieth century paint a fairly consistent picture of the music, its performers, and its social context. The songs employed many traditional verses that were the common property of singers, and these verses were arranged in a variety of stanza patterns from a single line endlessly repeated to groupings of three or four lines. The singing was usually accompanied by one or more musical instruments, generally a guitar or small string ensemble in the country and small towns, and a piano in the cities. The harmonica is also mentioned in connection with this new music. The singers were mostly male, some of them professional or semiprofessional. Popular stage singers, usually female, also began adopting these songs into their acts. The singers are consistently described as young, in contrast to those who sang the older songs of the slavery period. Odum associated this new music with the class of displaced migratory workers seeking cash work in the levee camps and lumber camps, building roads and railroads, picking cotton during the harvest season, hauling wood or coal, working on the riverboats, or seeking work in the towns and cities. Others associated the blues with pimps and gamblers, and still others found them among those who had run afoul of the law and landed in jail. The ideal of the blues singer was to be free to move about, riding in style when times were good and hoboing when times were tough, hiring himself out to the highest bidder for his manual labor or musical services or else hustling up a living by his own wits and charm, generally living as well as he could and leaving whenever he became dissatisfied or restless. He avoided being tied to the land, either as an owner or through a long-term sharecropping arrangement, as this meant the loss of mobility and acceptance of the social status quo. He preferred to sing and play for tips on street corners and in parks,

on passenger trains and riverboats, and at railroad stations, pool halls, bars, cafés, brothels, house parties, dances, and traveling shows. It was a dangerous life, but potentially a rewarding one and certainly always interesting.

The early observers tell us mostly about the music's social context and print samples of the song lyrics. They say little about specific blues singers, preferring to treat them all rather anonymously as members of a homogeneous social class. It is only in the era of commercial recording of this music that we begin to distinguish one artist from another in terms of musical career and musical style. Professional stage singers began to record blues as early as 1920, but most of the songs were the creations of sophisticated songwriters and were far removed in style from the folk blues of Texas and the Deep South. By 1923 these songs began to include a greater amount of folk blues material as a new crop of southern stage artists began to record. Among these were "Ma" Rainey, Bessie Smith, Ida Cox, and Sara Martin, who often sang their own compositions, which drew upon the folk blues tradition. Male blues singers also began to make recordings. The first of these, artists such as Sylvester Weaver, Papa Charlie Jackson, and Lonnie Johnson, displayed stylistic affinities with stage and jazz traditions. It was the 1926 recordings of Blind Lemon Jefferson, a true southern folk bluesman from Texas, that opened the floodgates for the recording of down-home blues. In the next six years, perhaps as many as two hundred solo artists and small groups made commercial records of this type of music.

Several factors converged during this period that promoted the recording of this largely underground music. One factor was the invention of the electrical recording process, which made the guitar easier to record, afforded the listener a wider acoustic range and less surface noise, and made it somewhat easier to distinguish the words of singers with regional accents and slurred diction. Electrical recording equipment was also easily portable. Soon after its invention many of the major recording companies launched field trips to discover and record regional talent. An enormous number of blues were recorded in the South, along with gospel music, jazz, hillbilly music, and other styles. Memphis, Dallas, Atlanta, and New Orleans became important regional recording centers during this period, with temporary studios set up by the companies for periods of up to two weeks. Further sessions were held in Bristol, Charlotte, Savannah, Nashville, Louisville, San Antonio, Richmond, Johnson City, Shreveport, Jackson, Birmingham, and Knoxville. The growing popularity of radio, which competed with the phonograph, prompted the record industry to undertake field trips in order to find new music and new markets radio did not serve. A further inducement to record folk blues in these years may have been the recent publication of several books on blues and black folk music by Dorothy Scarborough, W. C. Handy, and Howard W. Odum and Guy Benton Johnson that had drawn attention to the folk origins of the blues and had perhaps spawned an interest among the reading public for "the real thing." But while record company executives may have read these books, it was largely a nonreading public that bought most of the records, namely the black folk community in the South as well as recent migrants to the northern cities. This was the same community that had created the music in the first place, some three decades earlier, and had supported it all along. The extensive recording activity and field sessions lasted until 1932, by which time all of the major record companies had gone into bankruptcy as a result of the Depression. Although down-home blues artists continued to be recorded in later years as the record industry recovered, field sessions in southern cities were rare, and the companies were much more selective as to which artists they recorded. They sought proven hitmakers and artists who could

W. C. Handy, a pioneering musician in the realms of the blues and jazz, wrote "The St. Louis Blues," which changed the course of American popular music.

compose original songs on novel themes, sing clearly, and play a distinctive, often virtuosic, instrumental accompaniment.

Although the best blues artists possessed instantly recognizable personal styles, there was a certain degree of overall stylistic unity to the early recorded blues by artists from the Deep South and Texas. Since many of them were active musicians before the 1920s, we can safely assume that most of these common stylistic characteristics predate that period. They may well have been formed about the time when the blues first came into being around the beginning of the century. Probably the most striking feature of this music is its overall sense of intensity, urgency, seriousness, sincerity, and conviction. The performers give the impression of being at one with their music. They are not merely instruments who present a song. When one hears the song, one hears the performer. This is particularly the case in the Deep South. Here the blues often seems stripped to the bare essentials. There is little filler, little ornamentation, little wasted space. Every note is meant to be felt. The singing tends to be impassioned, with the voice coming from the back of the singer's throat and having a harsh, raspy quality. The melodies are often pentatonic or nearly so and sometimes are little removed from field hollers. Many of the verses are drawn from the shared body of traditional blues lyrics and are generally serious in tone, sometimes dealing with subjects of a spiritual nature, such as death or the singer's relationship to heavenly or diabolical forces. Texas blues has a similar level of intensity, but the singing tends to be breathier and less raspy, more melismatic, and somewhat less dependent on traditional lyrics. The instrumental accompaniments in the Deep South generally have powerful, driving rhythms, often accelerating in tempo over the course of a song. In this early period, rhythms are generally strongly duple with little sense of swing. The guitar or piano is often played very percussively. Strings are bent to obtain the flexibility of the human voice. Another commonly employed technique is that of sliding a glass or metal tube or ring (or a pocket knife) along the strings to produce a whining tone. Few passing notes or chords are played, and many of the pieces, in fact, display a modal character or have only one or two chords. Often the guitar plays an insistent repeated short phrase after the vocal lines.

Again, the Texas blues varies somewhat from this pattern. This blues tends to approximate more closely the standard three-line, twelve-bar structure. Some Texas guitarists feature a steady, thumping, often muffled bass, repeating a single note or chord overlaid by a rhythmic treble part. In other cases, however, the guitar drops out or becomes very subdued behind the singing, only to resume in a responsorial fashion. In such cases the playing is sometimes rather ornamented and rhythmically free, suggesting that the music may have been designed for listening as much as for dancing.

Many of these characteristics, such as the short repeated phrases, pentatonic tunes, acceleration, percussive playing, and the slide technique, can be linked to traditional African music, particularly that of the Savannah region of West Africa, where the music often assumes a similar degree of intensity. Some of the musical instruments found in the Deep South and Texas blues tradition also have an African origin, though they are often constructed from different materials and thus appear somewhat different from their African prototypes. Perhaps closest in form to an African instrument were the panpipes or "quills" played by Texas bluesman Henry Thomas. The five-string banjo used by Gus Cannon of the Memphis band Cannon's Jug Stompers was also based on an African prototype instrument. Jug bands, which were a prominent part of the blues scene in the cities of the Deep South during the

1920s and 1930s, served as important repositories of the African instrumental tradition. The jug and kazoo, which were found in most such bands, were derived from African "voice disguisers," which were used frequently in connection with masked rituals to represent spirit voices. By the 1930s the jug was often replaced by the one-stringed bass made from an inverted washtub or lard bucket. The original form of this instrument is the African ground harp, also known as an earth bow. The washboard, which was frequently heard in combination with these other blues instruments, is also based on African scraping percussion instruments. Many blues guitarists began on a one-stringed children's instrument made from a length of broom wire stretched on a board or on the side of a house and played by striking the string while sliding a glass bottle along its length. A somewhat similar children's instrument is found in Central Africa, with analogous forms in several Afro-Latin cultures. Although the American instrument was not recorded until the 1950s, many musicians have attested to its use in earlier years as a stepping stone to the guitar. Its geographical distribution is almost exclusively confined to the state of Mississippi and portions of adjacent states, precisely the same area where the slide guitar style enjoyed its greatest popularity.

Whistler's Jug Band was filmed in Louisville, Kentucky, in 1930 by a Twentieth Century-Fox/Movietone newsreel crew. Several minutes were shot—including some footage of barnyard animals—with the group playing "Tear It Down, Bed Slats and All," which they would record for RCA Victor in June 1931 as "Foldin' Bed." The final cut newsreel story ran approximately 30 seconds and was exhibited locally as a "news item." It was never shown nationally.

Some blues artists wandered freely over the South or even all over the country, especially after they gained a degree of fame through making records. Others remained strictly community musicians, usually holding a nonmusical job such as farming during the week, or settling in some city where they could find enough musical jobs to make ends meet. Many, however, worked a regional circuit. The most famous of these blues regions was the Delta, roughly the northwest quarter of the state of Mississippi. Much of this region's rich soil was not opened up to cultivation until the late nineteenth and early twentieth centuries, the time when the blues form was first emerging. Large plantations were established, and black workers streamed in from the surrounding impoverished hill country, most of them farming on a sharecropping arrangement with the landowner. The prosperity and opportunity of the Delta not only attracted farm workers but also musicians. Many workers were paid in cash and received settlements at the end of the fall harvest, and the blues musicians were there to give them a reason to spend some of their money.

In this environment musicians could learn from one another and develop styles that synthesized many musical ideas brought to the region from the surrounding countryside. No region of the South produced as many great blues artists as the Delta in the first half of this century. The cities and larger towns in and near the region were also magnets for blues musicians. Here, also, the people had some cash and could usually spare a bit of it for entertainment. Often certain streets were the centers of black commerce and entertainment, such as Beale Street in Memphis,

The Dockery Plantation contributed extensively to the development of the blues in Mississippi. Indisputably, its major contribution was Charley Patton.

Farish Street in Jackson, Fourth Street in Clarksdale, and Nelson Street in Greenville. Pianists especially gravitated toward the cities, where they could find work in the saloons and at rent parties. The towns and cities all along the Mississippi River developed an especially strong piano blues tradition, but pianists also found work in the levee camps along the river and in the lumber camps of the piney woods region of southern Mississippi and southeast Louisiana. Here the workers were often isolated far from town, and the companies had to import women and musicians for their entertainment on weekends. In Texas the towns and cities were generally spaced farther apart than in the states farther east. Blues musicians traveled by train, and the various railroads became prominent subjects in their songs. Here, too, the cities were important destinations, and certain streets or sections became known for entertainment, such as Deep Elm and the Central Tracks in Dallas, Dowling Street in Houston, and Fannin Street in Shreveport, Louisiana.

The state of Mississippi probably provided the greatest number of blues artists during the early era of recording, due largely to the preeminence of the Delta as a blues region. Perhaps sensing this, record companies made frequent stops on their field trips in Jackson and especially Memphis, which lie more or less on the southern and northern edges of the Delta. Two men played key roles in getting many of the Mississippi blues artists to these field sessions or to the permanent recording studios in the North. One was Ralph Lembo of Itta Bena in the Delta, and the other was H. C. Speir of Jackson. Both owned furniture stores that did a large business with black customers. An important item of furniture in that period was the phonograph, and along with it were sold the latest "race" records. Noting both the heavy demand for these records as well as the wealth of talented artists virtually just outside their doors, these two men undertook to serve as free-lance talent scouts, locating, auditioning, rehearsing, and sometimes managing blues singers, bringing them or sending them to recording sessions. For this work they were paid a fee and were assured that they would be able to sell plenty of records by locally popular artists.

One of the blues artists that H. C. Speir discovered was Charley Patton. In many ways he epitomized the musical and social patterns that shaped the Delta blues, and as one of the pioneers of this tradition, he served as a mentor, role model, and waymaker for many other Delta bluesmen. Patton was born in 1891 near Bolton in the hill country between Jackson and Vicksburg. Around the beginning of the new century, workers from this area were heavily recruited for the large plantations that were being carved out of newly cleared land farther north in the Delta. By 1905 Charley's father, Bill Patton, had brought his family to the huge Dockery's plantation in the Delta between Cleveland and Ruleville, where several of their old neighbors had also settled. Bill Patton was an ambitious man. He was attracted by the opportunity to raise large crops in the fertile Delta soil as well as by the possibility of additional cash income from the lumber business that was a byproduct of the clearing of land that had been forest and swamp. Patton rented a large spread, part of which he sublet to other workers whom he hired; on the side, he operated several timber-hauling wagons. Toward the end of the 1920s, he was able to buy over a hundred acres of his own near Dockery's and operate a country store. Charley could have helped his father in these enterprises, eventually inheriting them and perhaps building them into something even more grandiose. This, however, would have involved the acceptance of the social status quo in the Delta, one which was driven by rampant racism that assigned an inferior caste role to all people of African ancestry, no matter what their accomplishments. Charley wanted a greater degree of freedom than his father

The Mississippi Sheiks, seen here in a Bluebird Records catalog of 1936, were (left to right) Bo Chatman (a/k/a Chatmon or Carter), Walter Vincson (a/k/a Jacobs or Vincent) and Sam Chatman or Chatmon. This was a family band (Vincson was a cousin) of multi-instrumentalists with ever-changing personnel who played throughout the mid-South for white as well as black audiences. They all had extended recording contracts, both as individuals and as members of the Sheiks. Bo was particularly active as Bo Carter, a master of the double entendre as well as a superb guitarist who was rumored capable of playing each of his songs in every key.

had. He tried preaching, an activity that he pursued intermittently throughout his life. He even recorded several spiritual songs and a short sermon in the midst of his blues recordings. Preaching offered social status and some freedom of movement, but it was also closely tied to the social status quo of the black community. The same ambition that drove Bill Patton to seek opportunity in the new frontier territory of the Delta through enterprise and the acquisition of property impelled his son Charley to seek freedom of expression, freedom of action, and freedom of movement by abandoning an interest in physical property and land and becoming an itinerant blues singer. Keeping Dockery's as his primary home base, Charley Patton roamed the Delta for some twenty years up to his death in 1934, playing at every conceivable venue and for audiences of all sorts, rich and poor, young and old, black and white. There is hardly a town in the Delta where he is not recalled by those who were old enough to hear the blues in the 1920s and early 1930s. At times his travels took him farther afield, eastward and westward to Georgia and Texas, southward to Jackson, Vicksburg, Natchez, and New Orleans, and northward to Memphis, St. Louis, and Chicago. He made plenty of money, married at least eight times, had countless girlfriends, and generally lived quite well. The demand for his musical services and the grueling pace of his restless life-style eventually combined with a chronic heart condition to end his life at age forty-three. But for those whose lives were mostly spent behind mules and plows under the hot Delta sun, it must have seemed that Charley Patton lived a thousand lifetimes, practically a new one each day and in each Delta town.

Between 1929 and 1934 Charley Patton recorded over fifty titles. Among them were spirituals, folk ballads, ragtime dance tunes, and versions of popular hit songs, but the majority of his pieces were Delta blues. Patton had begun playing guitar in the hills, but his style was formed from listening to the older blues singers around Dockery's. These men were probably a few years older than Charley and would have been among the first generation of blues players. It was the blues that formed the core of Patton's repertoire and style and that shaped his approach to the rest of his material, even that which represented musical traditions slightly older than the blues. Patton's style practically epitomizes the Delta blues while at the same time displaying a distinctiveness no other musician ever came close to capturing. His voice was tough and raw, suggesting a rough-and-tumble life and a barely suppressed rage. Though he had a superb touch on the guitar and mastery of the subtleties of tone and timing, he often liked to snap and bend the strings and slide a knife over them to produce percussive and whining effects. These techniques were supplemented by other special effects, such as playing the guitar behind his head or between his legs. He often accented normally weak syllables and words of secondary importance for the song's meaning in order to give full weight to every part of his performance. He delivered a spoken commentary on many of his songs, seeming to create his own audience and context even in the recording studio. Although he drew heavily on the storehouse of traditional blues verses, many of his lyrics had a startling originality and contained highly personal references. His recordings had an extremely spontaneous quality, always seeming to be songs still in the making, never finished products delivered by the artist for their final embalming in shellac. One seems to be hearing Charley Patton at that very moment working on his musical repertoire, engaged in a high-energy process of reshaping and reworking.

The songs he recorded in his first session in 1929 express his restless spirit, as he mentions places far off and describes a turbulent life-style.

P. C. (Polk) Brockman, listed as the publisher of "The Jazz Fiddler," was an Okeh Records distributor in Atlanta. Much of the time he functioned as a talent scout/manager and was also responsible for the first recordings of Fiddlin' John Carson, swinging the deal by promising Okeh that he would take the first 500 records pressed.

(9-29-10M	MATRIX NO.	W403804					10 INCH
TITLE	THE JAZZ FIDDLER						
ARTIST	MISSISSIPPI SHEIKS		Jacobs + Carter	ACCOMP.			
SUB. NO.	RECORDED	SHIPPED	TEST RECEIVED	REPORTED	DISPOSITION		REMARKS
A	2-17-30	2-18-30	3-1-30	3-7-30		Old Time Tune-Vocal	
B	"	2-18-30	3-1-30	3-7-30			

COMPOSER Jacobs-Carter

AUTHOR

✓ PUBLISHER P.C. Brockman- 217 Whitehall St,S.W,Atlanta,Ga.

DATE OF COPYRIGHT 1930

DATE OF COPYRIGHT CONTRACT 3-7-30 W&P
3-24-30 W&P

DATE OF COPYRIGHT EXTRACT

CATALOGUE NO. 45436

MONTH LISTED

COUPLED WITH

RECORDING OPERATOR

Jackson on a high hill, mama, Natchez just below.
Jackson on a high hill, mama, Natchez just below.
(If) I ever get back home, I won't be back no more.

Oh, my mama's getting old; her head is turning grey.
Oh, my mama's getting old; her head is turning grey.
Don't you know it'll break her heart, know I'm living thisaway.

Oh, I'm going away, baby; don't you want to go?
Oh, I'm going away, baby; don't you want to go?

Between 1929 and 1941, Walter Vincson recorded for the Brunswick, Okeh, Decca, and Bluebird companies under the name Walter Vincent, with Chatman's Mississippi Hot Footers; as Walter Jacobs and The Carter Brothers; and solo as Walter Vincson, Walter Jacobs, and Walter Vincent—all of this in addition to his work as a member of the Mississippi Sheiks.

Spoken: *I know you want to go, baby.*
Take God to tell when I'll be back here any more.
> —*"Screamin' and Hollerin' the Blues"*

I'm going away to a world unknown.
I'm going away to a world unknown.
I'm worried now, but I won't be worried long.

I feel like chopping, chips flying everywhere.
I feel like chopping, chips flying everywhere.
I've been to the Nation [i.e., Indian Nation], hmm Lord, but
I couldn't stay there.

Some people say them overseas blues ain't bad.
Some people say them overseas blues ain't bad.
It must not have been them overseas blues I had.

Every day seem like murder here.
Every day seem like murder here.
I'm gonna leave tomorrow. I know you don't bit more care.

Can't go down the dark road by myself.
Can't go down the dark road by myself.
If I don't carry my high brown, gonna carry me someone's else.
> —*"Down the Dirt Road Blues"*

Hitch up my pony, saddle up my black mare.
Hitch up my pony, saddle up my black mare.
I'm gonna find a rider, baby, in the world somewhere.

I got something to tell you when I gets a chance.
I got something to tell you when I gets a chance.
I don't want to marry, just want to be your man.
> —*"Pony Blues"*

But Charley Patton went beyond the usual blues themes of love relationships and travel to sing about events that he had witnessed or participated in. In his songs he treated his life and his observations as news, believing it would be of interest to others. Twice he sang about arrest and incarceration, although in one case it was actually a bootlegger friend who had been arrested and in the other he was merely held as a witness to a murder in a Delta roadhouse where he was playing. He sang about a railroad strike in Chicago that inconvenienced his travel plans, and he sang about the plantation overseer who banished him from Dockery's for leading some of the farm workers' wives astray. He recorded a blues about the effects of a drought in the town of Lula, but his greatest topical blues was the two-part "High Water Everywhere" about the 1927 flood of the Mississippi River and its tributaries. As if reflecting the confusion brought on by the flood, Patton's perspective shifts among that of a terrified victim caught in the sudden rush of water, an objective observer, and one of the rescuers.

*Joe McCoy (Kansas Joe, the
Georgia Pine Boy, Hallelujah Joe,
Big Joe, The Mississippi Mudder,
Mud Dauber Joe, and Hamfoot
Ham), first husband of Memphis
Minnie, brother of Charlie McCoy
and one of the Harlem Hamfats,
was a multitalented singer-
composer-instrumentalist as well
as the organizer of countless
recording sessions.*

*The back water done rolled, Lord, and tumbled, Lord, drove me down the line.
The back water done rolled and tumbled, drove poor Charley down the line.
Lord, I'll tell the world the water done struck Drew's town.*

*Lord, the whole round country, Lord, creek water is overflowed.
Lord, the whole round country, man, is overflowed.
Spoken: You know, I can't stay here. I'm bound to go where it's high, boy.
I would go to the hill country, but they got me barred.*

*Now, looky here now, in Leland, Lord, river is rising high.
Looky here, boys around Leland tell me river is raging high.
Spoken: Boy, it's rising over there. Yeah.
I'm going over to Greenville. Bought our tickets, good-bye.*

*Looky here, the water dug out, Lordy, levee broke, rolled most everywhere.
The water at Greenville and Leland, Lord, it done rose everywhere.
Spoken: Boy, you can't never stay here.
I would go down to Rosedale, but they tell me there's water there.*

. . . .

*Back water at Blytheville, backed up all around.
Back water at Blytheville, done struck Joiner town.
It was fifty families and children. Tough luck, they can drown.*

*The water was rising up in my friend's door.
The water was rising up in my friend's door.
The man said to his womenfolk, "Lord, we'd better go."*

*An Okeh ad for two Bo Carter
blues tunes.*

Oooh, Lordy, women is groaning down.
Oooh, women and children sinking down.
Spoken: Lord, have mercy.
I couldn't see nobody home, and was no one to be found.

For a period of some twenty years off and on, Charley Patton had a partner, Willie Brown, a slightly younger man, who had learned guitar from Patton. Unlike Patton the perpetual tinkerer, Brown shaped the musical ideas of his mentor into perfectly polished creations while retaining Patton's rough and percussive texture in his voice and guitar playing. Patton brought Brown to his 1930 session, where he accompanied his mentor on several pieces and recorded four selections of his own, only two of which survive. On "Future Blues," while snapping the bass strings of his guitar, he sang:

Can't tell my future, I can't tell my past,
And it seem like every minute sure gonna be my last.

And the minutes seem like hours, hours seem like days.
And the minutes seem like hours, hours seem like days.
Seem like my woman ought to stop her low-down ways.

Another artist Patton brought to his 1930 recording session was Eddie "Son" House, who was born and raised near Clarksdale and was about ten years younger than Patton. Up until two or three years before this time, House had been a preacher, but the lure of whiskey and the sound of blues played with a slide guitar caused him to give up this career and become a bluesman. House had the rich voice of a gospel singer. His "Preachin' the Blues," was surely autobiographical:

Oh, I'm gonna get me religion, I'm gonna join the Baptist church.
Oh, I'm gonna get me religion, I'm gonna join the Baptist church.
I'm gonna be a Baptist preacher, and I sure won't have to work.

Oh, in my room I bowed down to pray.
Oh, in my room I bowed down to pray.
But the blues came along, and they drove my spirit away.

Oh, I wish I had me a heaven of my own.
Spoken: Great God Almighty.
Oooh, a heaven of my own.
I'd give all my women a long, long happy home.

I met the blues this morning walking just like a man.
Oooh, walking just like a man.
I said, "Good morning, blues, now give me your right hand."

Oh, I got to stay on the job, I ain't got no time to lose.
Oooh, I ain't got no time to lose.
I swear to God, I got to preach these gospel blues.
Spoken: Great God Almighty.

Son House: the church's loss was the blues' gain.

In the course of this 1930 recording session Son House and Willie Brown became fast friends. Both settled in the town of Robinsonville, working as a team and becoming kings of the blues in the northern Delta for the next thirteen years. In 1941 and 1942 they were recorded by a team of researchers from Fisk University and the Library of Congress, and the results show both of the artists to have been still at the top of their form. Shortly thereafter Brown died, and House took a railroad job in Rochester, New York. Here he found himself outside the mainstream of blues activity, and he gave up music for many years. In 1964 he was rediscovered by blues researchers and persuaded to resume his career. For several years he astonished audiences around the country and overseas with the power of his authentic Delta blues. Poor health forced him to end his concert career after several years, and he passed away in 1988 in a rest home in Detroit. He had been one of the greatest of the Delta bluesman, a major influence on younger musicians from the area, including Robert Johnson and Muddy Waters, and he was a man who brought Delta blues to new audiences and a new generation.

Two families, the Chatmons and the McCoys, supplied several important members of the Mississippi blues scene. Both clans were from the country between Jackson and Vicksburg, and the Chatmons were neighbors of Charley Patton's family. The patriarch of their family was Henderson Chatmon, a fiddler who had been born well back in the slavery period. He had several sets of children, most of whom became musicians. The youngest set, born of his last wife in the 1890s and early 1900s, became known collectively as the Mississippi Sheiks, principal recording performers being Lonnie and Bo. Lonnie Chatmon played the violin and was equally adept at country breakdowns and waltzes, popular and jazz tunes, and lowdown blues. Bo Chatmon sometimes played violin as well, but more often played guitar in a steady rhythmic pattern of bass notes and chords. Their music was popular with both white and black audiences. More of a blues quality was added by their neighbor Walter Vincson, who was a fine singer and a versatile guitarist. Another Chatmon

Robert Nighthawk, as he was popularly known, was actually Robert Lee McCoy, cousin of Joe and Charlie McCoy. He worked with his cousins as a mouth harp player —a spectacular one at that—but eventually made his reputation as a slide-guitar player. His recorded examples on harmonica, particularly those with Big Joe's Washboard Band, are just about the very best that the genre can provide.

brother, Sam, sometimes recorded with the group, and it was he who carried the sound and repertoire of the Mississippi Sheiks into the 1970s and early 1980s through many concert and festival appearances as well as recordings. Bo Chatmon also had a distinguished solo recording career between 1928 and 1940, performing many bawdy pieces accompanied by some very original, precise, and complex guitar playing. Titles like "Banana in Your Fruit Basket," "Ants in My Pants," "Ram Rod Daddy," and "Mashing That Thing" give a good idea of the typical content of his songs. Recording mostly under the pseudonym of Bo Carter, Chatmon appeared on more than a hundred titles. An occasional partner of Bo Chatmon was Charlie McCoy, a versatile mandolin and guitar player and an effective singer. McCoy's repertoire and tastes were similar to those of the Chatmons, and he was very much in demand as an accompanist. Later, in the 1930s and into the 1940s, he worked in Chicago with his brother Joe McCoy, a stronger singer and an excellent guitarist and songwriter, who, under the name of Kansas Joe, had earlier worked as a partner with his wife, Memphis Minnie. Later, the McCoy brothers would be known as Big Joe and the Mississippi Mudder. Their cousin Robert Lee McCoy sometimes worked with them on harmonica. Also known as Robert Lee McCollum, he subsequently switched to guitar and became well known in Chicago in the 1940s and 1950s as Robert Nighthawk.

Tommy Johnson

Before Charlie McCoy worked with the Chatmons and his brother Joe, he had already built a reputation in Jackson, Mississippi, as a guitar accompanist. His greatest work in this capacity was as a second guitarist on the 1928 recordings of Jackson bluesmen Tommy Johnson and Ishman Bracey. Johnson was from Crystal Springs, about twenty miles south of Jackson, but he learned his blues in the Delta from Charley Patton and Willie Brown, among others, in the years before World War I. Like Patton, he was a rambler, who used Crystal Springs as his home base and Jackson as his urban base when he wasn't traveling all over Mississippi and Louisiana. Johnson's blues, like Willie Brown's, was carefully structured from a musical standpoint, and each song featured a remarkable interplay of vocal and guitar lines. His most famous piece was "Big Road Blues," which contrasts a vocal line made up of descending phrases with a repeated ascending figure played on the bass strings of the guitar, all the while with Charlie McCoy weaving in and out and around with his own guitar. On "Maggie Campbell Blues" Johnson reversed the process, playing a descending bass figure against ascending vocal phrases. Perhaps his most distinctive song was "Canned Heat Blues," in which he celebrated his love for drinking cooking fuel, which he consumed along with shoe polish, hair tonic, rubbing alcohol, and almost anything else that could provide a kick.

> *Crying, canned heat, canned heat, mama, crying, sure, Lord, killing me.*
> *Crying, canned heat, mama, sure, Lord, killing me.*
> *Takes alcorub to take these canned heat blues.*
>
> *Crying, mama, mama, mama, you know, canned heat killing me.*
> *Crying, mama, mama, mama, crying, canned heat is killing me.*
> *Canned heat don't kill me, crying, babe, I'll never die.*
>
> *I woke up, this morning, crying, canned heat 'round my bed.*
> *Run here, somebody, take these canned heat blues.*
> *Run here, somebody, and take these canned heat blues.*

Johnson only recorded a bit more than a dozen pieces, but each one was a classic, and many were learned by other youngest artists. His influence in the southern half of Mississippi rivaled that of Patton in the Delta. Despite his severe drinking problem, Johnson kept up his musical career until the age of sixty, passing away in 1956 in Crystal Springs after playing music all night for his niece's birthday party.

Johnson's friend Ishman Bracey was discovered by H. C. Speir, and it was Bracey who then brought Johnson and Charlie McCoy to Speir's attention. Bracey was a master at bending notes, both with his voice and guitar. He sang with a harsh, nasal voice and played in a spare, uncompromising style. His music is an acquired taste for the modern listener, but, like Charley Patton's, it repays repeated listening. While his friend Tommy Johnson had reputedly made a pact with the devil for his musical talent and stuck with the blues up to the end of his life, Bracey underwent a religious conversion in 1950 and became a preacher. He continued to perform gospel songs with his guitar but never recorded again.

Three other Mississippi blues artists from this period deserve special mention. Mississippi John Hurt was from the community of Avalon, near Greenwood, and was recorded upon the recommendation of his neighbors, the white guitar and fiddle duo of Narmour and Smith, who were already successful recording artists. Hurt was strictly a local artist, and following his brief recording career in 1928 he returned to Avalon and obscurity. His songs, accompanied by lovely guitar picking in a bright, crisp, syncopated style, show the high level of development of Mississippi blues at this local level and also provide insight into the full range of folk music, of which blues was only a part. Hurt recorded spirituals like "Blessed Be the Name" and "Praying on the Old Camp Ground," the work song "Spike Driver Blues," and folk ballads like "Frankie," "Louis Collins," and "Stack O'Lee Blues." In the early 1960s Hurt was discovered by blues researchers, still in Avalon and still playing the same music he had recorded in 1928. For several years he toured all over the United States and recorded once again, showing no change in style or loss of skills. Booker T. Washington White, better known as Bukka White, was another rediscovery of the 1960s, whose later career lasted until his death in 1977. White was from the hills of eastern Mississippi but came to the Delta as a young man, where Charley Patton inspired him to pursue a blues career. White had a rich voice and a percussive guitar style, featuring repeated riffs played in the slide style. Discovered by Ralph Lembo, he was brought to Memphis to record in 1930, but most of the session remained unissued. "The Panama Limited," however, was released, and it has White performing a hobo recitation while his guitar imitates the sound of a fast train. Seven years later, White recorded again in Chicago and had a substantial blues hit with "Shake 'Em On Down." Back in Mississippi, however, he got in some trouble with the law over a shooting scrape, and he was sentenced to a stretch in Parchman Farm State Penitentiary while his record played on jukeboxes in the free world. White recorded in Parchman for a visiting researcher from the Library of Congress.

By early 1940 White was out and headed for Chicago, where he recorded once again. The twelve pieces he recorded that year were uniformly brilliant. Three of the pieces dealt with various aspects of his prison experience, while others treated unusual topics like illness, death, and mental depression. The music, though, was too far out of the popular blues mainstream for 1940, and Bukka White had to return south to a dwindling musical career and years of hard work as a manual laborer in Memphis. His rediscovery in 1964 found him still in good form, his voice more gravelly, but with undiminished poetic gifts and a new talent for making up "sky songs" on the spot. In the meantime, he had helped his nephew B. B. King get established in Memphis in the 1940s and launch a blues career that is still going strong today.

Nehemiah "Skip" James was the son of a prominent preacher from Bentonia, Mississippi, on the lower edge of the Delta, who turned to the blues and recorded some of the strangest music in this genre during 1931. He was equally adept on the guitar and piano. On the latter, instead of keeping up a steady beat with the left hand and a melodic line with the right, James played darting, stabbing runs with one hand or the other in a frantic, nervous style. His guitar playing employed a minor tuning and had an eerie, hollow quality coupled with great virtuosity and inventiveness. His blues frequently evoked bleak, morbid themes, as in "Little Cow and Calf Is Gonne Die Blues," "Cypress Grove Blues," "Hard-Luck Child," "Hard Time Killin' Floor Blues," and the classic "Devil Got My Woman."

> *I would rather be the devil than to be that woman's man.*
> *I would rather be the devil than to be that woman's man.*
>
> *Oh, nothing but the devil changed my baby's mind.*
> *Oh, nothing but the devil changed my baby's mind.*
>
> *I laid down last night, laid down last night, I laid down last night,*
>   *tried to take my rest.*
> *My mind got to rambling like the wild geese from the west, from the west.*

James's records were released in the worst period of the Depression and were commercial failures. Discouraged, he turned to church work with his father, but never quite seemed to make his mark in this career. He had given up music and returned to farm work when he was rediscovered in the early 1960s. Although he was battling cancer and was cynical about the lack of recognition his talent had received during

Bukka White was one of the true titans of the slide guitar, employing a vigorous, rhythmic, propulsive approach to playing. Possessed of remarkable imagination, he produced songs that amount to miniature operas. B. B. King, a relative, says that he developed his guitar tremolo in imitation of White's slide playing, since he found it difficult to adapt to the slide technique himself.

Walter Roland had an exceedingly brief recording career, spanning only 1933 to 1935, after which he disappeared completely. A great barrelhouse/blues/boogie-woogie pianist, he was also an excellent guitar player, and recorded several sides as such. As an accompanist he had few equals, and, along with Lucille Bogan (Bessie Jackson), he formed one of the premier blues associations of the 1930s.

his prime years, he still managed to make concert tours and do more recording before finally passing away in 1969.

Many other great Mississippi artists recorded during the late 1920s and early 1930s. Often they made only a handful of sides, and little or nothing is known of their lives. The music, however, is frequently overwhelming in its power and paints pictures of striking personalities and exciting scenes. Some of these bluesmen would undoubtedly rank among the greatest names of the blues if they had recorded more or had lived to be rediscovered. Among these fine artists were Freddie Spruell, Papa Harvey Hull, Blind Joe Reynolds, Kid Bailey, Rubin Lacy (who was rediscovered but had become a preacher and given up blues), William Harris, Garfield Akers, Joe Calicott (who died about a year after his rediscovery), George "Bullet" Williams, Blind Roosevelt Graves, and the ladies Rosie Mae Moore, Elvie Thomas and Geeshie Wiley, Mary Butler, Mattie Delaney, and Louise Johnson. The records of all these singers are well worth a listen.

The state of Alabama also contributed several fine blues artists who recorded during this period. Perhaps the most remarkable was Jaybird Coleman, who was one of the few blues singers ever to be recorded accompanied only by his own harmonica playing. Several of his blues had bleak-sounding titles, such as "Trunk Busted— Suitcase Full of Holes," "No More Good Water ('Cause the Pond Is Dry)," and "Save Your Money—Let These Women Go." With a voice almost breaking with emotion, Coleman would sing verses of only a single line followed by an extended harmonica passage. His playing displayed a beautiful pure tone and a mastery of the technique of bending notes. His style was far outside the mainstream of commercial blues, but he is said to have been quite popular in the Birmingham area.

Of the Alabama guitarists, perhaps the greatest was Ed Bell, who also recorded under the names of Barefoot Bill and Sluefoot Joe. He was from the town of Greenville in the southern part of the state known as the Black Belt, an area of plantations somewhat like Mississippi's Delta region. Bell liked to extend his guitar lines with rhythmic riffs following his singing, which was done in a plaintive voice that had a quality somewhat like Jaybird Coleman's. Bell's favorite themes were trains and hoboing, as in "Mean Conductor Blues" and "Frisco Whistle Blues," and crime and prison, as in "My Crime Blues," "Big Rock Jail," and "Bad Boy." In later years he gave up the blues and became a preacher.

Sonny Scott was another Alabama guitarist from Birmingham, who recorded several blues in 1933, some of them accompanied by Walter Roland on piano or second guitar. Scott had a lighter voice than Coleman or Bell and used more conventional blues structures for his songs, but he was a good songwriter and an excellent inventive guitarist. Another pair of versatile instrumentalists was Joe Evans and Arthur McClain, who recorded as the Two Poor Boys. They both played guitar and kazoo, but sometimes switched off to piano, mandolin, or violin. Their repertoire was as eclectic as their instrumentation, consisting not only of blues but also ballads, country music, breakdowns, and popular songs. A larger group was the Birmingham Jug Band, which consisted of two harmonicas, mandolin, guitar, and jug. All of their 1930 recordings were in a rough rhythmic style with extended instrumental passages following rhymed pairs of vocal lines. They were the roughest of the jug bands that recorded during this period.

Large parts of the state of Louisiana are unrepresented on records by country blues artists of this early period. Jazz was the dominant sound in New Orleans and the area along the lower Mississippi River. Only guitarist Richard "Rabbit" Brown seems to have represented New Orleans, and he may well have come there from another part of the state. His blues sounds somewhat dated for 1927, as if he might have been more at home with ragtime material. Creole music predominated in the southwestern part of the state, but little of it was recorded until the years following World War II. It was the northwestern part of the state in and around Shreveport that contributed the most to the blues tradition during this period. The styles of the artists from this region are varied, suggesting a deep pool of resources from which they could draw. There was Jesse Thomas, whose guitar playing showed a jazz influence and a sophisticated awareness of harmony, and King Solomon Hill, who avoided chord changes while picking out melodies on the guitar with a slider and singing in an eerie high-pitched voice. Oscar Woods was a Shreveport guitarist who also played in a slide style, but with chord changes and a discernible Hawaiian influence. Through the 1930s he recorded solo, in duets with another guitarist, and as a member of a small jazz/blues combo called the Wampus Cats. He also backed up country music singer Jimmie Davis, who would later go on to become governor of Louisiana.

Perhaps the greatest blues artist from this region was Huddie Ledbetter, better known as Leadbelly. Born near Mooringsport in 1889, he was practically of the first generation of bluesmen. Blues, however, was hardly the extent of his repertoire. He also performed church songs, breakdowns, children's songs, work songs, folk ballads, and versions of popular songs. He accompanied his singing on the twelve-string guitar, which he had acquired on his travels in Texas, using the instrument's booming sound to advantage in playing rhythmic chordal backgrounds and bass lines. He also occasionally played the piano and accordion, and his songs contained frequent spoken interpolations by way of explanation or expansion on the theme. Leadbelly was a

Because of his style as well as the great breadth of his repertoire, Leadbelly was really a songster and not exclusively a blues artist. Accomplished on both six- and twelve-string guitars, as well as the piano, mandolin, mouth harp, and accordion, he led a life that was the stuff of novels. One of the most influential figures in all of twentieth-century American popular music, his presence is still strongly felt more than four decades after his passing.

Huddie and Martha Ledbetter's wedding picture, Wilton, Connecticut, 1935. Martha Ledbetter was once asked why Leadbelly is seen with white hair in some photos, but had black hair in all of the wedding shots. She explained that, since there were twenty years between Huddie and herself, he had blackened his hair with shoe polish in an effort to appear younger.

strong and rambunctious young man, used to having his way, and it wasn't long before he got into trouble with the law. He served a term in a Texas county jail for assault, but escaped around 1916. Two years later, he was in the Texas State Penitentiary serving a life sentence for murder. In 1925, however, he was released after singing for the visiting governor Pat Neff and impressing him with a song pleading for a pardon. He returned home to Louisiana, but by 1930 was in the penitentiary there, convicted of attempted murder. His fortunes took a turn for the better, however, when folklorists John and Alan Lomax visited the penitentiary at Angola, Louisiana, in 1933, seeking to record black folk music. Leadbelly recorded another plea for a pardon, which the Lomaxes played for the governor of Louisiana. A year later he was out of prison and working as a chauffeur and assistant to John Lomax, driving him to other prisons around the South in search of folksongs and giving college campus concerts, which Lomax set up. Leadbelly married and moved to New York City in the late 1930s, where he continued to give concerts, make radio appearances, and participate in labor and left-wing political causes. He was the first folk blues artist to present this music in concert to white audiences outside the South. Shortly before his death in 1949 he made a short tour of France, once again the first artist of his kind to appear in concert in Europe. He could be said to have initiated the revival of interest in country blues and related folk music, and many of his songs have gone on to become standard items in the repertoire of folksingers in America and abroad. Among the best known are "Goodnight, Irene," "The Midnight Special," "Rock Island Line," "Cotton Fields," "The Grey Goose," "Pick a Bale of Cotton," "Mr. Tom Hughes' Town," "The Bourgeois Blues," and "Good Mornin' Blues."

Texas figured prominently in many of the earliest reports of blues, and the state contributed greatly to the number of outstanding country blues artists who recorded in the late 1920s and early 1930s. The oldest of these was Henry Thomas, born in 1874 in the northeast part of the state. His nickname "Ragtime Texas" not only indicated his geographical origin but also placed his music firmly in the era of popular ragtime at the turn of the century. His recordings, made between 1927 and 1929, include ballads, church songs, folk ragtime pieces, breakdowns, and what appear to be the first stirrings of the blues, preserved on record some thirty years after Thomas learned or created them. He played a rhythmic, strumming guitar and accompanied some of his pieces with a set of panpipes worn on a rack around his neck. He hated farming, which he ridiculed in his "Cottonfield Blues." Instead, he celebrated freight trains, hoboing, and riding the rods in songs like "Railroadin' Some." The few facts that we know of his life indicate that he was a hobo and adventurer, rather well educated for his place and time, one who was equally at home entertaining well-to-do passengers in the white cars of Jim Crow trains and playing around campfires in hobo jungles, one who was determined to live a life that knew no bounds. He is the archetypal first-generation bluesman.

The greatest virtuoso among the Texas guitarists of this period and the most popular recording artist of them all was Blind Lemon Jefferson. He was born blind in 1897 near the town of Wortham, about seventy miles south of Dallas. Determined to make his own way in the world, he took to the guitar and was already playing at house parties, picnics, and on the streets in his early teens. He was also traveling into Dallas, Waco, and other larger towns and cities, beginning a rambling life-style that he would maintain up to his death. It was a precarious existence, indeed, especially for a blind black man. His only skill besides singing was wrestling, a vocation he pursued briefly, exploiting his enormous size and strength. Fortunately, he was blessed with a strong, expressive, high, clear voice, a gift for creating poignant lyrics and for drawing others from the folk tradition, and a seemingly unlimited fund of interesting and often technically difficult ideas on the guitar. He was a true artist, obviously absorbed in making and creating music. He used both of the typical Texas styles of folk blues guitar, sometimes thumping rhythmically on a bass string while playing a rhythmically regular figure on the treble strings, at other times letting the sound of the guitar practically disappear behind the singing and then following the vocal lines with freely improvised, loosely rhythmic guitar figures. Mississippi bluesmen accused him of "breaking time" and playing music that wasn't danceable, but none of this lessened his popularity. His records sold well in the Delta, and he often performed there and in Memphis. No other artist ever came close to matching his sound, although many tried.

Late in 1925, Jefferson was discovered playing on the streets of Dallas by the owner of a music store, who sent him to Chicago to record early the following year.

His first blues records, like most that followed, were instant hits. He was the first southern self-accompanied folk blues artist to succeed commercially on records, and his success can be said to have opened the door to all the others who followed in the next few years. Although some of his blues about women contained images of tenderness or sexual boasting, many more were about deceit and abandonment, mistreatment, selfishness, and horror, such as "Got the Blues," "Beggin' Back," "Black Snake Moan," "Struck Sorrow Blues," "Gone Dead on You Blues," "Low Down Mojo Blues," "Competition Bed Blues," "Deceitful Brownskin Blues," "That Crawlin' Baby Blues," and "The Cheaters Spell." He sang about grinding poverty and homelessness in "Broke and Hungry," "Match Box Blues," "One Dime Blues," and "Tin Cup Blues." Perhaps because of his blindness, he seems to have felt a special affinity with prisoners. Many of his blues were about courtroom and jailhouse scenes, such as "Blind Lemon's Penitentiary Blues," "'Lectric Chair Blues," "Prison Cell Blues," "Lock Step Blues," and "Hangman's Blues." Further fears of sudden bodily harm and

Blind Lemon Jefferson was a veritable giant during his time and an unqualified commercial success to boot. Nevertheless, the photo seen here is the only known image of the artist. The autograph, by a blind man, is the work of a publicist.

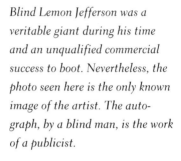

death came out in "Chinch Bug Blues," "Mosquito Moan," "Bootin' Me 'Bout," and "See That My Grave Is Kept Clean." His success as a recording artist enabled him to live well and indulge his pleasures in women and drink, but he remained a rambler between his home state of Texas and the recording studio in Chicago, in Memphis and down in the Delta during the cotton harvest season, in the coal camps of West Virginia, wherever there was money and a demand for his music. And the demand was everywhere, once he became a recording artist. After only four years of stardom and the recording of close to a hundred titles, the end came unexpectedly and horribly—just as he had apparently feared it would. Returning home from playing at a Chicago house party sometime in the winter of 1929–30, Jefferson apparently missed his ride or got lost and froze to death alone in the snow.

One artist who probably benefited from Blind Lemon Jefferson's success was Alger "Texas" Alexander. In fact, his home was just thirty or forty miles south of where Jefferson had been raised, and the two men probably knew one another before the 1920s. Alexander didn't play an instrument; he simply sang in a manner hardly removed from the field holler. The titles of many of his songs indicate that he had known a life of toil in the Texas bottomlands: "Long Lonesome Day Blues," "Corn-Bread Blues," "Section Gang Blues," "Levee Camp Moan Blues," "Farm Hand Blues," "Sabine River Blues," "Bell Cow Blues," "Work Ox Blues," "The Risin' Sun," and "Ninety-Eight Degree Blues." Others were more ominous, such as "Penitentiary Moan Blues," "Thirty Day Blues," and "Justice Blues." His rough singing style and seemingly inexhaustible supply of folk verses and images must have appealed because they sounded so familiar, so obviously drawn from the everyday existence that thousands had known in Texas and other southern states. He had only a limited sense of song structure and seems to have assumed that his accompanists would follow his meandering lines. Perhaps because of this he was privileged to have been accompanied by some of the cream of jazz and blues talent, versatile musicians like guitarists Lonnie Johnson, Eddie Lang, and Little Hat Jones, pianists Eddie Heywood and Clarence Williams, New Orleans trumpeter King Oliver, and the string band the Mississippi Sheiks. For a time he even had his own trio of piano, guitar, and saxophone, called the Sax Black Tams. Between 1927 and 1934 he had sixty-four sides released on records, and continued performing during this period at country suppers and house parties all over Texas and Oklahoma. As a recording artist with a familiar name, he had no trouble attracting guitarists or pianists who would try to accompany him. After serving a prison stretch for killing his wife in the early 1940s, he showed up in a Houston studio in 1950 with a guitarist and pianist and recorded two final pieces in the same style as his earlier songs, "Bottoms Blues" and "Crossroads." He lapsed back into the obscurity and anonymity from which he had come, and he died four years later. But it was not before he had left the world a remarkable portrait of life "in the bottoms."

Texas is a huge state, and it could be expected to produce blues artists of considerable diversity. Among those who recorded during this period were Willard "Ramblin'" Thomas, a native of northwest Louisiana whose austere guitar playing suggested an origin closer to the Mississippi Valley and who sang of tough times in Texas in "No Job Blues," "Hard Dallas Blues," and "Poor Boy Blues"; Dennis "Little Hat" Jones, who was from the San Antonio region and played a busy, nervous guitar style with odd changes of tempo; and J. T. "Funny Paper" Smith, also known as The Howling Wolf, an Oklahoma artist whose finely crafted lyrics and guitar work seemed to belie his preoccupation with themes of hoboing, whiskey, crime, voodoo, and sur-

The Reverend Robert Wilkins, also known as Tim Wilkins, circumspectly recorded some spectacular blues sides between the years 1928 and 1935, after which he turned to the church and refused to do further blues. He stayed active as a gospel artist until his death well into his nineties.

real imagery. There was Coley Jones, a fine guitar and mandolin player who, with his Dallas String Band, performed an eclectic repertoire of blues, folk ballads, rags, and popular tunes, and there was the Dallas Jamboree Jug Band, which recorded a more conventional blues repertoire.

Dallas also produced several fine women blues singers who were counterparts to Texas Alexander: Hattie Hudson, Gertrude Perkins, Ida May Mack, and Bessie Tucker. They sang forthrightly about life on the streets, rough men, fighting, and prison in such songs as "Black Hand Blues," "Wrong Doin' Daddy," "Penitentiary," and "Got Cut All to Pieces." Their accompanists Willie Tyson and K. D. Johnson provide us with some of the few examples of Texas barrelhouse piano playing in the 1920s.

The Texas harmonica tradition was also rarely recorded, but one record made in Dallas by William McCoy in 1927 had an enormous impact on other players. It was "Mama Blues" and "Train Imitations and the Fox Chase," pieces that would be emulated by countless others. Two years later another Texas player named Freeman Stowers, known as the Cotton Belt Porter, recorded some more fine blues as well as vocal imitations of animals in "Texas Wild Cat Chase" and "Sunrise on the Farm."

The cities of Memphis and St. Louis served as destinations for many black men and women seeking escape from the drudgery and oppression of farm life in the Deep South. They were also way stations for those who would migrate farther north. Memphis is still located within the Deep South, and its blues tradition naturally has much of the quality of the music of the nearby Delta and Mississippi hill country along with the closely related sounds of eastern Arkansas and western Tennessee. Most of the early blues musicians were migrants from the surrounding countryside. Typical of these were Reverend Robert Wilkins and Furry Lewis, both from northern

Mississippi but well established in Memphis by the time they recorded in the late 1920s. Wilkins's blues shows a seriousness and sensitivity for human feelings and relationships in the lyrics as well as a strong sense of craftsmanship in melodies and guitar work. Each of Wilkins's pieces is a distinct creation with its own structure, melody, guitar part, and lyric theme. He sang about rambling, longing, and escape in such blues as "Rolling Stone," "That's No Way to Get Along," "Long Train Blues," and "Get Away Blues." He also sang about the death of a loved one in "I'll Go with Her Blues," and about confinement in "Jail House Blues," "Nashville Stonewall Blues," and "Police Sergeant Blues." Not long after his 1935 recording session, which ended with his "Losin' Out Blues," he decided that the life he sang about wasn't for him. He became a minister in the Church of God in Christ and confined his guitar playing to gospel music. He was rediscovered in the 1960s and made some fine gospel recordings, but became embittered after failing to receive songwriter's royalties from one of his pieces that was covered by the Rolling Stones rock group. He went back to church work and died in the late 1980s.

Many people who are asked about their introduction to country blues invariably respond with the name of Walter "Furry" Lewis. Having lost a leg during his hobo youth, Lewis spent his working life as a street cleaner for the city of Memphis, working as a musician on the side. As a young man he was a Beale Street regular and was rumored to have played guitar in W. C. Handy's band.

The husband and wife team of Memphis Minnie and Kansas Joe—The McCoys—enjoyed great popularity between 1929 and 1934, recording countless sides in various settings and achieving commercial success during the worst of the Great Depression. RIGHT

Kansas Joe and Memphis Minnie pose mournfully in a promotion for their recording of "She Wouldn't Give Me None" and "My Mary Blues." BELOW

Furry Lewis lived almost as long but stayed with the blues throughout his life. His blues, like Wilkins's, had plenty of depth, but it was often laced with humor and irony. He played in the slide style on some of his pieces, and in general he displayed more looseness and spontaneity. In addition to his blues, he recorded distinctive versions of three familiar folk ballads about John Henry, Casey Jones (Lewis spells it

Kassie), and the gambler Stack O'Lee. Lewis's original recording career spanned only 1927 to 1929, but he was also rediscovered and recorded again starting in 1959. From this point on he toured occasionally, was visited in Memphis by countless musicians and fans, played many local festivals, served twice as an opening act for the Rolling Stones, appeared on the "Johnny Carson Show" and in a Hollywood movie with Burt Reynolds, and was made the first black Tennessee Colonel by the governor of the state.

Memphis not only presented to musicians the usual opportunities to play at house parties, corner saloons, and on the streets for tips; it was also a staging ground for many traveling tent shows and medicine shows. Some of these were large affairs with jazz bands and dancing choruses, but there were also many smaller shows with perhaps one or two musicians or a small string combo, a comedian or two, and perhaps a tap dancer. Under the leadership of a "doctor" who sold his own bottled remedies, these shows worked the smaller surrounding towns, setting up in the heart of the business district on weekends and shopping days, providing variety entertainment to draw a crowd for the doctor's sales pitch. The audiences were usually a mixture of blacks and whites, and so, at times, were the entertainers. Often, blacks as well as whites wore blackface makeup and performed minstrel show songs and comedy routines. They also performed blues as part of an entertainment meant to hold a mixed audience. One artist who specialized in working these traveling medicine shows was Jim Jackson. Born about 1890 in Hernando, Mississippi, not far from Memphis, and therefore equally familiar with ragtime and blues material along with some of the older folksongs like "Old Dog Blue," Jackson recorded between 1927 and 1930. His repertoire included folk and popular ragtime numbers like "He's in the Jailhouse Now," "I'm a Bad Bad Man," and "I Heard the Voice of a Pork Chop." Most of his blues were laced with generous doses of humor, while his guitar playing was often reduced to a simple strum with sometimes the imitation of a banjo rhythm. His biggest hit was the two-part "Jim Jackson's Kansas City Blues." So popular was this piece that he had to record another two parts, followed by two more parts with "Louisiana" substituted for "Kansas City" in the refrain. Jackson was at the height of his popularity when he wangled a bit part in King Vidor's film classic *Hallelujah*, which was partially filmed in Memphis in 1929. His career went downhill from there, however, as the Depression cut into his source of income from shows. He is said to have returned to Hernando, where he died in the late 1930s.

As was the case in other large cities, the solo blues artists of Memphis often found themselves at a competitive disadvantage with other, larger ensembles. Memphis had plenty of people with money to support musicians, but the image of "blues" held by the wealthy whites and the black bourgeoisie was W. C. Handy with his horn and his band of trained musicians, not the lone guitar picker or piano pounder. Even in the noisy saloons and at tenement parties and outdoors along Beale Street, a solo performer could barely be heard. Some of the solo guitarists simply joined with another guitarist. The resulting guitar duo sound became an important part of the blues scene in Memphis and has provided the nucleus for many larger ensembles even up to the present day. Like duos in other southern cities such as Jackson and Atlanta, those in Memphis featured the playing of two distinct musical lines that meshed with one another melodically, harmonically, and rhythmically. Usually one guitar played treble figures while the other played bass lines. The archetypical Memphis duo was the Beale Street Sheiks, comprised of Frank Stokes and Dan Sane. Stokes was born south of Memphis in 1887 but was resident in the city

Jim Jackson was representative of an older songster-entertainer tradition rooted in traveling medicine shows. His recording career was relatively brief, spanning 1927 to 1930, and his biggest success was his very first outing: the two-part "Jim Jackson's Kansas City Blues."

A local Memphis pick-up group plays at a party during the 1930s. The musicians are (left to right): Robert Burse, Dick Bowles, Little Laura Dukes, Louis Allen, Wilfred Bell, and Will Batts.

and active in music by the turn of the century. A blacksmith by trade, he was the vocalist of the group, who played the guitar with a powerful rhythmic chordal approach while hollering out his verses in a stentorian voice. Sane generally contributed rapid guitar runs in a lower register, sometimes doubling Stokes's playing and at other times playing a complementary line. They recorded mostly blues in several sessions between 1927 and 1929, but among their other selections were old minstrel and medicine show songs like "You Shall" and "Chicken, You Can Roost Behind the Moon." One of their most interesting pieces was "Mr. Crump Don't Like It," a critique of Memphis mayor E. H. Crump's reform politics, which were aimed at shutting down the city's "sinful" places of entertainment, a program that appealed to the black religious community. Ironically, a version of the tune had been used earlier by W. C. Handy as the main theme in his "Memphis Blues," a piece he published in 1912 and a tune that launched the blues into the realm of popular music. Crump himself had commissioned the tune three years earlier as a campaign song. It helped elect the man who would later impose curfews on places of entertainment in Memphis. Frank Stones continued to perform around Memphis through the 1940s, retiring in 1951 when his health began to fail. He sometimes performed with Dan Sane and sometimes with violinist Will Batts, with whom he also made a few recordings in 1929. Stokes died in 1955, and the other two musicians not long thereafter.

The guitar duo sound that enjoyed the greatest longevity on records featured a remarkable woman named Lizzie Douglas, who became better known as Memphis Minnie. She was born in Louisiana in 1897, the oldest of thirteen children. Her family worked its way up through the Mississippi Delta and settled outside Memphis around 1910. She began playing guitar at an early age and was already performing on the streets of Memphis and in traveling shows while still in her teens. In the 1920s she was a frequent sight on Beale Street as well as at juke joints and house parties down in the Delta. Usually she worked with a male partner on second guitar. When she began her recording career in 1929, her partner was Joe McCoy, a Mississippi bluesman who had recently settled in Memphis and the brother of Charlie McCoy, who had accompanied Tommy Johnson and Ishman Bracey. Joe McCoy came to be called Kansas Joe on his records with Memphis Minnie. In the next five years they recorded several dozen blues, with Minnie handling the vocals on the majority. Her first release, "Bumble Bee," was a hit, and she recorded it in four different versions. Minnie and Joe, who had married, then moved to Chicago, the center of blues recording activity in the 1930s. Both were fine guitarists and singers, and the fact that Minnie was clearly the star may have put a strain on their relationship; by 1935 they had gone their separate ways. Minnie worked with pianists and small combos for a while, now at the peak of her popularity. By 1939 she had teamed up with another Memphis guitarist, Ernest Lawlars, who became known as Little Son Joe. They remained together for the rest of their lives, and most of Minnie's many recordings from this point on were essentially duets with Lawlars, sometimes with an added bass or drums. Chicago was their main base of operations, though they made frequent trips back to Memphis. In the mid-1950s they moved back to Memphis and had a five-piece band there for a time. By the end of the decade, both were having health problems. Little Son Joe died of a stroke in 1961, and Minnie suffered a stroke herself about the same time. When she was rediscovered by researchers, she was in a nursing home, unable to play guitar and barely able to talk intelligibly. She never recovered and died in 1973.

Rufus Perryman was better known as "Speckled Red," king of the pound-them-down-to-the-bricks school of boogie-woogie piano.

The most spectacular ensembles on the Memphis blues scene were the jug bands. Such groups were found in nearly every city of the South and border states during the 1920s and 1930s, but it was in Memphis that they most proliferated and reached their peak of artistic development. Much of their success was due to the persistence and organizational ability of their leaders, including Will Shade, Charlie Burse, Gus Cannon, and Jack Kelly. They made liberal use of the upstairs room of Howard Yancy's pool hall on Beale Street, which served as a gathering place and practice room for musicians. Yancy would take calls for bands and act as a booking agent and clearinghouse, calling on one of these bandleaders to put together a group and fill engagements as they became available. In this way, his establishment functioned as an informal musicians' union.

The jug bands played at every conceivable kind of venue and function, at clubs on Beale Street and in the other black neighborhoods, at country juke joints and picnics in the surrounding region, on the streets and in city parks for tips, at birthday parties in private homes, at stag parties in hired hotel rooms, for gatherings of politicians and at civic events and campaigns, at the openings of stores and car lots, in

Two remarkable blues stalwarts jam together: J. D. (Jelly-Jaw) Short and nine-string guitarist Big Joe Williams. Williams, a traveling bluesman for his entire life, was a veritable walking encyclopedia of the blues, who always seemed to know who was where, who was living, and who had passed to the next world.

medicine shows, and on excursion trains and riverboats. Performing a mixture of blues, humorous pieces, ragtime tunes, and breakdowns, they were equally popular with white and black audiences. Even some religious songs were recorded with jug-band accompaniment. The instrumentation usually included the obligatory jug (although this instrument was occasionally dropped on recordings or replaced in the 1930s by the one-string bass), the kazoo, the harmonica, and the guitar. Other instruments that could be added or substituted were the banjo, violin, mandolin, piano, washboard, drums, saxophone, and even the musical saw. Instruments such as the piano, drums, and saxophone tended to show up mostly in the 1930s, as the jug bands tried to modernize in order to compete with other small jazz-influenced blues combos.

The first of the jug groups to record was the Memphis Jug Band under the leadership of Will Shade. Between 1927 and 1934 they recorded close to a hundred titles, sometimes under the names of various vocalists and, on one occasion in 1932, as the Picaninny Jug Band. Members of this group were probably also the artists who backed up Memphis Minnie on two titles in 1930 and recorded several additional numbers with Minnie and her husband Kansas Joe McCoy under the pseudonym of Jed Davenport and His Beale Street Jug Band. The band's personnel varied over the years it recorded, but at its core was always Will Shade, who was equally adept on harmonica and guitar and who sometimes handled the vocals as well. Another key member, who joined the band in 1928 after moving to Memphis from Alabama, was Charlie Burse, who enlivened the band with his tenor guitar playing, acrobatic dancing, and enthusiastic singing. Burse brought a more mainstream blues combo with some vestigial jug-band qualities, the Memphis Mudcats, to the studio in 1939, and his pelvic gyrations in performances in Handy Park on Beale Street during the early 1950s are said to have inspired the young Elvis Presley. Burse was only one of many talented players and singers Will Shade brought into the Memphis Jug Band. Among the others, many of whom went on to make records under their own names, were vocalist and kazoo player Ben Ramey; guitarist Will Weldon, who had a significant recording career of his own in the late 1930s; Vol Stevens, who played a banjo-mandolin and sang; vocalist Jennie Clayton, who was Shade's longtime girlfriend and also recorded under the name of Jennie Pope; violinists Milton Robie and Charlie Pierce, who brought a sophisticated trained musical sound to the group; jug blowers Charlie Polk and Hambone Lewis; Charlie Nickerson, who sang and sometimes played piano; vocalist Hattie Hart; Robert Burse, Charlie's brother, who played one-string bass and various percussion instruments; and Jab Jones, outstanding musician on both the jug and the piano, as well as an occasional vocalist. Will Shade continued to put jug bands together, often with Charlie Burse, through the 1930s and 1940s, and the two were rediscovered and recorded again by blues researcher Samuel Charters in 1956. Shade struggled with alcoholism, but continued to perform and put groups together until his death in 1966.

Perhaps the most distinctive jug band of Memphis was Cannon's Jug Stompers, made so by the presence of the five-string banjo played by its leader Gus Cannon. Cannon was born in 1883 in Red Banks, Mississippi, and spent his early years roaming around the Delta, perfecting his musical skills. He had a core repertoire of old breakdown pieces but gradually assimilated the ragtime repertoire and picking style and was performing mainly blues material by the time he recorded in the late 1920s. His first records, a mixture of ragtime and blues material, were made in 1927 under his familiar nickname of Banjo Joe, with Blind Blake backing him up on guitar.

Mary Johnson—known as "Signifying" Mary Johnson—was an excellent singer and songwriter who was married to Lonnie Johnson for several years. The couple never recorded together—an altogether curious situation, since Lonnie seemed willing to back up virtually any artist capable of finding his or her way to a recording studio. However, Mary did have the good fortune to record with such giants as Henry Brown, Tampa Red, Roosevelt Sykes, Kokomo Arnold, and Peetie Wheatstraw, all of whom added immeasurably to her recordings.

Two members of Whistler's Jug Band—guitarist Buford Threlkeld (the "Whistler") and tenor banjo player Willie Black, who for years was misidentified as a mandolin player.

During the next three years he recorded over two dozen pieces in a jug-band format. Usually his group was just a trio, featuring the extraordinary wailing harmonica of Noah Lewis, with guitar and vocal support by Ashley Thompson, followed by Elijah Avery and finally Hosea Woods. Cannon himself played the jug, suspended from a harness worn around his neck. The fine instrumental work of Cannon and Lewis and their soulful vocals, along with those of Thompson and Woods, resulted in music of a high artistic quality ranking with the best of country blues. Noah Lewis recorded a handful of harmonica solo pieces as well as some others with his own jug band in 1929 and 1930 before fading back into obscurity. Gus Cannon continued to perform in Memphis on a part-time basis into the 1960s. In 1963 he received belated recognition when a New York folk group called the Rooftop Singers remade one of his old recordings, "Walk Right In," into a number-one hit. Cannon was brought back to the studio once again to record an album for Memphis's fledgling Stax Record Company, on which he was backed by Will Shade on guitar and some other jug band veterans. He was in fine form for the session and recorded an excellent album, on which he largely reverted to his early breakdown repertoire. It was a fitting conclusion to a remarkable era of Memphis music. Gus Cannon played less and less as the years went on and died in 1979, close to the age of one hundred.

Jack Kelly and His South Memphis Jug Band didn't record until 1933. Long remembered as a buddy of Frank Stokes, Kelly used both of Stokes's main accompanists, Dan Sane and Will Batts, in his band along with a "Doctor" Higgs on jug. The group sounds more like a small country blues combo with added jug, and when Kelly returned to the studio in 1939, the jug was dropped. He had a fine voice and a strong rhythm on the guitar, which guaranteed his popularity on the Memphis blues scene into the 1950s.

Other Memphis artists recorded with jug band musicians or in styles that showed the influence of the jug-band sound. Among these were Too Tight Henry and Kaiser Clifton in the early years, and Allen Shaw, John Henry Barbee, Little Buddy Doyle, and James De Berry in the 1930s. Memphis was also reputed to have an excellent piano blues tradition, but little of it was recorded in the early years. The few pianists who recorded a handful of sides were total obscurities like Blind Clyde Church, anonymous backers of female vocalists, or artists like Jab Jones who worked mostly as members of jug bands. The great Speckled Red was based in Memphis and was in and out of the city in the late 1920s and most of the 1930s, but he was a journeyman pianist and not representative of the local area's traditions. It was not until Memphis Slim left the city and began his recording career in Chicago in 1940 that a major body of Memphis piano blues began to be committed to records.

Besides Memphis, the city of St. Louis was another major blues center on the way north from the cottonfields of the lower Mississippi Valley. Some of the artists, like J. D. Short, Lane Hardin, Blind Teddy Darby, and Henry Spaulding, were simply transplants from the Deep South who performed passionate down-home blues. Guitarist/pianist Henry Townsend was equally passionate in his delivery, but also displayed a degree of self-consciousness and urban sophistication in the outlook of his lyrics. These same qualities, in a more restrained and orderly approach, were displayed by guitarists "Hi" Henry Brown, Clifford Gibson, and Charley Jordan, while the sophistication reached its ultimate level in the prolific work of the great guitarist and singer Lonnie Johnson. Ever since the days of ragtime, St. Louis had been a major piano center. This instrument was well represented in blues by artists like Henry Brown, James "Stump" Johnson, and Barrel House Buck MacFarland, as well as others who will be discussed later. Some of the most interesting blues from St. Louis was provided by several female singers, most notably Edith North Johnson, Mary Johnson, Luella Miller, Alice Moore, and Bessie Mae Smith. Between them they recorded over a hundred titles, generally accompanied by a pianist and one or two other instrumentalists. Their songs combined elements of the cabaret-vaudeville style with the toughness of country blues, as they sang in an unaffected manner of violence, cheating men, the drudgery of their workaday lives, lovemaking, nightmare images, escape, and a whole host of other subjects. Many of their recordings displayed songwriting skills of a high order that deserve greater recognition and exposure.

Louisville and Cincinnati were other cities on the way north that had significant blues traditions. The sounds here were generally more sophisticated and oriented toward ensemble work rather than solo blues in the country manner. Even guitarists like Sylvester Weaver and Walter Beasley of Louisville were more at home on the vaudeville stage than in juke joints and house parties. Jug bands, string bands, and washboard bands predominated in these two cities on the Ohio River. Clifford Hayes, Earl McDonald, and Buford Threlkeld (better known as "Whistler") were the leaders and organizers of jug bands in Louisville. Those of Hayes and McDonald incorporated jazz instruments, and all three bands leaned heavily toward a popular and ragtime repertoire. Washboard Walter Taylor with sometime partner John Byrd led a more down-home type of ensemble in the city. In Cincinnati the ensemble traditions were represented by Stovepipe No. 1 and David Crockett, the Cincinnati Jug Band, and groups under the direction of James Cole, Walter Cole, Kid Cole, Bob Coleman, and Walter Coleman, all of whom may have been related. These groups tended to preserve more of a southern sound than their counterparts in Louisville.

Some Deep South and Texas blues artists from the 1920s continued to record in the 1930s, but by the end of that decade there were only a few still making records. These were generally artists like Memphis Minnie, who had modernized their styles and adapted to newer trends. Others had died, such as Blind Lemon Jefferson and Charley Patton, while others still, like Son House and Texas Alexander, were content to hustle a musical living on a local or regional level without benefit of current recordings to promote their efforts. Still more artists lost their audiences because they sounded dated or gave up the blues and joined the church in order to lead more settled lives. The Great Depression meant less money was available for entertainment, and for a time it virtually killed the blues recording industry. As the record companies reorganized, one of their responses to the new economic realities was to curtail drastically the on-location recording of blues. While a fair number of blues sessions were held in Texas and New Orleans after 1930, the only Deep South sessions consisted of one each in Jackson, Hattiesburg, Birmingham, and Memphis. By far the bulk of blues recording during the 1930s was done in Chicago and New York, and southern artists generally had to travel to these cities if they wanted to be recorded. Often they settled in the North and adapted their styles to the current trends, recording with the established studio artists in order to give their records a more mainstream sound. Styles and tastes were changing. Pure folk blues by self-accompanied solo artists were fading out, as were string bands and jug bands. The guitar-piano combination, pioneered in the late 1920s by Leroy Carr and Scrapper Blackwell, became more popular, and the new combos often included piano as well as a string bass and often one or two brass or reed instruments. The rhythmic quality of the music was also changing. Swing and boo-

William Bunch, variously known as Peetie Wheatstraw, the Devil's Son-in-Law, and the High Sheriff of Hell, was a tremendously popular pianist-singer who occasionally played guitar and was in constant demand as an accompanist. The limitations of his musical approach had no apparent effect upon his popularity.

gie rhythms predominated. Often there was a tension between duple and triple rhythmic feeling and sometimes a frantic quality to the beat. Instrumental virtuosity and versatility were stressed, and the artists who recorded the most during this period were those who could combine instrumental technique with a clear voice and strong songwriting abilities. Jukeboxes became more common, and artists were needed who could supply dozens of well-crafted blues on novel themes to keep the listeners entertained.

In spite of these important changes, a fair amount of country blues was recorded during the 1930s, some of it by artists who adapted to one or more of these modern trends. In general the pianists fared better than the guitarists during this era, perhaps because the piano was somewhat more easily adaptable to ensemble work and to producing the popular swing and boogie rhythms. The leading piano stylist of the 1930s was Roosevelt Sykes. Born in 1906, he was raised alternately in West Helena, Arkansas, and St. Louis. He was living in the latter city when he began his recording career in 1929. He was in the studio during all but two of the next twenty years, turning out one hit after another, usually performing solo or with a guitarist, bass player, or drummer during the 1930s, but increasingly with larger combos during the 1940s. Although he could play excellent fast pieces and boogies, it was in the slow and medium-paced blues that Sykes was especially innovative. He clearly separated the functions of the right and left hands, playing a deep rumbling bass to hold down the beat while darting all over the keyboard with his right hand, using the latter as a lead instrument in the manner of horn players and later electric guitarists. It was a style that worked well on a solo basis and with larger ensembles. During the 1930s he worked mostly in Memphis, St. Louis, and Chicago, but by the late 1940s he was touring more all over the South, doing one-nighters and short stints in clubs. As his popularity finally began to decline in the 1950s, he moved easily into the folk and blues revival scene, recording many albums and performing in concerts and festivals both here and abroad. He finally became resident in New Orleans and spent his last years there playing mainly for tourists, most of whom were unaware of his important place in blues history. Roosevelt Sykes died in 1983, having been a professional bluesman for over sixty years.

St. Louis, where Roosevelt Sykes got his start as a recording artist, was the home to other important blues pianists in the 1930s, including Walter Davis, who was born in Mississippi but had settled in St. Louis by the time he began recording in 1930. He sang in a sad, melismatic voice and was at first accompanied on piano by Roosevelt Sykes, but by 1935 he began playing his own piano in a simplified version of Sykes's style, yet with individual flourishes that included notes suggesting a minor tonality. During the latter half of the 1930s he was one of the country's most popular blues recording artists. He recorded much less during the 1940s and early 1950s and eventually faded into obscurity, dying in 1964. The other popular pianist of the 1930s was William Bunch, who lived across the Mississippi River in East St. Louis and called himself Peetie Wheatstraw, the Devil's Son-in-Law, and the High Sheriff from Hell. Wheatstraw had come up to St. Louis from Arkansas and also began recording in 1930, playing piano in a more rhythmic style and often working with a guitarist. He sang about the permanent problems and temporary pleasures of urban working-class life during the Depression and came across on records as a barstool buddy and "one of the guys." His voice was often slurred in the manner of someone who has had a few drinks, and he customarily rushed his lines, interjecting falsetto moans—a mannerism admired by countless fans and fellow musicians. His career came to an

Another important artist with a host of pseudonyms, Roosevelt Sykes—a/k/a Dobby Bragg, the Honeydripper, Easy Poppa Johnson, St. Louis Johnny, and Willie Kelly—was a masterful blues boogie-woogie barrelhouse pianist, an excellent songwriter and singer, and an accompanist nonpareil. He was very typical of artists active in St. Louis during the 1920s and 1930s, and he also served sporadically as a talent scout for Decca and RCA Victor.

Hersal Thomas was the youngest "star" of the musical Thomas family. Despite his death at the age of fifteen, he was extremely influential as a boogie-woogie piano player, with the likes of Albert Ammons and Meade "Lux" Lewis paying him homage.

Cow Cow Davenport printed up business cards to make it official: "The man that gave America boogie-woogie." Thanks, Cow Cow.

end on his thirty-ninth birthday in 1941, when the car in which he and his pals were riding was hit by a train.

Other important blues pianists lived farther south. The saloons in the towns and cities along the Mississippi River had always been a haven for pianists. Another important area was the lumber camps and towns of the piney woods district of southern Mississippi and southeast Louisiana. Many blues pianists worked these territories, playing for the workers who loaded and unloaded freight on the riverboats, built the levees, and cut and hauled timber. It was a rough environment, but there were plenty of saloons with pianos that needed players. One pianist who worked along the Mississippi River was Lee Green, one of the mentors of Roosevelt Sykes and the first pianist to record a number of traditional instrumental themes of the region, including the famous "Forty-Four Blues." Another product of this environment was Eurreal "Little Brother" Montgomery, who was born in the lumber town of Kentwood, Louisiana. Montgomery was a superb craftsman on the piano and a virtual library of the styles performed by the many other obscure pianists who roamed this territory. He spent much of the 1930s based in Jackson, Mississippi, working with a large jazz band, but he recorded mostly as a solo bluesman. In the 1940s he became part of the Chicago blues scene and worked successfully in concerts and tours in later years. Another pianist who worked in Jackson in the mid-1930s was Jesse Coleman, better known as Monkey Joe. He migrated to Chicago later in the decade and formed a small blues combo there known as his Music Grinders. Harry Chatmon, who was a brother of Bo, Lonnie, and Sam Chatmon of the Mississippi Sheiks, also recorded some piano blues during the 1930s. Perhaps the top pianist in the piney woods district of southern Mississippi was Cooney Vaughn, who had a reputation as one of the best, and the four pieces he recorded with the Graves Brothers in Hattiesburg in 1936 display a tremendous rhythmic drive coupled with marvelous technique. Another pianist from farther north, around Dyersburg, Tennessee, was Lee Brown, who was picked up by Sleepy John Estes and Hammie Nixon on their way to a session and given a chance to record. He scored a hit with "Little Girl Little Girl" on his first session in 1937, performing in a style somewhat reminiscent of Roosevelt Sykes's, and sustained a recording career for several years thereafter.

The Birmingham area was another center of piano blues activity, its steel mills and coal mines providing a rough industrial environment comparable to the river docks and the levee and lumber camps. Several of the top Birmingham pianists had gone north, such as Clarence "Pine Top" Smith and Charles "Cow Cow" Davenport, but one who stayed was Walter Roland, whose recording career only lasted from 1933 to 1935. During this time he recorded several dozen outstanding blues under his own name and as an accompanist to Lucille Bogan, Sonny Scott, and Joshua White. His style featured a rock-steady rhythm from the left hand and fast rhythmic tremolo figures and cascading runs from the right. He worked especially well with Lucille Bogan, who, under the pseudonym of Bessie Jackson, recorded some remarkable blues on themes of violence, sex, and underworld life. Later in the decade, another fine Birmingham pianist, Robert McCoy, represented the city's tradition as an accompanist to several singers. McCoy made further recordings under his own name in the 1950s and 1960s.

Texas was another area with a piano blues tradition well documented in the 1930s, due in no small part to the continuation of field recording sessions in the state during this era. Recordings made in the 1920s by Dallas artists Willie Tyson, K. D. Johnson, and Whistlin' Alex Moore and members of the Thomas family from

Houston had already demonstrated that the state was rich in blues piano stylists. The recordings of George W. Thomas had, in fact, given the first hints of boogie-woogie-style piano. George made only a few recordings, but his younger brother Hersal recorded prolifically, especially as an accompanist to his niece Hociel Thomas and sister Sippie Wallace, who were two of the stars of vaudeville blues during the 1920s. Another close associate of the Thomas family was Moanin' Bernice Edwards, who had learned to sing and play piano from Hociel and Hersal. Edwards as well as Alex Moore made further recordings in the 1930s, providing a continuity with the earlier period. Edwards joined the church shortly thereafter, but Moore continued to perform his raunchy saloon blues in Dallas until shortly before his death in 1989. The field recording in Texas took place between 1934 and 1937. In general the pianists played in a gentler and more harmonic style than their counterparts in the

Big Joe Williams, shown here with his homemade invention, the nine-string guitar, was a man of many contradictions. He could be quite gruff and dismissive one moment yet helpful and charming the next. This photograph is puzzling in that it shows Williams, a right-handed guitarist, playing with his left.

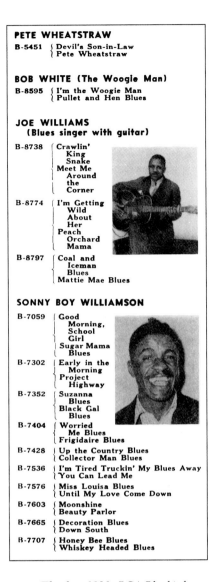

PETE WHEATSTRAW

B-5451 { Devil's Son-in-Law
{ Pete Wheatstraw

BOB WHITE (The Woogie Man)

B-8595 { I'm the Woogie Man
{ Pullet and Hen Blues

JOE WILLIAMS
(Blues singer with guitar)

B-8738 { Crawlin'
{ King
{ Snake
{ Meet Me
{ Around
{ the
{ Corner

B-8774 { I'm Getting
{ Wild
{ About
{ Her
{ Peach
{ Orchard
{ Mama

B-8797 { Coal and
{ Iceman
{ Blues
{ Mattie Mae Blues

SONNY BOY WILLIAMSON

B-7059 { Good
{ Morning,
{ School
{ Girl
{ Sugar Mama
{ Blues

B-7302 { Early in the
{ Morning
{ Project
{ Highway

B-7352 { Suzanna
{ Blues
{ Black Gal
{ Blues

B-7404 { Worried
{ Me Blues
{ Frigidaire Blues

B-7428 { Up the Country Blues
{ Collector Man Blues

B-7536 { I'm Tired Truckin' My Blues Away
{ You Can Lead Me

B-7576 { Miss Louisa Blues
{ Until My Love Come Down

B-7603 { Moonshine
{ Beauty Parlor

B-7665 { Decoration Blues
{ Down South

B-7707 { Honey Bee Blues
{ Whiskey Headed Blues

This late 1930s RCA Bluebird
catalog makes reference to "Pete"
Wheatstraw, an artist almost
always called "Peetie."

Mississippi Valley and Alabama. This may have resulted from the rich ragtime piano tradition in Texas, which had preceded the growth of the blues, or it may have represented an accommodation of the growing jazz movement in the Southwest. Rob Cooper from Houston may provide a link with the ragtime era by way of his "West Dallas Drag," but most of his recorded work was as an accompanist to Joe Pullum, who sang blues in a modernistic style. Another pianist known only as Andy Boy was born in Galveston but grew up in Houston, where he learned his piano skills from Hersal Thomas and other local players. The eight blues he recorded in 1937, as well as accompaniments to Joe Pullum and Walter ("Cowboy") Washington, are good examples of the Texas piano style of this period. Most of the other pianists from this period hustled a living in rough saloons in the towns along the Santa Fe Railroad in the area approximately bounded by the cities of Shreveport, Dallas, Abilene, San Antonio, Corpus Christi, Houston, and Beaumont. They hoboed on trains from town to town, showing up in saloons wherever there was an unoccupied piano stool. Most of their identities were disguised by monickers similar to those of their fellow hoboes. There was Son Becky, Black Boy Shine, Black Ivory King, Pinetop Burks, and Big Boy Knox. Little is known about any of them. Son Becky, Pinetop Burks, and Black Boy Shine all died young, the victims of tuberculosis and exposure brought on by rough living. With the exception of some sessions by Frank Tannehill, recording of Texas pianists on location ceased after 1937. In that same year Curtis Jones brought the style to Chicago, where he became an important recording artist over the next several years and a member of the elite among that city's blues figures. In the years following World War II, other Texas pianists based on the West Coast, like Ivory Joe Hunter, Charles Brown, and Amos Milburn, would develop a more sophisticated piano and vocal sound, bringing the Texas piano tradition into a more modern era and into more refined settings.

While Texas was well represented by pianists, the states of Mississippi and Tennessee were mainly represented by blues guitarists during the 1930s. In Mississippi the guitar styles displayed somewhat less local and regional isolation and more of a synthetic quality than those of an earlier era. Guitarists incorporated swing and boogie rhythms from the piano and jazz traditions. They also frequently displayed a frantic quality in their beat, possibly an influence of the urban jive music that had begun to be recorded by the Mills Brothers, Ink Spots, and many other vocal and instrumental groups in the 1930s. Some of the Mississippi artists were clearly updating the sounds and styles of earlier bluesmen. Otto Virgial, for instance, shows traces of the style of Charley Patton, while Willie "Poor Boy" Lofton offers rather frantic versions of songs and musical ideas recorded earlier by Tommy Johnson and Ishman Bracey. Mose Andrews shows the influence of both Patton and Johnson. Eugene Powell reflects the instrumental virtuosity of the Chatmon and McCoy brothers with a more swinging rhythm. The duets with Willie Harris that Powell recorded in 1936 under the pseudonym of Sonny Boy Nelson and their accompaniments to the singing of Powell's wife Mississippi Matilda are some of the finest two-guitar work ever recorded within the Mississippi tradition. Harris himself may have been the William Harris who recorded superb Delta blues in a rougher style in the late 1920s.

Big Joe Williams was another Mississippi artist influenced by Charley Patton, but he also brought a great amount of individuality to his music. He was born in 1903 in Crawford in the eastern part of the state, but left home early to begin a wandering musician's life that brought him first to Birmingham, where he played with a jug band in the 1920s, and eventually to the Delta, where he came under Patton's influence. He moved on to St. Louis and eventually came to record in Chicago in 1935. His records in this and the following years find him playing a nine-string guitar, something he invented himself, and performing in a frantic and improvisational version of Patton's style. He sang about travel in "49 Highway Blues," about the Depression in "Providence Help the Poor People," about mistreatment in "Stepfather Blues," and of course about women in "Little Leg Woman," "Somebody's Been Borrowing That Stuff," and his classic "Baby Please Don't Go."

Robert Johnson, whose spider-like fingers displayed a musical awareness far beyond the artist's years and era, was a giant now revered by people in all walks of musical life. The extensive mythology surrounding him includes the romantic notion of selling his soul to the devil—at the "crossroads" and on the stroke of midnight—in exchange for his unparalleled musical abilities.

People who both traveled and played with Robert Johnson say that he could carry on a conversation in a roomful of people while the radio was playing in the background, ostensibly paying absolutely no attention to the radio, yet the next day play note for note whatever songs had been on the air. He is quite possibly the most influential blues artist of all time.

Through the 1950s he was back and forth between St. Louis, Chicago, and Mississippi, keeping his name before the wider public by making some records every two or three years. Beyond adding an electric pickup, his basic style never changed, nor did his outlook or rambling life. Despite his tough demeanor, he moved easily into the folk and blues revival of the 1960s and made many concert appearances and tours. He was still performing well, traveling around, and living the same life-style as ever until shortly before his death in 1982.

Other artists who played frenetic and updated versions of older blues styles were Tommy McClennan and Robert Petway. Both had been active around Greenwood in the Delta, both sang in rough, heavy voices, and both played steel-bodied guitars. They had been influenced in the 1930s by Rubin Lacy, who had brought the older central Mississippi sound performed by himself, Ishman Bracey, and Tommy Johnson up to the Delta. McClennan was the more versatile and more prolific on records, recording forty blues between 1939 and 1942. His rowdy sound was quite popular on the jukeboxes, but his career never picked up again due to alcohol abuse, and he faded into obscurity. Less is known of Petway, who recorded only fourteen issued blues in 1941 and 1942, among them the earliest version of the Delta blues classic "Catfish Blues," which McClennan also subsequently recorded as "Deep Blue Sea Blues."

By far the most important of those Mississippi bluesmen who synthesized what had gone before was Robert Johnson. He was born in 1911 in Hazlehurst in the southern part of the state, but was brought to the northern Delta town of Robinsonville by his mother around 1920. An "outside child" who perhaps felt personally rejected, Johnson took an early interest in music. He came under the influence of Son House and Willie Brown, who moved to the Robinsonville area in 1930. Shortly thereafter he left and traveled through Mississippi, absorbing every influence he could. On his 1936 and 1937 recordings, one hears not only the influence of House and Brown but also Skip James, Johnny Temple, and Hambone Willie Newbern among artists he might have encountered personally in the South, along with popular recording artists like Leroy Carr, Peetie Wheatstraw, and Lonnie Johnson. Robert Johnson sang with slightly muffled diction in a passionate, agonized, and sometimes strained voice. His guitar work was brilliant. He could perform percussive bottleneck pieces incorporating and updating older strains of Delta blues found in the music of artists like Son House and Charley Patton, but he could also play walking bass figures and suggest the rich sound of guitar-piano duets of Leroy Carr and Scrapper Blackwell or even larger blues combos. Persistent themes in his blues were religious despair and pursuit by demons. These are expressed in such pieces as "Cross Road Blues," "Preachin' Blues," "If I Had Possession Over Judgment Day," "Stones in My Passway," "Hellhound on My Trail," and "Me and the Devil." Such themes led to rumors and reports that Johnson had actually made a pact with the devil for his mysterious musical powers. Johnson also painted images of constant rambling, degradation, and uninhibited sexuality in pieces like "I Believe I'll Dust My Broom," "Sweet Home Chicago," "Rambling on My Mind," "Terraplane Blues," "They're Red Hot," "Walking Blues," "Drunken Hearted Man," and "Traveling Riverside Blues." Yet he also showed a tender side in such pieces as "When You Got a Good Friend," "Come On in My Kitchen," "I'm a Steady Rollin' Man," "Little Queen of Spades," "Honeymoon Blues," and "Love in Vain." This musical and creative genius died an early death near Greenwood, Mississippi, poisoned by a man who believed Johnson was courting his wife. He had been scheduled to appear in a concert at Carnegie Hall a few months later. Johnson recorded only twenty-nine songs in his brief career, but he left an extraordinary musical legacy and personally influenced a number of blues artists who would carry the music forward over the next two decades. Among these were his stepson Robert "Junior" Lockwood, his partner Johnny Shines, David "Honeyboy" Edwards, Eddie Taylor, and two giants of the postwar Chicago blues scene, Muddy Waters and Elmore James. More than fifty years after his death, a reissue of his complete recordings went gold and won a Grammy Award.

While the Mississippi blues was being updated in the 1930s, a somewhat different evolution was taking place in the country blues of western Tennessee, which had developed in greater isolation in towns such as Brownsville, Ripley, and Jackson. A foretaste of this tradition was provided in 1929 on six recordings by Hambone Willie Newbern of Ripley, a rough-voiced singer who spent a good portion of his life in jails and workhouses. He sang of being arrested for vagrancy in "Shelby County Workhouse Blues"; another of his recordings was the earliest version of what would become a Deep South blues standard, "Roll and Tumble Blues." Newbern's cousin "Sleepy" John Estes began his recording career later that same year, but reached his peak of popularity in the 1930s. Estes was from Brownsville and spent most of his life there or in the city of Memphis, about sixty miles to the southwest. He sang in a distinctive high-pitched crying style and played a rather rudimentary rhythmic guitar, but he generally knew enough to record and perform with skilled accompanists. His first recordings made in Memphis in 1929 and 1930 find him with another outstanding Brownsville musician, James "Yank" Rachell, on mandolin and Jab Jones on piano. Jones was better known as a pianist and jug blower with the Memphis Jug Band. The sound of this trio was unique and especially remarkable for its shifting rhythmic focus. One of Estes's recordings, "The Girl I Love, She Got Long Curly Hair," used a melody similar to that of Newbern's "Roll and Tumble Blues," indicating that this tune was traditional in the blues of the Brownsville and Ripley area. Estes resumed his recording career in 1935, working with a second guitarist and/or harmonica player, generally from the Brownsville area, and recorded forty blues over the next six years. Many of these pieces are remarkable for their descriptions of people and events in Estes's life, and collectively they give the most complete portrait of the experience of a small-town southern blues singer in this era. Estes sang of poverty and the Depression in "Down South Blues," of government relief programs in "Government Money" and "Brownsville Blues," of a near-fatal accident in "Floating Bridge," of the perils of the hobo's life in "Hobo Jungle Blues" and "Special Agent," and of prominent businessmen and patrons in "Liquor Store Blues" and "Lawyer Clark Blues." He recorded more blues in a couple of sessions around 1950, which were not released at the time. By then he had become totally blind, and his career seemed over, but his fortunes took a turn for the better in 1962 when he was rediscovered in Brownsville along with his old harmonica partner Hammie Nixon. Together over the next fifteen years they recorded many times and toured all over the United States, Europe, and Japan. After Estes died in 1977, Nixon continued performing for another seven years until he died as well.

Yank Rachell separated from Estes after their 1930 sessions and began a recording career of his own in 1934. He played both mandolin and guitar on records, working with various second guitarists and eventually with Sonny Boy Williamson on harmonica. Between 1938 and 1941 he had several hits, which were distinguished for their close interplay with Williamson's harmonica and their exciting combination of

The mandolin was never one of the favorite or most frequently used instruments in blues, but perhaps if blues mandolin players all had the virtuosity of James "Yank" Rachell, it would have been a different story. Also an excellent guitar player, he is probably better known as the perennial associate of Sleepy John Estes than in his own right—a lofty enough position, to be sure, but also unfortunate, because he is an artist to be reckoned with.

rural down-home feeling and modern swing rhythm. Rachell himself was rediscovered in Indianapolis in the wake of Estes's rediscovery and has continued to perform blues on mandolin and guitar, offering a rare reflection of a style that was current over fifty years ago. Two other Brownsville guitarists recorded some excellent blues in the 1930s. One was Son Bonds, who sang in a manner rather like Sleepy John Estes, but displayed more dexterity on guitar. He recorded first with Hammie Nixon on harmonica in 1934 and later with Estes on second guitar. Bonds was shot to death while sitting on his front porch in Dyersburg in 1947 in a tragic case of mistaken identity. The other guitarist was Charlie Pickett, about whom little is known. He recorded only four songs in 1937, but his rich voice and intricate guitar work on such pieces as "Let Me Squeeze Your Lemon" and "Down the Highway" suggest that he might have been the best of an outstanding lot of guitar bluesmen from this area.

Sleepy John Estes was one of the most personal and anguished of all blues poets. His recordings are quintessential examples of the best of blues poetry, and some of his early efforts, particularly those with Jab Jones on piano and his longtime partner Yank Rachell on mandolin, are about as good as the blues gets.

Arthur ("Big Boy") Crudup—in an early RCA studio publicity shot. Note his amplifier, prominently displayed among his musical gear.

Tennessee was also noted for an extraordinary harmonica blues tradition. The earliest indications of this were the weekly radio broadcasts of De Ford Bailey on the Grand Ole Opry out of Nashville. Bailey made recordings of some of his best-known pieces in 1927 and 1928, which reveal an amazing technique; often it sounds as if two harmonicas are playing at once. Bailey continued broadcasting regularly into the 1940s and was imitated by many other players, both black and white. At the western end of the state were the harmonica players in the jug bands, most notably Will Shade and Noah Lewis, who was actually from Henning, Tennessee, in the Ripley–Brownsville area. When not working in Memphis, he often performed locally and was a major influence on Hammie Nixon, who recorded in the 1930s with Son Bonds and Sleepy John Estes.

While Lewis played entire blues tunes in an older style, Nixon adapted his ideas and techniques to an accompanying style that served as a second responsorial voice to that of the singer. This approach to the instrument was perfected and joined with updated swing rhythms by a younger player from nearby Jackson, Tennessee,

Crudup, from Midnight, Missis-sippi, was a superb songwriter, a fine singer, an elemental guitarist, and a great innovator. He was one of the "bridges" between pure country and the newer emerging "electric" blues of the early 1940s.

John Lee "Sonny Boy" Williamson. After learning the basics of Nixon's style, Williamson left for St. Louis, where he fell into the company of other blues artists and was brought to Chicago to record in 1937. His first records, some of which were modernized themes that had earlier been recorded by jug bands from Memphis and Brownsville guitarists, were hits and launched him on a career as one of the most successful blues recording artists for the next eleven years. Williamson recorded with many of the top stars and session men in Chicago and had hit after hit, displaying a fine songwriting ability. His harmonica playing and slightly lazy, lisping singing style were widely imitated. Williamson was on the verge of leading the transition to Chicago's postwar electric blues sound when he was brutally murdered there in 1948 during a robbery as he was returning home from performing at a club. It was left to successors like Little Walter and Billy Boy Arnold to carry his style forward into the electric blues era. Together with Roosevelt Sykes and Robert Johnson, Sonny Boy Williamson was one of the most important down-home blues artists of the 1930s, leading the transition from older solo blues styles to modern ensemble styles and making his instrument into a lead voice in an ensemble sound.

The styles created by artists like Robert Johnson, Roosevelt Sykes, and Sonny Boy Williamson brought the main country blues instruments of guitar, piano, and harmonica to such a degree of technical perfection that the only direction in which they could go was toward incorporation into an urban ensemble sound. The consolidation of the recording industry through domination by three major companies and the economic and social disruption of World War II also seemed destined to put an end to country blues as a viable commercial sound on records. Yet one of the very processes that aided in the creation of new blues ensemble sounds, electronic amplification, also served to breathe new life into country blues. This was particularly the case for the guitar and the harmonica, which, as acoustic instruments, could be overwhelmed by louder instruments in the various types of combos. When a magnetic pickup was attached to a guitar or when a harmonica was blown directly into a micro-

Meeting in Memphis (left to right), Willie Nix, Rice Miller (Sonny Boy Williamson II), and Robert Jr. Lockwood, 1949.

John Lee Hooker, from Clarksdale, Mississippi, burst upon the scene in the late 1940s like a gigantic meteor. He is still active today, approaching his music much as he always has. ABOVE

phone, the instruments produced a very different sound. They were once again loud, serious, aggressive voices in the blues.

One artist loomed especially large in the transition to electric country blues. Arthur "Big Boy" Crudup, a native of Mississippi who had hoboed his way north to Chicago, was discovered by the already established blues star Big Bill Broonzy and taken to the studio to make his first records in 1941. He sang with passion in a high, strong voice and played simple rhythmic figures on his amplified guitar in a style well suited to the new louder sound. He was an effective songwriter, able to tap the feelings of other southern migrants like himself who had known hard lives. Unlike most down-home blues artists, Crudup kept recording right through the war era. He added a string bass to his sound and, later, drums—an instrument rarely heard before in a down-home blues setting. But now the country blues guitar could compete with these loud instruments, which provided a heavy bottom as well as powerful rhythmic support. Using the new trio format, Crudup recorded "That's All Right" in 1946. Eight years later, a young white boy in Memphis named Elvis Presley would record a very similar version of this same piece on his first commercial record, launching a new era in American music with a new name: rock 'n' roll.

Crudup continued to make records into the early 1950s, but his career faded just about the time that Presley's was beginning. Discouraged, he worked outside music, transporting migrant farm workers up and down the East Coast until he was rediscovered in the mid 1960s. He toured widely and finally gained a measure of the recognition he was due before suffering a fatal stroke in 1974.

The revolutionary sound pioneered by Crudup was fostered in the years following World War II by the rise of many independent record companies in all parts of the country, often in cities that already had demonstrated strong blues traditions,

This is the earliest known shot of Elmore James and is a photograph of a photograph found on the wall of a rooming house in Mississippi where James had spent a great deal of time. BELOW RIGHT

such as Chicago, Detroit, Memphis, and Houston. Other companies, in cities like Los Angeles and Oakland, took advantage of new patterns of the migration of southerners who took their music with them. Many blacks from the rural South had moved to the cities during and after the war, driven by the lure of wartime and postwar industrial jobs, by the mechanization of agriculture that reduced the demand for farm workers on the plantations, and by a desire to escape from the entrenched patterns of Jim Crow. With postwar prosperity, these migrants, along with those who remained in the South, provided a ready market for country blues music, both live and on record. Another factor that aided in the popularity of country blues—indeed, of all blues styles—was the advent of black radio. Beginning with WDIA in Memphis in 1948, stations with an all-black music format or with significant blocks of time devoted to blues, gospel, and jazz reached every portion of the country that contained a black community. WDIA, with its powerful 50,000-watt signal, boasted that it reached one-tenth of the entire black population of the United States. Many of them were farm workers or city and town dwellers who had recently left the farms. Between 1948 and the mid-1950s there was an increase in the recording of down-home country blues, mostly performed by new artists. These records, almost all of them on various new independent labels, were played on the radio and heard on jukeboxes in urban taverns and rural honky-tonks.

As might be expected, the region of Mississippi, Arkansas, and western Tennessee, with its strong blues tradition, provided many artists who contributed to this movement. Few, however, made more than a handful of recordings in a country blues style. Although the results were often superb from artists like Luther Huff, Charley Booker, L. C. Green, Junior Brooks, Willie Nix, and a host of others, the record companies soon found that they could sell even more records by electric blues combos and other artists in urban styles. Many country blues artists, like pianist Willie Love or harmonica player Rice Miller (who took the name of Sonny Boy Williamson following John Lee Williamson's death), had already adopted a combo sound before they began recording. Others, like Muddy Waters, did so shortly after launching their recording careers. Many, like Elmore James, headed for the northern cities soon after enjoying initial success with down-home blues recordings, and quite a few were already based in the North when they began their careers. One of the latter was John Lee Hooker, the only artist from this region to record a large body of country blues material during this period. Hooker was from Clarksdale, Mississippi, but had settled in Detroit by the time he began making records in 1948. His first release, "Boogie Chillen," was a huge hit, and Hooker followed it up over the next few years with dozens of records of just him and his guitar. He recorded for a host of labels, often under such pseudonyms as The Boogie Man, John Lee Cooker, John Lee, Johnny Williams, Texas Slim, John Lee Booker, Delta John, and Birmingham Sam. His style stripped the blues down to its bare essentials of pentatonic tunes and raw guitar riffs in ferocious boogie rhythms. With a single guitar, Hooker could generate the rhythmic energy of an entire jump band. His moaning style of singing often dwelt upon themes of death, loneliness, and despair in the manner of Son House or Robert Johnson. Titles such as "Goin' Mad Blues," "Drifting from Door to Door," "Burnin' Hell," "Nightmare Blues," "Moaning Blues," "No Friend Around," and "Graveyard Blues" are typical of his material from this period. It was not until 1953 that Hooker began to record much with larger combos, but even after this time he frequently reverted to a simpler format. Although often viewed as a "primitive," Hooker pushed the blues as far forward as he pushed it back. His boogie rhythms

The great Muddy Waters (above), who went on to fame in Chicago and beyond, is seen here with Joe Hill Louis (below), a much neglected talent who died young.

Frankie Lee Sims from Texas was yet another neglected blues artist of great substance.

Doctor Isaiah Ross, truly a one-man band, is still active today and has been a great favorite with European audiences.

have continued to be a source of inspiration for many artists in both blues and rock 'n' roll.

An interesting adaptation of the country blues developed in Memphis. It was the one-man band, and its chief exponents were Joe Hill Louis and Doctor Isaiah Ross. Each artist played a guitar and a harmonica mounted on a rack around the neck while playing a bass drum and/or high hats with foot pedals. Although Louis could play some modern-style lead guitar, both he and Ross were at their best playing rhythmic riffs and boogie-woogie patterns, which gave a fuller sound. Both artists for a time hosted radio shows on WDIA, which enhanced their local popularity. Perhaps it was the surplus of country blues talent and the notorious competitiveness of the blues scene in Memphis that sustained these one-man bands, for they could simulate the sound of a larger combo while being hired to perform for the price of a lone musician. Ross moved on to Flint, Michigan, to work in the auto industry while performing music on the side. Louis died in 1957 of tetanus following an accident sustained while doing yard work.

Farther south, around Baton Rouge, Louisiana, a country blues scene developed in the 1950s and began to be recorded in 1954 at Jay Miller's studio in nearby Crowley. Miller entered into an arrangement with the Excello Record Company of Nashville to issue many of his recordings. Excello had a further tie-in with a local radio station that broadcast these and other blues records all over the South on a late-night program that included the advertising of packages of the latest blues hits by mail order. Through this means and through the jukeboxes, the sound of Baton Rouge blues artists was kept before the black public as late as the mid-1960s. The chief artists were all masked by quaint pseudonyms, including Lightnin' Slim, Slim Harpo, Lazy Lester, and Lonesome Sundown. They borrowed ideas from recent blues stars like Lightnin' Hopkins, John Lee Hooker, and Jimmy Reed, combining them with a lazy vocal delivery to forge a unique synthesis that came to be known as the

Louisiana swamp blues sound. The core of this sound was the combination of electric guitar and harmonica, but as time went on, piano, bass, and drums were often added. In the northwest part of the state, around Shreveport, the country blues tradition was sustained in the postwar years by several artists, chief among them James Bledsoe, who recorded some superb blues in 1949 and 1950 under the name of Country Jim.

Several blues artists from Texas had more success in recording a sustained body of country blues material in the postwar years than their counterparts from the Deep South, though they, too, often gravitated toward larger combo sounds. Many of them also relocated in California, just as the Deep South artists had moved to Chicago and Detroit. Lowell Fulson is a good example of these trends. Actually from Tulsa, Oklahoma, he was settled in the San Francisco Bay area by the time he began recording in 1946. Most of his records were in a small combo format, and he can be viewed as one of the leaders in the development of contemporary blues lead guitar. In his early years of recording, however, he occasionally performed only with his brother Martin on second guitar, providing a deep droning country blues sound that beautifully complemented his passionate crying vocals. Andrew "Smokey" Hogg was from east Texas and spent much of the 1940s going back and forth between his home state and Los Angeles. He had recorded a couple of sides in 1937 showing a heavy influence of Peetie Wheatstraw in his singing, but it was not until 1947 that he began to come into his own as a recording artist. Over the next six years he recorded approximately 150 titles in sessions in Los Angeles, San Diego, Houston, and Dallas for many labels. Hogg needed money to support his drinking habit and was always willing to record for any company that paid cash. He occasionally played piano, but his main instrument was the guitar, which he played in a rudimentary style. He was at his best by himself, though he often preferred to work with a pianist and sometimes with larger combos, which occasionally yielded chaotic results. Many of his pieces were personalized versions of previous blues hits, but he also recorded many fine original pieces as well as some that went back to the Texas folk tradition. His two-part "Penitentiary Blues," based on a prison work song, was one of his most effective pieces. He sang in a pleading voice that undoubtedly had great appeal for others like himself, who were torn between the rural South and the lure of the big cities. Although one of his last recordings was "No More Whiskey," liquor got the better of him. He got sick in Los Angeles in 1960 and went home to Texas to die of an ulcer hemorrhage.

Two blues artists based in Dallas displayed distinctive styles on their records made during this era. Frankie Lee Sims had served in the Marines during World War II and had been a schoolteacher for a time before that, but his blues sounds anything but scholarly. He played a raw, distorted electric guitar and had a voice to match. Although some of his playing suggested contemporary lead guitar, he simplified this style and often worked with just one or two other instruments. The excitement of his music makes it a shame that he only recorded a couple dozen tracks before his death in 1970. Melvin "L'il Son" Jackson fared somewhat better. He, too, had served in the military during the war and then made his way to Dallas. He had performed mostly with spiritual groups, but he sent a demonstration recording of his blues singing and guitar playing to a record company in Houston and was rewarded with a session in 1948. His first records sold well, and over the next six years he recorded over sixty pieces. He played an insistent rhythmic guitar and sang with evident sincerity of his successes and failures, hopes and sorrows, of bad men and cruel women. He recorded

Although he hails from Oklahoma, Lowell Fulson is generally associated with Texas blues. He is still very much active today.

both solo and with a band of three to five bebop musicians, who were oddly effective in following Jackson's sometimes unorthodox changes. L'il Son Jackson and his band toured all over the South, but in 1954 Jackson got tired of the rough-and-tumble blues life and returned to Dallas, where he rejoined the church. He was rediscovered by researchers and made one last solo album in 1960, but he never followed it up with personal appearances. He died in 1976.

The most prolific, successful, and consistently "country" of the postwar Texas country bluesmen was Sam "Lightnin'" Hopkins. He was born in Centerville, Texas, in 1912 and learned guitar and left home at an early age. He spent much of the late 1920s, the 1930s, and early 1940s roaming around east Texas and occasionally outside the state, sometimes performing as Texas Alexander's guitarist. In the 1940s he settled in Houston and began performing in the dives along Dowling Street. In 1946 he traveled to Los Angeles to record with Houston pianist Thunder Smith, from which association Hopkins got the nickname "Lightnin'." It was Hopkins who had the hit recordings from the session, while Smith soon faded into obscurity. Hopkins had been somewhat influenced by Blind Lemon Jefferson, but his guitar lines were simpler and more suited to the sustaining quality of the electric guitar. Hopkins was an extraordinary songwriter and seemingly could compose, on the spot, a song on any subject. He practically had to, for over the next six years he recorded close to two hundred titles in Houston, Los Angeles, and New York for a bewildering variety of labels. Like Smokey Hogg, Hopkins was inclined to record for cash rather than under a long-term contract. His songs offered a wry commentary on people and the world about him, as in "Short Haired Woman" and "Automobile Blues," but he could also comment on local and world events, as in "That Mean Old Twister," "European Blues," and "Sad News from Korea." "Tim Moore's Farm," "Groesbeck Blues," and "Penitentiary Blues" contained elements of protest against injustices in the southern social and prison systems. Hopkins's recording career had a brief lull in the mid-1950s, but by the end of the decade he had been located by researchers, still perform-

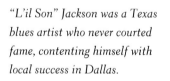

"L'il Son" Jackson was a Texas blues artist who never courted fame, contenting himself with local success in Dallas.

ing in Houston bars and at country picnics. He began recording albums at the same prolific pace for many companies and soon entered the folk and blues revival scene, where he was an instant hit. When not touring all over the world, he could be found back home in his usual haunts along Dowling Street performing for the homefolks. He even had records on southern jukeboxes as late as the 1960s. He passed away in 1982, having given the world an enormous legacy of fine country blues recordings.

Artists like Lightnin' Hopkins and John Lee Hooker brought the country blues through the 1950s. Just when it seemed that interest in this type of blues was once again fading at the end of the decade, blues researchers launched a new wave of recording on their field trips through the South. Samuel Charters, Harry Oster, Alan Lomax, and others who followed rediscovered many of the recording artists of an earlier period, like Sleepy John Estes, Mississippi John Hurt, Son House, Skip James, and Bukka White, while finding many great new artists like Mississippi Fred McDowell, Robert Pete Williams, and Mance Lipscomb. Largely as a result of their work, the sounds of country blues continued to be heard and recorded for another three decades and are still going strong today.

An unidentified twelve-string guitarist plays for the troops in Atlanta some time during the 1920s.

COUNTRY GIRLS, CLASSIC BLUES, AND VAUDEVILLE VOICES

WOMEN AND THE BLUES

RICHARD K. SPOTTSWOOD

◆◆◆

At first glance, it may seem odd that women once enjoyed such a high profile in the blues. Pianists Bertha Gonsoulin and Lil Hardin, who worked with King Oliver; pianist Mary Lou Williams of Kansas City and the John Williams and Andy Kirk bands; and Dolly Jones, whose vaudeville act included jazz trumpet specialties, were part of a small minority of working black female instrumentalists in the 1920s. Chicagoan Lovie Austin was better known, since her name appeared routinely on the Paramount label's blues releases between 1923 and 1926, both as pianist and as leader of Lovie Austin's Blues Serenaders, backing up the label's stars Ida Cox and "Ma" Rainey, and occasionally contributing some group instrumentals on her own.

But it was the singers who commanded center stage in the black vaudeville houses that sprang up in America's major cities during the years of prosperity created by World War I, especially those like the Pekin and Vendome in Chicago, the Lincoln and Lafayette in New York, along with the dozens of clubs, restaurants, and cafés that emerged alongside them, providing countless opportunities for aspiring talent. The comparatively egalitarian nature of the stage gave young women the opportunity to develop their talents and earn at least a precarious livelihood with them. As the blues became profitable, singers toured the country on the T.O.B.A. (Theater Owners' Booking Association) circuit, which linked stages in small towns with those in big ones, allowing residents an occasional evening with their favorites.

This studio glamour shot of Memphis Minnie hardly conveys her powerful approach to the blues. She was among the greatest blues artists of all time. CHAPTER OPENER

Mamie Smith, one of the several unrelated Smith girls, had the distinction of recording "Crazy Blues" in 1920, generally considered to be the very first blues recording. She also had a successful career in films. RIGHT

The story of the blues is inseparable from that of the phonograph record, which has played a crucial role in the dissemination of popular music in this century. Until 1920, the recording industry was all but closed to black American musicians and entertainers, with a handful of exceptions like comic Bert Williams, coon-shouter George W. Johnson, Jim Europe's and Ford Dabney's "society" orchestras, and a few spiritual singers, all of whom achieved a place in the white entertainment world early in the century. Oddly, the pioneering Victor, Columbia, and Edison companies had no compunction about recording black artists in Central and South America; black performances from Cuba, Puerto Rico, Brazil, and Argentina survive from 1910 and earlier, made during the companies' frequent field trips to record and distribute indigenous music from these and other countries of the Americas. In the United States, black music and musical style were usurped and "polished" by white vaudevil-

lians like Marie Cahill, Eddie Cantor, May Irwin, and Al Jolson, accompanied by record-company house orchestras. Popular white entertainers drew heavily on the compositions of James A. Bland, Gussie L. Davis, Creamer and Layton, Shelton Brooks, and other black writers, delivering them either in broad dialect or with other stylistic elements designed to be demeaning. (In fairness, we should remember that Jews, Hispanics, and others perceived as alien to white mainstream culture were also considered fair game for parody in the entertainment world.)

Given these conditions, the appearance of Mamie Smith on records in 1920 was truly a history-making event. She was thirty-seven at the time, a veteran of years of touring as a dancer, chorus girl, and cabaret singer. Her first few records, especially "Crazy Blues," sold exceptionally well, opening the way for other talented black vaudeville ladies—Edith Wilson, Mary Stafford, Lucille Hegamin, Trixie Smith, and Ethel Waters, to name a few—to supplement their incomes with record making.

Except for trips to ports of call below the border, virtually all recording in the early 1920s took place in New York, where sophisticated Harlemites (by and large) had little interest in the blues. Perry Bradford reported that W. C. Handy's band from Memphis was scorned when they attempted to play the blues at Harlem's Lafayette Theater in 1918. Some minds changed when early successes like "Crazy Blues," Ethel Waters's "Down Home Blues," and Lucille Hegamin's "Arkansas Blues" achieved hit status on records; still, these singers (with the very notable exception of Waters) had comparatively little success with the semiblues hybrid tunes turned out by hopeful Broadway writers and publishers throughout the 1920s with the aim of "improving" on the blues.

One exception to the rule was Atlanta-born Trixie Smith, whose "Trixie's Blues" merited first prize in a widely publicized blues contest and a subsequent recording contract in 1922. Though she was also a veteran of the stage, her southern

Edith Wilson appears with her Original Jazz Hounds.

roots kept her close to the blues. "Freight Train Blues," "My Man Rocks Me," "Railroad Blues," and "Mining Camp Blues" incorporated traditional elements into new compositions and served notice that there was a hearty appetite outside New York for nonvaudeville blues.

Though she was an excellent singer, Trixie Smith produced slight impact compared to that made by Bessie Smith, whose superbly resonant voice captured depths of emotion old to the blues but new to records when her first efforts were published in 1923. By then, she had worked southern minstrel shows as well as northern theaters, becoming a seasoned singer of both pop songs and blues. Rumors persist that recording auditions were made in 1921–22 and that she was turned down because of her earthy voice and her earthy behavior. True or not, such stories (and there are plenty more) have helped enshrine a great singer in even greater legend.

Bessie Smith is seen here as a young woman at the outset of her career. Thomas Edison, inventor of the phonograph and head of the world's first recording company, noted of young Bessie Smith in his talent audition file: "Voice n.g. 4/21/24."

Columbia Records producer Frank Walker did record Bessie Smith early in 1923 and promptly signed her to a one-year exclusive contract, despite the fact that her first record (and her first major hit) was a cover of "Down Hearted Blues," which Alberta Hunter had written and recorded two years previously. Pianist Clarence Williams, who brought Smith to Walker, was an active composer and publisher in his own right. Williams composed "Gulf Coast Blues" (on the reverse side) and had obtained publishing rights to "Down Hearted Blues." Obviously, his interest was in promoting his own catalog as well as a new singer.

Edison, Emerson, Black Swan, and Okeh have all been cited as companies that turned Bessie Smith down after auditions. Hindsight makes it easy to scorn their mistakes. However, the reasons for these early resections become clearer when Smith's first records are compared with those of her contemporaries, whose thinner voices were less of a threat to disk-cutting styli and whose dialects were far less pronounced. All the more credit, then, to Frank Walker, whose judgment was quickly vindicated in the marketplace. The pairing of "Gulf Coast Blues" and "Down Hearted Blues" sold almost 800,000 copies during 1923, a figure that probably exceeded even that of "Crazy Blues" three years earlier. Though her subsequent releases never outdid the first, she remained a prominent artist on the Columbia roster until the Depression. Frank Walker also remained with the company for several years and was still in the business as a producer for MGM Records in 1947. At that time he hit another home run when he signed an unknown Alabama honky-tonk singer named Hank Williams.

Bessie Smith's records were invariably made in New York, where optimal studio conditions prevailed and where the broad resonance of her magnificent voice could best be captured. She rarely used more than two or three musicians to back her; often she and Walker were satisfied with simple piano accompaniments, which allowed minimum distraction from her singing. Still, her best efforts usually involved larger groups, mostly drawn from pianist Fletcher Henderson's orchestra. Cornetists Joe Smith and Louis Armstrong provided memorable second voices on the few songs they played on; trombonist Charlie Green was an exceptionally fine blues soloist in Henderson's band and on his numerous accompaniments for Bessie Smith, who on one occasion even paid tribute to him with the song "Trombone Cholly." Green and Joe Smith also participated in a unique 1927 session devoted exclusively to Tin Pan Alley tunes; the Bessie Smith versions of "Alexander's Ragtime Band," "After You've Gone," and "There'll Be a Hot Time in the Old Town Tonight" remain definitive and unsurpassed.

On other occasions, her records are flawed by plodding accompaniments and funereal tempos, designed to give her powerful voice maximum leeway. Presumably, this kind of delivery worked well in live performance situations, when she performed without microphones in large halls, and musicians of the caliber of clarinetists Bob Fuller and Abraham Wheat or pianists Porter Grainger and Fred Longshaw were sufficient for the understated backings required. But on records these men fare poorly and are heard all too well. Smith's best records tend to be those with capable musicians who were better able to support her while providing interesting moments on their own.

Bessie Smith succeeded in part because she masterfully straddled the line between vaudeville and the blues, drawing on rural black vocal style to enhance material that sounded perfunctory by comparison when performed by her stage-oriented contemporaries.

Producer Frank Walker is seen here at the contract signing of one of his most important discoveries, Hank Williams.

"Ma" Rainey, one of the most important and influential of all female blues artists, seen with her Georgia Band, Georgia Tom Dorsey, piano.

Gertrude Pridgett "Ma" Rainey had worked the stage, too, with the carnivals, minstrel shows, and tent shows that were the forums for black entertainers in the Deep South even before the turn of the century. In a rare, perhaps unique, interview, she told folksong scholar John W. Work that she first encountered the blues

in 1902 in a small town in Missouri where she was appearing with a show under a tent. She tells of a girl from the town who came to the tent one morning and began to sing about the "man" who had left her. The song was so strange and poignant that it attracted much attention. "Ma" Rainey became so interested that she learned the song from the visitor, and used it often in her "act" as an encore.

The song elicited such response from the audiences that it won a special place in her "act" as an encore. Many times she was asked what kind of song it was, and one day she replied, in a moment of inspiration, "It's the Blues."

This account is fascinating because it inspires at least as many questions as it answers. Rainey also told Work that she had received comments in the press about her singing of "these strange songs" as early as 1905. If her memory was accurate, she had encountered the blues even before W. C. Handy first heard it in Tutwiler, Mississippi, in 1903. Most accounts place the origin of the blues in the first years of this century. If "Ma" (the name always appeared in quotes) Rainey's account is as plausible as it seems, she served as both midwife to the new music and as an important early champion, adopting the blues as a professional singer and introducing it throughout the South and Midwest in her popular shows. It would be interesting to know what sorts of songs the blues displaced in her repertory; there is little besides blues on the records she began to make twenty years later. It would also be nice if we knew what the song was that she heard on that Missouri morning, and could discover the 1905 press clips she cited to Work.

With three exceptions, the female blues singers who graced early 1920s recordings were born around 1895. Mamie Smith (1883–1946), Sara Martin (1884–1955), and "Ma" Rainey (1886–1939) were well into their thirties by the time they made records. Smith and Martin provided the innovative novelties their sophisticated audiences enjoyed. Rainey, by contrast, was steeped in the folk culture of her people. References to agriculture, hard times, superstitions, and, above all, loves won and lost, kept her appeal close to the ground.

This is not to say that "Ma" Rainey was nothing more than a bearer of tradition. The authorship, ownership, and copyrighting of songs were not such consequential matters as they have since become, so it is hard to know to what extent she composed her own material or simply borrowed and polished the efforts of others. The recorded songs suggest that they were deeply imbued with her own personality and outlook—that of the weary veteran who's been there and seen it all, whose vulnerability to pain and heartbreak is tempered by a residual toughness, if not cynicism, that gives her blues universality and timelessness. She used folk traditions creatively, setting her "Stack O'Lee Blues" to the Leighton-Shields "Frankie and Johnny" melody on one occasion and contributing one of the earliest recorded Titanic disaster songs on another ("Titanic Man Blues," 1925). She dealt frankly with social deviancy, combining humor with an expression of shock when she sang of finding her man with another man ("Sissy Blues"), but celebrating lesbianism in her first-person "Prove It on Me Blues" and bemoaning the life of a prostitute in "Hustling Blues." These and other tough-minded songs pull no punches. They're blues at their best, allowing humor to merge with grief, and candor in turn to displace vulgarity. No less superb are her lyrics on the themes of lost and betrayed love, as in the closing verse of what may have been her most popular song, "Bo-Weavil Blues":

> *I went down town*
> *I got me a hat*
> *I brought it back home*
> *I laid it on the shelf*
> *I looked at my bed*
> *I'm gettin' tired sleepin' by myself.*

Inevitably, "Ma" Rainey is compared with Bessie Smith; just as inevitably, the latter is seen to personify the blues of their era more than Rainey does. They were both supremely gifted performers; the chief difference between them is in the way their voices were recorded. Bessie Smith was fortunate to have placed herself in the hands of Frank Walker and Columbia Records. In Walker she found a supportive pro-

Sara Martin and Clarence Williams, as seen in a studio portrait. Martin had the good fortune to make numerous recordings in different settings. Similarly, Williams, a mediocre pianist at best, was much in demand as an accompanist during the 1920s. On the same day that he panned Bessie Smith in audition, Thomas Edison indicated of Sara Martin: "No, voice bad. 4/21/24."

ducer and, in Columbia, a state-of-the-art recording system, especially after May 1925, when Columbia licensed Western Electric's new electrical recording techniques.

"Ma" Rainey settled for considerably less when she signed on with the Paramount label in Chicago. By the time of her first records, in December 1923, the label had found a profitable niche in the emerging blues industry, especially after discovering that it could market a technically inferior product to minority consumers. As a result, the Rainey records are relatively inaccessible to modern ears. Her low, throaty contralto voice hadn't much volume to begin with, and the recordings have trouble capturing the nuances of her dialect. Sometimes one has to strain to catch words and even whole phrases, which threaten to disappear behind a curtain of inferior sound. Even so, the original products sound a good deal better than the reissues of them that began appearing even before her death in 1939. Those available today suffer from excessive noise filtering and "enhancing," both efforts to compensate for the limited availability of clean original pressings for copying. At this writing,

Columbia is making Bessie Smith's complete works available on compact disc; sadly, there is no comparable effort in sight for the magnificent music of "Ma" Rainey.

Another notable blues singer from the period was Ida Cox, whose career paralleled "Ma" Rainey's in some respects. Both toured with the same minstrel and tent shows in the 1910s, and both became established stars with large followings after they began to record with Paramount in 1923. Cox was also a gifted blues poet, whose songs of death and its attendant beliefs and superstitions became a prominent feature in her work after the 1923 hit "Graveyard Dream Blues." Follow-ups on this included "Bone Orchard Blues," "Death Letter Blues," "Marble Stone Blues," "Coffin Blues," and even a "Graveyard Bound Blues." Ida Cox was far from the first to find inspiration for song in death and burial, themes central to sacred music, to ancient ballads, and even to a good deal of popular music in the last century. Cox recorded "Graveyard Dream Blues" in June 1923 (the exact date is lost) at the same time that Fiddlin' John Carson was making the first genuine hillbilly record for Okeh in Atlanta, "The Little Old Log Cabin in the Lane," an 1870 composition about imminent death. Songs of death remained central to country music for decades, and the theme figures importantly in the country blues of Blind Lemon Jefferson, Leroy Carr, Charley Patton, Robert Johnson, and others, though not as prominently as in Ida Cox's music.

Cox's other memorable songs include "I've Got the Blues for Rampart Street," the first lyric on record to celebrate the music and nightlife of New Orleans, and "Wild Women Don't Have the Blues," a theme celebrated by contemporary feminists who know the idiom. "The Blues Ain't Nothin' Else But!" adroitly defines the genre, and "Hard, Oh Lawd" is an early version of "Hard, Ain't It Hard," a folk song later commemorated by Skip James, Roy Acuff, and the Weavers, among others.

Louisville-born Sara Martin was from the generation of Rainey and Mamie Smith. Though not gifted with a great voice, her showmanship and versatility made her a sought-after performer. Her first Okeh record from 1922, "Sugar Blues," became a classic, revived by Bob Wills and trumpeter Clyde McCoy in the 1930s. Martin also put early versions of W. C. Handy's folk-derived "Joe Turner Blues," "Hesitation Blues," and Tony Jackson's "Michigan Water Blues" on record. Her choice of accompanists revealed far-ranging tastes. Fats Waller was featured on two of her first three releases. Louisville guitarist Sylvester Weaver came to New York in 1923 to lend some rural flavor to several of her songs and cut several exciting instrumental pieces of his own, giving Martin the honor of sponsoring the first country bluesman to record. In 1924, Clifford Hayes and Earl McDonald brought a jug band from Louisville to play on her records and make some of their own. She retired from performing after 1928 to devote herself to church work. Even before then, she had recorded some exciting gospel music on several occasions with Sylvester Weaver, Arizona Dranes, the blind singer-composer-pianist from the Church of God in Christ, and, in 1927, with her future husband Hayes Withers.

The year 1923 brought Rainey, Cox, and Bessie Smith to the studios for the first time, marking at least a partial swing away from the vaudeville blues of New York. Rainey and Cox emerged from the Chicago milieu, specifically from the Monogram Theater, where Paramount Records recording supervisor Mayo Williams first heard them and persuaded them to record. Their success ensured that the focus of Paramount's blues-recording activity would remain in Chicago, where the company could mine the enormous reserves of black talent passing through on the T.O.B.A. circuit or living in the city itself.

Although she was not in the same league as "Ma" Rainey or Bessie Smith, Ida Cox was an extremely good singer and writer who recorded a number of outstanding items.

A member of the famous Thomas family of Texas, Sippie Wallace enjoyed a good deal of success her second time around, during the blues revival of the 1960s.

That same year saw the first major expansion of recording activity beyond the confines of New York. Though Victor, Columbia, and Edison had engaged recording teams to travel by water to Central and South America beginning in 1904–1905, New York remained virtually the only recording location in the U.S. until the early 1920s. The best remembered of these early field trips took the Okeh company to Atlanta and Chicago in June 1923, at the same time that Ida Cox was making her first recordings. To these were added other major southern and midwestern metropolises, as every record company with the means to do so took to the road in order to discovery blues singers, hillbilly bands, and other artists with popular regional appeal. Broadening the geographical recording base also allowed the appearance of so-called country blues on record for the first time. In 1925–26, performers like Blind Blake, Blind Lemon Jefferson, Lonnie Johnson, and Papa Charlie Jackson sang on record to their own guitar accompaniments in a folk-blues style whose appeal soon rivaled the vaudeville ladies of New York.

The term *country blues* is something of a misnomer, since it applies to all non-vaudeville blues, whether rural, urban, or something in between. Women singers were still featured in some quantity on records during the late 1920s, though in lesser number than before. The first of the regional singers to enjoy a hit was Texas-born Beulah "Sippie" Wallace, with her first coupling, "Shorty George" and "Up the Country Blues" in 1923. She was part of a highly productive musical family that included her brothers pianist Hersal Thomas and composer George Thomas. A niece, Hociel Thomas, was also a significant blues singer in the mid-1920s. Wallace herself survived to become a featured artist on the folk festival circuit from the 1960s until her death in 1986.

Victoria Spivey came from another musical Texas family; her sisters Addie (Sweet Pease) and Elton also had minor blues careers in the 1920s and 1930s, but Victoria became the star with her 1926 "Black Snake Blues," recorded for Okeh while she was living in St. Louis. The song also did well for Blind Lemon Jefferson the following year, when "That Black Snake Moan" became his own signature piece. Spivey's "TB Blues," "Furniture Man Blues" (with Lonnie Johnson), and "Funny Feathers" kept her in the limelight and helped keep her almost constantly active until her death in 1976.

St. Louis was home to many blues singers who found their way onto records after Lonnie Johnson and Victoria Spivey. Music retailer Jesse Johnson organized a number of trips to Chicago, Richmond, Indiana (home of Gennett Records) and Grafton, Wisconsin (Paramount Records, after 1929) for talented St. Louis blues musicians, who became prominent in catalogs after 1926. Guitarist/mandolinist Al Miller accompanied his wife Luella on a number of discs made for Vocalion between 1926 and 1928; Mary Johnson was married to Lonnie Johnson between 1925 and 1932, though they did not record together. The best of her all-too-few records contain remarkable blues poetry, some with accompaniments by extra-rough trombonist Ike Rodgers and the influential pianist Henry Brown. Edith North Johnson (married to Jesse Johnson) played her own piano on several of her songs; Roosevelt Sykes sat in for her on others. Her "Honey Dripper Blues" is the source of the name ("The Honey Dripper") by which Sykes was best known in the 1930s. Alice Moore (Little Alice from St. Louis) was perhaps the best of the city's female blues figures. Her tight, intense soprano voice lent special power to her songs, which included several versions of "Black and Evil Blues," a chilling statement of self-denial based on color. Equally compelling is "Broadway Street Woman Blues," a narrative piece about the arrest

and conviction of a prostitute. Ike Rodgers and Henry Brown worked on some of her best records; other St. Louis bluesmen like Peetie Wheatstraw, Jimmie Gordon, and Lonnie Johnson were also prominent in Moore's recording groups.

Alice Moore and her St. Louis contemporaries might have enjoyed more prominence had the list of their records been longer or had they been touring performers like "Ma" Rainey and Bessie Smith, thereby leaving behind something of a story about their lives and careers. As it is, little information about them survives; were it not for the recordings, even their names would be forgotten. Much the same is true of blues figures, male and female, throughout the South. Many were amateurs or semiprofessionals, who left little trace beyond a chance encounter with a recording microphone.

Though New York remained the focal point for recording activity in the 1920s and 1930s, it was never the only place where records were made. Regional phono-

Hociel Thomas, another member of the famed Thomas family, was a boogie-woogie pianist who carried on the tradition of her short-lived uncle, Hersal Thomas.

Addie (Sweet Pease) Spivey, who also recorded under the name of Hannah Mae, was generally found in the company of jazz players who had a bent for the blues. Here she looks more like a movie star than a blues artist.

graph companies were licensed under Edison's patents in the 1890s. Edison also recorded some Cantonese opera by Chinese immigrants in San Francisco in 1902, and Columbia took portable equipment to Chicago in 1915 to record Polish music. The first trip to the American South was long overdue by the time Okeh made the first of many excursions to Atlanta in June 1923, to record local musicians then receiving national prominence through exposure on station WSB, whose powerful signal covered a fair portion of the globe after it went on the air in March 1922. Okeh recorded local dance bands, spirituals by the Morehouse College Quartet, hillbilly tunes by Fiddlin' John Carson, and one side each by blues singers Fannie Goosby and Lucille Bogan. Both were summoned to New York for further recording soon thereafter, but their efforts made little impact at the time—primarily because Okeh already had a thriving catalog of blues singers competing for attention.

Lucille Bogan became an interesting figure. She lived in Birmingham, Alabama, where, as pianist Big Chief Ellis remembered, she had strong ties to the city's black underworld. She next appeared in Paramount's Chicago studios in 1927 and recorded again in Chicago for Brunswick between 1928 and 1930. In March of that year, she recorded "Alley Boogie" with pianist Charles Avery, which became a minor hit and remains noteworthy as one of the first pieces after the death of Clarence "Pine Top" Smith in 1929 to associate the name "boogie-woogie" with the blues piano style. Bogan also recorded an unsentimental song about the difficult economics of prostitution during the Depression. For some reason, it was titled "They Ain't Walking No More" on her March 1930 session and remade in a December session, this time correctly titled "Tricks Ain't Walking No More."

The latter was reissued in 1932, along with "Alley Boogie," on lower-priced labels intended for sale in five-and-ten stores. These issues credited Bogan as Bessie Jackson and did well enough to warrant her recording many more titles under this new name between 1933 and 1935. The "tough woman" stance she assumed in these songs was not new. Bessie Smith, "Ma" Rainey, and Victoria Spivey had made songs in the 1920s celebrating murder, dope, prostitution, and other "antisocial" activities

An Okeh ad for Spivey and Johnson's "Furniture Man Blues." ABOVE

Victoria Spivey's recording career started at around age sixteen, with her very first effort, "Black Snake Blues," quickly becoming a blues staple. She made numerous recordings and was accompanied by such musical giants as Lonnie Johnson, King Oliver, Louis Armstrong, and Henry "Red" Allen. She enjoyed renewed fame during the blues revival of the 1960s. LEFT

Lucille Bogan, whose recording career spanned 1923 to 1935, was one of the great blueswomen of all time. A provocative singer and extraordinarily talented writer, she generally teamed with Walter Roland on piano. Bogan moved to Los Angeles in the mid-1930s and was killed by an automobile during her first week in that city. Walter Roland was never heard from again after 1935.

as elements of power and independence in at least some women's lives. Rainey, as we've noted, added lesbianism to that list; so did Lucille Bogan, with "Women Won't Need No Men" in 1927 and "B.D. [i.e., bull dyke] Woman's Blues" in 1935. She also made understandably bowdlerized versions of the bawdy classics "Sweet Petunia" in 1927 and "Shave 'Em Dry" in 1935. The Cincinnati pianist Jesse James recorded a relatively unexpurgated version of the former in 1936, which was issued pseudonymously on an under-the-counter pressing in the 1950s. Bogan herself recorded a completely uncensored version of "Shave 'Em Dry," which was also pressed anonymously. It stands alone among recorded blues performances in its celebration of uninhibited sexuality and its potential to continue to surprise—if not shock—veterans of the sexual revolution in the 1990s.

The "Bessie Jackson" records were enhanced by the piano work of another Birmingham native, Walter Roland, whose spare, rolling accompaniments suited Bogan's moods perfectly. Their work together marks the last appearance of a major female blues singer in the grand 1920s big-voiced shouting style of "Ma" Rainey and Bessie Smith. Lucille Bogan was a fine singer of compelling blues, whose work deserves to be more widely heard in our own time.

By the late 1920s, male blues singers who provided their own guitar or piano accompaniment had come to dominate the blues record market. They were inexpensive to record, especially since most received cash payments instead of royalty contracts. Names like Alberta Brown (New Orleans), Bertha Ross (Birmingham), and Cleo Gibson (Atlanta) reveal exciting female voices on a handful of obscure recordings, but they prove exceptions to the rule. Two Dallas singers enjoyed brief recording careers in the late 1920s. Lillian Glinn recorded two popular tunes, "Doggin' Me Blues" and "Brown Skin Blues," on a Columbia coupling (14275-D) when the company made its first of several annual visits to Dallas in 1927. The latter title, with the refrain, "a brown skin man's all right with me," was one of all too few songs *celebrating* negritude during the era. Bessie Tucker's mournful, resonant contralto voice echoed the cottonfield hollering styles of Blind Lemon Jefferson and Texas Alexander. The few records she made in 1928–29 contain some remarkable songs, including a startling redaction of the children's favorite, "Ride and Shine on the Dummy Line." In "The Dummy," she tried to slip by without paying the fare, and the trainman "took me by the hand and led me to the door, he beat me 'cross the head with a two-by-four." "Key to the Bushes" is a defiant prison blues in the best Texas tradition:

> *Captain got a big horse-pistol*
> *And he thinks he's bad*
> *I'm gonna take it this mornin'*
> *If he makes me mad*

Like Lucille Bogan in Birmingham, Tucker had a reputation as a tough customer in the Dallas underworld, an image at odds with a surviving 1920s publicity shot, which shows a thin young woman with delicate features and a pleasant smile.

Along with a handful of bluesmen like Tampa Red and Big Bill Broonzy, Memphis Minnie was one of the few figures to make a successful transition from the rural, guitar-dominated blues of the 1920s to the urban nightclub styles of the 1930s. Born Lizzie "Kid" Douglas near New Orleans before the turn of the century, Minnie shared in the music activities of the streets and saloons in Memphis after the war. By

1929, she was on records with her equally gifted husband, Kansas Joe McCoy, with whom she made solos and duets against the background of their solid twin-guitar work. The McCoys went their separate ways in 1935; Joe founded the successful Harlem Hamfats band with his brother Charlie McCoy, while Minnie joined a loosely knit group of blues singers contracted by publisher/producer Lester Melrose to various labels for recording purposes. By 1935, she was working with rhythm sections on records designed for dancing and the tavern jukeboxes that were beginning to proliferate following the repeal of prohibition in 1933. Her first coupling for Vocalion, "Bumble Bee"/"I'm Talking About You," was a fair-sized hit in 1930. Minnie was the guest on a Memphis Jug Band cover of "Bumble Bee" later in the year. "I'm Talking About You" became a western-swing favorite of groups led by the Maddox Brothers and Rose, Bob Wills, and Milton Brown. "Fishin' Blues" from 1932 was not a big hit at a time when record sales were in a slump, but it made enough of an impact to be covered by Bumble Bee Slim in 1935 and country singer Lew Childre in 1936. Childre became a mainstay of the Grand Ole Opry in the 1940s and 1950s, and Minnie's song became more closely associated with him than any other. She married Little Son Joe (Ernest Lawlars) in 1939 and began working with him in a twin-guitar setting. Her next major hit came in 1941, after she acquired an electric guitar. "Me and My Chauffeur" made all the jukeboxes, as did "Black Rat Swing," which featured Joe's singing and was credited to *Mr.* Memphis Minnie.

With the exceptions noted, the 1930s saw the increased dominance of male blues artists who, with few exceptions, provided their own accompaniments, even when they were joined on record by Melrose-style rhythm sections. White and black singers like Ethel Waters, Ivy Anderson, Billie Holiday, Mildred Bailey, Ella Fitzgerald, and Teddy Grace included blues in their repertoires, but only as part of their larger mix of popular songs and show tunes. Even Helen Humes, who had recorded as a teenage blues singer in 1927, stuck to ballads and torch songs during the several years she worked with Count Basie, leaving the blues to Jimmy Rushing.

The same recording of "Black Rat Swing" was released in two curious permutations: by "Mr. Memphis Minnie," as shown here, and by Little Son Joe.

Alberta Hunter was more a vaude-villian than a blues singer. She enjoyed great success during the 1930s in Europe, then dropped out of sight for many years until she was rediscovered in her eighties, becoming the darling of New York nightclubs.

A few women did remain loyal to the blues in the 1930s, probably to the detriment of careers they might have enjoyed had they taken up pop music as well. Their preoccupation with suggestive songs had more to do with the marketplace and the demands of jukebox operators than with the desires of the singers themselves. Georgia White made an impact with revived older tunes like "Trouble in Mind," "Dupree Blues," "Alley Boogie," and "Your Worries Ain't Like Mine," but songs like "I'll Keep Sittin' on It" and "Daddy, Let Me Lay It on You" predictably fared better. Lil Johnson scored with "Hot Nuts (Get 'Em From the Peanut Man)" and "Press My Button (Ring My Bell)" in 1936, which set the pace for more of the same. Fortunately, many of her records are enlivened by the presence of pianist Black Bob (Hudson) and guitarist Big Bill Broonzy, who were surely encouraged by Johnson's good-natured raucous singing. Merline Johnson was dubbed "The Yas Yas Girl," as she let her public know precisely where she stood on sexual matters. Perhaps the choice of her nickname was a marketing device; ironically, some of her strongest songs, like "New Muddy Water Blues" and "Got a Man in the 'Bama Mines," don't offer much by way of jukebox eroticism.

As the 1930s drew to a close, so did the distinctive role of women in blues. With the deaths of Clara Smith in 1935 and Bessie Smith in a 1936 Mississippi automobile accident that has assumed the proportions of legend, the pioneers who had so decisively dominated the scene in the 1920s began to disappear. A few encores from singers like Alberta Hunter, Coot Grant (and husband Wesley Wilson), Trixie Smith, and a little-known 1920s singer named Rosetta Crawford were recorded for Decca by producer Mayo Williams, who had first encountered them when he produced for Paramount in the early days. Decca also recorded new versions of a number of early blues by the white Louisiana-born singer Teddy Grace that year. Western-swing bands had routinely included the blues as part of an eclectic mix offered to dancers in the Southwest, but Grace's efforts, aimed at the broader popular music market, initiated a pattern of pop covers of "race-record" hits, which extended well into the rock 'n' roll era. Columbia Records' John Hammond had produced a Bessie Smith reissue album in 1936, with carefully chosen material meant to appeal to a growing audience of jazz collectors, who were at least as interested in the sidemen as in the singer herself. Hammond had produced Smith's final recordings—and Billie Holiday's first ones—in 1933, surrounding each with all-star accompaniments.

When Hammond produced the first of his "From Spirituals to Swing" concerts at New York's Carnegie Hall in December 1938, he invited Bessie's niece by marriage, Ruby Smith, to do some of her songs by way of tribute. In 1939, he located Ida Cox in Knoxville for another Carnegie concert and surrounded her with hand-picked musicians for a productive record date as well.

Blues women in the 1940s combined popular song styles with the blues in much the same way as their ancestors had done in the Mamie Smith generation. In 1940, Chicago's Lil Green had a major success with "Romance in the Dark," followed

A studio portrait of two of Decca Records most recorded artists of the 1930s: Bumble Bee Slim (Amos Easton) and Georgia White.

"Wee Bea Booze" (Muriel Nicholls; right) and Sister Rosetta Tharpe (below) both recorded for Decca with substantial success during the late 1930s and 1940s. Tharpe was an extraordinary guitarist.

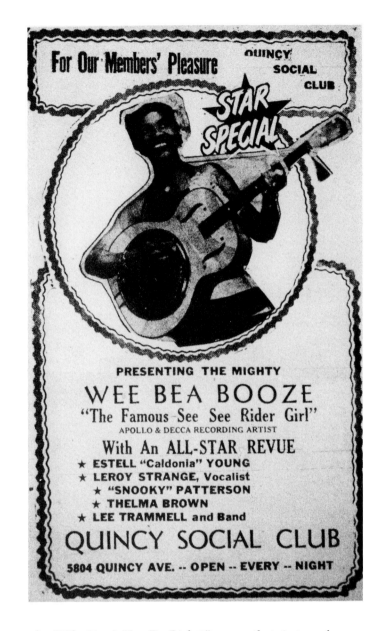

the next year by "Why Don't You Do Right?" a song that, in turn, became a catalyst for the career of young Peggy Lee, who recorded it with Benny Goodman in 1942.

The year 1941 saw another interesting crossover, when gospel singer Sister Rosetta Tharpe combined that career with another as a blues shouter in Lucky Millinder's big band. It was a bold move for the time and a successful one for a while, until pressures from the religious community forced Tharpe to abandon her secular forum. She was a powerful guitarist as well as an authoritative singer, and the loss of her instrument in the band context was keenly felt. Wee Bea Booze (Muriel Nicholls) also provided her own guitar backing on some 1942 Decca records, which included a hit with her revival of "Ma" Rainey's 1924 "See See Rider." The revived version turned the song into a standard, and it was the one Chuck Willis turned to in 1957, when he created still another hit version.

The 1940s saw the blues become almost an exclusively male music, the vehicle of urban shouters and jump bands and a new generation of southern singer/guitarists,

like John Lee Hooker, Muddy Waters, and Lightnin' Hopkins. Moses Asch recorded the blues of Sonny Terry, Brownie McGhee, and Huddie Ledbetter on his Asch, Disc, and Folkways labels, which he marketed to folk-music enthusiasts in the North, but he found no comparable women performers. Talented entertainers like Pearl Bailey, Una Mae Carlisle, Sarah Vaughan, Camille Howard, Savannah Churchill, and Dinah Washington would have sung the blues a generation before; in the 1940s, they merged more closely with the worlds of pop music, rhythm and blues, and jazz, discovering far broader audiences than the blues had ever attracted, even in its salad days of the 1920s.

In the 1950s and beyond, few women have opted to sing the blues. Among the notable exceptions are Chicago's KoKo Taylor, who has worked with most of the important bluesmen of that city since she began singing in nightclubs over thirty years ago; Willie Mae (Big Mama) Thornton, whose powerful 1952 "Hound Dog" was eclipsed by Elvis Presley's relatively restrained cover in 1956; and Big Maybelle, who remained closer to the blues than most R & B singers in the 1950s.

As folk festivals began to spring up in the 1960s, a few veteran survivors managed to receive some belated recognition and new recordings. Victoria Spivey was out front in these activities with her Spivey label, which featured her new recordings, along with vaudeville blues survivors Lucille Hegamin and Hannah Sylvester. Edith Wilson worked for Quaker Oats for many years as the media personification of their Aunt Jemima trademark, and appeared for a while on the coffeehouse and festival circuit before her death in 1981, reviving songs identified with her half a century earlier. A feeble but charming Sippie Wallace was doing the same in the 1980s, raising our collective consciousness with her "Women, Be Wise."

It seems safe to say that the era of women's blues begins around the turn of the century, or at least on the occasion when "Ma" Rainey first heard the blues in 1902. If the era didn't end in 1925–27, with the proliferation of southern recording trips and the introduction of electrical recording, those years did mark the end of the hegemony women singers had enjoyed. The Depression, jukeboxes, the war, and evolving public tastes further chipped away at their status within the idiom. Some musical stage productions in recent years, like "Bubbling Brown Sugar," "'Ma' Rainey's Black Bottom," and "One Mo' Time," have starred younger singers performing old blues as repertory set pieces of historic value, but without breathing into the genre the new life that would affect public taste. Today's blues singer is typically a male with a heavily amplified guitar and a saxophone-led band, who rarely looks back to the past for his songs. If it's true that what goes around comes around, women might find a way back to the blues again. Even if we've come ninety years since "Ma" Rainey's Missouri discovery, there's still a world of human feeling waiting for expression in the blues.

HOLY
BLUES

THE GOSPEL TRADITION

MARK A. HUMPHREY

◆◆◆

"Don't let the Devil steal the beat from the Lord!"
Mahalia Jackson

"Holy blues" is an evident oxymoron, "a figure of speech combining seemingly contradictory expressions" (*Oxford American Dictionary*). Holy blues is oxymoronic if we believe blues to be "the devil's music," a tenet held by many "reformed" blues singers and the "saints" of some African-American churches. Blues is unholy, and sacred music unbluesy. Blues celebrates pleasures of the flesh, while sacred music celebrates release from worldly bondage. One is oil to the other's holy water, unmixable. At least some would have it so.

Once viewed as the twin populist voices of African-American culture, blues and gospel music traditions have gradually come to be seen as existing on either side of a dualist divide crossed only at peril to one's soul. We have come to believe that the choices offered African-Americans were those of mutual exclusion: either blues or gospel music, God or the Devil, Heaven or Hell. The blues singer took the latter, sometimes striking Faustian bargains (or so Tommy Johnson is said to have claimed) for greater mastery of "the devil's music."

Today, many blues aficionados regard blues singers, especially the male blues singers of the Mississippi Delta, as twentieth-century African-American analogues to the nineteenth-century Romantic poets, who rebelled against social convention, stole Promethean fire with their art, and died young of laudanum addiction, tuberculosis, syphilis, or suicide (choose one). The myth of the Byronic poet—brilliant, defiant, and self-destructive—has sustained its great power and resonance for more than 150 years of Western culture. That myth is subtext to our continued fascination with such dissimilar icons of the 1950s as the beat poets and the country singer dubbed "the hillbilly Shakespeare," Hank Williams. It has been the raison d'être of many rock stars, living and dead. The myth tells us that life and art are inseparable. For the Romantic artist, life and art must both defy taboos, roil with internal and external conflict, and ultimately martyr the artist.

The problem with projecting this myth onto blues singers is that the culture in which they lived and worked was one with no tangible link to the Romantic tradition. If some bluesmen believed they were playing "the devil's music," and if a few bragged of it with such appellations as "The Devil's Son-in-Law," none seem to have equated "demonic defiance" with an alternate route to some higher truth, the evident goal of European Romantics (a goal voiced by the well-worn phrase from William Blake's *Proverbs of Hell*, "The road of excess leads to the palace of wisdom"). The Romantic deification of the individual is fundamentally foreign to African-American culture, and the projection of a Byronic character onto blues singers (most visibly, of course, onto Robert Johnson) tells us more about the observer than the observed.

This isn't to say that the dualism of "the devil's music" as stark opposite to "songs of praise" is something white intellectuals have merely imagined to recreate the bluesman in our own image. No, there is ample evidence to suggest that an either/or sensibility was one with which blues singers truly grappled. There is also reason to believe that the culture in which they lived was more forgiving of them than its religious rhetoric might, on the surface, suggest. How else can we explain the men who worked variously as blues singers and preachers, apparently without becoming pariahs in their communities?

Blues and sacred music served different social functions in African-American culture. The experiences (one could even say ideologies) they exemplified were in conflict, but the musics associated with this conflict were not as strictly segregated from one another as our paradigm of the Byronic bluesman may lead us to believe. Blues came into an African-American culture in which the ecstatic Holiness and Pentecostal churches were spreading, and those populist faiths embraced eclectic musical expression. Conversely, blues, a new idiom at the turn of this century, could not help but be in part shaped by the varied and venerable African-American sacred music traditions, nearly two centuries its senior.

Coming to terms with African-American music is impossible without addressing the anvil on which it was forged. Between 1505 and 1870, some ten million Africans were enslaved and brought to the Americas in the most extraordinary forced migration of human history. The English, initially repelled by slavery, enthusiastically embraced the trade when they saw the bountiful fruits wrought from slave labor by their hated rival colonists, the Spanish. England threw itself into slaving in the mid-seventeenth century, though Africans had been brought to the North American colonies as early as 1619 (a year before the Pilgrims landed), as indentured servants. In 1788, Alexander Falconbridge observed in *An Account of the Slave Trade* on the Coast of Africa: "The poor wretches are frequently compelled to sing also; but when they do so, their songs are generally melancholy lamentations of their exile from their native country."

That exile was followed by further dehumanization: the dissolution (via the auction block) of any tribal or familial ties that had survived the passage from Africa. Expressions of African culture and religion were largely suppressed, as were any gatherings that might be seen as a pretext for insurrection. Stripped of past cultural identity and denied all opportunity to form new ones, the African in America was without

Thomas A. Dorsey was the single most important individual in twentieth-century gospel music. He was originally known as Georgia Tom, the piano-playing and singing blues partner of Tampa Red. CHAPTER OPENER

A *Vocalion jacket touts an array of "race" recording stars.*

any institution offering a cultural core, a meeting place beyond the white purview and a world view—until the rise of the African-American church.

The first recorded baptism of an African in the North American colonies took place in 1641. Missionary zeal in North America was tempered by a troubling question: Did baptizing an African confer freedom upon him? Laws were passed to the effect that it did not, but there was still little rush to Christianize the colonists' human chattel. This changed in the 1730s with the Great Awakening, a religious revival that swept England and America and that at last deemed slaves worthy converts. Among the missionaries who came to America in the 1730s was John Wesley, founder of Methodism. His preachments were underscored by the hymns of Dr. Isaac Watts, an English minister, physician, and composer whose music was livelier and whose lyrics closer to the vernacular speech of the day than what the stiff psalms of the day then offered. Colonial editions of Watts's Hymns and Spiritual Songs first appeared in 1739 and proved particularly popular with slaves. The religious instruction offered them by Wesley and like-minded missionaries included both Holy Writ and hymns, which emphasized its lessons. In 1755, the Reverend Samuel Davies, a Presbyterian evangelist, wrote: "I cannot but observe that the negroes, above all of the human species that I ever knew, have the nicest ear for music. They had a kind of ecstatic delight in psalmody."

(Two hundred twenty-eight years later, I visited Los Angeles's Landmark Church, then pastored by Johnny Otis, rhythm and blues bandleader best known for the 1958 novelty hit "Willie and the Hand Jive." The choir's lead singer addressed the congregation, and, in recalling the music she heard as a child, made reference to "one of those ol' Dr. Watt hymns." The congregation uh-huhed in recognition. Generations later and on the far side of the continent from where Watts's hymns were first learned by slaves, this reference still rang a resonant bell. In 1760, the Reverend Mr. Todd, a missionary distributing hymnals to newly converted slaves, regretted that he had been "obliged to turn sundry empty away who have come to me for Watts Psalms and Hymns.")

Over a million blacks lived in the United States by 1800, comprising 19 percent of the nation's population. More than one hundred thousand were free, and among these freedmen were the founders of the first African-American denominations. Richard Allen founded the Bethel African Methodist Episcopal Church in Philadelphia in 1794, and in 1801, published the first American hymnal designed solely for a black congregation's use.

The creation of separate black churches was in part a response to white unease at a black (albeit segregated) presence in American houses of worship, but it also provided a true community center beyond white sanction and observation. That center proved a pillar of strength for generations and produced the community's leaders in its preachers, who took to heart Watts's advice: "Ministers . . . ought also to cultivate the capacity of composing spiritual songs and exercise it along with the other parts of worship, preaching and prayer."

A "Second Awakening" swept America in the early years of the nineteenth century, characterized by week-long encampments ("camp meetings") in wooded areas, with constant preaching, praying, and singing. The black presence (and enthusiasm) at these camp meetings often exceeded that of whites. An observer at an 1838 Pennsylvania meeting attended by seven thousand complained that "Their shouts and singing were so very boisterous that the singing of the white congregation was often completely drowned in the echoes and reverberations of the colored people's tumultuous strains." Worshipers were swept along by tides of mass ecstacy similar to those experienced in Pentecostal churches a century later. The camp meeting songs that were a significant part of the orally transmitted "spiritual" tradition took shape at this time.

Not all of these songs would have given white masters much comfort, had they understood them. In 1830, a visiting Scotsman, Peter Neilson, noted of black spirituals: "The downfall of the archfiend forms the principal topic of their anthems." One of the anthems Neilson heard, "Satan, Your Kingdom Must Come Down," would be recorded nearly a century later by Blind Joe Taggart. The time of Neilson's observation and the thinly concealed subtext of the song (the true person of the archfiend) are noteworthy. A year later, in 1831, Nat Turner's insurrection swept through Southhampton County, Virginia. In its aftermath, Virginia's Governor Floyd told his state's legislature: "The most active incendiaries among us . . . have been the negro preachers." In the days following Emancipation, a survivor of "the time of old Prophet Nat," Charity Bowery, would sing a hymn for a researcher:

There's a better day a-coming—
There's a better day a-coming—
Oh, Glory, Hallelujah!

"They wouldn't let us sing that," Bowery recalled of the tense days after Turner's revolt. "They thought we was going to rise, because we sung 'better days are coming.'"

In the autumn after the guns roared at Fort Sumter, a white woman named Mary Boykin Chesnut recorded in her diary a visit to a black church on a South Carolina plantation. The preacher "clapped his hands at the end of every sentence, and his voice rose to the pitch of a shrill shriek, yet was strangely clear and musical, occasionally in a plaintive minor key that went to your heart." Following an ecstatic service filled with "devotional passion of voice and manner," the congregation "broke out into one of those soul-stirring Negro camp-meeting hymns. To me this is the saddest of all earthly music, weird and depressing beyond my powers to describe."

During the Civil War, 186,000 black soldiers served in the Union Army as the "United States Colored Troops." Although the Army was segregated, black and white soldiers were brought into unprecedented contact, and a wider national awareness of African-American song resulted. Colonel Thomas W. Higginson of the South Carolina Volunteer Regiment wrote a memoir, *Army Life in a Black Regiment*, in which he noted the music heard in the black soldiers' camps: "The everlasting 'shout'

Bishop Grace—also known as Daddy Grace—was a very important and influential figure in the black gospel world of the 1920s and 1930s. By the 1950s, his New York City church was a musical feast in which performers played whatever instruments they carried in.

The holy blues grew out of the same evangelical grassroots revivalism that spawned mass baptisms like this one.

is always within hearing, with its mixture of piety and polka, and its castanet-like clapping of the hands. Then there are quieter prayer meetings, with pious invocations and slow psalms, 'deaconed out' from memory by the leader, two lines at a time, in a sort of wailing chant."

In 1867 the first collection of "spirituals" was published, *Slave Songs of the United States*, collected by William Allen, Charles Ware, and Lucy McKim Garrison. Among its contents were the hymns of Dr. Watts as well as folk spirituals, which would find their way, albeit in altered form, onto 78s in the 1920s.

In 1866, Fisk University, open to black students, was established in Nashville. From its ranks came the Fisk Jubilee Singers, the first group to "concertize" spirituals. The Fisk Jubilee Singers undertook their first national tour in 1871, and lecturer Henry Ward Beecher wrote of their New York City appearance, "They make their mark by giving the spirituals and plantation hymns as only they can sing them who know how to keep time to a master's whip." The group undertook a world tour in 1886 and vastly expanded appreciation of African-American sacred song, albeit in a smoothed-over and Europeanized form.

By the time blues began taking embryonic shape in the 1890s, African-American sacred song was already a tradition older than the American republic. White commentary from the eighteenth and nineteenth centuries presents an incomplete picture of this music, but at least tells us that many elements still characteristic of black sacred music and services were firmly established prior to the Civil War. "Interested, and yet at the same time shocked" at a "spectacle" observed at a black church in Chattanooga in 1859, the Reverend Robert Mallard wrote: "The whole congregation kept up one loud monotonous strain, interrupted by various sounds: groans and screams and clapping of hands." The Reverend Mallard (whose concession to liberality was that "Some allowance, of course, must be made for the excitability of the Negro temperament") could have been shocked by similar "spectacles" more than a century later.

Elements of African-American worship and sacred song remained constant for generations (the "deaconed out" slow psalms Higginson noted during the Civil War derived from the practice of "lining out" used by our English Puritan forefathers as early as 1644 to teach psalms to the unlettered), but this tradition was by no means impervious to change. Change has tremored more rapidly and radically through it in the past hundred years than during any other epoch, beginning in the 1890s with the challenge the new Holiness churches posed to the established Baptist and Methodist denominations. Populist and ecstatic, the Holiness churches shook with "shouts" and primitive jazz bands. An even more virulent strain of experiential Christianity emerged prior to World War I with the spread of Pentecostalism, emphasizing trance states and speaking in tongues. Unlike the black music that accompanied the Great Awakening of the 1730s and the Second Awakening (with its camp meetings) some seventy years later, the music of these religious upheavals is audible to us, thanks to Edison's invention of 1877.

In 1902, the Victor Talking Machine Company issued six single-sided records by the Dinwiddie Colored Quartet, their authenticity asserted in Victor's 1903 catalog: "These are genuine Jubilee and Camp Meeting Shouts sung as only negroes can sing them." Male quartet singing was a tradition in long standing. Visiting South Carolina from Sweden in 1850, Fredrika Bremer wrote in her diary: "I heard the negroes singing . . . their hymns sung in quartette were glorious."

The six Dinwiddie Colored Quartet performances were among the rare representations of "genuine Jubilee and Camp Meeting Shouts" at the dawn of commercial recording. The Fisk Jubilee Singers and other performers of "concertized" spirituals took their place on wax cylinder and disk alongside popular racist minstrel skits and "coon songs" (often, though not always, performed by whites), but examples of black music which were neither offensive parodies nor smoothed for white consumption were scarce on record prior to 1921. The widely circulated black newspaper, the Chicago Defender, declared in 1916 that "Records of the Race's great artists will be placed on the market" when record companies comprehend "how many Victrolas are owned by members of our Race." This realization became fact five years later.

The runaway success of Mamie Smith's Okeh recording "Crazy Blues" created an instant vogue for women who sang vaudeville-influenced "classic" blues. "Every phonograph company," Metronome announced in 1922, "has a colored girl recording blues." It soon became evident that blues was not the only black music the record companies could exploit successfully. The labels began recruiting black preachers for recordings of three-minute sermons punctuated by congregational shouts and

Mamie Smith put on the glamour during her "Crazy Blues" time.

Reverend Gates was probably the most successful of all recorded preachers, a fact that failed to impress Thomas Edison, who noted in his talent file: "This fellow might be a wonder but I can't use him. 9/10/26."

Columbia *"New Process"* Records
REG. U. S. PAT. OFF.

REV. J. M. GATES

I N Rev. J. M. Gates, Columbia has brought one of the South's great preachers in contact with the world. To hear him at his very best be sure to get his Columbia New Process Records. They are "like life itself."

DEATH'S BLACK TRAIN IS COMING . .
NEED OF PRAYER—*Sermons with Singing* .   14145-D   75c

singing. Calvin Dixon's "As an Eagle Stirreth Up Her Nest" was the first of these recordings in 1925, and it may be said that the genre prospered well into the time of the LP. The recording of preachers singing and sermonizing to congregational encouragement soared after 1926, when the Reverend J. C. Burnett's "The Downfall of Nebuchadnezzar" sold over eighty thousand copies, and Reverend J. M. Gates's debut, "Death's Black Train Is Coming" likewise made cash registers ring. Paul Oliver, writing in Songsters and Saints: Vocal Traditions on Race Records (1984), reports, "Eventually, in the space of approximately a dozen years, 750 sermons by some seventy preachers were released."

Gates was the most popular and prolific of them. He waxed some two-hundred titles between 1926 and 1941. Some, like "The Need of Prayer" (1926), include moving examples of the "deaconed out . . . wailing chant" Higginson heard at Civil War camps. Others surely captured buyers with sensational titles, including "Dead Cat on the Line," "Manish Women," and "Speed On, Hell Is Waiting for You," an admonition to reckless drivers. Gates used both topical themes and then-current slang as part of his appeal. His 1930 message about the Depression, "These Hard Times," used the expression "It's tight like that" to indicate the national paucity of jobs, money, and food, but Gates's audience would have recognized it as a reference to Tampa Red's immensely popular 1928 hokum blues "It's Tight Like That," as well as the sexual connotation of the term.

While the recorded sermons with song of such Baptists as Gates and the Reverend A. W. Nix were bestsellers, strong competition came from the fiery exhortations (with music to match) of such "Sanctified" preachers as Reverend D. C. Rice and F. W. McGee. The Sanctified (Holiness or Pentecostal) preachers might be accompanied by syncopated piano, or cornets, trombones, and tambourines, or guitars and even mandolins, harmonicas, jugs, and washboards (a Holiness jugband appears in the 1928 recordings of Elder Richard Bryant's Sanctified Singers). Musically heterodox, the Sanctified denominations also differed from the Baptists and Methodists in granting women roles of leadership. The full fury of Pentecostalism was unleashed in the half-dozen 1928 recordings (among them "God's Warning to the Church") of Missionary Josephine Miles and Sister Elizabeth Cooper. Missionary Miles, accompanied by Cooper's piano and moaning, delivered blood-and-thunder sermons in a hoarse, rapid-fire shout punctuated by exhortations to "Bless God's great name." She wrung down wrath on the unholy with an ecstatic conviction many male evangelists might have envied.

In addition to evangelists, the Sanctified women included in their numbers many impassioned singers and musicians. In 1927, Jessie May Hill sang in an urgent

Reverend Gates preaches in a publicity shot for Okeh.

Reverend Campbell and Reverend Burnett were two preachers who recorded numerous sermons during the 1920s and at least as late as 1945.

style anticipating that of Sister Rosetta Tharpe more than a decade later. (The similarity in the two artist's phrasing is uncanny on Hill's "This World Is Not My Home," a performance that swings with a modernity exceptional for its time.) From Columbia, Mississippi, the deep, growling shout of Bessie Johnson was heard on a dozen sides waxed in 1928–29. One of her accompanists, guitarist/singer Lonnie McIntorsh, remembered Johnson as "the singingest woman I've ever known." In a performance with the Memphis Jug Band's Will Shade on guitar, she led the Memphis Sanctified Singers in a song bespeaking her Sanctified affiliation. "He got the Holy Ghost fire," she shouted of her savior in "He Got Better Things for You."

The Sanctified sisters were fearless. Sister Cally Fancy didn't flinch from chastizing the mighty in her 1931 recording, "Death Is Riding Through the Land— Pts. I & II."

Presidential life is in God's hands,
This message is for you, too;
And, Governors, remember,
When you are sentencin' men,
My God is watching you.

In "Part II" of her song, Sister Fancy turned prophetic:

You think the War is over
Because the U.S.A.
Have joined the League of Nations,
But the War is on her way.

In 1931 Japan invaded Manchuria, and Hitler's rise in Germany was only two years away. Fancy warned that men should put their faith in God rather than armaments: "He can face the Huns without machine guns," she sang. Her piano accompanist may have been Thomas A. Dorsey, who, having recorded ribald hokum blues with Tampa Red, went on to become one of the prime movers in shaping modern gospel music.

The Texas-born blind pianist and singer Arizona Dranes was only twenty-one when she made her recording debut for Okeh in 1926. A favorite at the annual convention in Memphis of the Church of God in Christ, Dranes performed in churches from Texas to Chicago, where she inspired the young Rosetta Tharpe. Hearing Dranes's combination of the four-square and the syncopated in such piano show-pieces as her instrumental "Crucifixion," it is easy to imagine a lineage from Dranes to such later Pentecostal-turned-rocker pianists as Jerry Lee Lewis. Holiness and Pentecostal services were sometimes integrated. Even when they were not, the music that accompanied black and white services was similar. In 1929, a white Holiness singer, Leader Cleveland, recorded "Babylon Is Falling Down" in a highly rhythmic style with guitar, harmonica, and shouted asides. The song sprang from African-American tradition and was also waxed by Reverend F. W. McGee.

Along with preachers and Sanctified sisters, the record factories of the 1920s sought out the religious street singers who eked out meager sustenance from the sidewalks and sympathy of Herbert Hoover's America. Many of these men (and a few women) were blind. Most played a readily portable instrument, the guitar, and have come to be dubbed "guitar evangelists" by collectors of prewar black recordings.

Blind Joe Taggart takes pride of place as the first of them on record in November 1926. Taggart was probably from the Southeast, but little information has surfaced about the guitar evangelist with the longest recording history (1926–34). His premiere recordings feature him and his wife singing a cappella, and are among his most moving performances. The popular "death's black train" theme rumbled through "I Wish My Mother Was on That Train," which offered a stark admonition:

Oh, sinner, your train is comin',
I know she's goin' to flag;
I know her by her rumblin',
For she's always draped in black.
I'll bid you fare you well,
For you made your bed in Hell.

Arizona Dranes was one of Okeh's more obscure but more appealing artists in the gospel tradition.

Taggart later recorded this song with guitar accompaniment, changing the lyrics and the title to "Wonder Will My Trouble Then Be Over." One of Taggart's "lead boys" and accompanists, Joshua White, went on to considerable fame and influence as a folk-blues popularizer.

Hard on Taggart's heels into the recording studio was Edward Clayborn, who first recorded in December 1926. His initial success was "The Gospel Train Is Coming," which Vocalion credited to The Guitar Evangelist. "The record sold well enough," Robert Dixon and John Godrich wrote in Recording the Blues, "to be repressed over the years, with label attributions to Edward W. Clayburn, Edward W. Clayborn, and even Rev. Edward W. Clayton!" Who the artist was, however, remains a mystery: Nothing is known of Clayborn. His rather urbane and relatively restrained approach suggests a less "countrified" background than that of other guitar evangelists, but this is conjecture. His vibrato-laden tenor voice was accompanied by a guitar style both brilliant and idiosyncratic. He was among the cleanest, most accurate slide- or bottleneck-style guitarists to record, yet his fluid melodic lines on the top string were accompanied by an unchanging "boom chang" bass. Clayborn favored hymns with frequent chord changes, yet he never fretted the guitar or otherwise indicated that his tunes weren't monochordal.

Lyrically, he could be quite inventive. "Your Enemy Cannot Harm You (But Watch Your Close Friend)" was a paranoid warning that anticipated the O'Jays' "Back Stabbers" by nearly fifty years:

> People, I want to tell you
> Just how your friend will do;
> They'll work to get your secrets,
> And dig a pit for you.

And Clayborn could be chillingly topical. On January 18, 1928, he recorded "God's Riding Through This Land." Half speaking and half singing in the carefully modulated chant of a preacher, Clayborn droned:

> Aaah, nineteen hundred twenty-seven,
> Fourteenth day of November,
> God rode through Pittsburgh,
> Over on the North side.

On the date Clayborn mentions, a gas tank in the Pittsburgh plant of the Equitable Gas Company exploded, demolishing a mile-square area. Twenty-eight people were killed and six hundred hurt. Five thousand were left homeless. Fresh in his mind two months later, Clayborn saw this as a terrible retribution from a God of Justice:

> He don't ride like a natural man,
> He has all power in his hand.

Cataclysmic events—the sinking of the Titanic, World War I, the influenza pandemic of 1918–19, tornadoes, the 1927 Delta flood—were celebrated as evidence of God's wrath in black sacred songs recorded in the late 1920s and early 1930s. Colonel Higginson may have heard similar songs during the Civil War; certainly he heard songs in which, as he noted, "the lurid imagery of the Apocalypse is brought to bear. This book, with the books of Moses, constituted their Bible." The vivid symbolism of Revelations had already inspired African-American psalmodists for generations. Richard Allen's 1801 collection for his Bethel African Methodist Episcopal Church included these verses:

> But who can bear that dreadful day,
> To see the world in flames:
> The burning mountains melt away,
> While rocks run down in streams.
>
> The falling stars their orbits leave,
> The sun in darkness hide:
> The elements asunder cleave,
> The moon turn'd into blood!
>
> Behold the universal world
> In consternation stand,
> The wicked into Hell are turn'd
> The Saints at God's right hand.

Similar sentiments thunder with feverish intensity from the recordings of a blind Texan born nearly a century after Allen's hymnal appeared. Blind Willie Johnson recorded at a time when black vernacular music beyond jazz and "classic" blues was little noticed by whites, but his work was striking enough to cause Bookman reviewer Edward Abbe Niles to note "Blind Willie Johnson's violent, tortured and abysmal shouts and groans and his inspired guitar in a primitive and frightening Negro religious song 'Nobody's Fault But Mine!'" The confrontational urgency of Johnson's music has been no less startling to those today who listen to the thirty recordings this itinerant street singer made for Columbia between 1927 and 1930.

They constitute an incomparable body of work, at once universally expressive of African-American tradition and uniquely expressive of an extraordinary intuitive genius. Johnson's oeuvre may be the single most cogent and compelling exemplification of the black sacred music that evolved from the conversion of slaves up to the advent of professional gospel music in the 1930s.

A unifying force galvanizes Johnson's work, but through it runs considerable diversity. There are folk spirituals of fine vintage. Higginson heard "The United States Colored Troops" sing one of the songs Johnson recorded, "Keep Your Lamp Trimmed and Burning." Though blind, Johnson learned texts and tunes from hymnals, perhaps by hearing them in church or as they were performed by other street singers. Some he learned from the instruction of his wife, Angeline. Sam Charters found her in Beaumont, Texas, living in pathetic poverty but surrounded nonetheless by a wealth of music. "There were over a hundred song books in an old trunk beside Angeline's shack in Beaumont," he wrote. Among them was a hymnal published in 1881 with over five hundred songs.

The anthems of Holiness revivals also entered Johnson's repertoire, songs celebrating the cleansing blood of Jesus and the "latter rain" that would bring revival to spiritless churches. Such Sanctified symbolism, coupled with the furious intensity of many of Johnson's recordings, always seemed at odds with Angeline's insistence on Johnson's Baptist affiliation. Research by Dan Williams unearthed another woman in Johnson's life, Willie B. Harris, who claimed she was the female vocalist on two of Johnson's sessions. Significantly, she linked Johnson with the Church of God in Christ.

The Victrola may have influenced Johnson's repertoire to a slight degree. Prior to Johnson's recordings of the songs, "Bye and Bye I'm Goin' to See the King" had been recorded by both Arizona Dranes and Blind Mamie Forehand, and "Take Your Burden to the Lord and Leave It There" had been waxed no less than four times (by Blind Joe Taggart, the Pace Jubilee Singers, Washington Phillips, and Blind Roosevelt Graves). Other songs Johnson recorded have no known precedent and were probably original with him. Some are rife with topical references and suggest that the anger in his voice was seeking a worldy target. Others present a unique view of a God more immanent than transcendent. Whether original or learned, Johnson's performances welded these songs to him. His versions became definitive, and were the ones later emulated.

Like the vocals of Sanctified preachers, Johnson's performances were emotional outpourings rippling with vibrato, growls, and other effects aimed at exciting believers. Robert Palmer suggests a lineage from African sacred ritual to Johnson's celebrated "false bass" voice. "The masker was often believed to be possessed by a god or spirit," Palmer wrote in Deep Blues, "so his voice had to change along with his appearance. . . . Other masked singers, especially in the slave coast region, mastered deep chest growls, false bass tones produced in the back of the throat, strangulated shreiks, and other deliberately bizarre effects." Survivals of African ecstatic religion may have informed the practice of African-American ecstatic religion and the singing that accompanied it.

Johnson was an extraordinary guitarist, especially when playing bottleneck style. Fluid and accurate, delicate yet driving, his melodic lines on the top string formed a second (and, when he had a singer with him, third) voice. Sometimes Johnson would drop the end of a sung phrase and let the bottleneck "sing" it, a technique also favored by many Delta blues slide guitarists.

FOUR RACE ARTISTS SIGNED FOR COLUMBIA

Four new race artists were signed to record exclusively for the Columbia Phonograph Company during the recent Southern trip of Frank Walker, executive in Columbia's recording studios.

Blind Willie Johnson is reported as a new sensation in the South in singing sacred songs to a fine guitar accompaniment of his own.

Lillian Glinn is a new singer of blues, full of pep and personality. She possesses an extraordinary voice, of which every word gets over on the phonograph.

Washington Phillips presents gospel records that are different. His songs are admired for the significant meaning he gives them, and he accompanies himself on an instrument never before heard.

Laughing Charley is the latest addition of race contributions to the "Joy Note" in living. He sings blues with a laugh.

The first releases of all these artists have just been listed for Columbia's next monthly supplement of race records.

While many contemporary listeners admire Johnson's guitar mastery and fiery vocals even as they dismiss his message, there's little doubt that, for Johnson, his artistry was primarily a means to a conviction-filled end. From the age of five, his widow told Charters, his goal was to be a preacher. Johnson's songs suggest a thorough knowledge of scripture, perhaps gleaned from hearing innumerable sermons. Many of his songs were shaped along the lines of sermons. "Jesus Is Coming Soon" used the influenza pandemic that followed World War I as a sign of the Second Coming much as a preacher might, stating a contemporary problem and relating it to scriptural precedent.

Between October 1918 and the end of February 1919, an estimated 21,642,274 people perished in a worldwide pandemic that, for its brevity and severity, has no recorded equal. More than a half-million deaths occurred in the United States, including five thousand in a single week in New York City. Futile precautions were taken—the wearing of masks, the closing of public places (as Johnson notes in his song)—but nothing stemmed the fury of the disease, which disappeared almost as mysteriously and suddenly as it had appeared. On December 5, 1928, Johnson, joined by a female vocalist who may have been Willie B. Harris, warned of God's wrath to the unrighteous in a furious shout:

> *Well, we done told ya,*
> *God done warned ya,*
> *Jesus comin' soon . . .*

Alone, Johnson delivered his sung sermon:

> *In the year of 19 and 18,*
> *God sent a mighty disease;*
> *It killed a-many thousand*
> *On land and on the seas.*

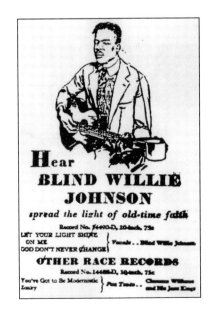

Selling Blind Willie Johnson and others on disk.

The verses that follow note that the epidemic "floated through the air," and that doctors, military leaders, even "nobles" were helpless before this divine scourge. "God is warning the nation," Johnson growls and ends his song by citing scripture:

> *Read the book of Zechariah,*
> *Bible plainly say,*
> *Says the people in the cities dyin'*
> *'Count of they wicked ways.*

"Jesus Is Coming Soon" moves in the rhetorical style of a sermon. A contemporary crisis is observed, the thesis is stated that it is a punishment from God and omen of the Second Coming and Judgment, and scriptural authority is cited to defend the thesis.

While Johnson preached "old-time religion," his songs embraced an innovation that mirrored closeness with God. The ferocious 1927 recording "Jesus Make Up My Dying Bed" mingled ancient Christian symbolism (the marriage of Christ to His church, suggested by Revelations 19:7) with a then-popular metaphor, telephonic communication with Heaven:

Since me and Jesus got married,
Haven't been a minute apart;
With the receiver in my hand,
And religion in my heart.
. . . I can ring him up easy; Ahh . . .

Johnson's alliterative parallels—receiver, religion; hand, heart—indicate an ear for the poetry of the pulpit. The metaphors were still fresh twenty years later when the great Texas quintet, the Soul Stirrers recorded Johnson's song as, "Well, Well, Well." To its earliest users, the telephone must have seemed mediumistic in its ability to "conjure up" the voice of a person miles away. As a metaphor for prayer, it proved irresistible. F. M. Lehman's anthemic "The Royal Telephone" (published in 1919) urged the saints to:

Telephone to glory,
O what joy divine!
I can feel the current
Moving on the line;
Built by God the Father
For his loved and own,
We may talk to Jesus
Through this royal telephone.

Reverend Sister Mary Nelson made a rousing a cappella recording of this in 1927, and two years later Blind Roosevelt Graves and Brother waxed it. There were varied uses of the metaphor—Johnson's rival guitar evangelist, Blind Joe Taggart, employed it in "Wonder Will My Trouble Then Be Over":

Call up Jesus in Heaven,
He will answer you;
He will come to the phone,
Put your feet on solid stone.

The novelty of this symbolism would not wear off soon. As late as 1953, the superb Texas quartet the Pilgrim Travelers used it in "I've Got a New Home":

I've got a telephone,
Doncha know now boys
It's way down in my bosom . . .

Lead singer Jess Whitaker chanted: "I tell operator to give me long distance; tell long distance to give me Heaven, and I'll tell Heaven I want my Jesus. When I get Jesus, I'll tell him my troubles."

Other metaphors welcoming twentieth-century innovation appear in Sanctified recordings. In 1930, Mother McCollum sang:

Oh, Jesus is my air-o-plane,
He holds this world in His hands;
He rides over all,

He don't never fall,
Jesus is my air-o-plane.

McCollum also sang a song acknowledging the concept of leisure time, "When I Take My Vacation in Heaven," which Tampa Red would parody in 1935 as "When I Take My Vacation in Harlem." The Sanctified singers seem to have had one foot firmly in the present and the other in an Old Testament epoch. Certainly one senses that of Blind Willie Johnson. In a single verse of "Jesus Is Coming Soon," he seemingly recalls both the 1918 influenza pandemic and some Biblical plague:

Well, the noble said-a to the people,
"You better close your public schools;
To prevent this empire's ending,
Better close your churches, too."

Perhaps Johnson viewed the United States as an empire, a modern version of a despotic Babylon that Jehovah would surely smite. Legend has him being arrested for "inciting to riot" for singing his ferocious "If I Had My Way I'd Tear the Building Down" in front of the Customs House in New Orleans. He illustrated God's judgment on mortal pride in "God Moves on the Water," an account of the 1912 sinking of the Titanic. (Legend has a Titanic deckhand boasting, "God Himself could not sink this ship.") And Johnson mixed patriotism with protest in "When the War Was

Blind Willie Johnson is pictured here in his only known photograph. Note the tin cup at the top of his guitar, an essential accoutrement for the street singer. Johnson took gospel music to a level that has yet to be equaled.

Washington Phillips poses about 1927 with two zither-like instruments in a photograph accompanying an announcement that he will sing gospel records for the Columbia Phonograph Company. Phillips's musical approach was quite gentle in comparison with other recorded religious artists of the time.

On," his only recording without religious references. It is the single most detailed account we have in song of African-American reaction to the War to End All Wars.

No prior international event can be said to have significantly touched the lives of poor southern blacks. Suddenly, they were being called to join the fight against the dreaded Hun, a figure who must have seemed incredibly remote. Conscripted, they would prove themselves able soldiers (a contemporary recruitment poster shows a black doughboy saying goodbye to his sweetheart above the legend "Coloreds Are No Slackers"), but they must have wondered about their role in defending a nation that so severely curtailed their social mobility.

Johnson acknowledges the racial "equality" of the draft (blacks served in segregated units commanded by white officers), but also concedes the complaints of those at home over rationing, increased taxes, and the high price of food. In a coherently progressive narrative recorded eleven years after the rout of the Kaiser, Johnson recalled the ambivalence of the disenfranchised.

> *Well, just about a few years*
> *And some months ago,*
> *United States converted for war,*
> *Sammy called the men*
> *From the East and West,*
> *"Get ready, boys, we got to do our best."*

Johnson's familiarity with Uncle Sam ("Sammy") suggests satire. So, more pointedly, does his second verse:

> *Well, President Wilson,*
> *Sittin' on his throne,*
> *Makin' laws for everyone.*
> *Didn't call the black man,*
> *Leave out the white . . .*

Johnson failed to sing what would have been the final line in the verse. Instead he substituted a dazzling phrase on guitar. This omission suggests self-censorship (nothing like it occurs in any other Johnson recording). If he felt he was treading through a mine field by mentioning race, Johnson went on to specify the rationing that caused ill will toward "Sammy":

> *Yes, you measure your boiler [possibly coffee],*
> *Measure your wheat;*
> *Half a pound of sugar*
> *For a person a week.*
> *Folks didn't like it,*
> *They blamed Uncle Sam,*
> *A-got to save the sugar*
> *For the boys in France.*

Future blues singers were among "the boys in France," but none would record much more than a fleeting reference to "them overseas blues." Indeed, social commentary this pointed remained rare in blues. Not until J. B. Lenoir's 1954 hard-times

complaint, "Eisenhower Blues," would anything so striking as Johnson's swipe at
"President Wilson, sittin' on his throne" appear in blues. It was the African-
American church, not the juke joint, that provided a forum for discussion and criti-
cism of the mighty and their impact on the meek. Johnson's "When the War Was
On" illustrates why it was the church that would produce the dynamic leadership of
the Civil Rights movement.

More than any other sacred singer of his era, Blind Willie Johnson left a palpable imprint on American music. What came to him from folk tradition went back to
it molded in his likeness. Such disparate artists as the Reverend Blind Gary Davis,
Fred McDowell, and Roebuck Staple listened, bringing traces of Johnson's repertoire
and style to the 1960s folk/blues revival. Twenty-one years after Johnson's death in
1949, a reissue of his 1927 recording, "Mother's Children Have a Hard Time" (the
performance that inspired Edward Abbe Niles to call Johnson "apparently a religious
fanatic" in a 1928 review), was again played on southern black gospel radio stations.
Some were reportedly deluged with calls from listeners who wanted to know how to
book the singer for their church! Blind Willie Johnson performed with an urgency
that has remained compelling for over sixty years now.

Ironically, the Johnson performance that has occasioned the most comment
and has been most often reissued is also his most atavistic. "Dark Was the Night,
Cold Was the Ground" is a largely wordless monody of moans accompanied by a
restless, singing slide. Beautiful and austere, the performance uses the silences
between notes to create a tension both oppressive and elevating. In the liner notes to
the Yazoo label reissue album Praise God I'm Satisfied, Steve Calt observed: "His
most unusual creation is the amorphous 'Dark Was the Night'. . . . It is one of the
few folk pieces that cannot be related to a specific genre, as its emphasis is on pure
sound rather than form."

Johnson's performance is a reverential mood piece that may recreate the part of
Baptist services Leadbelly recalled for the Library of Congress: "The Amen corner sisters, the ones who do this moanin', starts out . . . and when the men is prayin', to

*Two guitar-playing religious
artists who started as bluesmen,
Gary Davis (above) and Pops
Staple (left) came from disparate
blues backgrounds. Davis, of the
East Coast Piedmont school, was
a contemporary of Blind Boy
Fuller, while Staple, from Missis-
sippi, was greatly influenced by
Charley Patton.*

give 'em some spirit, they'd moan behind 'em and that would make 'em pray." Angeline Johnson sang "Dark Was the Night" a cappella for Sam Charters in a recreation of the old "lining out" style. Each line of the hymn is sung relatively quickly, with minimal ornamentation (the leader's role), and is sung back slowly, with ample melisma (the congregation's role). Angeline repeated each line and effectively sang both parts. Impressionistically, her husband's bottleneck guitar and moaning may have reflected "lining out" the hymn or the dialogue between "Amen corner sisters" and praying men.

Nathaniel R. Dett published a version of the hymn in *Religious Folk-Songs of the Negro as Sung at Hampton Institute*, a volume that appeared in 1927, the year of Johnson's recording. It appeared again in Newman I. White's 1928 collection *American Negro Folk-Songs*, which noted the field collection of the song as early as 1905. Widely known, Blind Joe Taggart would make it part of his "Been Listening All Day Long" in 1928:

> *Dark was the night and cold the ground*
> *On which my Lord was laid;*
> *Sweat-like drops of blood ran down,*
> *In agony He prayed.*

White noted the song's frequent appearance in "hymn-books of the white churches from the early nineteenth century." George Pullen Jackson tells us in *White Spirituals in the Southern Uplands* (1933) that it "was well liked by the fasola folk" (i.e., white shape-note singers). The original author of Blind Willie Johnson's "amorphous" masterpiece was Thomas Haweis, who, like Dr. Isaac Watts, was an eighteenth-century English physician and clergyman. Haweis penned several theological tomes and one collection of over two hundred hymns, *Carmina Christo; or, Hymns to the Saviour, Designed for the Use and Comfort of Those who Worship the Lamb that Was Slain*. Published in Bath, England, in 1792, *Carmina Christo* contains "Dark Was the Night and Cold the Ground" under the title "Gethsemane." The hymn's transformed appearance at a Dallas recording session 135 years later bears witness both to Blind Willie Johnson's intuitive genius and to the enduring strength of the threads woven into the African-American sacred music tradition.

Guitarist and film scorer Ry Cooder adapted Johnson's version of the Haweis hymn in his moody score for the 1985 film *Paris, Texas*. In a move that would likely please the heaven-minded Johnson, his 1927 recording was included among the artifacts of earth culture on the spacecraft Voyager. Beethoven and Chuck Berry were beamed at the auditory receptors of curious aliens; alongside them, Blind Willie Johnson's elegiac masterpiece "Dark Was the Night, Cold Was the Ground" played at the stars.

The day before Blind Willie Johnson made his recording debut (December 3, 1927), another remarkable sacred artist recorded for the first time at the same Columbia field trip to Dallas. Washington Phillips sang in a gentle voice devoid of Johnson's righteous rage, and the strange "plucked piano" (called a Dulceola or Dolceola) he played produced music tinged by an innocent ethereality, quite unlike Johnson's jagged earthiness. But, like Johnson, Phillips used the recording medium to comment on his world, especially the quality of its believers. He found much that was wanting in "The Church Needs Good Deacons," which pointed a finger at lecherous deacons ("All that some of them is fittin' for/Is to run 'round at night"). Worse still in Phillips's eye was the splintering of Christians into competing denominations, each believing its "elect" would be Heaven's sole occupants. The fault lay with church leaders. In "I Am Born to Preach the Gospel," Phillips sang:

> *Oh, preachers ought to stand together,*
> *But you see yourself they have split;*
> *Now what all the churches is needin' right now*
> *Is a regenerated pulpit. Oh yes!*

His most celebrated comment on the top was "Denomination Blues—Pts. 1 & 2," a title likely suggested by the record company and not the artist, who may have blanched at the notion he was performing blues. He was and he wasn't. Phillips's tune is derived from W. C. Handy's 1915 hit "Hesitation Blues," but his lyrics detail the differences among various Baptist, Methodist, and Holiness churches in practices of Baptism and Communion:

> *Now the Church of God*
> *Have it in their mind*
> *That they can go to Heaven*
> *Without the sacramental wine.*

Columbia promoted Washington Phillips as a gospel singer as well as an "occasional" blues artist.

A *studio card from the recording session that yielded the two-part tour de force "Denomination Blues."*

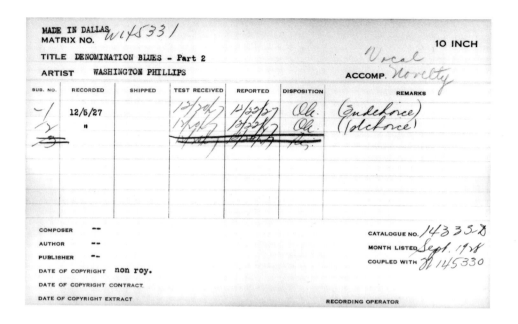

Denominational differences of worship were also manifest in the music heard in services, a topic illustrated by Leadbelly in his Library of Congress recordings. "Long years ago when they sang," Leadbelly recalled of the Baptists, "they carried it slow." He demonstrated with a stately rendition of "Let It Shine on Me," much as Blind Willie Johnson had introduced his recording of it in 1929. "Now the Methodists," Leadbelly continued, "they picked it up a little bit." He sang the chorus over, sprightlier now, and added, "Now the Holy Ghost, they picked it up and carried it on." His final rendition "rocked," again almost as Johnson had performed it, moving from the Baptist to the Holiness styles of expression.

Denominational differences had a bearing not only on performance styles within the church but also on degrees of sanction against performing "worldly" music. This came to light during the blues revival of the 1960s, when some rediscovered bluesmen adamantly refused to sing "the devil's music" again while others were heard singing both blues and spirituals. Eddie "Son" House variously preached, plowed, and sang blues during his early adult years. Rediscovered in 1964, House spent much of the next decade treating his young white admirers to both unadulterated Delta blues and such ancient spirituals as "John the Revelator." Robert Wilkins was rediscovered the same year as House, and though he recast some of his superb prewar blues in sacred garb ("That's No Way to Get Along" became the twenty-two-verse epic, "The Prodigal Son"), the Church of God in Christ minister never again performed blues. "Oh, I could," Wilkins told Pete Welding. "If I was in the Baptist Church, I could play those songs and be accepted, but they won't accept me in the church I'm in."

House was a Baptist, and an important tenet of Baptist faith is "Once in grace, always in grace." A believer "fully saved" in this denomination might believe that a little blues singing wouldn't jeopardize his soul, while members of "hardshell" Holiness and Pentecostal churches would find such liberality untenable. Reverend Gary Davis was a Baptist, which may explain why he could perform both "Twelve Gates to the City" and "Cocaine Blues."

But not all Baptists were so tolerant. Leadbelly once "got religion" but continued to play for dances, which branded him a backslider and got him banished from church. Remembering this more then thirty years later for Alan Lomax, Leadbelly was evidently still stung by the experience: "The church people raise more hell than any twenty people I ever seen," he said bitterly, "because they go to church all the time and the next week they runnin' all around over the country, tending to somebody else's business." The "saints" objected to Leadbelly's playing reels. Asked by Lomax what he meant by reels, Leadbelly defined them as "love songs and blues and one thing and another like that. But they want me to sing all spirituals." In the 1960s, Fred McDowell likewise used reel to describe the earliest blues he heard and remem-

Son House recorded both secular and religious songs with equal intensity.

bered old folks saying "'Uh-uh! He ain't got nothin'! I heard him play a reel,' see." These men remembered reel as a catchall for social music, and whether it was blues in the 1920s, reels at the turn of the century, or "corn-shuckin' songs" in slavery times, all dance tunes were equally "the devil's music."

This attitude was communicated, along with Watts's hymns, to slaves during the Great Awakening. Thomas Symmes voiced it in 1720 in Boston, when he advocated the singing of psalms for its "Tendency to divert . . . from learning Idle, Foolish, yea, pernicious Songs and Ballads." Little wonder that, in the nineteenth century, Helen W. Ludlow would record this comment (albeit in racist dialect) from a former slave: "Nuffin's good dat ain't religious, madam. Nobody sings dem corn-shuckin' songs after dey's got religion."

If such exclusion from the world was the believer's ideal, many fell short of it. One finds no scarcity of religious titles in the discographies of the more prolific blues recording artists of the 1920s and early 1930s, especially among the guitar-playing men. The stringently secular repertoires of a Lonnie Johnson or Blind Blake are somewhat exceptional. And while we may smile at the ruse of a Blind Lemon Jefferson performance of "All I Want Is That Pure Religion" issued under the pseudonym Deacon L. J. Bates, legend has Jefferson piously refusing to play blues on Sundays. We don't know enough about these men to assume either that their sacred performances were cynical attempts to cash in on the success of the guitar evangelists, or that their religious sentiments were genuine. We only know that many of the best prewar bluesmen were nearly as well acquainted with the Lord's music as with the Devil's. Of the fifty-four surviving titles by the Delta's Charley Patton, ten are religious songs.

Like many other blues artists from the Mississippi Delta, Charley Patton recorded a number of religious items—some with Bertha Lee, who was his wife at the time.

Some, in the manner of Blind Willie Johnson, feature a female second vocalist (Patton's wife, Bertha Lee) and bottleneck guitar. Both artists knew some of the same songs: Patton's "Jesus Is a Dying Bed Maker" is a version of the song Johnson recorded as "Jesus Make Up My Dying Bed." "You're Gonna Need Somebody When You Die," a variant of Johnson's blues of the same title, finds Patton intoning to a congregation:

> *Well, friends, I want to tell you, they tell me*
> *when He come down His hair gonna be like lamb's wool,*
> *and His eyes like flames of fire, and every man gonna*
> *know He's the son of the true living God . . .*

Archetypally, Patton drew the text of his verse from what Higginson called "the lurid imagery of the Apocalypse," taking his startling, vividly evocative vocabulary from the Book of Revelation.

In the Delta, Patton was known variously as a blues singer and a preacher. Perhaps this mixed reputation brought him together with a "backslid" Baptist preacher, Son House. The two "holy bluesmen" were joined by Willie Brown and Louise Johnson for a long trip to Grafton, Wisconsin, in the spring of 1930 for one of the most celebrated recording sessions in blues history. On a single day—May 28, 1930—Patton recorded the darkly moving "Moon Going Down" with Willie Brown, who waxed his stunning "Future Blues," and Louise Johnson recorded the boisterous "On the Wall." Son House recorded ten titles for Paramount that day, and the seven that survive bespeak a fascinating ambivalence toward his Baptist faith. In "My Black Mama—Part I," House seemingly proclaims himself an atheist:

Hey, tain't no heaven,
Tain't no burnin' hell;
Say, where I'm goin' when I die,
Can't nobody tell.

He then contradicted this with an emotional plea to God for rain in "Dry Spell Blues—Part II," an apocalyptic account of the devastating drought of 1928–30 ("I believe to my soul this ol' world is 'bout to end"):

Oh, Lord have mercy, if you please;
Oh, Lord have mercy, if you please.
Let your rains come down,
And give our poor hearts ease.

The celebrated "Preachin' the Blues—Parts I & II" seemed both to ridicule fake piety and to confess, in religious terms, the frailty of its singer:

Oh, coulda had religion,
Lord, this very day;
Woh, I'd had religion,
Lord, this very day.
But the womens and whisky,
Well, they would not let me pray.

Though House admits he isn't equal to the task of "having religion," he nonetheless has a mystical encounter:

Now I met the blues this mornin'
Walkin' just like a man;
Woh, walkin' just like a man.
I said, "Good mornin', blues,
Now gimme your right hand."

A divine visitation during prayer might bestow on a Christian the calling to preach. House suggests he's received a "calling" of another order and states that his is a mission of some urgency:

Oh, I'm gonna have to stay on the job,
I ain't got no time to lose;
Hey, I ain't got no time to lose.
I swear to God
I got to preach these gospel blues.
(Spoken: Great God A'mighty!)

Thirty years later House's disciple, Muddy Waters, would enjoy great success with a buoyant blues that combined a gospel shout with lyrics about an unsuccessful hex. If Waters felt any of House's ambivalence about juxtaposing blues and gospel in "Got My Mojo Working," he never expressed it. He did, however, tell James Rooney: "I was a good Baptist, singing in the church. . . . So I got all of my good moaning

and trembling going on for me right out of the church." And his blues? "It's from the heart," said Waters. "That's my religion." The implied priesthood House presented in "Preachin' the Blues," the sense that the bluesman answered a calling and delivered a powerful message, was a legacy Waters brought into the era of rock 'n' roll, a time when Ray Charles was often introduced as "The High Priest of Rhythm & Blues."

House would often revise "Preachin' the Blues" during his rediscovery (at least three substantially different versions were recorded in the 1960s), but the one constant was the song's striking first verse:

> Woh, I'm gonna get me religion,
> I'm gonna join the Baptist church;
> Woh, I'm gonna get me religion,
> I'm gonna join the Baptist church.
> I'm gonna be a Baptist preacher,
> And I sure won't have to work.

If we understand "work" as the hard physical labor of a subsistence agrarian economy in which Delta blacks scrabbled at the bottom rung, then the verse suggests more than a dig at the clergy. House describes what, in a middle-class context, we would call a career opportunity. If your aspirations transcended fieldwork, the pulpit was one of the few available options. "I wanted to be an outstanding man," Muddy Waters told James Rooney. "I believe I would have made a good preacher." The premier blues singer of his generation considered preaching the likeliest path to becoming "an outstanding man." Though the road he chose was different, Waters apparently felt that the role he played onstage and the one he might have played in the pulpit were analogous.

For bright and artistic black men of the Depression-era Delta, the roles of preacher or performer of social music were the primary alternatives to agrarian indentured servitude, and the personality traits that contributed to success in either role were similar in this environment. Blessed with strong lungs and rhetorical flair that might turn either to biblical exegesis or to the spinning of blues lyrics, a man could make his way in the world as something other than field laborer. Small wonder that some of the most celebrated early bluesmen—Charley Patton, Son House, Reuben Lacy, Ishman Bracey, Skip James, Robert Wilkins—would variously preach and play blues. Little wonder, too, that elements of "churchy" delivery began to bleed into blues performance, or that blues phrasing would creep into church.

House employed the declamatory, vibrato-laden style of a "straining" preacher in "Preachin' the Blues," a revolutionary symbiosis of the sacred and profane. The radical element of the song is less its lyrical content than the musical context in which House's "sermon" is delivered. In *Songsters and Saints: Vocal Traditions on Race Records*, Paul Oliver presents detailed evidence of a large body of songs from minstrelsy and ragtime traditions that satirize preachers as thieving, lecherous hypocrites. By the time of House's "Preachin' the Blues" in 1930, the untrustworthy preacher of ragtime song had become an antic figure of folklore, and ragtime itself a socially accepted medium for satire. The medium effectively defanged the message, telling listeners, "This is a fun song: Only kidding."

House demonstrated that he knew ragtime when he recorded for the Library of Congress in 1941–42 and probably did when he recorded for Paramount. That he chose instead to frame "Preachin' the Blues" in the newer, harder Delta blues idiom accentuated its dramatic tension. Delta audiences familiar with Patton and similar performers knew that this style conveyed much of the artist's world view—it expressed what he perceived to be the truth. The musical context framed House's lyrical message with a sense of urgency that told listeners: "The singer means what he says. He isn't kidding." Delta audiences would have recognized the echoes of the pulpit in House's delivery. Using his region's musical vocabulary of secular truth, a preacher's emotive vocal style, and an ambivalent "sermon" filled with both self-confession and blasphemy ("Oh, I wish I had me a heaven of my own . . ."), House crafted one of the timeless masterpieces of "holy blues."

"Preachin' the Blues" was among the last great country blues to be recorded before the full brunt of the Depression crippled the recording industry. Nehemiah "Skip" James would have a single extraordinary session for Paramount in 1931, commenting on the Depression in "Hard Time Killin' Floor Blues":

Skip James was one of the most intensely personal artists ever to have recorded blues or gospel music. His virtuosity on guitar as well as piano was exceptional.

The Tindley Quaker City Gospel Singers are pictured here about 1932.

Hard times here an' everywhere I go,
Times is harder than ever been before.
People are driftin' from door to door,
Can't find no heaven, I don't care where they go.

Not long thereafter, James turned from blues and was ordained a minister in the Missionary Baptist Church. (Rediscovered more than thirty years later, James remembered his old blues and played it.) Paramount, considered by many to have been the greatest prewar blues label, folded in 1932.

The Depression was a watershed in both the history of blues and of African-American sacred song. The silence that fell over the recording industry masked changes that must have taken place in blues performance in the early 1930s. By 1936, they were manifest in the recordings of Robert Johnson, obviously indebted to Son House while clearly moving toward the sound Muddy Waters would mold in Chicago more than a decade later. The Depression was the stimulus for far more drastic change in black sacred song. It was the kiln in which modern gospel music was fired. Not surprisingly, a "born again" bluesman was feeding the fire.

Thomas Andrew Dorsey was the offspring of the union of a Baptist minister and a church organist. Dorsey took to the keyboard and church songs in his child-hood, later pointing to pioneering black hymn composer Dr. Charles A. Tindley ("I'll Overcome") as his chief inspiration. But "the world" lured him in the 1920s, when he married "Ma" Rainey's wardrobe mistress, Nettie Harper. As Georgia Tom, Dorsey accompanied Rainey and other blues singers on dozens of recordings, including a notorious handful of hokum titles with Tampa Red and female impersonator Frankie "Half Pint" Jaxon. "I was one of the great bluesmen who traveled the country over," Dorsey recalled in the 1983 documentary film *Say Amen, Somebody*. "In the blues business, I wrote over three hundred." Dorsey expressed no regrets over his worldly past and, in fact, seemed to relish it. "I'm not ashamed of my blues," he told Anthony Heilbut, author of the definitive *The Gospel Sound: Good News and Bad Times* (1971). "Blues is a part of me, the way I play piano, the way I write." Dorsey freely acknowledged the cross-pollination of the Lord's music with the Devil's.

"There are moaning blues that are used in spirituals," he said, "and there are moaning spirituals that are used in blues."

In 1930, Dorsey turned his back on "the blues business" and formed the Thomas A. Dorsey Gospel Songs Music Publishing Company. Joined two years later by Sanctified singer Sallie Martin, the pair stirred Chicago churches, and in 1933 the Dorsey–Martin team invited throngs of the faithful to Chicago's Pilgrim Baptist Church for the first gathering of the National Convention of Gospel Choirs and Choruses.

As they built their organizational power base, Dorsey and Martin toured the country, galvanizing churches with Dorsey's songs ("Take My Hand, Precious Lord," "If You See My Savior") and selling the sheet music for them. At a nickel apiece, Dorsey's songs were cheaper than 78s, and inspired a generation of singers who loved their folksy and florid lyrics, as well as the combination of hymnal, barrelhouse, and

Thomas A. Dorsey poses with members of his flock, including Sallie Martin, at right.

A *1939 photograph shows Thomas A. Dorsey boarding a train for a gospel convention. The identities of the other individuals are unknown.*

Tin Pan Alley in the music. The Depression's depths created an audience eager for Dorsey's hopeful messages, though not every church embraced his songs. "When I first started out singing gospel," Willie Mae Ford Smith told Chris Albertson, "the churches didn't want it—'We don't want that coonshine stuff in here, we don't want no ragtime singing in here.'" To Viv Broughton, she recalled, "They said I was bringing the blues into the church."

But the church walls crumbled before popular acceptance, and Dorsey's songs were even urbane enough to enter the pop mainstream. Guy Lombardo made a hit of "My Desire," and Red Foley was the first of many country crooners to record "Peace in the Valley." Dorsey's songs and organization brought sweeping change to African-American sacred music. The free-form congregational singing heard in sacred recordings of the 1920s would be supplanted by arranged choral singing (a development parallel to that in eighteenth-century New England church singing). The new songs of Dorsey and his contemporaries were wedging out the songs of the oral tradition and turn-of-the-century revivals. Dorsey and Martin understood the power of publishing, and a black gospel song industry was born. "Mother" Willie Mae Ford Smith organized a Soloists' Bureau at Dorsey's National Convention of Gospel Choirs and Choruses, and her example and tutelage produced a generation of disciples (including Mahalia Jackson) who sharply defined the gospel style well into the 1960s.

The Depression that devastated the recording industry provided the catalyst for modern gospel. A fortuitous melding of direction, discipline, and timing produced one of the more significant (if least celebrated) revolutions in twentieth-century American popular music.

The Depression also made radio America's most popular form of mass communication. Radios were cheap enough and common enough by the 1930s to make them the foremost medium of popular culture. Harmony vocalists made warm sounds especially suited to the home-and-hearth instrument of glowing cathode tubes. Radio brought the new gospel and "jazzed" spirituals to national audiences when "jubilee" quartets became radio stars in the late 1930s.

Most popular of all was Norfolk, Virginia's Golden Gate Quartet, which created a fresh approach to spiritual singing about the same time Robert Johnson was redefining blues. A school of imitators followed in the Gates' wake, and quartet singing was never quite the same thereafter. "I think with this quartet what we tried to create was what I used to call 'vocal percussion,'" founding father Willie Johnson told researcher Doug Seroff. Johnson likened the Gates' vocal percussion to "a bunch of guys beating a tom-tom somewhere. . . . It all had to be done sharply and together, along with the harmony, and we sang simple chords." But if the chords were simple, the precisely syncopated vocal percussion was not. The Gates' 1937 Bluebird recordings presented a new development in spiritual singing, one which retained the

The Golden Gate Quartet virtually set the standard for quartet gospel singing.

137

style's folk roots while stepping in sync with the Swing era. In 1938, John Hammond invited the Gates to participate in the legendary From Spirituals to Swing concert series at Carnegie Hall, and soon they were swinging the spirituals for the Beautiful People at New York's Café Society Downtown nightclub. National radio exposure brought their voices to millions, and the Gates quickly became such a beloved national institution that, in 1941, President Roosevelt had them perform at his inaugural gala.

If most of their material was freshly arranged spirituals, the Gates weren't afraid of being topical as well. In 1942, they sang "No Segregation in Heaven," and later revamped "The Preacher and the Bear" into a celebration of the Soviet rebuff of "the beast of Berlin" entitled "Stalin Wasn't Stallin'."

The early 1940s was a time when several black male vocal groups were widely heard singing both secular and sacred songs on national radio programs. The Delta Rhythm Boys, praised by jazz vocalist Jon Hendricks as "a vital link between spiritual and jazz harmonies," could be heard singing both the traditional "Dry Bones" and the Strayhorn/Ellington standard, "Take the A-Train" (with lyrics added by the Rhythm Boys' bass, Lee Gaines). The Charioteers were regulars on Bing Crosby's radio programs and sang everything from "Joshua Fit de Battle of Jericho" to "On the Sunny Side of the Street." Such largely secular groups were surely regarded with disdain by the "saints" of the growing gospel subculture, but they pioneered a trend that many of that subculture's purest voices would exploit in future decades: the performance of gospel outside the church for entertainment.

The stellar trailblazer of this trend was Sister Rosetta Tharpe, a flamboyant showstopper who, in 1938, stunned patrons at the Cotton Club by singing Dorsey's "Rock Me" with Cab Calloway's Orchestra (she also sang "I Want a Tall Skinny Papa"). Tharpe was born in Cotton Plant, Arkansas, but raised in Chicago (and on the road) by her singing Church of God in Christ mother, Katie Bell Nubin. She learned to pick a jazzy blues guitar in the manner of Lonnie Johnson and developed an urgent vocal style that swung. Like the Golden Gate Quartet, Tharpe appeared at the 1938 From Spirituals to Swing concert. "She sang holy roller hymns that had the rhythm and beat of less sacred subjects," smirked Howard Taubman in his New York Times review.

A decade before any but the faithful few had heard of Mahalia Jackson, Tharpe was a national star. Her recordings with Lucky Millinder's Orchestra were hits, she headlined at both Café Society Downtown and the Apollo, and she was profiled by Life. Along with the Golden Gate Quartet, she was the only gospel artist offered on V-Disc to inspire World War II soldiers. Some of her recordings featured the great boogie-blues pianist Sam Price, and it could be said that her performances were spirited without necessarily being spiritual.

She beamed and projected across the footlights, presenting a Swing-era jazzed version of Sanctified passion. Watching Tharpe dazzle and sway in an early 1940s "soundie," surrounded by scantily-clad "shake" dancers, it's easy to see why some saints took umbrage at her act. (Scorned by the Sanctified who were her original constituency, Tharpe eventually became a Baptist.) Tharpe never denied the bluesiness of her music, often singing "Trouble in Mind" and, in later years, touring Europe with the likes of Muddy Waters. "There's something about the gospel blues," she mused to Tony Heilbut, "that's so deep the world can't stand it."

But the world plainly loved the theatricality of gospel performance. Mahalia Jackson understood this and took her songs to the concert hall, while Clara Ward

Mahalia Jackson, the undisputed queen of all gospel singers.

*Sister Rosetta Tharpe slipped
easily back and forth between
secular and religious music.*

presented a gaudy parody of gospel in Las Vegas nightclubs and at Disneyland.
Ward's parting gesture to Jackson—tossing a mink cape at her casket—spoke volumes about the distance these women had come from the poverty and storefront
churches of their youths.

Jackson was raised Baptist in New Orleans, but learned much musically from
the Holiness churches and Bessie Smith. Her 1937 debut recording, "God's Gonna
Separate the Wheat from the Tares," was a Judgment Day warning waxed earlier by
Blind Joe Taggart. In the 1940s she toured nationally with Dorsey, who tried to
repress her Sanctified abandon, to no avail. (It was later squelched by the formality of
the concert hall.) Jackson's reputation on the gospel circuit led to some superb
recordings for the Apollo label in the late 1940s. White jazz buffs discovered her in
the early 1950s and hailed her as a sacred Bessie Smith. A contract with Columbia
followed, and with it came both fine gospel recordings and quasi-religious novelties
like "Rusty Old Halo." Jackson became a regal presence, the matriarchal gospel
archetype, but purists felt her concessions to the mainstream diluted her artistry.

139

Mahalia Jackson broadcasts her gospel sound.

"Mahalia, the musical daughter of Bessie Smith," wrote Heilbut, "was effectively modified into a black Kate Smith."

Such accusations of excessive properness were never cast at Clara Ward. She was the daughter of a formidable gospel stage mother, Gertrude Mae Murphy Ward, who first brought Dorsey and Martin to Philadelphia in the 1930s and who was a fierce inspiration to her singing daughters, Clara and Willa. The Ward Singers first came to national prominence at the National Baptist Convention of 1943. By the late 1940s the Ward Singers had become the hottest act on the gospel circuit, thanks in part to the addition of such nonfamily talent as the extraordinary Marion Williams. Nothing like Jackson's crossover success came to the Wards in the early 1950s, but gospel hits (Reverend W. Herbert Brewster's "Surely God Is Able" was one of their biggest) were frequent, and Clara was earning a reputation among the saints as Jackson's closest rival, even though the world had yet to hear of her.

That soon changed. In 1961, swirling in multicolored robes and brandishing tambourines, the Ward Singers, crowned by mountainous wigs, marched onto the Vegas nightclub circuit. Their act seemed like a surreal self-parody of gospel abandon. Surely some of the faithful wondered how this differed from the nineteenth-century minstrel show in which black musicians and singers were employed in "happy darky" plantation life parodies. But for better or worse, the shameless Clara Ward and the stately Mahalia Jackson were the gospel singers who got booked on the Ed Sullivan Show. They were the voices heard by those who never set foot in a black church.

Far from the glamorous venues offered Jackson and Ward, there were scores of tireless crusaders on the gospel highway. Tony Heilbut calls 1945–60 gospel's golden age, and it was an era when such extraordinary women as Bessie Griffin, Dorothy Love Coates, Edna Gallmon Cooke, and the Georgia Peach were heard "shouting" the faithful into ecstacy, alongside such stunning male groups as the Five Blind Boys of Alabama, the Dixie Hummingbirds, the Pilgrim Travelers, the Spirit of Memphis, and the Swan Silvertones. These were the standard-bearers and inspiration to the soul singers who, in a manner different from Jackson and Ward (somewhat more in the spirit of Son House), took the world to church during the heady years of the 1960s.

But there were still other voices, more atavistic, keening in country churches and urban storefronts and street corners, voices akin to the guitar evangelists of the 1920s. A few were recorded, though their recordings excited little of the enthusiasm collectors lavished on their blues-playing contemporaries. As a result, as little is known of the sacred artists who were stylistically nearest the blues. At least their music speaks eloquently. Listen to the two recordings Dennis Crumpton and Robert Summers made in 1936. The deft interplay of their guitars (one played bottleneck-style) rivals the best country blues guitar duets of the 1930s. Their vocals on "Go I'll Send Thee" lope with a down-home swing that suggests the folk roots of the syncopated vocal percussion of the Golden Gate Quartet and their contemporaries.

Eight years later in New York City, Reverend Utah Smith, "the Traveling Evangelist," made some extraordinary recordings that were easily as raw as anything waxed by the preachers and congregations of the 1920s. (Smith reprised some of these performances for Chess in the 1950s.) At the height of World War II he clamored, "See how war done broke out throughout the whole world" in "God's Mighty Hand," a half-sung, half-shouted exhortation. Smith, encouraged by a ragged female chorus that shouted and supplied handclaps, bellowed in a hoarse voice and played distorted electric guitar in a nervous, anarchic manner, "sock" jazz chords interrupted by swooping slides up the neck. His most celebrated performance is (with good reason) "I Want Two Wings," which offers all of Smith's quirks raised to the tenth power. In a quasi-intelligible, vein-popping shout (one makes out "cherubim flyin' from heaven"), Smith turns to the Book of Revelation for his two wings: "They put ol' John on the isle of Patmos," he shouts, "for the word of God and the testimony of JEEEEsus! He saw the end of time . . ."

If, during the age of Rosetta Tharpe, Smith seemed to have come from another time, others were just as anachronistic later. Sister Matthews's sole 1948 test pressing, "Stand By Me," bears Tharpe's imprint, though Matthews's relatively flashless reading is closer in spirit to the merger of blues and spiritual in rural environs. Matthews's affecting performance underscores the blues bones on which hymnist Tindley (writing before Handy's earliest published blues) molded spiritual muscle. Heilbut noted of "Stand By Me" that "the melody is a blues variant, the sixteen-bar blues, the form so ubiquitous in mournful gospel that I have dubbed it the Baptist blues."

In 1950, Willie Mae Williams made a record in Philadelphia, "Don't Want to Go There" (backed with "Where the Sun Never Goes Down"), which recalled such female bottleneck guitar evangelists of the 1920s as Blind Mamie Forehand. Intriguingly, Williams's vocal vibrato and driving guitar suggest the approach Bukka White used on religious songs in the 1930s. Coincidence or influence? We'll never know, though one could hazard a guess that Williams was originally from Mississippi.

We have a fuller picture of the repertoire of Sister O. M. Terrell, who waxed six titles in Nashville in 1951. Terrell played a steel-bodied National guitar bottleneck-

Clara Ward—before she donned her trademark wigs and joined the Ward Singers.

The Swan Silvertones earned an enduring niche in the gospel firmament. Claude Jeeter, their great lead singer, is seen front and center.

style and sang with a voice influenced by Tharpe, yet far less polished than hers. Fittingly, Terrell waxed earthy sermon-songs, epitomized by her indignant aside to the unclean of mouth in "The Bible's Right":

> *You snuff dippers, tobacco chewers,*
> *When you get to heaven*
> *You won't have nowhere to spit!*

There were other anomalies, men and women seemingly from another era, who were recorded in gospel's golden age. In the 1950s Elder Wilson waxed a stunning "Stand By Me" accompanied by two harmonicas blown in a deep blues wail. Nothing quite like it had appeared since the extraordinary 1927 harmonica duo performance of Jaybird Coleman and Ollis Martin on "I'm Going to Cross the River of Jordan Some o' These Days." The Two Gospel Keys recorded a spirit-filled "You've Got to Move" with rhythmic tambourine and guitar backing, a performance purely in the manner of the 1920s guitar evangelists who recorded with a female second vocalist. Later, Fred McDowell would perform "You've Got to Move," a traditional "shout," at a deliberate snail's pace (he recorded it several times in the 1960s, once on a wonderful Testament album recorded in a Como, Mississippi, church). The evident irony of McDowell's slow "shout" appealed to the Rolling Stones, who copied McDowell's performance of "You've Got to Move" for their 1971 *Sticky Fingers* album.

The work of another gospel-era anachronism inspired the Stones' "The Last Time," revamped from the Staple Singers' 1954 United recording, "This May Be the Last Time." The Staples would enjoy a success surpassing that of most mainstream gospel performers, though their music often drew from the same murky backwaters as the artists who remain discographical question marks. Had Roebuck "Pops" Staple been a solo, he might have left a handful of intriguing titles before disappearing into the obscurity that envelops Sister O. M. Terrell or any of several decades' worth of guitar evangelists. But Staple had gifted children, especially daughter Mavis, one of the most compelling voices in a genre noted for great singers. With Mavis soaring in front, the Staples conquered both the church and the world without ever sounding much removed from Roebuck's Delta roots or the Chicago storefront churches where they had honed their craft. Melding ancient and archetypal material with a fresh mode of delivery, the Staple Singers were uniquely adaptable and accepted by the saints in the 1950s, the folk roots audience in the 1960s, and the pop world in the 1970s.

Roebuck grew up in deepest blues country, Drew, Mississippi, where he learned guitar from Charley Patton. Patton's darkness, the sometimes ominous spatial tension of his music, Staple transformed into gospel. He even plays identifiable Patton guitar licks on some records; after Staple's introduction to "Don't Knock," one expects instead to hear "Pony Blues." The economy of the notes he plays is broadened by an effective and evocative use of tremolo on his amplifier—along with Mavis's sensuous contralto, a much-emulated hallmark of the Staples' sound. And there is much in this sound—spare, deeply emotional, but never florid—that suggests music drawn from a deeper well than that of many of the Staples' gospel contemporaries.

This brought the Staples to the notice of the 1960s folk/blues audience, for whom they recorded such atavistic performances as a medley of "Nobody's Fault But Mine" and "Samson and Delilah" entitled "Tribute to Blind Willie Johnson." Write that off to a producer's glib bid for rootsiness if you can, knowing that the producer was Nashville's Billy Sherrill. Best known for his blue collar Sturm und Drang production of Tammy Wynette, Sherrill may not be the likeliest person to suggest a tribute to Blind Willie Johnson. The songs probably came from Roebuck's repertoire. The

The Reverend Utah Smith during the 1950s, playing—probably—at a Dallas church.

The Staple Singers were one of the greatest of all family gospel aggregations. Mavis Staple is at the microphone.

Staple Singers had recorded songs of equal or greater vintage in the 1950s, before the folk audience knew they existed.

"A Dyin' Man's Plea" was Blind Lemon Jefferson's primordial holy blues "See That My Grave Is Kept Clean." The doomy "Downward Road" was a song that predated even the most venerable holy blues. "Oh, the downward road is crowded," the Staples intoned, "with unbelieving souls." Mavis, charismatically engaged with her sermon song, spun a chilling tale:

> *Young people who delight in sin,*
> *Tell ya what I lately seen,*
> *A poor ungodly woman died,*
> *She didn't have Jesus on her side.*
>
> *Well, she laughed and played*
> *Her time away,*
> *And still put off her dyin' day.*
>
> *Lord God Almighty had his plans all fixed,*
> *Friday mornin' the woman took sick.*
> *Well, she called her mother to her room,*
> *To listen to her dyin' doom.*

> Say, "The prayers are lost you prayed for me,
> My soul is doomed, I plainly see.
> So mother and father, fare you well,
> Your wicked daughter is doomed to hell."

In the 1925 collection *The Negro and His Songs*, Odum and Johnson published a version of this. As "Wicked Polly," the song was widely circulated among southeastern whites as a warning to frivolous youth who would "go to balls and dance and play." In 1921, Edward S. Ninde published an eight-verse version of the song in his *The Story of the American Hymn*. The following three verses speak for the whole.

> O young people, hark while I relate
> The story of poor Polly's fate!
> She was a lady young and fair,
> And died a-groaning in despair.
>
> "My loving father, you I leave;
> For wicked Polly do not grieve;
> For I must burn forevermore,
> When thousand thousand years are o'er.
>
> Your counsels have I slighted all,
> My carnal appetite to fill.
> When I am dead, remember well
> Your wicked Polly groans in hell."

This vivid Victorian doggerel has been traced at least to the 1830s, and legend has it growing from a broadside circulated following the agonized death of an actual "Wicked Polly" in prerevolutionary Rhode Island. If true, the song's 180-year journey to a Chicago ghetto recording studio is little less remarkable than the voyage of "Dark Was the Night, Cold Was the Ground."

The Staple Singers may have had a special penchant for penetrating the deeper recesses of their tradition, but, as their later move into pop illustrates, they weren't afraid of innovation. In their Vee-Jay recording "Ain't That Good News," "Pops" opens with a guitar figure traced around Ray Charles's "What'd I Say," and the tune is a thinly veiled sacred revamp of "I Got a Woman." Some "saints" must have smiled; Charles had taken the structure and spirit of gospel to the world, changing only the lyrics. The Staples were merely reclaiming what the saints knew was theirs in the first place.

Ray Charles's career breakthrough came via 1954's "I Got a Woman," and its upfront usurpation of gospel convention in an R & B context shocked some bluesmen as much as saints. "He's got the blues," Big Bill Broonzy huffed, "but he's crying sanctified. He's mixing the blues with the spirituals. I know that's wrong . . . he should be singing in a church."

But Charles wasn't a gospel singer fallen to the world's wiles. His eclectic background included stints playing country, jazz, and R & B. He never sang gospel even semiprofessionally, though he clearly knew the idiom from the inside out. In his 1978 autobiography (with David Ritz), *Brother Ray*, Charles fondly recalls singing informally with gospel groups he encountered on the road: "Just the way I liked to jam with jazz players, I also loved jamming with the gospel boys." Among the voices he singled out for special praise were those of Ira Tucker of the Dixie Hummingbirds, Archie Brownlee of the Five Blind Boys of Mississippi, and Claude Jeter of the Swan Silvertones. "These guys have voices which could shake down your house and smash all the furniture in it."

Though Charles is often credited with starting the trend toward "sanctified" R & B in the 1950s, which blossomed into soul music in the sixties, he was over a year behind the Five Royales, whose gospel-drenched "Baby Don't Do It" claimed the number-one spot on *Billboard*'s R & B charts on January 17, 1953. The Royales started in North Carolina as the Royal Sons Quintet, and it was in their sacred robes that the group first recorded for Apollo in 1951. ("Bedside of a Neighbor," their debut, had been the first Dorsey song to be waxed by a quartet, the Blue Jay Singers, twenty years earlier.)

The blues has spawned a great many "Blind Boy" groups—one of the best known and most accomplished are the Five Blind Boys of Mississippi.

It soon became evident that the Royal Sons were a fine, if unexceptional, sacred group, while the often raunchy Five Royales were something special. The holy blues "Give Me One More Chance" was recorded at the Royal Sons' 1951 debut session, Johnny Tanner shouting intense secular pleas to the encouragement of his quartet. It didn't take Apollo long to discern which of the group's incarnations had more to offer. Along with the Royales' churchy vocals, they became famous for a stage show enlivened by gospel theatrics. The Five Royales were the blueprint for James Brown's Famous Flames (also originally a gospel group). Hearing Brown's 1956 "Please, Please, Please" is like hearing an echo, three years later, of the Royales' "Baby Don't Do It." Underappreciated beyond the small fraternity of vocal group fanatics, the Five Royales should be toasted as the unheralded fathers of soul.

The 1950s was a decade when the gospel groups gave the devil his due. Defections occurred at an alarming rate. The former pianist for Willie Mae Ford Smith, Ruth Jones, had become the new queen of the blues, Dinah Washington. The handsome young replacement of the revered R. H. Harris in the Soul Stirrers, Sam Cooke, became a pop star in 1957. While the saints clucked disapprovingly at the backslid ("The devil ain't got me," the tragic Cooke said defensively), the gospel imprint on pop music was growing exponentially. By the early 1960s the rhythms, inflections, and even the vocabulary of gospel were flowing through mainstream pop.

Bobby "Blue" Bland is no gospel singer, though he reportedly was tutored by the Dixie Hummingbirds' Ira Tucker. In 1962, Bland had a national hit with "Yield Not to Temptation," as fine a marriage of gospel shout and metaphor with the pop blues idiom as you'll hear. Marvin Gaye, the son of an Apostolic preacher, had a 1963 smash that took its chorus from the oft-heard church exhortation, "Can I Get a Witness." The Impressions sang "Amen" and "People Get Ready." The fabulous Solomon Burke, raised as the "Wonder Boy Preacher" in his Philadelphia family's House of God for All People, turned his church's offering march into the joyous "Everybody Needs Somebody to Love" (covered, like much else, by the Rolling Stones). Before soul music became a cause célèbre in the mid-1960s as America's only foil to the British Invasion, the language and nuance of gospel had already permeated pop.

And in the 1950s rock 'n' roll was surely, in part, holy blues. Richard Penniman had idolized gospel singer Brother Joe May, "The Thunderbolt of the Middle West," and recalled in Charles White's 1984 biography, The Life and Times of Little Richard, "I used to like going to the Pentecostal Church, because of the music." His earliest performances were with a family gospel group, the Penniman Singers, and a boyhood encounter with sister Rosetta Tharpe made a deep impression. Appearing at the Macon City Auditorium, where Penniman sold Cokes, she invited him onstage to sing with a star. The applause, he recalled, "was the best thing that had ever happened to me."

The applause turned deafening when, as Little Richard, Penniman loosed the falsetto whoops of Sanctified sisters with fevered abandon in "Good Golly Miss Molly," "Tutti Frutti," and "Lucille." In 1957, Penniman left "the world" and cloistered himself in an Alabama Holiness seminary. He preached and made sacred recordings for a few years, including a 1961 album for Mercury produced by Quincy Jones. "He was preaching it," Jones told Penniman biographer Charles White. "Here was a serious young gospel singer." But a year later, the singing preacher had returned to the world, where he would remain another fifteen years. When the rock revival circuit began flourishing in the early 1970s, Penniman put on his most unhinged dis-

Little Richard made many journeys from the holy universe of gospel music to the carnal world of rock 'n' roll.

McKinney Jones of the Sunset Travelers.

plays, sometimes festooned in a silver robe and sporting an outrageous pompadour. Little Richard looked like a drag parody of the Ward Singers and peppered his bizarre patter between breakneck rockers with religious overtones ("Man's extremities are God's opportunities").

The manic energy had subsided by 1979, when a more subdued Penniman could be seen quoting the Book of Acts on the "Mike Douglas Show" and "700 Club." An Associated Press wire service story that year reported Little Richard selling the *Black Heritage Bible* door to door in Dallas. At a Seattle crusade, Penniman was introduced by the flamboyant white Pentecostal evangelist R. W. Shambach as "the former king of rock 'n' roll. Now he's got his feet on the rock and his name on the roll!" Penniman informed the faithful, "God told me to tell all of you to give up rock 'n' roll!" The crowd roared its approval. "It's holiness or hell, ladies and gentlemen!"

Regaling the saints with tales of drugs and debauchery, Penniman turned to a topic he must have heard preached often as a boy. "Do you think God wants you to have the blues?" asked the man whose "Directly From My Heart to You" was one of the great blues recordings of the 1950s. "The blues make you lie. The blues make you cry about somebody else's wife, about somebody else's husband. The blues make you make phone calls that you know you can't pay for. Do you think God wants you to have the blues? God don't want you to have no blues!" By the end of the 1980s, Penniman was again singing rock 'n' roll.

Not all children of the gospel highway have felt the need for such public either/or declarations. Aretha Franklin, aptly crowned the Queen of Soul, is the daughter of the Reverend Charles L. Franklin, who pastored Detroit's 4500-member New Bethel Baptist Church. Her first recordings were pure gospel in the Clara Ward mold, but such 1960s hits as "I Never Loved a Man the Way I Love You" and "Chain of Fools" were drenched deep in both blues and gospel. "Spirit in the Dark" (1970) may have been her crowning glory, a sensuous and powerful evocation of either a lover or the Holy Ghost. Two years later Franklin recorded a stunning two-LP *Amazing Grace* with James Cleveland and the Southern California Community Choir. For Lady Soul, neither the church nor the world could stake exclusive claim on her artistry.

In a few brief years after Franklin's *Amazing Grace*, the church-inspired soulfulness that had imbued black popular music throughout the previous two decades appeared to wither. What remained of soul by the mid-1970s had largely been sweetened and orchestrated beyond recognition. Funk and disco were the popular idioms, and even though they (and, later, rap) acknowledged the influence of such secular shouters as James Brown and Sly Stone, in this new music the storefront church, as much as the juke joint, seemed a dim and distant memory. Perhaps the church had ceased to mean much to the African-American youth who came of age in the mid-1970s. If the black church's promise had been epitomized by the Civil Rights movement, and if that movement's promise lay largely unfulfilled, then perhaps the church itself was past its prime, irrelevant.

No doubt churches, black and white, have long ceased being the compelling shapers of culture they once were. A secular culture with the attention span of a TV newsbite has little patience for the continuity of ritual and the rhetorical ripeness of the pulpit, though many of us apparently miss the community and constancy the church promised. If aerobics is the substitute religion of some and TV sports that of others, there are still "saints" who tend the ancient flame.

In Dallas, a black religious radio station still broadcasts frenzied services of a Fire Baptized Holiness Church, the preacher exhorting and the congregation responding in a manner little changed from that heard on Pentecostal sermon 78s of the 1920s. The music has changed; but then it always was changing. The contemporary gospel recordings the station airs are dominated by funk bass lines and singers deeply indebted to the smooth melisma of Stevie Wonder. Similar stations can be heard across the country, and they wouldn't exist if there weren't still a subculture of saints to support them.

Vestiges of tradition often appear in unexpected places. A New York "gangster" rapper, Diamond Shell, brags of besting his rivals in an OK Corral–style shootout on Brooklyn's mean streets and says you can mark the body count when you hear the church's "Tollin' Bells" (his rap's title). The death bell image is ancient and was used in the sacred recordings of Blind Willie Johnson, Charley Patton, and the Golden Gate Quartet, who waxed "Toll the Bells" in 1941. Sometimes metaphors outlive messages, and sometimes eternal messages reappear in new robes: Hammer's 1991 hit album, *Too Legit to Quit*, finds him rapping about his love for the Lord as Tramaine Hawkins sings "Do Not Pass Me By." This, too, may be holy blues.

BRIGHT LIGHTS, BIG CITY

URBAN BLUES

MARK A. HUMPHREY

◆◆◆

Bright lights, big city, gone to my baby's head . . .
Jimmy Reed

Fond as we are of celebrating centennials (even quincentenaries), it seems odd no one has yet hailed the hundredth birthday of the blues. Maybe it's due to a vague birth date ("formed in the 1890s" is as specific as scholars get), or maybe it's the absence of a dramatic delivery scene. We know of no single performance that shook the world in the manner of Stravinsky's *Le Sacre du printemps*, disturbingly new enough at its 1913 premiere to spark a riot. The nearest thing we have to a genesis scene is W. C. Handy's account of his 1903 encounter with the blues in the form of a "lean, loose-jointed Negro" who, in a Tutwiler, Mississippi, train station, played slide guitar and sang a primal Delta blues ("the weirdest music I had ever heard," wrote Handy in his autobiography, *Father of the Blues*).

But no less than Stravinsky's departures from "classical" rhythm and harmony shaped modern art music, the deceptively simple blues form revolutionized twentieth-century popular music. Blues became arguably the most-often-used song structure of the century, appealing for its straightforward simplicity, sensuous familiarity, and an openness that allowed such diverse composers as George Gershwin and Aaron Copland—as well as generations of pop, rock, country, and even gospel artists—to make it part of their sound.

Where did blues come from? The short-form answer gives us postbellum field workers hollering work songs that, musically and lyrically, contain the seeds of the blues. We fast-forward a decade or two and see Handy's "lean, loose-jointed Negro" hammering out the bones of Delta blues. Next, this prototypical bluesman's son

ry, and journalistic matter-of-factness, these songs report the daily drudgery, dangers, and fleshly pleasures of slum life. So, too, did blues as far back as we can hear it: for every 1920s blues recording about a balky mule or banty rooster, there were others that discussed such timeless urban themes as drugs and prostitution.

The blues Jelly Roll Morton recalled from 1902 was a whore's lament:

> *I stood on the corner, my feet was dripping wet,*
> *I asked every man I met . . .*
> *Can't give me a dollar, give me a lousy dime,*
> *Just to feed that hungry man of mine . . .*

The woman who sang and played this on piano, Mamie Desdoumes, was "a hustlin' woman," Morton told Alan Lomax, "a blues-singing poor gal." Some female blues singers, like the earliest Portuguese *fadistas*, may have been prostitutes who entertained customers with song as well as sex. Prostitution is the theme of enough early recordings of female blues singers to suggest either firsthand experience or an empathy with "hustlin' women." In her 1937 recording, "Walking the Street," Georgia White turned in a heartfelt performance of the song Morton heard thirty-five years earlier:

> *Stood on the corner till my feet got soakin' wet,*
> *Stood on the corner till my feet got soakin' wet,*
> *These are the words I said to each and every man I met.*
> *"If you ain't got a dollar, give me a lousy dime,*
> *"If you ain't got a dollar, give me a lousy dime,*
> *I've got to beg and steal to please that man of mine."*

White's "man" is clearly a pimp, a character reported matter-of-factly in several female blues about prostitution. Men who earned more conventional livings might

This session card was made out for an unreleased Lonnie Johnson recording.

GENERAL PHONOGRAPH CORPORATION

Record Laboratory

W 81188-a
W 81188-B

Laboratory No.   Size   10

DATE *August 5* 192*7*

Recorded by *N. 4.*

Catalogue No.

Coupled with

Special Catalogue No.

Selection *I Love You, Mary Lou*

By *Lonnie Johnson*   Accompanied by

Composed by *Lonnie Johnson*

From

Publisher *Lonnie Johnson*   Copyright *Yes*

Address *225 West 27 th St. — for 5 months*
N. Y. C.

Remarks *Race*
Guitar & Voice

BRIGHT LIGHTS, BIG CITY

URBAN BLUES

MARK A. HUMPHREY

◆◆◆

Bright lights, big city, gone to my baby's head . . .
Jimmy Reed

Fond as we are of celebrating centennials (even quincentenaries), it seems odd no one has yet hailed the hundredth birthday of the blues. Maybe it's due to a vague birth date ("formed in the 1890s" is as specific as scholars get), or maybe it's the absence of a dramatic delivery scene. We know of no single performance that shook the world in the manner of Stravinsky's *Le Sacre du printemps,* disturbingly new enough at its 1913 premiere to spark a riot. The nearest thing we have to a genesis scene is W. C. Handy's account of his 1903 encounter with the blues in the form of a "lean, loose-jointed Negro' who, in a Tutwiler, Mississippi, train station, played slide guitar and sang a primal Delta blues ("the weirdest music I had ever heard," wrote Handy in his autobiography, *Father of the Blues*).

But no less than Stravinsky's departures from "classical" rhythm and harmony shaped modern art music, the deceptively simple blues form revolutionized twentieth-century popular music. Blues became arguably the most-often-used song structure of the century, appealing for its straightforward simplicity, sensuous familiarity, and an openness that allowed such diverse composers as George Gershwin and Aaron Copland—as well as generations of pop, rock, country, and even gospel artists—to make it part of their sound.

Where did blues come from? The short-form answer gives us postbellum field workers hollering work songs that, musically and lyrically, contain the seeds of the blues. We fast-forward a decade or two and see Handy's "lean, loose-jointed Negro" hammering out the bones of Delta blues. Next, this prototypical bluesman's son hops a Chicago-bound freight; in the years following World War II, the music becomes crisper, harder—more of a piece with the urban landscape.

We trace blues evolving organically from the African-American work song to become a new dance and party music of the countryside, replacing slavery-era banjo and fiddle music. The free-floating verses and idiosyncratic meters of country blues were struck into something both more formal and flashy on the forge of city streets.

This evolutionary model moves smoothly. The amorphous a cappella field hollers get refined into an entertaining song *form*, which becomes increasingly sophisticated as its exponents move into an urban environment, where they compete in the arena of professional show business. We can neatly graph this evolution chronologically: nineteenth-century "arwhoolies" (field hollers) become varied styles of "country blues" by the teething years of the twentieth century, and an amplified "urban blues" emerges after World War II.

Inherent in this model is the assumption that "city blues" is a more recent phenomenon than "country blues," and that city blues evolved along a straight stylistic

Jimmy Reed was at the height of his popularity when he appeared in one of the least elegant publicity photos of all time—note the tape at the bottom of the cushion.

This 1930s photo features three bona-fide southern blues artists then resident in Chicago (left to right): Little Bill Gaither, Memphis Slim (Peter Chatman), and Big Bill Broonzy.
CHAPTER OPENER

A handbill for a blues tour.

line from country blues. Yet Jelly Roll Morton recalled hearing a sophisticated blues
in New Orleans by 1902, predating Handy's rural crossroads experience by a year. The
earliest recorded blues performers, the so-called "classic" female singers of the 1920s,
presented a formalized music no less arranged than anything Bobby "Blue" Bland has
performed more recently. Wasn't their studied "vaudeville blues" an essentially
urban idiom, even though it existed contemporaneously with the country blues of
Blind Lemon Jefferson and Charley Patton? While the Delta-to-Chicago sounds of
Muddy Waters and similar migrants clearly show an urban blues style developed
from a rural one, it may be that other city blues developed parallel to—and largely
apart from—its country cousins.

    Blues wasn't the only folk music to emerge in the nineteenth century that
spoke plainly of the pleasures and pains of a poor underclass. The tango of Argentina,
the fado of Portugal, and the Greek *rebetica* all grew from urban subcultures and
voiced the taboo—sex, drink, drugs—in vernacular frequently compared to urban
African-American "jive talk." Tango, fado, and *rebetica* have each been called the
blues of their respective countries, in part for a quality of musical mournfulness, but
more importantly for their vivid descriptions of a life-style that, by polite standards,
was deemed scandalous. What makes such varied musics blueslike is the manner in
which they express urban experience. In lyrics comprised equally of slang, lurid poet-

ry, and journalistic matter-of-factness, these songs report the daily drudgery, dangers, and fleshly pleasures of slum life. So, too, did blues as far back as we can hear it: for every 1920s blues recording about a balky mule or banty rooster, there were others that discussed such timeless urban themes as drugs and prostitution.

The blues Jelly Roll Morton recalled from 1902 was a whore's lament:

> I stood on the corner, my feet was dripping wet,
> I asked every man I met . . .
> Can't give me a dollar, give me a lousy dime,
> Just to feed that hungry man of mine . . .

The woman who sang and played this on piano, Mamie Desdoumes, was "a hustlin' woman," Morton told Alan Lomax, "a blues-singing poor gal." Some female blues singers, like the earliest Portuguese *fadistas*, may have been prostitutes who entertained customers with song as well as sex. Prostitution is the theme of enough early recordings of female blues singers to suggest either firsthand experience or an empathy with "hustlin' women." In her 1937 recording, "Walking the Street," Georgia White turned in a heartfelt performance of the song Morton heard thirty-five years earlier:

> Stood on the corner till my feet got soakin' wet,
> Stood on the corner till my feet got soakin' wet,
> These are the words I said to each and every man I met.
> "If you ain't got a dollar, give me a lousy dime,
> "If you ain't got a dollar, give me a lousy dime,
> I've got to beg and steal to please that man of mine."

White's "man" is clearly a pimp, a character reported matter-of-factly in several female blues about prostitution. Men who earned more conventional livings might

This session card was made out for an unreleased Lonnie Johnson recording.

view the flamboyant pimp with envy or scorn; Lonnie Johnson's "Crowing Rooster Blues" vehemently protests the pimp's parasitic high life:

> *What makes a rooster crow every mornin' 'fore day?*
> *What makes a rooster crow every mornin' 'fore day?*
> *To let the pimps know that the workin' man is on his way.*
>
> *We up before sunrise, slavin' sixteen hours a day;*
> *We up before sunrise, slavin' sixteen hours a day;*
> *We pay our house rent and grocery bills,*
> *And the pimps get the rest of our pay.*
>
> *Men, we got to get together; something's got to be done!*
> *We make money while the pimps really have the fun.*
> *And where there's only house rent and grocery bills,*
> *No mon, no fun.*

When Johnson recorded this in 1941, he could readily empathize with the urban clock puncher: he had known the drudgery of steel mill labor no less than the acclaim brought by his recording success. It was like that, off and on, for six decades of Johnson's remarkable life. Whenever musical opportunities dried up, he quietly found other means to pay "the house rent and grocery bills." Running on deep reserves of dignity and determination, Johnson renewed his musical career at least four times after the Depression flattened his initial stardom of the 1920s. "I've lived

Working under the auspices of the Farm Security Administration, noted photographer Russell Lee took this shot of Lonnie Johnson (at extreme left) with Dan Dixon on guitar and Andrew Harris on bass playing Squares Boulevard Lounge in Chicago during April 1941.

155

An Okeh promotion for Lonnie Johnson's "Baby, Will You Please Come Home."

a very beautiful life," he told Folkways Records' Moses Asch in 1967. "I've seen it very sweet and I've seen it very hard. . . . But somehow or other I managed to make it." Johnson drew extraordinary music and ironic poetry from his bittersweet life's experiences, and he is remembered as the first influential—and quintessential—urban bluesman.

Like that of the blues itself, the birthdate of Alonzo "Lonnie" Johnson is subject to conjecture: it has been variously given as 1889, 1894, 1899, and 1900. We know he was born into a musical family in New Orleans and began playing in his father's string band when he was fourteen. Though he became a guitarist of such subtlety and drive that his riffs would be echoed by generations of blues as well as jazz guitarists (Charlie Christian and Django Reinhardt no less than T-Bone Walker and B. B. King), the violin was his primary instrument in early years. (Johnson also played piano, passably well on record, and reportedly played a variety of stringed instruments in his youth.)

After the influenza pandemic of 1918 wiped out much of Johnson's family in New Orleans, he and his brother James "Steady Roll" Johnson (also a multi-instrumentalist, though primarily a pianist) moved to St. Louis, where they found employment with cornetist Charlie Creath's Jazz-O-Maniacs. The group often played on Mississippi River steamboats: "I played every excursion boat out there for five years," Johnson told Asch. It was with Creath's band that Johnson made his recording debut ("Won't Don't Blues") in St. Louis on November 2, 1925. Two days later, Johnson appeared as leader on the first of some 130 sides he waxed for the Okeh label before the Depression drew the curtain on the first era of blues recording in 1932. His trademark guitar style, already fully mature, graces "Mr. Johnson's Blues," but it was the other side of his first record, on which he sang and played violin, that Johnson would recall forty-two years later as "a big hit." "Falling Rain Blues" was popular enough (and well enough remembered) to prompt several rerecordings of it during Johnson's long career. His tremulous violin ("It's hard to play violin and sing at the same time," he said) breaks into an extended crying solo after the original recording's final verse:

> *Blues, falling like showers of rain;*
> *Blues, falling like showers of rain;*
> *Every once in awhile, I think I hear my baby call my name.*

Johnson's recorded violin playing lacks the smooth certainty of his guitar work, but it may be that ideas he first developed on the bowed instrument later reached maturity on the plucked one. The violin, by its nature, is a lead instrument; a singing vibrato naturally flows from an accomplished player's hands. This vocal quality was less evident in the guitars Johnson heard strumming rhythm backup—and little else—in the string bands of his youth. As he simultaneously discovered his greater affinity for the guitar and realized the limits of his violin virtuosity, Johnson transferred a violinist's sensibility—an emphasis on single-line playing enhanced by slurs and vibrato—to the guitar, on which such playing was new. Johnson was first not only to improvise as a jazz guitarist, but to use the guitar as a "crying" counterpoint to lyrics in the matter elaborated on by hosts of blues guitarists inspired by T-Bone Walker and, later, B. B. King.

Before this revolutionary departure, Johnson may have played music like that presented in the instrumental "Five O'Clock Blues," in which his wailing violin and kazoo are joined by De Loise Searcy's piano and brother James Johnson's banjo, giving this 1926 recording a rural jug-and-string-band feel. It was probably just such music that Johnson played in his father's string band, sounds rooted in the nineteenth century, when fiddle and banjo were popular in African-American music and the guitar little known. The opposite was becoming the norm by 1926, and no individual was more responsible for this trend than Lonnie Johnson.

In 1927, Johnson's unique guitar style caught the ear of another musical visionary, Louis Armstrong, who invited him to join Armstrong's Hot Five to record "I'm Not Rough," "Hotter Than That," and "Savoy Blues." A year later, he sat in with Duke Ellington & His Orchestra for one of the legendary recordings of the early Ellington Jungle Band, "The Mooche." (A 1960 reunion of Johnson and Ellington at

Captured in the most elegant studio portrait ever made of any blues artist, Lonnie Johnson is seen here with the twelve-string guitar that was made expressly for him by a luthier in Mexico.

New York's Town Hall was heralded by a *New York Daily News* headline emphasizing their contrasting fortunes at the time: "The Janitor Meets the Duke.") The year 1928 also saw Okeh pair Johnson with pioneering jazz guitarist Eddie Lang, best remembered for his work with violinist Joe Venuti, which inspired the Django Reinhardt–Stephane Grappelli duo. (Lang was also a steady presence in Paul Whiteman's Orchestra, and served as accompanist to Bing Crosby.) Johnson's instrumental duets with "Blind Willie Dunn" (Lang's *nom du disque* for the sessions) set a stunningly high standard for future jazz and blues guitarists. As a sideman, Johnson was in constant demand for blues recordings in the late 1920s, and his guitar graces many memorable vocals by (among others) Clara Smith, Victoria Spivey (including the infamous "Dope Head Blues") and Alger "Texas" Alexander, the primitive country bluesman whom Johnson ruefully recalled as being especially difficult to accompany, given his erratic sense of time.

The quirks of country bluesmen struck Johnson as merely unprofessional. At a time when most male blues singer/guitarists were playing rural dances, urban street corners, or, at best, medicine shows, Johnson was touring the black vaudeville circuit in the company of Bessie Smith and other female stars. During the blues revival tours of the 1960s, Johnson was quick to distance himself from the "primitives" in whose company he was sometimes displayed. "I sing city blues," he told Valerie Wilmer in 1963. "My style of singing has nothing to do with the part of the country I come from." Johnson was hip to the regional subdivision of blues styles, and having lived in New Orleans, St. Louis, Cleveland, Chicago, New York, Cincinnati, and Philadelphia, he firmly rejected the notion that his music was merely snipped from a region's folkloric fabric. It was, he insisted, an individual creation: "It came from my soul within."

Today we praise Johnson's individuality as an influential guitarist, but there's little doubt that his initial audience was won by the persona that emerged from his lyrics. He was indeed an urban bluesman, bluntly cynical about love, as evidenced by such early 1930s titles as "Not the Chump I Used to Be," "Beautiful but Dumb," and "Men, Get Wise to Yourself." There was a citified cool and ironic humor as he sang, with heavy-lidded detachment, "I'm gonna take my razor and cut your late hours" in "She's Making Whoopee in Hell Tonight."

Feminine deception was Johnson's idée fixe. It was the theme of 1928's "Crowing Rooster Blues" ("She will get ramblin' on her brains, and some triflin' man on her mind"), the song he later revamped to scorn pimps. With an urbane knack for self-deprecation, Johnson waxed "I'm Just Dumb" in 1940, admitting he was easily duped by womanly wiles ("Your ways is so sweet, but, oh! what a rotten mind!"). The theme was picked up again a dozen years later in an extraordinary King label recording with Todd Rhodes's Band, "You Can't Buy Love." Johnson had evidently studied some of his pupils as they had studied him; the performance opens with T-Bone-style chordal vamps, and Johnson's intensely up-front vocals (he'd heard the blues shouters, too) pled familiar cautions against Eve's daughters:

> *You can give your woman plenty money,*
> *Dress her up in fancy gowns;*
> *You can give your woman plenty money,*
> *Dress her up in fancy gowns;*
> *She will tell her outside man*
> *She's got the dumbest, the dumbest man in town!*

When Johnson recorded that, in 1952, he was an elder statesman competing with a horde of Young Turks weaned on his recordings from twenty years earlier. Remarkably, Johnson doesn't sound like a voice out of time trying feebly for a final hit. He would never sound like that. The recordings that mark his successive comebacks—for Decca in 1937, for King in 1947, for Bluesville in 1960—all seem assured, marked by a signature sound that hadn't changed in essence since 1925 and yet proved adaptable to any new challenge, whether it was a horn section or an electric pickup for Johnson's guitar. Johnson updated fluidly without compromising his musical personality, and this, even more than his virtuosity and influence as guitarist, may be the quality that makes him one of the truly heroic figures of the blues. Without sounding antiquated, he continued to make music that was not so much unchanged as it was timeless up to his death in 1970. Certainly the quality that made him heroic to the young men who would reshape the blues beginning in the 1930s was his urbanity, his frank discussions of deceitful women, pimps, even the gangsters who ruled Chicago in the Capone era (for example, "Racketeer's Blues"). These were songs of the city, blunt and spicy as a dime novel.

Via record, Johnson's aural cityscapes reached listeners in such remote rural environs as Robinsonville, Mississippi. It was there that Robert Johnson patiently studied Lonnie Johnson's Okeh 78s, blending their smoothly urban guitar licks and vocals with sounds gleaned from such local role models as Eddie "Son" House and Willie Brown. As he became more competent in his imitation, the young Mississippian began to claim he was related to the famous bluesmaster with whom he shared a last name. His traveling companion, Johnny Shines, heard Robert Johnson—feeling bolder still—tell some rural audiences that he actually was the man they knew only from record, Lonnie Johnson!

Such idolatry and imitation of recorded "stars" was radically changing blues by the late 1930s, chipping away at the distinct regionalisms that, a decade earlier, had made Mississippi's Charley Patton, Georgia's Blind Willie McTell, and Texan Blind Lemon Jefferson sound like products of sharply different worlds. Growing up with the phonograph he used as sexual metaphor in "Phonograph Blues," Robert Johnson was free to learn as much from men he might never meet as he was from the ones he routinely studied at Delta dances. His recorded repertoire evidences a cross-hatching of influences—the "cool" urbanity of Lonnie Johnson no less than the "hot" intensity of Son House. By the late 1930s, singers like Robert Johnson were making urban blues less a matter of geography than of attitude.

An attitude of persistent longing—for a woman, for a distant home, for rest or money or inner peace—pervaded many of the best blues of Leroy Carr, a pianist and singer whose recordings had a profound effect on Robert Johnson, among others. Carr was born in Nashville in 1905, but spent most of his life in Indianapolis, where he established a reputation as the city's best blues pianist and singer. The barrelhouse life-style drove the easygoing Carr to early alcoholism, alluded to in many of his recordings ("Corn Likker Blues," "Straight Alky Blues 1 & 2," "Hard Times Done Drove Me to Drink," and so on). His recording partner, guitarist Francis "Scrapper" Blackwell, was a bootlegger who told Theodore F. Watts that he first met Carr while "selling my corn . . . he bought all the alcohol I had. That put me out of business."

But a new business opened when Carr suggested they record together. Their initial 1928 Vocalion label waxing, "How Long, How Long Blues," featured Carr's restless yet resigned inquiry ("How long, baby, how long . . .") underpinned by the insistent, doomy bass in Carr's left hand and Blackwell's heavy thumb. The sound

Leroy Carr's many recordings were not only vastly influential but readily available, in contrast to performances of most of the period's country blues artists of the deep South. Sadly, Carr lived only to age thirty.

and the attitude evoked such a responsive chord in black listeners that the record reportedly sold a million copies and had to be rerecorded when Vocalion wore out the master. (Carr and Blackwell recorded six variants of "How Long, How Long Blues" in the course of some 114 recordings together. Muddy Waters recalled "How Long, How Long Blues" as one of the first songs he learned to play.)

There would be other notable piano-guitar teams throughout the history of the blues, but none exceeded the success or influence of Carr and Blackwell. "They showed an almost telepathic sympathy in their duets," Giles Oakley observed in *The Devil's Music: A History of the Blues* (Taplinger, 1977), and their popularity was such that they continued to record through the depths of the Depression when other blues artists were silenced.

For every downcast "How Long, How Long Blues," Carr and Blackwell would offer an ebullient celebration of their raucous barrelhouse world. Their 1930's "Sloppy Drunk Blues" ("I'd rather be sloppy drunk," Carr sang, "than anything I know") packed enough punch to be recast as a tough Chicago blues twenty-four years later by Jimmy Rogers, with Little Walter Jacobs blowing hard harp as if to say he knew whereof Rogers sang. "Barrelhouse Woman" chided a woman who frequented the establishments where Carr played ("I wish that I could cure her barrelhousin' ways . . ."), though the song's rollicking rhythm takes the sting from Carr's chides:

Scrapper Blackwell, one of the most unusual guitar-playing blues practitioners of the 1920s and 1930s, was a marvelous stylist and a magnificent artist in his own right as well as Leroy Carr's faithful partner.

She struts around all day,
She barrelhouses the whole night through.
She struts around all day,
She barrelhouses the whole night through.
But when she loves me, I forget that I ever was blue.

Two of the giants of urban blues meet at the RCA Victor Recording Studios in Camden, New Jersey, about 1934. Tampa Red is on the left; Leroy Carr on the right.

"Barrelhouse is noted from barrel whiskey," Texas pianist Edwin "Buster" Pickens told Paul Oliver in *Conversation with the Blues* (Horizon Press, 1965). "Back in the late 'twenties, early 'thirties, it would be nothin' strange to see a man have a keg of bootleg whisky. Probably half a barrel of whisky . . . that's why they call it the barrelhouse. . . . You had your tin cup—just dip down in the barrel."

As much as Carr's molasses vocals and pungent lyrics, Blackwell's guitar was an essential part of the sound record buyers loved, and Carr knew it, shouting encouragement to Blackwell in the midst of an inspired solo ("Boy, this is gonna be a killer!"). Blackwell's crisply snapped treble lines anticipated both Robert Johnson and T-Bone Walker. If less commercially successful, Blackwell's solo recordings of the era were no less impressive than many of his duets with Carr. He was still living in Indianapolis at the time of his rediscovery in 1958, and remained an able and fiery

161

guitarist. His second musical career was only beginning to gain momentum when Blackwell fell to a murderer's bullet in 1962.

For Carr, the road was even shorter: booze got the better of him, and he succumbed to acute nephritis on April 29, 1935. Two months later, Blackwell was called to record a tribute, "My Old Pal Blues":

> *The day of his funeral, I hated to see Leroy's face.*
> *The day of his funeral, I hated to see Leroy's face.*
> *Because I know there is no one could ever take his place.*

At the same session, Blackwell accompanied Amos Easton, who was best known as Bumble Bee Slim, on "The Death of Leroy Carr." For this performance, Easton was dubbed Leroy Carr's Buddy:

> *Now people I'm gonna tell you, as near as I can*
> *Now people I'm gonna tell you, as near as I can*
> *About the death of Leroy Carr, he was my closest friend.*

Bumble Bee Slim, with his steel-bodied National guitar, poses with Honey Hill (left) and Bill Gaither (right).

Easton recorded two other blues dedicated to Carr's memory, and Bill Gaither's "Life of Leroy Carr" was waxed five years after Carr's death: The people remembered.

For a man who drank himself to death at age thirty, Carr cast a long shadow. Scores of 1930s blues recordings reflect his influence, though those of Robert Johnson are probably best known to today's blues audience. Carr's "Midnight Hour Blues" hangs heavily as backdrop to Johnson's "From Four Till Late"; "Blues Before Sunrise" was recast by the young Mississippian as "Kind-Hearted Woman," and Carr's "When the Sun Goes Down" provided the framework for "Love in Vain." Carr's impact didn't end in the 1930s. Twenty years after "Midnight Hour Blues," Antoine "Fats" Domino echoed Carr's piano riffs from the piece in Lloyd Price's "Lawdy Miss Clawdy," and Ray Charles recorded "How Long, How Long Blues." But the Carr disciple who best reflected his spirit—while dressing it in sharper threads— was Charles Brown, whose smooth 1940s recordings were dubbed after-hours blues. Brown's coolly intimate 1948 recording of Carr's "In the Evening When the Sun Goes Down" is a polished reflection of Carr's message in refined medium. It could be suggested that Carr invented, or at least anticipated, the after-hours blues; a *noir* cast hangs over his brooding urban blues, songs dealing with inner doubts and an anxiety heightened by the night:

> *In the wee midnight hours, long 'fore the break of day,*
> *In the wee midnight hours, long 'fore the break of day,*
> *When the blues creep up on you and carry your mind away.*
>
> *While I lay in my bed, and cannot go to sleep,*
> *While I lay in my bed, and cannot go to sleep,*
> *While my heart's in trouble, and my mind is sinking deep.*
> —*"Midnight Hour Blues"*

Some scholars believe that the alienation that has transcended race and class in twentieth-century urban America was first given populist voice by blues singers. Among them, Leroy Carr seemed to make alienation almost a credo of his best songs:

> *I just feel dissatisfied, baby,*
> *Now sometimes don't know what to do.*
> *I just feel dissatisfied, baby,*
> *Sometimes I don't know what to do.*
> *Have you ever had that same feeling, babe,*
> *To come over you?*
> —*"Blue Night Blues"*

Such questions were far from the minds of another popular piano-guitar duo of the era, "Georgia Tom" Dorsey and Tampa Red. Their recordings were bawdy evocations of good-time flats and urban barrelhouse nightlife, unmitigated by any of Carr's after-hours introspection. In fact, they parodied "How Long, How Long Blues," using female impersonator Frankie "Half-Pint" Jaxon to pepper the lyrics with sly asides and bedroom moans, which added a dimension to the song Carr certainly hadn't foreseen. The raucous and ragtimey records of Georgia Tom and Tampa Red were among the earliest assertive blues to emerge from the African-American experience in Chicago.

From the heyday of the racial stereotype: sheet music art for "It's Tight Like That."

"Ma" Rainey with Georgia Tom.

Both men joined the flood of southern migrants who streamed into Chicago following World War I. Georgia was their birthplace, though Tampa Red (Hudson Whittaker) was raised by his grandmother's family in the Florida city that, along with his light complexion, gave him his name. Thomas A. Dorsey's aspirations as a song-writer led him to study music at the Chicago College of Composition and Arranging, while Tampa Red was content to sing and play guitar on the Windy City's streets. They met around 1925, but would not record together for another three years; Dorsey was busy making a name for himself as a blues songwriter for the likes of Trixie Smith and as leader of "Ma" Rainey's band. Tampa Red, meanwhile, was honing a singing bottleneck guitar style that became his instrumental signature and earned him the moniker "The Guitar Wizard."

When they did team up to record for Vocalion in 1928, it was to wax the infamous "It's Tight Like That." Jivey and risqué, the song was a runaway success that epitomized a sound tagged "hokum." Big Joe Williams, who hoboed across the country, would tell *Living Blues* founding editor Jim O'Neal, "'Tight Like That' went just about to the four corners of the United States. Went through both races, white and black. You'd hear little kids mumblin' it everywhere you went."

As Carr and Blackwell did with "How Long, How Long Blues," Georgia Tom and Tampa Red frequently rerecorded "It's Tight Like That," along with other "good-time" titles ("Selling That Stuff," "Beedle Um Bum") built around more or less the same tune. It was a rare popular blues act of the late 1920s that didn't perform some "Tight Like That" variant, and even the Reverend J. M. Gates incorporated the metaphor into a Depression-theme sermon, "These Hard Times Are Tight Like That." Big Joe's assertion that the song "went through both races, white and black," is borne out by the appearance of "It's Tight Like That" in the repertoire of western swing bands a decade after it was a "race" hit.

The good times played out in 1932: "The bell had tolled on the blues," Dorsey declared dramatically many years later. Personal tragedy (the death of his wife and baby in delivery), coupled with the realization that there wouldn't be any more hokum hits, led Dorsey to abandon blues for sacred music (his role in modern gospel is discussed elsewhere in this book). Tampa Red weathered the lean years and resumed recording blues in 1934 for Bluebird and Victor, an association that continued until 1953 and yielded more than two hundred titles. Some were leering double entendres ("Let Me Play with Your Poodle") in the manner of his pre-Depression heyday, others ("Nobody's Sweetheart Now") were straight pop tunes, and still others ("Forget about Me") spare and bitter blues.

Tampa Red understood the advantages of a varied repertoire as well as that of a novelty gimmick like the "jazz horn" (kazoo) he blew on many of his records. He refused to be a relic and was among the first bluesmen to perform with electric guitar. His fluid bottleneck style fit well on the new instrument, and he used it on his influential recordings of "Black Angel Blues" (later "Sweet Little Angel"), "Love Her with a Feeling," "Crying Won't Help You," and 1940's "Anna Lou Blues," in which Tampa Red sang:

> . . . I'm going to Louisiana,
> Just to get me a Hoodoo Hand;
> And I won't stop trying
> Till I get you under my command.

Muddy Waters probably heard that, and reworked it a decade later in his "Louisiana Blues." Another Mississippian, Robert Lee McCoy (better known as Robert Nighthawk), drank deep drafts of Tampa Red, and the renamed "Anna Lee" became his signature song. Nighthawk's mournful vocals and distinctive weepy slide were well-suited to Tampa Red's "Crying Won't Help You" and "Sweet Little Angel," the latter a song that came to be associated with B. B. King.

Tampa Red wasn't content merely to influence the younger men who transformed urban blues after World War II. Toward the end of his tenure with Bluebird, his star still in the ascendant, he made them his accompanists, among them pianist Johnnie Jones and harmonica player Big Walter Horton. The influx of blues artists to Chicago in the 1930s and 1940s prompted Tampa Red to host a sort of blues hostel

Tampa Red, dressed, as always, with conservative dignity.

in his house at Thirty-fifth and State. The arrangement was made in part by Bluebird's A & R man Lester Melrose, who needed a place to house visiting performers. "Melrose'd pay him for the lodging," pianist Blind John Davis told Jim O'Neal, "and Mrs. Tampa would cook for 'em." Willie Dixon offered fond memories of the place in his autobiography, *I Am the Blues: The Willie Dixon Story*: "Tampa Red's house was a madhouse with old-time musicians. Lester Melrose would be drinking all the time and Tampa Red's wife would be cooking chicken and we'd be having a ball." A who's who of the era's bluesmen were often either bunking or rehearsing at the house: Big Bill Broonzy, Memphis Slim, John Lee "Sonny Boy" Williamson, Doctor Clayton, and Big Maceo Merriweather were among the guests.

Twenty-one years after "It's Tight Like That," Tampa Red managed to crack the then-new rhythm and blues charts with the moody "When Things Go Wrong

Big Bill Broonzy posed for a studio portrait elegantly commensurate with his wonderful Gibson cutaway scroll guitar.

with You (It Hurts Me Too)." The song would later become identified with Elmore James, whose intense vocals and amped-to-distortion slide guitar better suited the blues world of the 1950s. The 1954 death of his wife, Frances, devastated Tampa Red, and his 1960 "rediscovery" recordings were dim reflections of his past glory. Accounts of the years prior to his death in 1981 are sad portraits of a sweet but vague old man still loved by such long-time associates as Blind John Davis, who remembered Tampa's reign in the 1930s. In his prime, Tampa Red was a kingpin of prewar Chicago blues, a position he shared with his close friend, Big Bill Broonzy.

Like Lonnie Johnson, Mississippi-born, Arkansas-raised William Lee Conley Broonzy played fiddle before picking up guitar. "I was a fiddler back in them days," Broonzy told Studs Terkel in a 1950s radio broadcast. "Used to play schottisches and glides and waltzes . . ." His music making and farm labor in Arkansas were interrupted by the draft in 1918. Broonzy served two years in the military, which made Arkansas look unappealing after the cities of Europe. He was probably in his mid-twenties when he arrived in Chicago, where he enhanced his guitar skills by studying Papa Charlie Jackson, who played an archaic ragtime/minstrel style on the six-string banjo-guitar. Broonzy updated it effectively in his 1930 recordings with the Famous Hokum Boys, a group that included the ubiquitous Georgia Tom. "Some wanna know just what we got," Tom shouted. "We got good hokum and we serve it hot!" The Hokum Boys' anthemic "Eagle Riding Papa" was revamped by western swing's Light Crust Doughboys as a radio theme in the early 1930s. When that band splintered, vocalist Milton Brown waxed "Easy Riding Papa" with his Musical Brownies, and Bob Wills adapted it as the Texas Playboys' theme.

 With fellow Hokum Boy Frank Brasswell, Broonzy cut some wonderful ragtimey guitar duets ("Saturday Night Rub," "Guitar Rag," "Pig Meat Strut"), while "hokum girl" Jane Lucas encouraged dancers: "Ah, shake 'em, folks!" she shouted in "Hip Shakin' Strut," a party favorite. "Shake 'em fast!" Broonzy added. "Can't shake your shimmy, shake your yas-yas-yas!" If there was a Depression on, you'd never know it from the records Broonzy and the Hokum Boys made in 1930. "Can you sing the blues?" Steele Smith asks Broonzy in "Brownskin Shuffle." Broonzy answers firmly, "Boy, these blues ain't supposed to be sung, they're supposed to be *barrelhoused!*"

 If the ferocious pace ever lessened, it was only for Lucas to sing something like the leering "Pussy Cat Blues":

> *You can play with my pussy, but please don't dog it around;*
> *You can play with my pussy, but please don't dog it around;*
> *If you gonna mistreat her, no pussy will be found.*

But the urban party blues was only a part of Broonzy's repertoire. Robert Johnson would become a country bluesman with urban aspirations, but Broonzy was a truly urban bluesman with one foot forever planted in the country. You hear it in his late 1920s Paramount recordings ("Down in the Basement Blues"), but it remained an element of his repertoire during the hokum years ("My girl caught the train and left me a mule to ride," he lamented in 1930's "Grandma's Farm"), and he was still intermittently "country" even as he was waxing barrelhouse swing in the late 1930s with the Memphis Five, a group that included piano, trumpet, and alto sax. A decade later, with a new Chicago blues sound impatiently waiting in the wings, Broonzy could still be country. Despite the horns and what is essentially an R & B rhythm section,

Rosetta Howard and Big Bill
Broonzy in performance.

Rosetta Howard's 1947 recording of Broonzy's "Plow Hand Blues" (with Broonzy on guitar) is a pungent evocation of the sharecropper's plight. "Plow hand has been their name," Howard sang, "seems like a thousand years or more," and "Every night I'm hollerin' 'Woh, gee! Get up!' [mule-driver's commands] in my sleep."

Like hillbilly stars who, despite the trappings of mainstream success, insist on singing about their childhood mountain shacks and humble beginnings, Broonzy, the kingpin of Chicago blues, reminded his audience of the southern poverty whence they all came. Perhaps Lester Flatt sang across racial boundaries when he advised, "Don't Get above Your Raisin'."

Broonzy never forgot "C. C. Rider" and other blues he learned down home before becoming a black doughboy. In Chicago, he would never stop listening to the down-home blues brought north by the likes of Bukka White, whose 1937 hit "Shake 'Em on Down" Broonzy would cover ("New Shake 'Em on Down") a year later with his trademark holler accompanied by the smooth electric guitar of 16-year-old jazzman George Barnes. But his best songs were scarcely country; they were as cleverly crafted as anything to come from Tin Pan Alley:

> I dreamed I had a million dollars,
> Had a mermaid for a wife;
> I dreamed I winned the Brooklyn Bridge,
> On my knees shootin' dice.
> But that was just a dream,
> Just a dream I had on my mind.
> Now when I woke up, baby, not a penny could I find.
>
> I dreamed I was in the White House,
> Settin' in the President's chair;
> I dreamed he shaken my hand, says,
> "Bill, I'm glad you're here."
> But that was just a dream,
> Just a dream I had on my mind.
> Now then, when I woke up, baby,
> Not a chair could I find.
>   —"Just a Dream," 1939

King of the washboard players:
Washboard Sam.

Not only for their lyrics were Broonzy's works striking. Broonzy was recording with drums by early 1937 and, like his friend Tampa Red, he was an early exponent of the electric guitar. Imagine a wailing harmonica in place of the trumpet on some of Broonzy's Memphis Five recordings and you'll hear, well in advance of Muddy Waters and his contemporaries, a blueprint for postwar Chicago blues. Unlike Tampa Red, who rarely accompanied other artists, Broonzy often played as sideman on sessions by Washboard Sam (Robert Brown), Jazz Gillum, John Lee "Sonny Boy" Williamson, and Lil Green, whose delicious pop blues, "Romance in the Dark" (1940), was illuminated by Broonzy's guitar. Despite the ascendancy of a new generation of Chicago bluesmen, Broonzy waxed a session for Chess in 1953, sounding remarkably contemporary and yet as countrified as ever. But by then the blues audience had found new heroes, and Broonzy himself was courting a new group of listeners.

Critics have disdained Broonzy's late performances and recordings for a white "folk" audience, deeming them an attempt of a once-great bluesman to masquerade as a secondhand Josh White. Certainly Broonzy's recordings of the 1950s are neither the punchy jive of his Memphis Five sides nor the ragtimey hokum he served in the early Depression days. At their best, they were his country side, unmitigated by much else. He seems to have highlighted the aspect of his repertoire and style he knew would appeal to the folk crowd, and he pruned everything else back. This was really no more dishonest than his previous adaptations to changed circumstances and sounds. Songs he learned from Papa Charlie Jackson would have seemed archaic in a late-1930s Chicago bar, and neither ragtime nor hard urban blues would have gone down well with earnest collegiates who fancied Broonzy to be an archetypal Delta sharecropper. Broonzy understood this intuitively, and found what worked every time.

It's hard *not* to admire the marketing savvy of a man who knew the value of scarcity sufficiently to promote himself in Europe as the last living bluesman in America! Europe fell hard for Broonzy. His tours there were sensations, comparable to the visits of such jazz aristocracy as Louis Armstrong and Duke Ellington, but with the added mystique that he was the self-proclaimed last of his line. In the Netherlands, Yannick Bruynoghe collaborated with Broonzy on the autobiography, *Big Bill Blues* (1955), and, in 1956, produced a documentary film of the same name. Broonzy even married and fathered a son there. In Britain, his music was transformed by young guitarists who looked to Broonzy as the heroic ancestor of all they heard in American rock 'n' roll. Ask any English guitarist who came of age in the early 1960s— the folk revival's Martin Carthy and the Rolling Stones' Keith Richards among them—and most will say their first important influence was Big Bill Broonzy.

He was not forgotten back home, either. When Broonzy died in 1958, Memphis Minnie participated in a memorial concert—and she was a tough woman, who had even beaten Broonzy in a 1930s blues singing contest. A year after Broonzy's death, Muddy Waters recorded a tribute album, *Muddy Waters Sings Big Bill Broonzy* (Chess LP 1444). It was in part a bid for the white folk audience Broonzy intuitively understood and that initially found Muddy too strident (the English gently suggested he unplug on his first tour there, and did he know any of Big Bill's songs?). But it was also a genuine tribute, as Broonzy had championed Waters when he was the new kid in Chicago and Broonzy was still king.

There's a 1940s photo of them in a club, Broonzy beaming, arms spread wide in a gesture of inclusion beside Muddy, seemingly diminutive and demure, the crown prince in waiting. Different as their styles were, Broonzy recognized Waters's power and promise, and nurtured both. It was an example Waters would never forget, as he himself played mentor to scores of young men freshly arrived from the South to make music in Chicago. Such disparate artists as Buddy Guy, Robert Cray, and Johnny Winter recall Waters "like a father," and a few he affectionately called "my sons." In the midst of Chicago's hard ghetto and the sharp competition of its music scene, promising young musicians found caring mentors. This spirit of inclusion, as much as his music, was Big Bill Broonzy's legacy to Chicago's blues.

Outside Chicago and beyond whatever circumstance brought the shellac seductions of the Famous Hokum Boys to the attention of young men like Bob Wills, Broonzy's big break came by means of the death of Robert Johnson. In 1938, John Hammond was planning a massive concert for Carnegie Hall, From Spirituals to Swing, which would celebrate the varieties of African-American music and illustrate its influence on the pop music of the day, swing. Hammond hoped to bring Robert Johnson to New York as an exemplar of country blues, but Johnson had already been murdered.

Big Joe Turner, Blues Shouter Deluxe and the Pride of Kansas City—two poses, separated by some years.

With strict orders to "just sing the blues," Broonzy was slotted into Johnson's place for the legendary December 1938 concert. Hammond was satisfied with the substitution, according to his autobiography, *John Hammond on Record* (Summit Books). "Bill, who farmed in Arkansas with a pair of mules, shuffled out and sang about a dream he'd had in which he sat in President Roosevelt's chair in the White House," Hammond wrote. "The audience screamed. It had never heard anything like this." Nor had it heard anything like another extraordinary blues singer who also appeared that night, Big Joe Turner.

Born in 1911, Joseph Vernon Turner was acting as "lead boy" to blind street singers in Kansas City at about the time Broonzy and Tampa Red were settling in Chicago. Turner sang on the streets in a jugband, and at home listened intently to the 78s of Bessie Smith, Leroy Carr, and Lonnie Johnson. A special favorite of the man who would one day (in 1953) record "Oke-She-Moke-She-Pop" with Elmore James on guitar was Ethel Waters's 1929 recording, "Shoo Shoo Boogie Boo." The sound as much as the sense of a lyric was what mattered to Turner, who never learned to read or write, but who learned the blues vocabulary so thoroughly that he later became famous for tirelessly ad-libbing verses for hours on end.

Just as Robert Johnson urbanized his repertoire by recorded osmosis, city-born Turner countrified his by the same process. When he sang "Blues Jumped the Rabbit" in 1950, he echoed Blind Lemon Jefferson, and it's easy to sense an affinity in Turner's style with the man who was really the first blues shouter on record, Texas Alexander, whose songs were little more than field hollers in Saturday night suits. Turner was assertively urban and, in his New York Café Society days, even urbane, but he loved earthy metaphors: "I'm like a Mississippi bullfrog, settin' on a hollow stump," he

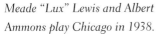

shouted in "Flip, Flop and Fly," a hit for him in 1955. "I like to keep 'em smiling," Turner said, and his down-home references were a strong part of his poetic humor.

By the time he was sixteen, Turner was sneaking into Kansas City's Backbiters' Club to hear pianist Pete Johnson play. Johnson was initially wary of this kid eager to sing the blues with him ("He was a rough dude," Turner affectionately recalled decades later), but Turner's wall-flattening bellow won him over. They became a team, fixtures of the nightlife in a city that Count Basie, Lester Young, and countless jazz greats called home. Turner combined blues singing with tending bar in a wide-open atmosphere nurtured by the corrupt benevolence of Boss Pendergast. "At the peak of the Pendergast era," Arnold Shaw wrote in *Honkers and Shouters*, "nearly 500 palaces of pleasure served a combination of music, liquor, girls, and marijuana."

But the time Tom Pendergast was convicted of tax evasion and his political machine collapsed in 1938, Turner and Johnson were on their way to Carnegie Hall. Somehow John Hammond had heard them from New York City, and little wonder. "When I started out," Turner recalled years later, "they didn't have no mikes, so I had to learn to sing without 'em. Fill up a room without a mike." Anyone who ever saw Turner shouting a microphone into distorted abeyance sensed he viewed them as mere props for lesser mortals.

Following the Carnegie Hall triumph that gave the world "Roll 'Em Pete," Turner and Johnson settled in for an extended stay at the newly opened Café Society Downtown, where Turner belted to the accompaniment of the Boogie Woogie Trio—pianists Albert Ammons, Meade "Lux" Lewis, and Pete Johnson. The twenty-eight-year-old singer "was tall and slender and moved around a lot," recalled Café Society owner Barney Josephson, "and he drove the women mad." Turner's charisma, propelled by the thirty fleet fingers of his accompanists, quickly became a sensation that made "boogie" the byword of the day.

Boogie piano was nothing new. It had been popular since the early 1920s in Chicago, where George and Hersal Thomas composed the influential "The Fives" in 1921. Five years later, Charles "Cow Cow" Davenport had a hit on both piano rolls

Elvis Presley, with Scotty Moore on guitar, made this appearance when he left Sun Records to join RCA. The Victor mascot, Nipper, sits to Presley's right.

and 78s with "Cow Cow Blues," and Clarence "Pinetop" Smith's "Pinetop's Boogie-Woogie" became the most influential and imitated of the 1920s boogie piano records (Tommy Dorsey's Orchestra was performing it on radio in 1938). But it was the uptown popularity of Turner and the Boogie Woogie Trio that ignited the boogie craze of the late 1930s, sending bobbysoxed teens jitterbugging to highly arranged jive: Ella Mae Morse's revision of Davenport's "Cow Cow Boogie," Will Bradley's "I Boogied When I Should Have Woogied," and Louis Jordan's "Choo Choo Ch'boogie."

By the mid-1940s, hillbillies had picked up the beat, and records like the Delmore Brothers' "Hillbilly Boogie" were the direct antecedent of rockabilly. The sound was still fresh to white Americans in 1943 when Pete Johnson tried to explain it to a *Milwaukee Journal* reporter: "Boogie is really a blues fugue," said Johnson. "You play something with the left hand and then you play the same thing with the right, and then you play them against each other, like counterpoint."

Johnson was only one of several great pianists who played counterpoint to Turner in the late 1930s and early 1940s. Sam Price, Freddie Slack, Willie "The Lion" Smith, and Art Tatum all recorded with Turner, who singled out Tatum as "a genius." (Jazz collectors still speak in rapt tones of their 1941 masterpiece, "Wee Baby Blues.") By the mid-1940s, Turner was waxing R & B for the National label, and both the sound and lyrics were grittier than his boogie-era jazz-tinged blues. He bragged in "I Got My Discharge Papers" (1946) of carving "U.S.A." on the enemy's "yas-yas-yas," and in "Playboy Blues" bellowed: "Some people call me a pimp and a gambler, but I ain't neither one; I'm just a hip little playboy, and love to have my fun."

Turner was widely influential during this time, and to musicologist Arnold Shaw he represented "the new black man" celebrating "self-respect and a sense of his worth." Certainly, he was a role model to such blues shouters as Roy Brown and

Wynonie Harris, responsible as writer and performer of "Good Rockin' Tonight." That song was one Turner could easily have created, and when Elvis recorded it in 1954, it became apparent that "The Hillbilly Cat" was essentially a blues shouter in whiteface.

"We kicked off that rock 'n' roll mess," Turner said some thirty years after punting "Shake, Rattle and Roll" through the goalposts of glory. "They said it wasn't going to last," he recalled, referring to the new music's enemies. "They talked about it like I had a tail." (It was, after all the "Devil's music.") "But it kicked over. Got the whole world at it."

Turner's Atlantic label recording of "Shake, Rattle and Roll" roared up the R & B charts in April 1954 and was a hit for nearly seven months. A western swing singer with a hankerin' for R & B named Bill Haley heard it, and in June he and his Comets cut a less lascivious "Shake, Rattle and Roll." Haley's version soared up the pop charts as Turner's faded from the R & B charts, but if Turner felt slighted, he bore no grudges. "It was alright with me," he said of Haley's cover. "He done a pretty good job at it."

And Turner would hear worse: Pat Boone's pallid cover of "Chains of Love" (Turner's first hit for Atlantic) and Johnny Ray's version of "Flip, Flop and Fly" (Turner's 1955 follow-up to "Shake"). Despite white covers of his songs, Turner himself became an unlikely rock 'n' roll star for a brief while, transforming that ancient blues "Corrine, Corrina" into a pop hit and appearing in the 1956 teen flick, *Shake, Rattle and Rock.* Turner was beefy, black, and forty-six when he hollered about a "teenage city, rock 'n' roll state" in the loopy "Teenage Letter." Neither Turner nor

T-Bone Walker plays a "Charlie Christian" model electric guitar manufactured by the Gibson Company. Freddie Slack, a great boogie-woogie pianist, looks on in admiration.

Atlantic was completely committed to such silliness, as evident in the 1956 album, *Joe Turner Sings Kansas City Jazz: The Boss of the Blues* (Atlantic 1234), which reunited Turner with his old friend, Pete Johnson. They reprised one of their earliest recordings, "Piney Brown Blues," along with Leroy Carr's "How Long Blues" and the boogie that shook Carnegie Hall in 1938, "Roll 'Em Pete." Turner and Johnson returned to Carnegie Hall for a final appearance together at the 1967 From Spirituals to Swing concert. The years had been kinder to Turner than to Johnson, who had "suffered a series of paralytic strokes and had not played piano for many years," according to *Downbeat* reviewer Dan Morgenstern. "His old buddy, Turner, took him by the hand, and for a moment the two middle-aged men looked touchingly like little boys." Johnson died later that year.

Big Joe Turner continued to shout the blues for the better part of eighteen more years, outliving not only most of the blues shouters he directly inspired, but Elvis as well. There were deep doldrums during this period, along with well-intentioned, if not entirely successful, attempts to record him as a jazz singer for the Pablo label. Turner could certainly sing jazzy blues, as evidenced by his recordings with Art Tatum. (He told this writer he composed Billie Holiday's "Fine and Mellow" when they were friends during their Café Society days, and it certainly sounds like Turner of that vintage.) But his ebullient nature steered him less toward the subtleties of jazz and more toward the elemental energies of boogie-woogie, rhythm and blues, rock 'n' roll—the labels changed with the decades, but Big Joe in essence did not. "I like to keep 'em smiling," he said. "Keep everybody jumping." So it was natural that, in the early 1980s, Turner was shouting to the children of the kids who made him an unlikely teen idol during rock's first flush in the 1950s. He often sang in Los Angeles–area "nu wave niteries," accompanied by such retro-hip bands as the Blasters. His great bulk deliberated to and from the stage on crutches; Turner evidently had enjoyed life a bit too much for his own good. But the infirm flesh became irrelevant when his mountain-moving spirit was manifest through a life-affirming shout: "My baby's a jockey, she's teaching me how to ride." When Turner's great heart finally gave out in 1985, songwriter Doc Pomus sent his old friend this message: "The angels are all going to have to sing a little louder to keep up with you.

"I must be a travelin' man," Turner mused late in life. "I got around. I never let any grass grow under my feet." After more than two vibrant years with the Boogie Woogie Trio at Café Society ("That was really a bang-up time," he recalled), Turner joined Meade "Lux" Lewis for a West Coast tour. They were sending Christmas cards from Hollywood's Swanee Inn in December 1941; three months earlier, pianist Freddie Slack helped Turner record "Blues on Central Avenue," the first recording to celebrate what was becoming one of the most dynamic black music scenes in America: "I'm in the land of sunshine," Turner sang, "standin' on Central Avenue." More than just the climate agreed with him: "Never had so much sport anywhere in my life," he boasted.

Industry was drawing blacks to the West Coast from the same Depression-ravaged states—Texas, Oklahoma, a few more southerly states and others in the Midwest—that gave California its Okies. There were approximately seventy-five thousand black Angelenos in 1940, the year Raymond Chandler made note of shifting demographics in his *Farewell, My Lovely:* "It was one of those mixed blocks over in Central Avenue," he wrote, "the blocks that are not yet all negro." The influx of southwestern migrants accelerated with World War II and ample employment in defense plants, factories, and oil fields. The housing crunch was eased by the wartime internment of the Japanese. A Los Angeles neighborhood near Central Avenue that had been dubbed "Little Tokyo" soon became "Little Harlem." By 1950, there were more than two hundred thousand blacks living in Los Angeles.

Clubs mushroomed along Central during the 1940s for the entertainment of the locals, servicemen, and the occasional show biz "swells" gone slumming. Unlike southern or midwestern cities with long-established black populations, Los Angeles was untested territory, and the musicians who ventured there seemed inspired by the open terrain to try new ideas. Central Avenue was nearer to the fabled Hollywood and Pacific beaches than it was to sharecropper farms or cold northern tenements, so blues musicians freely broadened their palettes, painting at times in dreamy hues and often with a jazzy sophistication. Bebop no less than blues could be heard on Central in the 1940s, and the close proximity produced some exciting hybrids.

T-Bone Walker was perhaps the most influential exponent of the new sound. "He'd get a blues guy on piano sometimes," recalled Marili Morden, one of the founders of the Jazz Man Record Shop, "but always jazzmen for the band." Walker's guitar playing was bluesy in a jazzlike way: crisply articulated notes interspersed with sexy slurs in the manner of a jazz trumpeter. His storming chordal vamps, often echoed by the horn section, were a six-string imitation of blaring brass and reeds. He created an approach to guitar that seemed intended to compensate for an absence of horns, despite there being plenty on his records. It was an extremely influential attack well-suited to small combos without Walker's resources. His imitators were legion, though few ever equalled Walker's impeccable phrasing, subtle syncopation, and the thoughtful depth of his lean guitar monologues.

Aaron Thibeaux Walker was born in 1910 in Dallas, where he was destined to lead Lemon Jefferson and follow Huddie Ledbetter. He danced and passed the hat at the performances of his stepfather's string band; when he was twelve, his mother bought him a banjo. A 1929 amateur contest in Dallas won him a week's work with Cab Calloway's band. He was granted a solo spot doing the splits while he played banjo. That same year Columbia recorded two sides by "Oak Cliff T-Bone," but the nineteen-year-old had yet to find his mature style. The guitar playing on "Trinity River Blues" and "Wichita Falls" offered little to distinguish it from sundry Texas country guitarists, and the vocals tell us only that T-Bone was listening to Leroy Carr. Columbia wouldn't call Oak Cliff T-Bone again.

Sometime in the 1930s, Walker was tutored by Oklahoma City's Chuck Richardson, whose other star student, Charlie Christian, developed an equally impressive hornlike approach to electric guitar. Whether Walker, Christian, or their teacher were playing electric guitars at the time is not clear. Rickenbacker introduced its Electro Spanish guitar in 1932, but only a handful were ever sold. By the time Gibson's electric ES150 (popularly known to collectors as "the Charlie Christian model") appeared in 1936, Walker was en route to L.A.

He was hired to drive a car and pull another from Texas, and arrived well in advance of the wartime boom ("You had mud streets in Watts back then," he recalled years later). Walker was hired as a dancer by saxophonist/bandleader Big Jim Wynn, but soon was singing and playing guitar as well. He honed an impressive act, which had him doing splits and picking guitar behind his head—sure crowd pleasers so close to Hollywood.

Veteran L.A. bandleader Les Hite caught Walker's act and hired him in 1939. Hite's band had provided soundtracks for several films and boasted many stellar

T-Bone Walker strikes a characteristic pose, holding his guitar flat.

alumni prior to Walker, including Lionel Hampton, who was a drummer for Hite in the 1920s. Walker quickly became an important draw for Hite, as indicated by a February 1, 1940, *Downbeat* report of Hite's first New York tour: "His new star is T-Bone Walker with choruses on 'I Wonder Why She Don't Write to Me.'" Later that year, Les Hite and His Orchestra recorded "T-Bone Blues" for Varsity. "I love my baby," Walker sang in an assured and relaxed voice quite unlike Oak Cliff T-Bone's, "she's so mean to me." The hornlike vocal phrasing, underscored in the performance by a trumpet echoing each line, has less of Leroy Carr and more of Billie Holiday in its sinuous architecture. There's impressive guitar here, too, but not T-Bone's. Frank Pasley (later one of Joe Liggins's Honeydrippers) plays a bluesy amplified Hawaiian steel at the outset. Its dreamy tone anticipates the electric bottleneck guitar recordings of Robert Nighthawk and Earl Hooker in the 1950s. Simultaneously, it suggests the southwestern roots of both the musicians and their audience, who doubtless had heard bluesy steel guitar in the popular western swing bands of the day, notably Bob Dunn's recordings with Milton Brown's Musical Brownies and Leon McAuliffe's with Bob Wills's Texas Playboys.

Walker's guitar would wait two more years to be recorded, but it appears in mature glory on 1942's "I Got a Break Baby" with Freddie Slack on ivories, playing close to the vest, and Walker's guitar up-front. The guitar is, in fact, so much the star of the recording that it gracefully bobs and weaves a full minute before Walker sings, "It was way last winter, baby, and the ground was covered with snow . . ." This performance set the pattern for many of Walker's best blues, and if his spurned lover's lament was old as the blues itself, his tasteful setting and burbling electric guitar were then freshly minted.

As much as slow blues, Walker was expert at "jump" blues, and was one of the idiom's first popular exponents. Jump blues was an extension of the boogie craze. Walker's earliest jump recordings were cut in 1945 for Chicago's short-lived Rhumboogie label, though the lyrics of "T-Bone Boogie" jibe with what the *Downbeat* writer heard Walker sing with Les Hite in 1940 ("I Wonder Why She Don't Write to Me"), suggesting he had been jumping for some time. The tempos and bands varied throughout the 1940s, when Walker recorded for Capitol, Mercury, Black & White, and its subsidiary, Comet. The song destined to become such an overworked standard of the blues world, "Call It Stormy Monday," first appeared on Black and White in 1947. Overfamiliar today, the song was bitterly powerful when new, capturing the weary disillusionment many West Coast blacks felt in the years after World War II.

By the time Walker began his four-year stint with the Imperial label in 1950, he was without question the most popular and influential blues guitarist of the day. Many of his disciples shared his southwestern roots and had also moved to California, among them Lowell Fulson, who once accompanied Texas Alexander and was the first to record "Everyday I Have the Blues" (1949); Pee Wee Crayton, another fine guitarist, who celebrated the L.A. scene in "Central Avenue Blues" (1948); and Pete Lewis, whose string bending was the highlight of many Johnny Otis Orchestra records (for example, "Boogie Guitar," 1949). Crowded by Walker would-bes and more aggressive R & B acts, Imperial tried Walker in new settings: with Dave Bartholomew's New Orleans R & B band in 1953; with echo on his vocals ("Pony Tail"); with a mambo beat ("Hard Way"); with drums heavily up-front in an attempt to beat Joe Turner at the white pop market just opening to R & B acts ("Yes, I got a teenaged baby, she likes to wear her sloppy Joes," Walker sang in 1954). None of this met with great commercial success, so Walker simply continued to sing the blues to a dwindling following.

Meanwhile, Chuck Berry was becoming a teen idol on the strengths of riffs recycled from Walker's repertoire, a liberal helping of his grandstanding, and some of the poetic humor of the old man. "Sweet Little Sixteen" recast Walker's "Bobby Sox Blues" (1946): "Bobby sox baby, I've got to let you go; you've got a head full of nothin' but stage, screen, and radio." Walker remained intermittently active in music until his death in 1975. The immense turnout for his funeral indicated how many still remembered his heyday in the Los Angeles of the 1940s.

Walker's success was phenomenal; but those who had neither his talent nor his luck sometimes turned bitter when they found L.A.'s promise illusory. In 1947, Crown Prince Waterford recorded "L.A. Blues," which featured Pete Johnson on piano and lyrics that seemed to mock Big Joe Turner's "singing postcard" from six years earlier:

> *Some call it the land of sunshine,*
> *Some call it old Central Avenue;*
> *Some call it the land of sunshine,*
> *Some call it old Central Avenue;*
> *I call it a big ol' country town,*
> *Where the folks don't care what they do.*

Walker at the microphone in an appearance with the Les Hite Orchestra at the time of his hit, "T-Bone Blues."

A slick Charles Brown at the piano.

If a man can make it in Los Angeles,
He can make it anywhere;
If a man can make it in Los Angeles,
He can make it anywhere;
But you've got to have a used Cadillac car,
Yes, boys, and you can't stay square.

Waterford lampooned the trendy materialism that has always been part of the California Dream, one which had seemed attainable to many blacks during the euphoria of wartime employment. A darker mood descended not long after V-J Day (August 15, 1945), evidenced by the fall 1945 success of Johnny Moore's Three Blazers' Aladdin recording of the moody "Drifting Blues":

Well I'm driftin' and driftin',
Like a ship out on the sea.
Well I'm driftin' and driftin',
Like a ship out on the sea.
Well, I ain't got nobody
In this world to care for me.

A fortune-teller had predicted the record's success to Charles Brown, who wrote the song while still in high school in Galveston, Texas. Brown's intimate, silky vocals

with the Three Blazers were indebted to Nat King Cole and would influence such
disparate artists as Amos Milburn and Ray Charles. After Brown split from guitarist
Johnny Moore's group in 1948, he continued to have some success: 1951's compelling "Black Night" echoed the *noir* patina of Leroy Carr's best blues. But his polished and introspective blues ballad style, perfectly tailored to L.A.'s club scene of
the 1940s, became anachronistic in the brasher climate of the 1950s, and Brown
slipped into undeserved obscurity. He has enjoyed a renewed career in recent years,
sounding as good as ever, reaping the rewards of tours with pop star Bonnie Raitt,
and winning a Grammy nomination for the 1990 album *All My Life* (Bullseye Blues
CD BB 9501). Brown's career has been brightened by some remarkable songs
(decades of fireside smooching have been inspired by 1947's "Merry Christmas
Baby"), but there could be only one "Drifting Blues." Johnny Otis called it "the black
national anthem of the late forties."

This is the point in our tale when most chronicles of "urban blues" only just begin.
Muddy Waters waxed his first important sides in 1947, and a year later Memphis
radio station WDIA adopted a black music format that became a catalyst for much
of the significant blues recording in postwar Memphis. In their enthusiasm for this
music, some chroniclers have painted everything that preceded it in rather dim hues
and left the impression that the giants who emerged in the Chicago and Memphis of
the 1950s did so from a virtual void. In fact, the young men who arrived in Chicago
in the 1940s encountered a vibrant blues scene, which had been going since the
1920s. They were more eager to join the fray than rout the veterans, who often
(especially Tampa Red and Broonzy) provided much-needed help and encouragement. That there would be a natural changing of the guard was inevitable, just as it
was certain that the generation most recently come from the South would sound
different from men who had settled in Chicago after World War I. The process of
change was more one of evolution than revolution.

The charisma of artists like Muddy Waters and the mystique of Sun and Chess
Records have likewise obscured the importance of all modern urban blues that preceded them. If our broad notion of modern urban blues is tied to a band with a
strong rhythm section punctuated by stinging electric guitar, let's not forget the
recordings T-Bone Walker was making in Hollywood not quite eight months after
the bombing of Pearl Harbor. So much for neat prewar/postwar demarcations. A
highly developed modern urban blues was being played in California well in advance
of other regions, and it was also West Coast entrepreneurs who pioneered the trend
toward small independent labels that played such a crucial role in the development
and dissemination of postwar blues. (Oakland's Gilt-Edge Recording Company was
the first in 1945, with Cecil Gant's "I Wonder.") Credit for the development of
modern urban blues must be shared in several quarters, but this in no way diminishes
the power and impact of the sweet thunder that was rolling in the late 1940s from
Chicago and Memphis.

The year 1943 was when Muddy Waters took a train from the Delta to
Chicago; it was also the year Charles Brown arrived in L.A. from Texas. Both men
quickly found work, though for Waters it was labor in a paper factory rather than performing in a nightclub. Brown had a national hit within two years, while Waters's
star was slower to ascend: 1948's "I Can't Be Satisfied" was his first hit.

It would be hard to find two more dissimilar temperaments or stylists, yet there
is something of the urban *angst* epitomized by "Drifting Blues" in Waters's "I Can't

Be Satisfied," except that it is framed in a very different way. Boozy ennui is replaced by a nervous agitation; Ernest "Big" Crawford's bass provides a country shuffle rhythm on which Waters weaves a web of slippery exclamations from his slide guitar. Both men are in motion ("Goin' back down south," sings Waters, "child, don't you want to go?"), but Brown's is a somnambulist's stroll while Waters seems to be riding a freight with poor shocks (and enjoying it). Brown's song is an intimate after-hours confession, while Waters's dissatisfaction is an extroverted street-corner shout. Brown turns his dissatisfaction inward, while Waters threatens violence ("Well, I feel like snappin' pistol in your face"). Both men sing from somewhere in the night, Leroy Carr's insomniac "wee wee hours" seeming not far in the background for Brown, while Waters recalls "hainted" Delta nights ("My doorknob keeps on turnin'," Robert Johnson sang in "Malted Milk Blues," "must be spooks around my bed . . ."):

> Well, now, all in my sleep,
> Hear my doorbell ring;
> Lookin' for my baby,
> I didn't see not a doggone thing.
> Lord, I was troubled,
> I was all worried in mind.
> Well, honey, I couldn't never *be satisfied!*
> And I just couldn't keep from crying.

With different musical vocabularies understood by two very different urban populations (one uprooted from the Southwest, the other from the Delta), Brown and Waters variously expressed the rootlessness and anxiety many urban blacks felt after World War II. It's worth noting that both men wrote their songs *before* their migration. Waters recorded "I Can't Be Satisfied" as "I Be's Troubled" in Mississippi for the Library of Congress in 1941. Beyond their common theme, "Drifting Blues" may have set up the success of "I Can't Be Satisfied" in another way. The urbanity of Brown and similarly smooth West Coast stylists provoked a reaction among blacks who knew more of rough juke joints than genteel bistros, and wanted music to match. As David Evans notes elsewhere in this book, such down-home bluesmen as Lightnin' Hopkins, John Lee Hooker, and Frankie Lee Sims were suddenly popular at the end of the 1940s—precisely when the elegant after-hours blues peaked. Unintentionally, Charles Brown may have opened the door for Muddy Waters.

McKinley Morganfield was born in Rolling Fork, Mississippi in 1915. Robert Johnson was only four years older, and while the two never met, they shared a common mentor in Eddie "Son" House. Both Johnson and Muddy Waters (Morganfield's boyhood nickname) recorded variants of House's "Walking Blues"; Aristocrat titled Waters's 1948 version "I Feel Like Going Home." From House, Waters gleaned a bottleneck guitar technique and a dramatic "churchy" singing style. "He'd always call Son 'the ol' man,'" said guitarist Johnny Winter, who worked extensively with Waters late in his career. "Muddy had a lot of respect for Son House. You could tell that he had learned a lot from him and looked up to him."

The lessons were deeply ingrained by the time Alan Lomax caught up with Waters on the Stovall's plantation near Clarksdale, Mississippi, in the summer of 1941. One of the recordings Lomax took back to the folk song archives of the Library of Congress from this field trip he entitled "Country Blues," but it was essentially

House's "Walking Blues." House, in fact, had recommended Waters to Lomax, who recalled decades later that the twenty-six-year-old blues singer had neither a guitar nor shoes.

But what he lacked in possessions he made up for in ambition: "I wanted to be known," Waters told James Rooney. "I wanted to be an outstanding man." He had already earned a local reputation for the blues he sang and the whisky he made, but Waters wanted more than Clarksdale could offer him. By the late 1940s, he was pursuing his goals aggressively in Chicago. "Little Walter, Jimmy Rogers and myself," Waters told *Downbeat*, "we would go around looking for bands that were playing. We called ourselves The Headhunters, 'cause we'd go in and if we got a chance we were gonna burn 'em."

Waters's fire was searing Chicago's clubs before it ignited on record. His 1946 sessions for 20th Century and Columbia went nowhere, and he first appeared on the Chess brothers' Aristocrat label in 1947 as a sideman to Sunnyland Slim. Albert Luandrew was the name Slim was given in Vance, Mississippi, in 1907. He made a reputation playing piano in Memphis barrelhouses with the likes of Doctor Clayton and Sonny Boy Williamson (Rice Miller) before arriving in Chicago about the same

Muddy Waters, one of the architects of Chicago's electric blues, turned a vast audience onto the blues in the postwar era.

Muddy Waters appeared in a pompadour at the popular Los Angeles rock venue, the Kaleidoscope, in 1968.

time as Waters. The song Slim sang with Waters as sideman, "Johnson Machine Gun," was a harbinger of the flair for bravado violence that enlivened the lyrics of many postwar Chicago blues:

> *I'm gonna buy me a Johnson 'chine gun,*
> *And a carload of explosion balls;*
> *Yes, I'm gonna be a walkin' cyclone,*
> *From Saginaw to the Niagra Falls.*

Seven years later, Waters would shout Willie Dixon's lyric about "an axhandle pistol on a graveyard frame" in "I'm Ready." Incredibly, Sunnyland Slim closed his "Johnson Machine Gun" with a quotation from Lonnie Johnson's 1930 recording, "She's Making Whoopee in Hell Tonight":

> *Yes, the undertaker been here,*
> *Darlin', I give him your height and size;*
> *Now if you don't be making whoopee with the Devil*
> *Tomorrow this time,*
> *Baby, God knows you'll be surprised!*

Aristocrat 1301, by Sunnyland Slim and Muddy Waters, was followed by Aristocrat 1302, by Muddy Waters with Sunnyland Slim. "Gypsy Woman" wasn't a hit, but it was archetypal Waters in both theme and delivery:

> *Well, now, you know I went to a gypsy woman*
> *To have my fortune told;*
> *Say, "You better go back home, son,*
> *and peek through yo', your keyhole!"*

Waters was establishing a signature sound and a persona that was alternately menacing and celebratory, brooding and boastful. Describing how his style differed from the music of such Chicago predecessors as Tampa Red and Big Bill Broonzy, Waters told *Guitar Player*'s Tom Wheeler: "Mine was a rustier sound, a grittier sound." It was the sound that made a hit of "I Can't Be Satisfied" in 1948, and the Chess brothers emphasized it on Waters's releases for the next two years. His sole accompaniment, except for his own distinctive guitar, was often Ernest "Big" Crawford's bass, and the songs dipped deep into the Delta wellspring. "Rollin' and Tumblin'" was a Delta standard first recorded by Hambone Willie Newbern in 1929 (seven years later, Robert Johnson recorded it as "If I Had Possession Over Judgment Day"), and Waters's "Rollin' Stone" was a reworking of Robert Petway's 1941 hit, "Catfish Blues." Petway drummed out a danceable rhythm on his metal National guitar, while Waters played the sparest notes possible on his Gibson electric, stripping the tune to bare essentials and creating a palpable tension over which he sang:

> *Well, my mother told my father*
> *Just before, hmmm, I was born;*
> *"I got a boy child's comin',*
> *Gonna be, he's gonna be a rollin' stone . . ."*

Waters would later tag this sound "deep blues," a dramatic reinvention of the Delta's most essential elemental music. For stark power, Waters never exceeded these early sides, which seem to gaze into his past (and that of his fellow Delta migrants), not with nostalgia, but with a stunning passion. Yet the past was not where Waters truly lived. He was anxious to record with his Headhunters, the terror of Chicago's blues clubs.

Ironically, the earliest recording of the "classic" Waters band was not on a Waters session but on a 1949 Jimmy Rogers side of "Ludella," which included the guitars of Rogers and Waters, Little Walter on harmonica, and Sunnyland Slim's piano backed by "Big" Crawford's bass and an unknown drummer. The Chess brothers shelved the recording, and when Rogers cut his hit version a year later, Waters was absent. Little Walter's earliest appearance on a Waters recording is 1950's intense "You're Gonna Need My Help I Said." Waters's Headhunters—they never recorded under this name—were not grouped all together on a Waters date until late 1951, when "They Call Me Muddy Waters" was cut. "They call me Muddy Waters," he sang, "I'm just restless, man, as the deep blue sea . . ." Later in the song, Waters announces: "I'm the most bluest man in this whole Chicago town."

With Waters as its charismatic core, his band was creating an ensemble sound that heightened "deep blues" traditionalism with a punch and urgency. Rogers was the quintessential sympathetic sideman, unobtrusive but ever ready. Born James A. Lane at Ruleville, Mississippi in 1924, Rogers encountered Rice Miller and Howlin' Wolf in Memphis and was playing with Sunnyland Slim in St. Louis before he moved to Chicago around 1945. His no-frills guitar playing and lazy down-home vocals were superbly supported by Little Walter's harp on 1950's "That's All Right," his first hit for Chess. Walter was still with him on his final Chess waxing, "Can't Keep from Worrying," nine years later, but Rogers had left the Waters band in 1956 to be replaced by the fiery Pat Hare.

The mercurial Little Walter split from Waters's band in 1952 following the success of his instrumental showpiece "Juke," though he was in and out of Water's recording sessions throughout the 1950s. Walter has been likened to Charlie Parker for his visionary improvisations, but a closer parallel is to be found in the folk pop idiom: Earl Scruggs's reinvention of the banjo in bluegrass. Both Little Walter and Scruggs took an instrument deemed old-time and created a modern approach so stunning as to make the "old-time" instrument the showy centerpiece of most ensembles playing their chosen genre. They created new techniques and musical vocabularies for what had been considered rather limited instruments, and it was their example all future players sought to emulate.

Marion Walter Jacobs was born in Marksville, Louisiana, in 1930. He was the youngest of Waters's early musical compadres, so it seems appropriate that he brought the most modern ideas to the group and, as leader, was best able to compete with the aggressive R & B competition (Walter had a record in the R & B charts every week of the year in 1954). Walter was playing guitar before he discovered his knack for the harmonica. Legend has him wanting to play saxophone but, unable to afford one, he settled for the lowly harp and created his saxlike sound for it. Like many legends that attempt to explain the development of a genius, this one may be half true, but it's as likely that Walters's meeting with Rice Miller in Memphis influenced his early harp technique.

Walter arrived in Chicago in 1947, where he was soon playing for tips on Maxwell Street, a bustling open-air market where "musicians lined all up and down

Little Walter Jacobs, seen in a studio publicity shot, was an extremely erratic individual, but one of the great mouth harp geniuses.

Otis Spann, a marvelous boogie-woogie and blues pianist and an essential player in Muddy Waters's band, did not live past his fortieth year.

"Crazy For My Baby"
(W. Dixon)

7874
Time: 2:45
Arc Music
B.M.I.

LITTLE WALTER
CK-986

CHECKER

MANUFACTURED BY CHESS PRODUCING CORP., CHICAGO, ILLINOIS, U.S.A.

the street," according to singer/guitarist/mandolinist Johnny Young. Walter honed his craft in this competitive milieu, where his talent garnered fatherly advice from Broonzy and Tampa Red as well as an early waxing, "I Just Keep Loving Her," on the short-lived Ora Nelle label in 1947. Jimmy Rogers soon introduced Walter to Chicago's clubs, and eventually to Muddy Waters.

Walter was playing unamplified harp on such down-home sides as Waters's "Louisiana Blues" (1950), but a year later his well-amped, distorted wail was blowing against Waters's stinging slide on "Country Boy," in which Waters slyly excuses his failings to a lover with, "I'm a country boy, and I always will treat you wrong." Walters's long, lean lines were a perfect foil to Waters's intense vocals and trembling slide; all the great harp men—Junior Wells, James Cotton, Big Walter Horton—who succeeded him in Waters's band followed his blueprint. Troubled, fractious, and too fond of drink, Little Walter Jacobs died in 1968 from injuries sustained in a fight.

Another core member of Waters's classic Chicago blues band did not join him on record until 1953, but he was the one with whom Waters enjoyed the closest and longest relationship. Otis Spann was born in Belzoni, Mississippi, where a local barrelhouse pianist named Friday Ford offered inspiration. By his midteens, Spann had already become a regular performer in Jackson, Mississippi, juke joints. He was the same age as Little Walter and arrived in Chicago the same year, 1947. Spann adapted easily to the Chicago piano tradition embodied by Big Maceo Merriweather, then crippled by a stroke (Spann sometimes helped him play). Spann's breadth and depth as blues and boogie pianist weren't showcased on record until his 1960 recordings for the Candid label, but a sixteen-year stint with Waters's band began in 1953, when he played close to the vest on the recording of "Blow Wind Blow."

Coincidentally or not, the addition of Spann to the Waters band came at the time of his greatest success on the R & B charts. The second Waters session on

Big Maceo was one of the best of all boogie-woogie pianists. His career was cut short by a stroke. Maceo is seen here with his daughter and his niece.

185

which Spann played yielded his single biggest hit, "Hoochie Coochie Man." It stayed in the national Top Ten roster from March to early summer 1954 and received the following enthusiastic rave from the editors of *Cash Box*: "The chanter throws every one of his tricks into his job and he receives ork backing that is certainly not the least important part of the disc's success." In his 1975 history of Chicago blues, *Chicago Breakdown*, Mike Rowe writes: "Spann's contribution was a magnificent rolling bass, or, in the band passages, crashing treble work which perfectly fit the new sound of the city."

Aside from working with Waters, Spann was in constant demand to record with other Chess artists. The year 1955 was especially busy for him: he played on Sonny Boy Williamson's "Don't Start Me to Talkin'," Chuck Berry's "You Can't Catch Me," and Bo Diddley's "Bo Diddley." Spann accompanied Little Walter on the 1958 classic, "Key to the Highway," and two years later accompanied Waters's archrival

An early photo of Howlin' Wolf, one of the great Delta blues singers.

Howlin' Wolf on three of his best: "Wang Dang Doodle," "Back Door Man," and "Spoonful." Willie Dixon, who often called the players for these sessions, explained why he tapped Spann so often: "He was a *good* musician. You see, a good musician knows how to make the other fellows sound good. Otis was the type of guy who could play with anybody, and play behind you enough to make you sound good. When it came his time, he would do his thing, but he would get out in time to let *you* do yours." Waters appreciated this, and came to call Spann his half-brother. The last of the great barrelhouse pianists died in 1970, little more than a month after his fortieth birthday.

By 1954, Willie Dixon had replaced "Big" Crawford as bass player on Waters's records and was asserting his influence more critically as songwriter. "I really wasn't well known as a songwriter until 'Hoochie Coochie Man,'" Dixon said in his 1989 autobiography, *I Am the Blues*. The song was tailor-made for Waters; Dixon lifted the "gypsy woman" from Waters's debut Aristocrat single and added a prenatal prediction borrowed from "Rollin' Stone":

> *The gypsy woman told my mother*
> *Before I was born,*
> *"You got a boy child's comin',*
> *He's gonna be a son-of-a-gun . . ."*

"Hoochie Coochie Man" blended down-home references to conjurers ("I got the John the Conqueror root," Waters warned, "I got to mess with you") with Waters's blustery urban persona. It was a perfect refinement and distillation of everything Waters had created on Chess, and Dixon wrote two other hits for him in 1954 that were equally effective. "Just Make Love to Me (I Just Want to Make Love to You)" was a straightforward come-on, and the aggressive "I'm Ready" tempts "pretty little chicks" and dares "some screwball" to choose off the mighty Muddy, armed with "tombstone bullets wearin' balls 'n chains."

Dixon had a genius for crafting songs that highlighted the personas of Chess label artists. Wolf was the first to record "Wang Dang Doodle" in 1960, but the ebullient Koko Taylor owned it with the 1965 recording that made it her signature song. Dixon better nailed Wolf's dark menace with "Back Door Man" (1960). Wolf had just turned fifty when he growled:

> *I am a back door man;*
> *Well, the men don't know,*
> *But the little girls understand.*

Howlin' Wolf became Waters's chief rival on the Chicago blues scene, though he would have been content to have stayed in West Memphis, where his live afternoon broadcasts in KWEM had earned him a loyal following. "Howlin' Wolf drew more people in a club than anybody that's ever been in town," Rufus Thomas told Hugh Merrill. "Drew more people than Ray Charles." All Memphis loved the Wolf, but Chicago beckoned: "Leonard Chess kept worryin' me to come to Chicago," Wolf reported to David Booth. "I moved to Chicago in 1952 or 1953. I had a four thousand dollar car and $3900 in my pocket. I'm the onliest one drove out of the South like a gentleman." Before leaving, he waxed a kind of aural postcard for fans, "House Rockers." "You know I'm just out of California," Wolf said calmly over his band, storming through a breakneck jump tune. "I'm on my way to Chicago. The people have never *seen* the Wolf there. I'm in your town when I get there."

But it had been a long journey. Chester Arthur Burnett was born in West Point, Mississippi, in 1910. His parents were working a plantation in Ruleville, not far from Will Dockery's plantation, where Charley Patton resided. The flamboyant Patton taught Wolf the rudiments of Delta blues guitar, and while Wolf never became much of a guitarist, he squirreled away verses learned from Patton and his contemporaries for future use.

When grown, Burnett stood 6 feet 3 inches and tipped the scales at more than 270 pounds, earning him such nicknames as Bull Cow and Big Foot Chester (Sam Phillips recalled the impression Burnett's enormous feet made on him). There are sundry stories about the source of the name Howlin' Wolf, though the truth may be less important than the way Burnett came to embody the role implied by the name.

Chester Burnett, "The Howlin' Wolf."

Big, fearsome, solitary, and mysterious, the Wolf was already an imposing figure in the Delta by the late 1930s, according to Johnny Shines. "I was afraid of Wolf," he told Peter Guralnick, "just like you would be of some kind of beast or something. . . . Well, it wasn't his size, I mean what he was doing, the way he was doing, I mean the sound that he was giving off."

Wolf roamed the Delta for a while in the company of Robert Johnson and Rice Miller, who married Wolf's sister and taught him harmonica. But mostly he farmed with his family, an unremarkable life interrupted by his enlistment in the Army in 1941. He never saw combat, but he did entertain troops while stationed in the Seattle area. After the war, Wolf returned to farming in Mississippi, but he must have sensed something brewing and, in 1948, formed the nucleus of his band in West Memphis. His gig as disc jockey and live performer on KWEM soon followed.

"A disc jockey from West Memphis told me about [Wolf's] show on KWEM," Sam Phillips told Robert Palmer. Phillips was a disc jockey himself on Memphis's WREC and, in 1950, opened the Memphis Recording Service, offering souvenir transcriptions of weddings, funerals, and civic gatherings. Sensing a market for local blues talent, Phillips was recording B. B. King for the Bihari brothers' West Coast RPM label by 1950. He soon began looking for additional blues acts. "When I heard him," Phillips told Palmer about Wolf, "I said, 'This is for me. This is where the soul of man never dies.'" Phillips had Wolf in his studio for the first time in the spring of 1951. "His eyes would light up and you'd see the veins on his neck and buddy there was *nothing* on his mind but that song," Phillips recalled of the man he would call his greatest discovery. "He sang with his damn soul."

While not the first performance Phillips captured on tape, the first the world heard of Wolf was "Moanin' at Midnight." It opens with a thunderous a cappella hum seemingly erupting from *inside* the microphone. Hearing this distorted bay, one can well imagine Phillips's dismay as he watched his VU meter needle nosedive into the deepest end of the red zone. Willie Johnson then joins Wolf with his electric guitar, also highly distorted, playing a repetitive guitar figure Wolf probably taught him, one derived from Tommy Johnson's "Cool Drink of Water Blues" (1928). Wolf then unleashes a spine-chilling falsetto howl, another vestige of Johnson's influence. Next he blows harp, simple but effective, laying in with Johnson's jagged guitar and Willie Steele's flapping drums, chaotic but right on time. The sound is a molten blur of harp, guitar, and drums (the piano that discographies list is inaudible or lost in the fray). The effect is an auditory fever dream, heightened by Wolf's paranoid lyrics:

> *Well, somebody knockin' on my door;*
> *Well, somebody knockin' on my door.*
> *Well, I'm so worried, don't know where to go.*

Wolf sings the standard I-IV-V changes, but the band, as if hypnotized by its groove, never leaves the I chord. This can't be dismissed as a matter of technical deficiency, since, on earlier sessions, the same musicians played standard blues changes, and guitarist Johnson even displayed a penchant for jazzy takeoff solos. No, "Moanin' at Midnight" wasn't a mistake. It was a conceptually daring reduction of the blues. "On those early records," Wolf told Pete Welding, "I was the one who told the guys what to play, how the music was to go. Now, the bass patterns on those records, they are mine—that's my bass. Some of those numbers are just one chord. There's no changes to them; that's something I got from the old music."

Wolf has been called a primitive, but his primitivism was willful and might be likened to that of cubist painters who, by juxtaposing "primitive" elements in unexpected ways, created the art of the avant-garde. Wolf understood what he was doing with his blues deconstructions. In order to rebuild this music, he first had to raze it to its very foundations.

His singing standard blues changes against a single chord and repetitive riffs became a favorite device and appears in many of his most powerful records. One of the grimmest was "No Place to Go" (1954), on which the band relentlessly plays a five-note riff, laying into the beat hard at the front of each repetition like a needle stuck in a skipping record. Bitterly, Wolf sings:

> Now I'm old and gray,
> Got no place to go.
> You got yourself a young stud,
> And you can't stand me no more.

Sonny Boy Williamson II was one of the certifiable "characters" of the blues.

The monotony of the underlying riff is primitivism with a vengeance; the syncopated bounce that announces each five-note phrase echoes the fall of a sledgehammer in the manner of a prison work song. Waters may have sung "deep blues," but Wolf tapped roots that were deeper still. In "Smokestack Lightnin'" (1956), he abandons the A-A-B blues verse structure altogether for what is essentially a field holler.

"Smokestack lightnin' means a train," Wolf said, and the earliest train blues may have grown from pronouncements like Wolf's:

> Woh, stop your train!
> Let a po' boy ride.
> Oh, don't you hear me cryin',
> Wooh . . .

Sam Phillips sent his Memphis recordings of Howlin' Wolf to Chess, adding fuel to a dispute with the Biharis at RPM, already miffed that Chess had been given Jackie Brenston's "Rocket 88," which topped the R & B charts in June 1951. Phillips's betrayal of the Biharis was repaid when they hired the entrepreneurial bandleader Ike Turner, who led the "Rocket 88" session, to record Wolf for RPM. "Moanin' at Midnight" (Chess 1479, issued August 15, 1951) became "Morning at Midnight" on RPM, and entered the national R & B charts in September. While Wolf enjoyed the attention, both the Chess and Bihari brothers threatened Phillips with lawsuits. The acrimony faded when it was mutually agreed that up-and-coming Memphis R & B singer Roscoe Gordon became RPM's property and that Wolf would go to Chess. But to be safe, Leonard Chess urged Wolf to move to Chicago, where his legend loomed large for more than two decades. Anachronistic in Memphis in 1951, he became even more so in the quickly changing Chicago blues scene of the later 1950s and 1960s. Yet Wolf never strayed far from his course and was cutting compelling one-chord wonders as late as 1966's "Commit a Crime," with Hubert Sumlin's slashing guitar recalling the urgent chaos of 1951 Memphis. Wolf, as ever, was gruffly vigilant of malefactors, and he details the sins of "the evilest woman I ever seen":

> You mix my drink with a can of Red Devil lye;
> Then you set down, watch me,
> Hopin' that I might die.

Cancer claimed one of the Delta's greatest bluesmen in 1976. Howlin' Wolf was inducted into the Rock and Roll Hall of Fame as a "forefather" in 1991.

Like the Wolf, Rice Miller, his brother-in-law by a short-lived union, went by a number of monikers in his lifetime: Little Boy Blue was an early performing name befitting the Delta wanderer who made a big impression with his belt of Hohner "horns" in various keys. Footsie came from his habit of carving slits in his boots literally to cool his heels. And The Goat? If you've seen a late photo of Miller with his goatee and leer, it's self-explanatory.

The name that occasions controversy is the one by which he's best known, Sonny Boy. Suggestions that he lifted the name from John Lee "Sonny Boy" Williamson, an immensely popular harmonica player and singer whose Bluebird hits commenced in 1937 and who was murdered in Chicago in 1948, propelled Miller into a defensive rage, proclaiming, "I am the original, and the *only* Sonny Boy!"

Perhaps. But the truth for Miller was a matter of convenience, which ought not interfere with a good story—like his version of Robert Johnson's death, culminating with the dying singer cradled in Sonny Boy's arms. Miller would be remembered by some as a charming con man and by others as a violent drunk. Searching his memory for an accolade, KFFA announcer Sonny Payne told Hugh Merrill, "He never stabbed

Elmore James, influential slide guitarist, made a huge hit with his electrified version of Robert Johnson's "Dust My Broom."

anybody that I know of." But he never failed to make an impression, either, and Miller is the third member of the triumvirate of Delta "elder statesmen" who made compelling new/old blues at the Chess label in Chicago.

Miller was older than either Waters or Wolf, having been born sometime before the turn of the century near Glendora in Tallahatchie County, Mississippi. We know nothing of his early influences, though one account has him playing only religious tunes when he first took up harmonica. He is reported to have farmed with his mother and stepfather until he was thirty, at which time an argument with his stepfather put him on the "bummer road." This may have been in 1930, at which time the Delta was reeling from drought and the Depression. Miller learned to live by his wits and to play harmonica well enough to earn some spending change on his travels.

He crossed paths with a series of promising young guitarists similarly adrift, including Robert Johnson, Elmore James, and Robert "Junior" Lockwood. By 1941, Miller and Lockwood were playing on the streets of Helena, Arkansas. Lockwood had only recently returned from Chicago, where he recorded four sides for Bluebird, home of the *other* Sonny Boy. One of his songs, "Little Boy Blue," was probably inspired by his partner, who still used *that* name. Miller and Lockwood heard that a radio station was opening in Helena, and they proposed to KFFA owner Sam Anderson that they perform daily on his station free, provided they could plug their gigs in the area. Anderson called Max S. Moore, who he knew was looking for a way to promote his King Biscuit Flour. KFFA made its first broadcast on November 19, 1941, and the fifteen-minute "King Biscuit Time" quickly became a hit. Moore claimed he gave Miller the Sonny Boy name to make it sound like a national recording star was promoting his flour. Lockwood played electric guitar, the first to be widely heard in the Delta, and Sonny Boy was blowing amplified harp, perhaps the first to be heard anywhere. Soon they were joined by drummer James "Peck" Curtis and pianist Robert "Dudlow" Taylor, making for a rocking Delta quartet, probably the first grouping of its kind to be heard outside the juke joints. With the irascible Sonny Boy at the helm, the group was widely popular; Robert Palmer calls them "the Delta's first media-made blues stars."

Despite the security of the radio show and the success it brought his live performances, Sonny Boy grew restless and, by 1944, was "on the wander" again. He might be seen anywhere from Florida to Texas, though he settled for a while in Belzoni with his friend Elmore James (Sonny Boy was hawking an alcohol-based elixir called Talaho on area radio stations), then moved on to West Memphis, where he spent perhaps six months pitching another nostrum, Hadacol, on KWEM. Sonny Boy never stopped for long between 1949 and 1951, which was when Lilian McMurry finally cornered him long enough to record for her Jackson, Mississippi-based Trumpet label. Sonny Boy was more than fifty by the time he recorded. His eccentric, insinuating vocals and harp prowess were well-seasoned by that time. So, too, was his wit and knack for spinning memorable tales, mostly about women. He knew one lady so cruel she put him out when it was "Nine below Zero," and another whose sexual feats brought "Eyesight to the Blind" and similar cures ("Every time she start to lovin', the deaf and dumb begin to talk").

It was also during his stint at Trumpet that Sonny Boy blew harp on the first recording Elmore James made of "Dust My Broom," the Delta standard Robert Johnson had recorded back in 1936. James lacked the subtlety and range of other electric slide guitarists of his generation (Robert Nighthawk, Muddy Waters, Earl Hooker), but he played and sang with an intense conviction that made "Dust My

Broom" an enduring (and danceable) blues standard, as well as his signature tune up to his death in 1963.

Ever restless, Sonny Boy continued to travel, though now in a more northerly orbit that took him as far as Detroit, where he worked for a time with Baby Boy Warren's band. In 1955 Chess bought out Sonny Boy's Trumpet contract, and he belatedly found himself in the thriving Chicago blues scene. There he was reunited with Lockwood, who had become a session guitarist at Chess. The personnel were different, but the basic grouping—guitar, piano, bass, drums, and Sonny Boy on harp and vocals—was essentially the one he had pioneered at KFFA in 1941. Pushing sixty, Sonny Boy felt free to let his bizarre imagination run amok. He offered paranoid warnings against the "Unseen Eye," wove a baffling fantasy about a girl he meets in an otherwise-deserted "Little Village" ("She's got a pad like a palace, and everything was cruisin' kind . . ."), and, in "Have You Ever Been in Love," sang the praises of a woman whose attributes included "hydraulic hips" and an "air-conditioned stomach." The blues idiom never knew a finer surrealist poet.

"Don't Start Me to Talkin'" of 1955 would be Sonny Boy's biggest single hit, climbing to number three on the R & B charts, but his greatest success came in 1963

A WDIA broadcast featured a youthful B. B. King and one-man band Joe Hill Louis.

when he toured Europe to wild acclaim, especially from the English. The Animals and the Yardbirds were the best known of the young "beat" groups who performed and recorded with the sly sexagenarian. In Copenhagen, he made some intimate and affecting recordings for the Storyville label (reissued in the U.S. as *Keep It to Ourselves*, Alligator ALCD 4787) with pianist Memphis Slim and Matt "Guitar" Murphy as his sole accompanists. Even they were silent on "When the Lights Went Out," where we hear only Sonny Boy singing and playing harp, alone as he'd been when he first struck the "bummer road" decades earlier:

> *When the lights went out,*
> *So dark I couldn't see . . .*

The lights went out for Aleck (also known as Alec and Alex) "Rice" Miller in 1965, not long after he'd resumed his leadership of the King Biscuit Entertainers. "I just came home to die," he told his friends in Helena.

B. B. King, his band, and his tour bus on Beale Street, Memphis, about 1951.

Sonny Boy's brief stint at KWEM in 1948 inadvertently launched the career of a then-skinny kid named Riley King. He had provided inspiration earlier when he and Lockwood would play around Indianola, Mississippi, where King heard them in his

teens and was impressed by the crowds they drew. Grown and living with his cousin, Bukka White, King showed up at KWEM in hopes of landing a spot like Sonny Boy's. Instead, Sonny Boy let King perform one song and then enlisted him in getting Sonny Boy out of a jam. He had managed to book himself two gigs that night; would King mind covering at the lower-paying one? King made a favorable impression that night on Miss Annie, who ran the Sixteenth Street Grill in West Memphis. She said that if King could muster a radio show like Sonny Boy's, she would hire him at the princely sum of twelve dollars a week, plus room and board. That was all the incentive the twenty-three-year-old needed.

Legend has a drenched Riley King showing up at the studios of WDIA after a long walk from the Memphis bus station in a thundershower, his guitar wrapped in newspaper. "He looked so sad," WDIA's female program director Chris Spindel recalled to Louis Cantor, "but when he began to play, we all knew he had it." King was hired for a fifteen-minute Saturday afternoon slot, where he was introduced as "The Beale Street Blues Boy." The fans just called him B. B.

WDIA was the big time, the self-proclaimed "Mother-Station of the Negroes," which pioneered a format for black listeners earlier in the year of King's arrival. Like Sonny Boy, King was initially hawking a curative elixir, Peptikon, but in time his professionalism and popularity attracted a national sponsor, Lucky Strike cigarettes. While this may not look like a major career milestone today, it was WDIA's first national advertiser. Recording opportunities soon followed.

The first came for the Nashville-based Bullet label in 1949, with King unpacking his guitar to record "Miss Martha King" with an R & B band that included trumpet, trombone, and two saxes. The Biharis in L.A. heard the records and contacted Sam Phillips about recording him for RPM, thus making King the first bluesman to record at the Memphis Recording Service.

"B. B. Blues" (1951) is dominated by Solomon Hardy's searing sax, and Phineas Newborn, Jr.'s tack-hammer piano is the instrumental star of the rocking "She's Dynamite":

> She carries a pearl-handled pistol,
> A knife and a razor, too;
> You don't tell her nothin',
> She'll always tell you.
> She's dynamite . . .

By 1952, King's guitar was asserting itself in sessions that yielded his first real hit, "Three O'Clock Blues." The song was Lowell Fulson's, for whom it had done well in 1948. (King looked to Fulson's recordings again four years later when he recorded "Everyday I Have the Blues," written by Memphis Slim.) With a national hit under his belt and the Biharis urging him onto the road to promote his recordings, King's Memphis days were numbered. He reluctantly quit WDIA in 1953 and closed the Memphis chapter of his prolific recording career in September 1952 with "Boogie Woogie Woman," a raveup featuring Ike Turner's storming piano and a theme that echoed Leroy Carr's "Barrelhouse Woman" from two decades before:

> Well, she's a boogie woogie woman, she boogies all the time,
> Well, she's a boogie woogie woman, she boogies all the time,
> Well, now if she keep on boogiein', she's bound to lose her mind.

B. B. King strikes a pose well-nigh scholarly, as if in contemplation of his future.

Once on the road, King never stopped. By 1954 his endless one-nighters were already grossing him $480,000 a year! His success would be unequalled, though it was challenged by a man who once played rhythm guitar for King's band at the Sixteenth Street Grill, Bobby "Blue" Bland.

Robert Calvin Bland grew up in Rosemark, Tennessee, but made it to Memphis about the same time as everyone else: 1947. Just seventeen, he worked in a garage and sang in a gospel group, but soon Bland was singing the blues at Palace Theater amateur shows and "hanging around Beale Street with a bunch of guys," he told Peter Guralnick. The guys included Johnny Ace, Roscoe Gordon, and B. B. King, whose singing style Bland emulated. Gordon brought Bland along for a session he was doing at Phillips's Memphis Recording Service in August 1951, and his "Love You Til the Day I Die" wound up as the B side of Gordon's "Booted," a romping hit on

Chess. Four months later, Gordon and Bland were back in Phillips's studio for another session, which yielded the topical "Letter from a Trench in Korea." Typically, the Biharis got wind of Bland's talent, and were waxing "Crying All Night Long" for their Modern label in early 1952. But the Biharis didn't keep Bland long, for Memphis disc jockey James Mattis had signed him to his newly formed Duke label before the end of 1952. To their mutual chagrin, another bidder then requested Bland's talents, as witnessed by the doleful "Army Blues":

> *Sorrow this mornin', that awful day has come;*
> *Sorrow this mornin', that awful day has come;*
> *Uncle Sam has got me, I ain't having no more fun.*

Bobby "Blue" Bland

Bland's military service lasted two and a half years, and by the time he returned to performing, Duke (and Bland's contract) were owned by Houston's Don Robey. Whatever his army stint had cost his career, the time off seemed to have allowed Bland to mature as a singer. His swooping falsetto soars wildly on his first Houston recording, "Lost Lover Blues" (1955), and he whoops appreciatively at Roy Gaines's T-Bone twangs in the tough "It's My Life Baby" from the same session:

> *Woh, it's my life, baby,*
> *Don't try to change my ways . . .*
> *Well, if you want my loving,*
> *Don't make no graveyard plays.*

Gaines and, later, Clarence Holloman were the guitarists who propelled Bland's 1955–58 Duke performances, Texas-style string bending wrapped around R & B horns and Memphis-born vocal intensity. The comparisons with King were inevitable, though Bland's records had an edgier fervor and an urban toughness. In "You've Got Bad Intentions," Bland snarled:

> *Well, you say you can't go on living*
> *If you can't be by my side;*
> *Gonna send you a bottle of poison,*
> *Please commit suicide!*

The fire was cooling by 1957, the year Bland recorded "Farther up the Road," a soulfully gospel-tinged blues in which his youthful anger was submerged in sorrow. The record was a huge hit and a natural turning point in Bland's style, which became smoother. The King parallels receded as Bland emerged as a new kind of blues shouter, simultaneously intimate and powerful, in such songs as the bitter "I Pity the Fool" (1960). Bland has never enjoyed the media saturation that has followed King since the late 1960s, but he has never ceased touring or recording, either, and has probably retained the most faithful black following of any blues singer of his generation.

Bland toured for years with Junior Parker, another Memphian who was on the Duke label. After the army and before his hits started coming, Bland even worked as Parker's valet. Herman Parker was born in West Memphis in 1927 and became "Little Junior" after a stint blowing harmonica for Howlin' Wolf. The band that became Little Junior's Blue Flames was forming by 1950, and two years later the enterprising Ike Turner was recording them for the Biharis' Modern label. Sam Phillips heard the Blue Flames and contacted them to record for *his* new label, Sun. "Fussin' and Fightin' (Blues)" was the sort of thing Parker wanted to record, Deltafied after-hours blues with purring sax and smooth vocals. But Phillips wanted something rawer, so the Blue Flames laid into an infectious groove lifted from John Lee Hooker's "Boogie Chillun" (1948), and Parker talked, then sang, then talked and sang his distinctive wrinkle on the endless boogie, "Feelin' Good." It was the summer of 1953, and the vibrant Memphis blues scene that flowered as WDIA "went black" in 1948 was already dispersing. Howlin' Wolf, B. B. King, and Bobby Bland scattered from the River City, but there were still some good records to be made, like Parker's "Mystery Train" later that year. A sax blows in imitation of a dark and distant locomotive, while the guitar, piano, and drums lay down a repetitive hypnotic bounce familiar in the Delta since the days of Charley Patton and Tommy Johnson. Parker's vocals ooze a smooth modernity against lines about women-stealing trains that are as old as the Delta's earliest blues:

Proving that blues is a truly universal music, Jimmy Reed appears with a diminutive troupe of extraterrestrials.

Train I ride, sixteen coaches long;
Train I ride, sixteen coaches long;
Well, that long black train carried my baby from home.

Two years later, Elvis would record this for Sun, symbolically linking the label's blues and rockabilly eras. There would be many more rockabilly covers of "Mystery Train," but their spirit was really that of the highballin' hillbilly train grooves set in the '40s by Roy Acuff ("Freight Train Blues"). They missed the mystery of "Mystery Train," a resignation to the inevitable so strong as to become the rhythmic heart of the Delta's blues.

Phillips's Sun label continued to record fine blues in 1953 and 1954—Walter Horton's lonesome and lithesome instrumental, "Easy," James Cotton's protest against sharecropping, "Cotton Crop Blues," and the early sides of James Milton Campbell, best known as Little Milton. A phenomenal singer and guitarist still active and widely popular, Milton had yet to find his style when he was recording for Sun. Even if he had, the time was short for the blues there when he cut "Alone and Blue" in March 1954. Elvis's first session was only four months away, and his success pointed Phillips in another direction. By the year's end, blues activity at Sun had virtually ceased. "For a black person," Sun alumnus Rufus Thomas told Hugh Merrill, "when Sam Phillips heard Elvis and those people, it was all over."

But the blues scene in Chicago was still bubbling, and opportunities to record flourished as new labels popped up, hoping to emulate the success of Chess. Vee-Jay came nearest to giving Chess a serious run for the money, especially with the recordings of Jimmy Reed. James Mathis Reed was born in Leland, Mississippi, in 1925, where he received encouragement from his harmonica-playing father. After a wartime stint in the navy, Reed moved to Chicago, working in an iron foundry by day and hitting the clubs at night. It wasn't uncommon for two people from a tiny Mississippi hamlet to run into one another in Chicago, which is how Reed encountered childhood chum Eddie Taylor, who had become a far better guitarist than Reed. Together, they created a lightly bobbing back-porch boogie groove on their two guitars, punctuated by Reed's crying harp and thick-tongued vocals. Infectious and likable, Reed's sound was an instant hit, especially with the jukebox trade. "You Don't Have to Go" (1954) garnered this rave from *Cash Box*: "Jimmy Reed is really in there pitching as he handles the slow bouncy blues with feeling and gusto. Effective wax." Reed's "slow bouncy blues" never varied much from record to record, but it was a winning formula. In 1956 he had five consecutive hits, while Muddy Waters mustered only one that year. Reed's were among the last urbanized down-home blues to achieve such widespread popularity. There was a friendly accessibility in his songs, which appealed beyond boundaries of race and region, and, before his death in 1976, Reed would hear covers of his simple songs by Elvis and the Rolling Stones, among others.

Darker sounds rumbled from Chicago's West Side, newly settled as the city's black population expanded from the South Side. The hospitality that had welcomed many of the bluesmen who hit town in the 1940s was absent now, and these younger men were less indebted to the Delta's traditions than Waters or Wolf or Sonny Boy had been. They hit meaner streets and had perhaps even less to lose than their predecessors, so they made correspondingly hard music. Their tough sound was in part a matter of necessity. "There's a thing with most of the West Side boys," singer/guitarist Jimmy Dawkins told Mike Rowe. "What we're doing is playing with a bass, drums, and guitar, but we're *thinking* of a horn or two horns and when we throw those heavy chords that's what we're doing. It's a creative thing. It makes us get this heavy sound as we call it substituting for a full band."

In August 1956, Eli Toscano started a West Side label to wax the "heavy sound" and chose a name and emblem of fitting power and menace: Cobra. The ubiquitous Willie Dixon was Cobra's A & R man and session leader, as well as songwriter for Cobra's first and most successful release, "I Can't Quit You Baby." The artist was a twenty-two-year-old singer/guitarist named Otis Rush, whose impassioned vocals pushed "I Can't Quit You Baby" into R & B Top Ten. The Mississippi-born Rush must have been sufficiently awed by his good fortune to acquiesce when Dixon gave him a follow-up song that was a baffling mismatch of artist and repertoire, an unusual goof for the usually savvy Dixon. "Violent Love" is structurally a 1920s Tin Pan Alley song (Dixon even has Rush "makin' whoopee") with cornball horns and lyrics that

Buddy Guy (left) in concert with Johnny Winter.

seem jauntily to endorse date rape. Having Rush record "Violent Love" made as much sense as offering "Smokestack Lightnin'" to Bing Crosby, and it was only the first of many wrong moves in a career that has been dogged by setbacks. It was with genuine anguish that Rush sang (his own lyrics this time):

> *I lay 'wake at nights, false love, just so troubled;*
> *It's hard to keep a job, laid off, I'm havin' double trouble.*
> *Hey, hey, yeah, they say you can make it if you try.*
> *Yes, some of this generation is millionaires,*
> *It's hard for me to keep decent clothes to wear.*

Magic Sam

"Double Trouble" (1958) was one of Rush's last releases on Cobra. (The searing guitar on the song was played by Ike Turner, who made his mark on Chicago in the 1950s, as well as Memphis and St. Louis.) The best of Rush's Cobra sides were as intense as anything to come from the second wave of postwar Chicago bluesmen, though others quickly lined up to shoot for his high standards as Rush's career foundered in "Double Trouble."

Sam Maghett was only twenty when he became Magic Sam for his first Cobra single, "All Your Love" (1957). Like Rush, Sam had a piercing high voice, albeit without Rush's ferocity. Rush's initial Cobra releases tended to downplay his distinctive guitar and pushed the horns upfront, but Sam's featured guitar-based minimalism from the gate. Shimmery tremolo riffs sparkle alongside Sam's pleading cry in "All Your Love," the band laying into a sinuous groove likely lifted form Ray Charles's "Lonely Avenue," which in turn was copped from the Pilgrim Travelers' "I've Got a New Home." In Sam's hands, the heaviness of the plodding gospel groove is sheared down to a relaxed whiplash, sexy and perfect for slow dancing. "All Your Love" became the foundation of many of Sam's fine Cobra sides in the same groove, among them "Easy Baby" and "Love Me This Way." It defined a new city blues style perfect for small combos working tiny taverns. The singer/guitarist was the center, supported only by an able rhythm section (bass and drums). The format was old, of course, but to it Sam brought something new—a kind of cool intensity. His blue flame smoldered undiminished on his fine Delmark albums of the 1960s, but flickered out—too soon—in 1969. He was only thirty-two.

Eli Toscano had realized sufficient success with Rush and Magic Sam on Cobra to try a third promising young singer/guitarist, Buddy Guy, on his newly formed Artistic subsidiary in 1958. Guy was from Louisiana, so it is not surprising that the influence of New Orleans-based Guitar Slim hangs heavy behind the early Artistic side, "You Sure Can't Do." But there was much of Rush's urgency on Guy's first Artistic recording, "Sit and Cry," tenor and baritone saxes chopping out a foundation over which he proclaims:

> *Blues all in my bloodstream;*
> *Blues down in my home;*
> *Blues down in my soul;*
> *I got blues all . . . in my bones.*

West Side toughness and the requisite command of the guitar were bountiful in Guy's self-assured recordings. Very much a man of the moment, there was something

Like many another blues artist, Freddy King, an exceptional Texas blues guitarist, died young.

else in the flamboyant Guy's work, urban and up-to-date, which harkened back to the Delta, to Robert Johnson and his mentor, Son House, who personified the blues as a living spirit. Blues continued to be a dialogue between the present and past. Guy moved to Chess in 1960, where he recorded "First Time I Met the Blues," a striking song about the malevolent blues spirit, but for all its right-now West Side intensity, the song was essentially "The First Time I Met You," waxed twenty-four years earlier by singer/pianist Little Brother Montgomery (he was from Louisiana, too):

> The first time I met the blues, mama,
> They came walking through the wood.
> The first time I met the blues, baby,
> They came walking through the wood.
> They stopped at my house first, mama,
> And done me all the harm they could.

By the late 1950s, the blues had been a long time out of the woods. It had never stopped changing, nor had it ever stopped referring back—in a lyric or a lick—to markers that were seemingly timeless and transcended neat rural/urban lines of demarcation. Eighteen years after finding Muddy Waters, Alan Lomax returned to the rural South "with hi-fi stereo equipment," he wrote, "to offer the singers of mountain, bayou, prison and cotton patch the best of modern sound technology." Among his discoveries in 1959 were fife and drum bands playing a deeply African proto-blues, music that was generations old when the blues "came walking through the wood" sixty-some years earlier. On the same trip he also recorded singers imitating the latest Sonny Boy Williamson records. Down South, the ancient and the modern were juxtaposed with ease, given that there was little commercial imperative to make a hit. In Chicago it was different, as the competitive blues scene was saturating its market, one which had essentially peaked. The young lions of the West Side were still in their twenties, but the kids who should have been practicing to take their place often weren't playing the blues at all.

As always, it wasn't clearly the end of an era, but a new one was shaping up by the time Muddy Waters became the toast of the Newport Jazz Festival in 1960. And, as before, technology was a catalyst. It had been the phonograph in the 1920s, then, belatedly, radio some twenty years later. Now it was television's turn to transform the blues—and its audience.

By 1963, Sonny Boy Williamson, decked out like a Fleet Street barrister, could be seen on the BBC singing "Fattening Frogs for Snakes" to adoring young Britons while the scruffy Rolling Stones, in 1965, sang Willie Dixon's "Little Red Rooster" to American teens on *Shindig*. The exchange seemed surreal. What did the country metaphors—of sexual deceit in the one song and prowess in the other—mean to Anglo-American adolescents in an era of napalm and naugahyde? Perhaps it didn't matter; for the medium, we learned, *is* the message. Pop music would soon contain collages of blues interwoven with Indian ragas and baroque fugues. We had come to live in a global village, Marshall McLuhan assured us, and the era's collage-pop was less the product of psychedelic epiphanies than of globe-shrinking television.

Feeling bewildered and betrayed, some bluesmen protested that young Englishmen (and, in their wake, white Americans) were stealing their music and making fortunes. Music critics echoed their outcry. If the charges were partly true, they were also ultimately irrelevant. One may as well protest any inexorable historic

tide that sweeps some away and others forward. (Hadn't Broonzy railed against Ray Charles's mixing of blues and gospel textures a decade earlier?) Neither the bluesmen who were exported to Europe in the 1960s to great acclaim nor their English admirers who conquered America had much control over the currents in which they swam.

By the 1970s, Buddy Guy, who first met the blues in the woods, was playing music imitative of Jimi Hendrix, who became a legend by imitating the guitar pyrotechnics, stagy histrionics, and freaky fashions of Anglo-American rockers deeply indebted to the likes of Buddy Guy. Some say Hendrix and Guy were sellouts, while others count them as savvy journeymen who swam with the prevailing current. Either way, the blues was now an international music responding to far-flung influences. Questions of regional city-by-city schools were primarily historic ones. By the time it entered the global village, the blues had endured an arduous and amazing journey from the Tutwiler, Mississippi, train depot where, in 1903, W. C. Handy first tasted "the weirdest music I had ever heard."

Backstage at a blues festival (left to right): B. B. King, Fred McDowell, Big Mama Thornton, Junior Wells, and Roosevelt Sykes, among others.

TRUCKIN' MY BLUES AWAY

EAST COAST
PIEDMONT STYLES

BRUCE BASTIN

◆◆◆

IN THE BEGINNING

In 1940 Edgar Rogie Clark, director of the Third Annual Arts Festival held at Fort Valley State College in Perry County, Georgia, sent a letter to "the musicians and music lovers of the state" regarding a "Special program" to be held on April 6 at 8:00 P.M. It was a momentous occasion, little noticed at the time, and afforded even less interest since.

The occasion was to be a gathering of *folk* performers—an open invitation by Clark to "all banjo players, guitar players, jug bands, fiddlers, mouth organ, harp players and string bands." Clark's invitation had been reinforced by the college president, Horace Mann Bond, who had enjoyed the singing in a local church. The musicians came and performed, and a genuine folk music festival was added to the existing Agricultural Show for a decade or so.

For any college to organize such a folk festival during the 1940s was remarkable in itself. This one was unique for the South, let alone Georgia, for Clark was black, and so was Bond. Fort Valley was a college for black student teachers. *All* the performers were black. The music was black. Never before had a black establishment shown the remotest interest in documenting grassroots black folk music in this manner. Sadly, its uniqueness remained. Never again did any black establishment concern itself with such documentation. Not until the late 1970s, apart from the Library of Congress, were institutions of any sort anywhere to show interest; but they remained few.

If this is an unorthodox preamble to an overview of the emergence and history of blues in the southeastern states, it will serve to show that as a musical genre it went unnoticed at all stages in its development by people outside the social and economic groups for whom the music held relevance. That these groups were largely nonliterate meant that the music was either ignored or scorned, and that such documentation as occurred came from individuals motivated by nonacademic and nonestablishment factors, and usually at a late date.

The emergence, growth, and changing patterns of blues in the southeastern states needs to be viewed from different (and sometimes conflicting) angles. Whether or not there was to be *any* future documentation at all, the music evolved according to social, economic, historical, and geographical factors—as with any genuine grassroots music. It would also die out, governed by the selfsame factors. Superimposed upon this was the tenuous influence of commercial recordings; these both altered areas of growth and expansion, and granted some documentation of the processes that were evolving in the music, albeit seriously restricting early attempts at ethnocentric explanation, as the recordings became *the* statement of the music to analytical minds and ears—the medium was the message.

During the time of commercial documentation—documentation being secondary, naturally, to commercial viability—there were attempts to document areas of the music, thanks largely to individuals operating through the Archive of American Folk Song at the Library of Congress. At a much later date, commencing really during the 1960s, there were separate, uncoordinated areas of documentation by interested individuals, linked neither to institutions nor to commercial activities. Out of their research came links to both commercial release of recorded material (really only for collector consumption) and to minor institutional involvement.

Perhaps the separate strands that wove the fabric of blues emerging in the Southeast were not noticeably different from those in other regions of the South, but it is salutory to appreciate that a music that today is taken for granted as an art form in its own right, and about which many people proclaim themselves knowledgeable enough to instruct others in its rudiments, would have had virtually no documentation had it not been for a handful of individuals, operating in largely unconnected areas. Today's acceptance sits hard on the heels of yesterday's ignorance and frequent outright rejection. Today a black generation might acknowledge this musical form as having a validity, although remaining wary of it, but other than the performers themselves, most past generations stubbornly refused to acknowledge any merit whatever. This is, of course, the stuff of bandwagons—and bandwagons are only there for some people to ride.

Given the restrictions upon documentation suggested above, any assessment of the emergence of blues in the southeastern states can only come from the limited overview of its assessor, and from the biases that assessor attributes to elements of growth. Parallel themes existed; black folk of a certain socioeconomic level derived blues from emphases upon their own lives and from the influence of outsiders. Few of these were capable of being documented in any serious sense; only by talking to "survivors" could one assemble a concept of musical evolution and change. Some of these performers became documented in the slipstream of commercial recordings and, by these, their lives and musical emphases became available to many. Others, usually far outside the commercial flow of recording, were documented by the sheer energy and foresight of folk-song collectors like John A. Lomax, Alan Lomax, and Zora Neale Hurston. Lawrence Gellert, in *his* collecting, was making a conscious political statement about the treatment of blacks in the South. All helped fill in the spatial fabric. The later collectors, from the folk-boom years of the 1960s and

Musicians in performance at the Fort Valley, Georgia, Folk Festival in 1944 include Buster Brown (with harmonica, in white jacket), Gus Gibson (with guitar, in front of Brown), and Buz Ezell (in the center with harmonica and guitar). Spectacles like this were called "ham and egg" shows. Note the presence of both in this photograph. CHAPTER OPENER

onward, recorded the continuing patterns of musical evolution—although they often consciously sought the little-changed survivals of earlier, passed styles. Others looked for historical origins of a deceased music, only to find it alive but largely invisible. All, conscious or otherwise, brought their prejudices to bear; but without them there would be no telling of the story. The story would have existed without them, but no one would have known, and no one would have asked about it. It would have been the folk memory that people from time to time suggest exists.

The background contributing to the emergence of blues in the Southeast has been well-enough documented already; sufficient here for us to appreciate that it grew out of markedly changing conditions for blacks in the South, roughly in the decade following the mid-1890s. Perhaps the music came to the Southeast later than elsewhere (e.g. Mississippi), and a case can be made for its emergence really only in the decade before World War I, and its firm establishment by about 1920.

Blind Blake, possibly the greatest of all ragtime-blues guitarists, enjoyed a good deal of popularity through his recordings, but this is the only known photograph of him.

Writing at this late date, it is perfectly logical to make a case for a regional style for blues in the Southeast, but in the early days at least (and quite possibly throughout its history) it is probable that the performers in the region, when exposed to blues on commercial disk, thought no more about region than anything else. They bought what they liked. The first musical giant from the Southeast to record was Blind Blake. Rather a vague picture of the man is all we have, mythically fitting the pattern of the traveling legend, passing ever onward, leaving music and awe behind. Between the summers of 1926 and 1932 he cut some eighty titles for release on the Paramount label, a feat that is something of a legend in the recording business. We have no knowledge of his background. We don't even know his name for certain. Nonetheless, this wizard of the guitar was one of the great influences from commercial disk before the stock market crash, which terminated his recording career. Just the same, he may well have sold no more records in the Southeast than the Texan Blind Lemon Jefferson, from whom Paramount issued rather more disks than Blake, in half the time.

Blind Blake was one of the supreme blues guitarists and we are fortunate that he recorded so extensively, but he was also a consummate ragtime performer, highlighting an important strain in the style that portrays blues from the Southeast as being distinct from other regions. One of the region's finest guitarists, who commenced a recording career a decade later than Blake, stated: "I ain't never heard anybody on a record yet beat Blind Blake on the guitar. I like Blake because he plays right sporty." "Sporty" is just right. Blake exhibits a panache, a stunning statement born of overwhelming technique and utter confidence. "Blind Arthur's Breakdown" (1929) will show what the Reverend Blind Gary Davis meant by "sporty," but you can place your pin anywhere at random in his discography and still come up with Blake at his best. A handful of shadowy references place Blake at times between Jacksonville, Florida (his possible birthplace), and Chicago (where he recorded). We hear tell of him in

Promoting an array of Piedmont luminaries.

208

Charleston, West Virginia, Savannah, Atlanta, and New York City. At least five cities were supposedly where he died, usually in an accident but once reportedly murdered. Almost true to fable, evidence neither of birth nor death has been uncovered.

Blind Blake's mobility exemplifies other patterns in the evolution of blues in the Southeast. Undoubtedly, the music was polygenetic, having different sources and chronological origins if generally similar inputs. Music came in from outside the region but it also spread within the region along geographical and historical lines.

During World War I considerable numbers of southern blacks moved north, and by the early 1920s, push-pull factors depleted rural areas and concentrated rural blacks in southern urban centers. Agricultural depression and the advent of the boll weevil broke down patterns of farming and rural settlement. With work unavailable, there was no economic alternative to migration to urban centers, even if work there was uncertain. Then again, the urban center offered broader opportunities for social and economic improvement; almost wholesale, rural dwellers moved to the city and took with them rural customs. The persistence of folk traditions in the city was not a myth.

Even before the drift to towns had become a flood, rural communities were able to experience some of the extra things in life which rural stores were not able to offer. Mail order catalogs came into being by the 1890s, Sears Roebuck supreme among them, and a bewildering array of goods could be ordered, C.O.D., by rural free postal delivery. Among the pages were many advertisements for musical instruments, and most important were advertisements for guitars. The spread of the guitar among blacks, its replacement of the banjo, and its role in blues can hardly be overstated. In the Southeast blues became a guitar-oriented music, facilitating its swift and easy dissemination.

By the 1920s, a series of socioeconomic and historical shifts had thus helped breed circumstances in which blues were able to prosper and spread. Large numbers of rootless blacks had settled in urban centers in the South, which were themselves on the road and railroad links from Florida in the South toward New York in the Northeast. The Appalachian Mountains, running southwest to northeast from northern Georgia through the Carolinas into Virginia, effectively provided a physical barrier to the Mississippi Valley and the Tennessee-Kentucky plateaus to the west. Migration was rural to urban, South to North, tapering off along that route in major centers like Atlanta, Charlotte, Durham, Richmond, Washington, Baltimore, Philadelphia, and Newark–New York.

Racial tensions of the mid-1890s to mid-1900s had eased—or perhaps had simply fallen into a more rigid pattern, understood by both sides. Until the stock market crash of late 1929, many of those who had settled in the urban centers found themselves with more money, and with the advent of a black phonograph industry after 1920—albeit usually white-owned—records were sold of black artists, aimed specifically at the black market. For perhaps the first time ever, black artifacts were aimed at a section of the black consumer public that could perhaps afford the goods, without having to read the goods. Records could be bought and heard, and a new breed of entrepreneur hit the scene, capable of determining that at least some rural blacks with undeniable musical talents could be recorded. The traditional folk pattern of passing on music to a younger set was to be enhanced by pure fortuity of circumstance; traditional folk could be recorded and their records heard by thousands of others, miles away from the home of the recording artist. This enabled a rapid dissemination of music that otherwise could have come only from the slow passage of itinerant artists or the even slower projection of the music from generation to generation.

Shrewd middlemen in the music scene in New York saw to it that a market existed for blues records among a black public. As always with a simple musical catch-all term, "blues" denoted a wide range of black music, from Mamie Smith's "Crazy Blues" to Blind Blake's picked guitar solos, but sales were there. Hardly a bluesman interviewed in the Southeast in the 1960s and 1970s failed to mention Blake or Blind Lemon Jefferson, if their blues origins were rooted in the 1920s. The projection of the music by means of the phonograph record cannot be overlooked, and yet its influence remained a parallel development of the music itself.

Not everyone had a phonograph player, or access to someone else's. Many musicians learned their styles directly rather than poring over a disk; many learned both ways. To some, music learned from disk was in addition to what was learned in more traditional methods. Anyway, forty years later, who would be able to attribute influence with any accuracy? Probably not the performers themselves; certainly not the visitors who came to document.

If Blind Blake was the first to exemplify the style that has become associated with the Southeast, even a cursory assessment of his style will pinpoint factors in recognizing regional traits. One annotator of his music stated that "playing with a terrific flair for improvisation . . . he is at once subtle and ornate. No other blues guitarist has a more complicated or sophisticated style."

"CROW JANE, WHAT MAKES YOU HOLD YOUR HEAD SO HIGH?"

As well as recording sessions in the North, there were also field trips into the South to record. Atlanta was an early center; Victor was there in 1927, 1928, and 1929, drawing artists from far afield but also recording local bluesman Blind Willie McTell. Julius Daniels came from Charlotte to record the same year that South Virginian Luke Jordan and Andrew and Jim Baxter from Georgia were recorded in Charlotte. Consistency counted less than opportunity. Charlotte became a center for Decca's southeastern recordings in the 1930s. In late 1927, Victor recorded on a trip from Bristol, Tennessee, to Savannah, Georgia, but this enterprising experiment presumably posed too many problems, as established recording centers were used in the future.

Columbia and Okeh also used Atlanta as a base as early as 1925, though they failed to capitalize on this early date. They recorded more local bluesmen like Peg Leg Howell, Barbecue Bob and his brother Charlie Lincoln, Curley Weaver, and Buddy Moss, as well as the omnipresent McTell. Instrumental in organizing these sessions were such A & R (artists and repertoire) men as Art Satherly and Dan Hornsby in Atlanta, and their overall boss, Frank Walker, who also went on southern field trips. The full role of A & R men and company agents may never be assessed, but their role in recording certain Atlanta bluesmen has been documented, as has that of the American Record Company agent, J. B. Long, in Durham, who discovered such major bluesmen as Blind Roy Fuller, Sonny Terry, Brownie McGhee, and Gary Davis. Charles Rey, a Richmond dealer, organized a 1929 Okeh session in town, and a fascinating description of the activities of local distributors Harry Charles and Polk Brockman in Atlanta has been given.

Without doubt, had it not been for such men many of the region's major bluesmen would never have recorded. Just the same, many of the best never did record; anyone who has done fieldwork research can name bluesmen held in local awe, whose names would be otherwise unknown. Sheer chance entered into the story. Traveling bluesmen who didn't especially want to be located easily fell through the net, like a Georgian named Blind Log. Agents were few and could have heard only a small number of musicians, certainly few outside urban centers. Thus we pay too much attention to the recorded evidence, exaggerating the distortion even more. William Moore cut some sides for Paramount in 1928, of which eight were released, but he lived in the remote Virginia tideway area. Gary Davis always rated Blind Simmie Dooley as a musician, although his four-title session in 1928 for Columbia with Pink Anderson gives no hint of prowess. Willie Walker (also blind) cut two titles for Columbia in Depression-bound 1930 but was a local South Carolina legend. The reaction to his music on cassette from people who had not heard it in well over forty years had to be seen to be believed. Listen to "South Carolina Rag" and you will understand. Bluesman Baby Tate initially flatly refused to try to play Willie Walker tunes but later promised to record "South Carolina Rag" for Pete Lowry. He died of a heart attack, quite unexpectedly, just before the session.

Every city held at least one bluesman with a reputation shrouded in legend, about whom we often have only a name. Around Atlanta it was Clifford Lee, Jonas Brown, or Buddy Keith. Brown was discovered, totally incapacitated by a stroke, but Buddy Keith was fit and capable of playing when I saw him in 1972. Whether or not he was one of those past his peak who could play but would rather not, or whether he chose not to play out of sheer intransigence (as was his right!) I'll never know. I spent hours trying to interview and record Ephen Lee in North Carolina. Everyone around Tarboro and Rocky Mount said he was *the* man. If he had been able to play guitar as well as he could skin a squirrel, he must have been superb. We'll never know.

A few remarkable artists were encouraged to record. Ernest Scott of Atlanta was one, though nothing has been released to date. Henry Johnson from South Carolina was another, and he remains the finest country blues guitarist I've ever seen and heard. His premature death deprived us of one of the more remarkable persisters with the faith, when his skills had hardly yet been transferred to tape. He had been

MADE IN ATLANTA MATRIX NO. W146 065							10 INCH
TITLE C. C. & O. BLUES.						*Vocal*	
ARTIST PINK ANDERSON & SIMMIE DOOLEY					ACCOMP. *by Two Guitars*		
SUB. NO.	RECORDED	SHIPPED	TEST RECEIVED	REPORTED	DISPOSITION		REMARKS
1	4/14/28		4/26/28	6/8/28	OK	2nd	
2	"		4/26/28	"	OK	1st	
COMPOSER					CATALOGUE NO. *14401.*		
AUTHOR					MONTH LISTED *April 192*		
PUBLISHER					COUPLED WITH *W146 064*		
DATE OF COPYRIGHT							
DATE OF COPYRIGHT CONTRACT							
DATE OF COPYRIGHT EXTRACT				RECORDING OPERATOR			

This Columbia Records session card was filled out at the time of the Anderson-Dooley recording session.

Barbecue Bob, one of Atlanta's blues giants, died before he reached thirty, but nevertheless left a rich recorded legacy.

"found" by bluesman Baby Tate, although his name was never mentioned by anyone else, which was hardly surprising, as he had never moved beyond three adjoining South Carolina counties. He did work with Arthur "Peg Leg Sam" Jackson, a remarkable harmonica player who worked the last medicine show to go on the road. That this truly amazing pair worked together around Jonesville, South Carolina, for years, including a fifteen-minute musical spot on WBSC, Union, in the early 1970s to sell cars, without anyone taking the slightest interest suggests either that by extraordinary good luck we had found the only such pair in the entire South or that they were not an isolated phenomenon.

The first significant Atlanta bluesman to record was Peg Leg Howell, who was spotted playing on Decatur Street late in 1926 by Wilbur C. Brown, later Columbia's assistant manager at the studios. By early 1929 Howell had cut over two dozen sides and then was dropped. His "Gang" were rough, country musicians; typically, they did not mix with the slicker set of Buddy Moss, McTell, and Curley Weaver.

Robert Hicks's first title was "Barbecue Blues," released under the name of Barbecue Bob, so christened by Columbia scout Dan Hornsby because Hicks worked at a barbecue stand. Over fifty sides were issued by the time of the final session in December 1930, although four titles were then cut by the Georgia Cotton Pickers, which included a young Buddy Moss on harmonica—and which provided perhaps the best recordings ever by a small juke-joint combo.

Barbecue Bob's brother Charlie Lincoln also cut a dozen titles for Columbia, while another from their set, Curley Weaver, recorded both on the Georgia Cotton Pickers sides and under his own name. Weaver, who teamed up with twelve-string guitarist Blind Willie McTell until the latter's death in the late 1950s, was the only one of Barbecue Bob's set to record after the war. Oddly, it was Weaver's mother who taught the Hicks brothers their idiosyncratic style, which Weaver rarely emulated.

Sadly, Barbecue Bob died of pneumonia in 1931, and his brother was unable to adjust. Eventually he was committed to jail, where he died in 1963.

Blind Willie McTell, like Blind Blake, was the stuff of legends, and had it not been for the determined efforts of a small band of people, he would also have drifted onto the scene, recorded, and vanished. David Evans cracked the nut, and McTell's story has been told in full. Born shortly before the turn of the century, he was recording for Victor by 1927 and by 1935 had also recorded for Columbia, Okeh, Vocalion, and Decca. Late in 1940 he ran across John A. Lomax, who instantly knew he had an artist of true stature in front of his portable machine. McTell loved it! He was a perfect foil for Lomax, who shrewdly allowed him to record monologues as well as ballads and blues.

McTell recorded after World War II for a variety of labels, most notably Atlantic, having heard from their distributor in town that McTell had just recorded for a rival, Fred Mendelsohn's Regal label. McTell's final session was in 1956, completing a recording career which spanned three decades.

Stories about McTell were legion. Pete Lowry and I spent many hours following leads—usually pretty fruitless. McTell died in 1959, but people told us he had been seen at Curley Weaver's 1962 funeral, and in 1972 we were shown where he'd sung in a storefront church on Highland Avenue not so long before. He'd been sighted in countless places—probably all true, as he was an inveterate traveler. Buddy Moss told me how he followed McTell on the New York subway in awe of the blind man's unfailing "radar." McTell directed Lomax back to his hotel in his car, much to Lomax's surprise. People called him "ear-sighted," and there were many similar stories. I rather wish he hadn't been so well documented, imagining him still heading for Chicago or California.

Despite the prolific recording careers of Robert Hicks (Barbecue Bob), Blind Willie McTell, and Curley Weaver, the most influential Atlanta bluesman of the 1930s was undoubtedly Buddy Moss. His recording career began just short of his twentieth birthday—the Georgia Cotton Pickers sides of 1930—but he did not record under his own name until 1933. Over fifty titles were recorded by mid-1935, when he "got in trouble." By the time Moss went to jail he had replaced South Carolinian Josh White as the most influential southeastern bluesman, even joining him for duets on his final 1935 sessions. Then the emphasis moved farther north.

The southern field trips largely ended during the Depression, and it was cheaper for talent scouts to send artists to northern studios. When Vocalion persisted in

Blind Willie McTell is seen here with his wife, Kate, in Atlanta during the late 1920s.
ABOVE LEFT

McTell sits for an RCA Victor Records publicity shot in an Atlanta studio, about 1930. The original of this photograph was rescued from the trash bin of a New York City building moments before being consigned to oblivion.
ABOVE RIGHT

recording in the field during the mid-1930s, many of its masters were ruined by engineering mishaps, including the entire McTell–Piano Red session of 1936 in Augusta, Georgia.

Joshua Daniel White had an early upbringing in the blues, enough for him in later years to turn his back and be active in social awareness movements, imbuing his music with pointed social comment. At the age of eight he was lead boy for a blind singer from his home town of Greenville, South Carolina. On their first tour he witnessed a lynching and was later beaten up and jailed in Florida, having been mistaken for a fugitive. He was hired out by his mother to other blind singers, recording with one, Joe Taggart, in Chicago when he was fourteen. His fast finger-picking style both epitomized the music of his region and became a role model for future bluesmen. More than one learned "Low Cotton," an early example of his social commentary, by heart. His first session under his own name was in 1932, and by the time of his last session as a rural bluesman (1936), he had released over sixty titles. Symbolically, his last coupling was "No More Ball and Chain" and "Silicosis Is Killin' Me," about a coal miner's disease, although he had no firsthand knowledge of it.

White settled in New York and rapidly became part of the leftist social-protest school following a stint at the Café Society Downtown, where he was earning $750 a week in 1947. After his early experience with southern life, one can hardly blame him for his politics. His success on the folk circuit in later years was the envy of Buddy Moss, whose postwar promise had evaporated in bitterness and recrimination.

In the summer of 1936, as Buddy Moss went to jail and Josh White to New York, yet another blind bluesman came onto centerstage. Fulton Allen, living then in Durham, North Carolina, came to the American Record Company's studios to record his second batch of sessions—his first having been the previous summer. By a remarkable coincidence, Allen, Josh White, and Buddy Moss were to be linked by another of the white southern scouts upon whom the major record companies depended to no small degree. Indeed, James Baxter Long, a store manager from the Carolinas, almost single-handedly reshaped the evolution of blues in the Southeast during the half-dozen years before World War II. While Long also "discovered" the best-known of all southeastern duets, Brownie McGhee and Sonny Terry, and perhaps the supreme guitarist of all (once Blind Blake had passed), Gary Davis, but Allen and Long were inextricably linked.

Long became interested in folk music while managing a store in Kinston, North Carolina, in 1934. Intrigued by the popularity of white accident ballads, usually concerning railroad mishaps, he decided, with the aid of an enterprising local newspaperwoman, to write his own about a wreck at nearby Lumberton. Armed with the song, Long held a singing contest to find a group capable of recording it for ARC, whose 78s he sold in the store. The Cauley Family recorded "Lumberton Wreck," and Long was in the record business.

Long was also impressed by the way that black farmers would come to his store and sing the first few lines of blues songs, expecting him to know what they were, so that they could buy the record from him. A natural entrepreneur, he quickly came to learn which was which, and to like the music. Josh White's "Low Cotton" prompted him to run a black quartet competition. The winning group was one of the finest from the Southeast, Mitchell's Christian Singers, who (thankfully) recorded in depth. Blues was recorded at that session, but never released. With two recording groups under his belt and a distinct liking for his new activity, Long was fortunate to be promoted to manager of a store in Durham, a city that held abundant blues talent. It was only a matter of time before the two connected.

Traveling round the tobacco salerooms to promote goods in his store, Long heard Fulton Allen singing and playing guitar and told him to come to the store. Allen arrived with two other guitarists, Gary Davis and an albino whom everyone knew as Red. Some months later, when Long's daughter was on summer vacation from school and he was able to take leave from his job, his family, together with their three newly discovered bluesmen, headed for the ARC studios and their English-born A&R man, Art Satherly, in New York.

Arguably, Fulton Allen was to become the best-known and probably most influential of all bluesmen from the Southeast. As Blind Boy Fuller—he became blind about eight years before he began to record—he cut 130 titles, all of which were released in the six years before his premature death in 1941, at the age of thirty-three. His "Step It Up and Go," from his penultimate sessions in March 1940, became a barometer for country bluesmen everywhere. When white researchers were investigating the music in the 1960s and 1970s no one with a pretense to playing country blues failed to know the tune.

Even more than Blind Lemon's "One Dime Blues" had for an earlier generation, Fuller's "Step It Up and Go" epitomized his era for eager-to-learn youngsters. It also neatly encapsulates the music of the region: joyous, finger-picked dance tunes, clearly sung. This might not be the moment to stress that a significant percentage of blues is actually good-time, Saturday-night dance music rather than blues as Art.

Willie Perryman, also known as Piano Red and Doctor Feelgood, made a number of recordings with Blind Willie McTell in 1936. Unfortunately, malfunctioning recording equipment ruined the entire session.

Someone once said that being black was wanting to be in Harlem on a Saturday night. All single-line statements carry an element of the inaccurate, but a high number of Fuller's blues were none other than black rural dance music—and they sold.

More remarkable than Fuller's recordings made at his first session were those made by Gary Davis. Blind from birth, like McTell and Jefferson, he was stubbornly mobile. His first coupling was blues, and he backed Fuller on a few titles, but when next he came to record under his own name he refused to sing blues and sang only religious songs. They are tough and uncompromising. Sadly, he fell out with Long, who was never able to persuade him to record again before World War II. A stunning example of his guitar work can be heard on "I Saw The Light," where the vocal is by Red. Ordained and credited as Reverend Gary Davis, he was to record voluminously from the 1950s on, and almost every release can be acquired with satisfaction.

In 1936 Fuller made sessions on his own, but his first recordings of 1937 again included Red (on washboard) and another guitarist, Floyd Council. Along with the South Carolina songster/bluesman Pink Anderson, Council's name would be preserved in the history of popular music in the rock group Pink Floyd. Later, in 1937, a harmonica player began to appear on Fuller's records, Saunders Terrell, better known as Sonny Terry.

As a teenager, Terry suffered damage first to one eye and then the other, leaving him "like looking through a spider web." Instead of earning a living as his friends did—he would have farmed—he found himself thrust, like Fuller, into an alien world. It is no accident that many of the major figures from the Southeast were blind: Blake, McTell, Fuller, Terry, Davis. McTell and Davis spent brief spells in vocational blind schools, but Fuller balked at the notion. Some idea of the problems that beset Fuller and Davis during the 1930s in Durham were revealed when files from the state department of public welfare were located. If a musician was out of

work, he received limited welfare relief; if he worked, no matter for how little, he received no welfare payment. However, the welfare department staff was not hard hearted. One staff member recorded: "He admitted he had been out playing but wouldn't say where. . . . I urged him to play me a number. His ability as a guitarist is unbelievable. I have never heard better playing. . . . I wonder if he might be playing around some times to pick up a little change."

Fuller made his last recording session in June 1940—the usual dozen titles, but all on the same day. The disintegration of his voice can be heard on the prophetic "Night Rambling Woman": "My left side jumps and my flesh begin to crawl," he sang. It was not his first autobiographical comment by far, but it was his last. Some of his closest friends felt he should never have made the trip, as a month later he was in the hospital. After frequent hospital stays, he was finally sent home to die in peace—of a bladder infection—with his adoring wife, Cora Mae, in February 1941.

Joshua White—Pinewood Tom, "The Singing Christian"—was one of the very best of all East Coast Piedmont blues artists. He was a wonderful guitarist and singer whose musical approach typified the genre. In later years he cast off the mantle of blues artist to become the darling of folk enthusiasts in and around New York City.

*Blind Boy Fuller's manager
J. B. Long poses in front of his
Kingston, North Carolina, record
store for a 1934 newspaper photo.
This image was captioned: "5,606
records at one time. Largest ship-
ment ever received in a North
Carolina store."*

About the time of Fuller's last session, a competent young guitarist breezed into town, having worked his way over from Tennessee, where his father knew A. P. Carter of the famous Carter Family. A. P. was glad to collect from black songsters and traveled with this young guitarist's fellow Knoxville musician, Lesley Riddle. Walter Brown "Brownie" McGhee was to make his mark in New York during the war years, but J. B. Long, having seen his best-selling bluesman die, was quick to fill the gap with McGhee, even calling him "Blind Boy Fuller No. 2," which McGhee never did appreciate. Nonetheless, McGhee has always fairly acknowledged Long's role in his rise to fame and has never uttered a word to Long's detriment, something that cannot be said of all of Fuller's friends. McGhee came to town with his own harmonica player, but a year after the initial recording sessions he had teamed up with Sonny Terry to produce a duo that was synonymous with blues for a vast number of people. And that's no small achievement.

Also about this time, Long heard of the predicament of Buddy Moss, still in jail in Georgia. Eventually, Moss was paroled into Long's custody, moving to Long's house near Durham. Here he worked for Long for ten years. According to local bluesmen, Moss had a comfortable life there, and the Longs were devoted to him, although Mrs. Long found him moody. Moody he certainly was; proud and resentful, too. He must have possessed considerable restraint to remain a decade in that role. Local bluesmen met him, but none knew him well.

Late in 1941, Moss and McGhee went to New York to record separate sessions, though each appeared on some of the other's sides, too. If anything, Moss's performance skills were better. His solo version of "You Need A Woman" is magnificent.

Sadly, half a dozen titles were never released and, unlike other recordings from the period, have never turned up even in test form. Six weeks after his New York sessions, the Japanese Navy torpedo-bombed the battleship *Arizona* and Moss's career. The shortage (and, later, rationing) of shellac from which to press records and an American Federation of Musicians recording ban in 1942 marked the end of the recording industry as it had been known for a quarter of a century. For Moss it was a cruel blow.

Genial when it suited him, Moss could nonetheless be very difficult at times. Even the most loyal of local bluesmen, like Roy Dunn, found their friendship greatly challenged. A projected major comeback session cut for CBS in 1966 was never released, after which it became impossible to record him; while documenting blues in the Southeast in the 1970s, Pete Lowry spent an undue amount of his time trying. He and I both remember bad experiences, but none of ours can have been a patch on Moss's, and it was perhaps amazing that he gave us the time of day at all. I'd sooner remember him one sweaty July afternoon in 1969, legs crossed, finger-picking his well-worn but beautiful-sounding guitar, grinning to himself, while he let us eavesdrop on a song he'd written, "Chesterfield." I'm just sorry you never got to hear him.

Blind Boy Fuller plays one of his steel-bodied National guitars in one of two known photographs extant.

"First Time I Was Ever in Trouble"

We are fortunate that there was considerable recording activity without commercial constraints, allowing a variety of recordings over a long period. These noncommercial recordings were made mostly by two men, John A. Lomax, within the establishment, and Lawrence Gellert, outside it.

Lomax has yet to receive his just deserts in an assessment of his work in documenting black folk music throughout the southern states. He was not an easy man to get along with, but he had a keen ear for the genuine article. Harold Spivacke, one-time head of the Library of Congress Music Division, accompanied Lomax on a field-recording trip to a Virginia penal institution. Lomax had early on appreciated that traditions were likely to survive in jail longer than outside. In any case, the repositories could be located with ease. Lomax shrewdly left Spivacke enmeshed with the warden's black vocal quartet while he slipped away to record a stunning bluesman, Jimmie Strothers. Years later, when I spoke to Spivacke about this trip, I used the term blues "artist" to describe Strothers. "Artist!" Spivacke exploded. "He killed his wife with an axe!" Well, Blind Jimmie Strothers may have done just that, but listen to his "Goin' to Richmond."

Joshua White—a dapper twenty-two year old.

Lomax was far more shrewd an operator than his somewhat hesitant southern drawl might suggest, as he is briefly heard on recordings made for the Library of Congress Archive of American Folk Song. Keen to record black ballads (hence so many versions of "John Henry") he also asked inmates to sing about how they came to be in the penitentiary, and some of the most remarkable autobiographical blues were recorded. Jesse Wadley thus recorded "Alabama Prison Blues" in Atlanta's Bellwood Prison Camp in 1934, suggesting that it might not have been a spontaneous creation, but Blind Joe's "When I Lie Down," caught the same year in Raleigh's Central Prison, was clearly fresh. "The first time I was ever in trouble was in 1934," he sang, with such conviction on December 19. "I got you charged here, Joseph, with bigamy," he has his judge say. It just *has* to be true! Hear also a guitarist who succeeded in emulating Blind Blake.

Contra F-141.		DATE MADE
EXCLUSIVE		1936 11'19
BLIND BOY FULLER		1937
DEPT. American - Race		2'11
LANG.		
CLASS.		
CODE		2'23
DATED	April 30, 1936	8'27
TERM	1 year	9¢8
COMMENCING	April 30, 1936	12-18
ENDING	April 30, 1937	
		12016
RECORDINGS	1 session 12 sel. or more	1-31
ROYALTY		4-6
ADV.-ON-ACCT.		
FLAT PAYM'T	$100.00	12-20
GUARANTEE		12-29
OPTION	1 year	
NOTICE	30 days	
KS:		

This recording contract summary for Blind Boy Fuller shows that he earned $100 for a day's worth of performances—that is, twelve selections "or more." ABOVE

A fascinating offshoot of John Lomax's field trips came in 1935 when his son, Alan, decided to follow in his footsteps. Together with a white professor of English from New York, Mary Elizabeth Barnicle, and the black writer Zora Neale Hurston, Lomax recorded many black performers on the idyllic Georgia Sea Islands north of Brunswick. The location was no accident. Robert Winslow Gordon had been based in nearby Darien when he recorded hundreds of cylinders of folksongs (no accompanied blues) in the spring and summer of 1926. As Lomax wrote me in 1983: "In those days blues were one of the best recorded musics. So we seldom bothered to record those blues singers that turned up. We were interested in the older level of secular music." Be that as it may, they did record some blues, but their documentation of the dance music or guitar "jooking" pieces was crucial in piecing together the fabric of the

J. B. Long gave Brownie McGhee Blind Boy Fuller's brown steel-bodied National after the artist's death. One Friday, finding himself short of funds, McGhee pawned the guitar. On the following Monday, he returned to redeem his pledge and get the guitar back, only to find that the guitar had been sold. It has never surfaced. RIGHT

The instrument of choice for Blind Reverend Gary Davis was a Gibson Super-400. Davis was in large measure responsible for making this instrument a popular big seller for Gibson.

music of the region. That they seldom bothered to record "those blues singers that turned up" manifestly proves they existed—and in an area from which no bluesmen were ever recorded, before or since.

Hurston had conducted research earlier in Florida and probably located bluesmen. With Lomax, she also traveled to Orlando, where they recorded a most enigmatic bluesman, Gabriel Brown. Two long slide-guitar pieces, "Education Blues" and "Talking in Sevastopol" (a slide-guitar tuning), show Brown at his best. His career is worth following at length, because it warns us not to draw inaccurate conclusions from scattered materials, but also suggests that other factors, at present hidden from us, must be tucked away in improbable locations for future exposure. Hurston probably modeled her Bubber Brown in *Mules and Men* upon him.

Brown, then twenty-five years old, had graduated from Florida's Agricultural and Mechanical College and studied medicine, but, coming from a poor family, had to take jobs on the side. In 1934 he represented Florida at the National Folk Festival in St. Louis, where he won first prize as the outstanding singer of folk songs and as a guitarist. This information comes from a note located among the effects of New

A studio portrait of Sonny Terry, blind harmonica virtuoso from North Carolina.

York–based music publisher and record company owner, Joe Davis. Davis had record-ed Gabriel Brown at a studio session in August 1943 and wrote to Brown, then living in Asbury Park, New Jersey, in November 1944 offering a renewal contract for "anoth-er year . . . and you will notice that for the second year I have again increased your recording fee." How many remarkable facts are tucked away in those sentences!

Is there somewhere written documentation of Brown's selection to represent Florida, his travel to St. Louis, and his entry into and winning of at least one class at the festival? Unanticipated written sources may well hold valuable clues for future research. If Hurston was involved, it does not appear in her biography. It was known that in New York Brown acted and performed in stage shows written by Hurston, and Lomax suggested that she might have brought him to New York to perform in a "bal-lad opera based in a turpentine camp," but she did not commence writing that (*Polk County*) until 1944, by which time Brown had recorded for Davis, and was holder of union card 3253 from Local 802 of the American Federation of Musicians—one of the

most difficult unions to break into. Davis's contract also stated that for the "second year" he had increased recording fees, so the first year in which fees had been increased must have been 1943. In that case, they must have been increased from an initial agreed fee in 1942. Presumably, then, the August 1943 recording session was not the first.

Lomax was correct in that Hurston hired Brown in 1944 because he was an actor; he had been a member of the Federal Arts Theatre since 1935, when Lomax and Hurston recorded him in Florida. His director was Orson Welles. In 1939 Brown appeared over Cincinnati radio with Richard Huey, whose gospel group, the Jubileers, was issued on disk by Davis in the early 1940s. Brown worked for U.S.O. shows during World War II.

The extent of the recordings Lawrence Gellert made in the field during the 1920s and 1930s only came to light in the mid-1980s, when they were placed in a university archive for safe keeping. Gellert was unique in that he recorded black folk-songs specifically as protest songs. Afforded special insight because he was living with a black woman in North Carolina, he also preserved the complete anonymity of his informants. He never once wrote down a name, recording dates are subject to question, and the locations are seldom given in greater detail than by state. Asked to sing without fear or pulling punches, Gellert's performers provided a core of blues lyrics with no parallel. "We Don't Get No Justice in Atlanta" and "Gonna Leave Atlanta" are searing, tough social commentary. The singers are fine, reminiscent of those whom Lomax found in Texas, but Gellert often recorded guitarists, too. Since no one is named, perhaps a few of those unrecorded bluesmen actually were recorded.

Gellert sometimes recorded from chain gangs, but whereas Lomax (in the Southeast) recorded in penitentiaries, Gellert recorded wherever he found his sources. Of socialist leaning, Gellert was born to Hungarian immigrants. One brother had been murdered in jail awaiting trial as a conscientious objector during World War I; his brother Hugo was involved with the socialist magazine *New Masses*, where Gellert found an outlet for lyric transcripts of his field recordings. Nancy Cunard included some for her anthology, *Negro*, in 1934. Even now, Gellert's work has gone largely unremarked. Two record companies issued albums from the startling Gellert collection, thanks to folklorist Bruce Harrah-Conforth, but they were only preaching to the converted.

By the 1940s, the only noncommercial recordings made of black folk music in the Southeast were recorded at Fort Valley, Georgia. The Library of Congress no longer turned its eye in this direction, although we are fortunate that copies of some (but not all) recordings made in the 1940s at Fort Valley were sent to the Archive of American Folk Song. In 1941, care had been taken to invite three major white investigators: the sociologist pair from the University of North Carolina at Chapel Hill, Howard W. Odum and Guy Benton Johnson, who were the earliest analysts of blues in the region, and Alan Lomax. None of them came. John W. Work came from Nashville's Fisk University, and Willis Lawrence James from Atlanta's Spellman College. W. C. Handy came as "Chief Judge"—the role he'd held the previous, introductory, year—accompanied by the white pianist J. Russel Robinson, a member of the Original Dixieland Jazz Band in 1919, who managed Handy's music-publishing business and had long been involved with black musicians.

It is to Work we owe a debt for preserving some of this music on disk, and for proving conclusively that the folk music sought out and judged "best" by this panel was indeed genuine grassroots music. Later, possibly inspired by the presence of

Handy, performers turned up to play "Stardust" on trumpet, but in 1941 the winners were Gus Gibson's "Milk Cow Blues" with delicious slide guitar, Allison Mathis' "Bottle Up and Go," just a year after Blind Boy Fuller's classic "Step It Up and Go," and the Smith band's "Fort Valley Blues," to say nothing of the highly individual songster and rack-harmonica player/guitarist Buster "Buzz" Ezell, who seems never to have missed a show until, presumably, his death.

Recordings also survived from 1943 at the Library of Congress, of which two were by a harmonica player from Cordele, Georgia. In 1959 Buster Brown was to record "Fannie Mae" in New York for the gutsy, pioneering, black-owned Fire label, hitting Number One on the national R & B charts, where it stayed for twenty-five weeks before crossing over onto the pop charts, ensuring that the bouncy harp sounds of the Southeast could be heard everywhere in the early 1960s.

It is also clear from publications in the mid-1940s, and from interviews with musicians, that recordings were made at most festivals, even if they seem not to have survived. Pete Lowry and I located Fort Valley guitarist Jack Hudson, who had recorded "Chain Gang Blues" at the festival in 1943; his uncle was even able to quote the first lines of the song, which I checked against a lyric transcript made at the time of recording. Two years earlier we had located washboard player Arthur "Popcorn" Glover, whose only claim to having recorded was once at the Fort Valley festival.

The Smith band's leader, C. W. Smith, was known locally as Blind Billy, but around Atlanta, where he was a good friend of McTell's in the 1950s, he was Blind Cliff. Harmonica player Jesse Stroller, who recorded in 1941, teamed up in 1945 with guitarist Charlie Smith, who had appeared solo before. One 1936 coupling from the ill-fated Augusta, Georgia, session in which the McTell/Piano Red sides were ruined was by a guitar-harmonica duet, Smith and Harper. Could they have been Charlie Smith and Jesse Stroller, a harper?

By the early 1950s, the festival was fading, ultimately killed by scornful black students who ridiculed the older performers. One string band that appeared in those early years was led by fiddler Elbert Freeman. Georgia folklorist John Burrison recorded the band in 1967. The line between recording and not was a very thin one.

"TOO MUCH COMPETITION"

From August 1942 until September 1943, the American Federation of Musicians recording ban prevented new commercial recordings. Doubtless the scene would have changed anyway, with the wartime restrictions on the availability of shellac, but the major companies balked at the notion of paying a royalty to the AFM. Decca was the first to relent, followed swiftly by Capitol, but Victor and Columbia refused to follow. Almost immediately, they lost their preeminence in the field of race recordings as a myriad of minor labels—some black owned—sprang up. The two majors surrendered in November 1944, but by that time they were out of step. Their management, unable to appreciate that new social forces were afield during and after the upheavals of World War II, failed to catch the new wave of black consciousness and increased wealth.

Most independent labels ("indies") looked to gospel or rhythm and blues, but the prewar blues scene was not utterly forgotten, particularly by the two latecomers, though neither of these looked to the Southeast. Instead, Chicago became the undisputed Mecca for postwar blues. Superficially, the regionalism that had characterized blues in the Southeast before 1942 seemed to have vanished during the war. As the blues scene generally shifted emphasis, with the introduction of electrification, reeds, and horns, it began to be more obvious that a massive change had taken place. In the decade following the Wall Street crash of 1929, there had been little shift in the overall blues pattern, although the roots of R & B had clearly become visible. In the next decade, however, the shift was enormous. For the Southeast, it was effectively terminal.

Nonetheless, viewed without prejudice, there *were* commercial recordings of bluesmen from the Southeast, and it is fair to state that hints of regionalism in blues remained more apparent in the New York metropolitan region longer than else-where—except, perhaps, Texas. Brownie McGhee and Sonny Terry surfaced on a slew of New York–New Jersey labels: Savoy, Alert, Disc, Sittin' In With, Jax, Derby, Harlem, Old Town, Red Robin, Grammercy, Jackson . . . McGhee appeared with his brother, Granville "Stick" McGhee, on the growing Atlantic label and Decca, which released "Baby Baby Blues" in 1947—as fine a blues from the Southeast as you could hope to find.

The McGhee Brothers, "Stick" and "Brownie," jam.

Gabriel Brown and Rochelle French play for the Library of Congress, Eatonville, Florida, June 1935.

Alden "Tarheel Slim" Bunn, from North Carolina, recorded "Too Much Competition" for Bobby Robinson's sharp little indie, Red Robin, in 1954, giving us an excellent idea of how Blind Boy Fuller might have sounded had he survived. He would only have been in his mid-forties. Joe Davis was recording Gabriel Brown at length; some thirty titles were released at the time. The final session by this solo acoustic bluesman was in 1952. Alec Seward and Louis Hayes, under numerous pseudonyms, including Guitar Slim and Jelly Belly, and the Back Porch Boys, cut fine regional blues for Tru-Blue, Apollo, and even MGM. The Newark-based Manor/Regis labels recorded superb bluesmen like Boy Green and Skoodle Dum Doo and Sheffield (Skoodle Dum Doo being Seth Richard, who recorded in 1928 for Columbia). Dennis McMillon recorded a stunning four-track session for Regal to provide bus fare back to North Carolina. Ed Harris, also from that state, cut many titles under a host of pseudonyms, including Carolina Slim, for Savoy and King in the 1950s. And the list goes on.

Recordings in the Southeast were extremely rare, and one just barely savors the pattern of persistence of the regional style in the immigrant blues of northern cities. One significant exception was the Philadelphia-based Gotham label, whose owner, Ivin Ballen, epitomized the generation of postwar entrepreneurs. Almost without exception, these white music-biz hustlers—who had an ear for the music and enjoyed it—spread their nets wide and, in so doing, caught some excellent bluesmen. Sonny Terry and Brownie McGhee recorded for Gotham, as did Dan Pickett, a superlative performer in the style of the Southeast and high on my list of most exciting bluesmen ever. Rather too lightly dismissed by some as derivative, he was no more so than, say, Titian or Breughel. Ballen had also recorded another excellent assimilator of the southeastern blues style, Alabama guitarist Ralph Willis, for his 20th Century label. Willis also cut several sessions in New York, mostly with Brownie

McGhee in accompaniment. Ballen even recorded and released one local bluesman, the improbably named Doug Quattlebaum.

The obscure Orchid label recorded one prewar bluesman, Sonny Jones, a friend of Blind Boy Fuller's—a 78 rare enough to kill for. Guitarist Marylin Scott recorded gospel music under the name of Mary DeLoach and sang with the tough R & B band of Johnny Otis, but in 1945 she had recorded for the embryonic Free label in Charlotte and later cut one stunning blues coupling, playing slide guitar, for Lance. "I Got What My Daddy Likes" has uncompromising lyrics, but it is really her delivery that generates murmurs from her male audience, not always of embarrassment. She plays her fine, blues-tinged guitar on some of her gospel renditions, but if only she had recorded more straight blues.

The southeastern blues style lived on in recognizable form into the 45-rpm era with Charles Walker, Lee Roy Little, Johnny Ace, and Larry Johnson, but by this time the music was regarded, by the few people who cared, as dead and gone. Record collectors entered the scene, concerned with artifacts, but these early collectors were also interested in more than just the music; intellectuals in the best sense, they were also interested in what lay behind the music. An interest in the social roots of the music grew into a desire to see the music documented. The early collectors were in closer harmony with the concepts of Gellert and Lomax than were the brash, self-made producers of the post-AFM ban.

These concepts gave rise to a series of documentary releases on Moses Asch's Folkways label, such as those compiled by Harry Smith and Frederic Ramsey, Jr. To those of us who came along a while later and were not among the batch trading Charley Patton 78s for three dollars, this was how we became aware of the breadth of black music in the United States.

"Cryin' for the Carolines"

The earliest preoccupation with blues documentation in the 1950s concentrated on the Deep South. Ramsey's fieldtrips were to Alabama, Louisiana, and Mississippi, as if nothing significant existed in, say, Georgia. In fairness, one can only do so much; I never reached Florida during my field trips to the Southeast, but then the Guggenheim was not backing me. Nor was anyone else. For such reasons, early documentation took place outside the Southeast.

Samuel B. Charters saw his *Country Blues* published in 1959, and written documentation of blues moved up a gear. I received Paul Oliver's *Blues Fell This Morning* for a Christmas present in 1960, and suddenly the music I had on a few albums became more accessible. He set the music in a social and historical context. Oliver's 1960 field trip through the Deep South with California collector/enthusiast/emergent record producer Chris Strachwitz kicked open more doors, making it possible for others to contemplate traveling south. Sam Charters recorded Pink Anderson and Baby Tate in South Carolina in the early 1960s, and we were able to hear this music on the Bluesville albums produced by Kenneth Goldstein (now Professor of Folklore at the University of Pennsylvania), who had an abiding interest in field work.

Acting independently, George Mitchell began recording in rural Georgia. He had been recording bluesmen in the Mississippi Delta during 1967, but the following year he moved to Georgia, near the Alabama state line. One Sunday, he and his wife Cathy set off to see if they could locate any local musicians. Expecting little success,

Buddy Moss relaxes at home during the early 1960s.

227

Buz Ezell on guitar and harp.

they "never visited a town where we were not led to at least one blues musician."
Mitchell continued to research blues in central and southwestern Georgia for years,
producing fascinating festivals for local consumption, like the Georgia Grassroots
Festival in Atlanta, which helped make whites aware of fast-vanishing musical traditions, black and white.

In 1969 I was planning to travel through the Southeast, junking for 78s during
my summer vacation from teaching. I'd had success the previous summer in Georgia
and was thankful that, this time, blues collector-enthusiast Peter B. Lowry came
along, too. His Rover 2000 was a distinct improvement on the Greyhound bus, even
if it lacked air-conditioning. In Atlanta he suggested we should look up Buddy Moss,
whom he'd met at a gig in New York. This was done without the object of research,

which had driven these earlier enthusiasts, but we had our Godrich & Dixon along to ask questions, and we had a good working knowledge of what had been recorded from southeastern bluesmen. Moss mentioned that he had lived in North Carolina for a while, naming two bluesmen brothers, Richard and Willie Trice, whom he thought lived near Hillsboro, not far from Durham. They had made one session for Decca in 1937.

The follow-up is worth description at some length. Returning north, we pulled in one night close to Chapel Hill, just south of Durham. There was a spare day on my itinerary before my charter flight back to England, so we decided to go to Hillsboro to see if we could trace Moss's blues-playing friends. We had names, a town, and a connection to the 1940s. Thirty years afterward, our thinking was purely historical. Three hours after we arrived in Hillsboro our lives had been transformed.

Buz Ezell (left), Buster Brown, and Jack Hudson: three men, two guitars, two harps.

Mebane, North Carolina, 1939.
The posters on the side of the
building advertise minstrel shows.

Assuming that one or the other of the Trice brothers might have died, we checked death records in the courthouse and found a death certificate for a Willie Trice: black, a laborer, and in his sixties. Perhaps we could find the brother, Richard. The postmaster knew no such name, but suggested we drive down to Chapel Hill, where the Trices lived. The postmaster there knew of no Richard Trice, so we checked the listings for Trice in the phone book. The fifth Trice we found suggested we contact Thurmon Atkins, who ran the "colored" cab company in town. Atkins was manning his cab company phone, but was happy to direct us to his old school friend, Richard Trice, who was working in Durham. While we were at it, did we want him to try to locate another old-time musician who had also recorded blues? There and then, in a bizarre three- or four-way conversation with his drivers and various clients, and after calls to all and sundry, he came up with an address in nearby Sanford for Floyd Council, Blind Boy Fuller's recording partner of 1937. Thirty minutes later, we were talking to a bemused Richard Trice in the gas station where he worked. Before the end of the afternoon we were talking to his brother, Willie. A different Willie Trice accounted for the death certificate we found in Hillsboro.

This day's investigations encompassed a number of issues. The music and the musicians were still there, and, with luck, they could be uncovered, but that luck came with perseverance, enthusiasm, and expense. That they were there was beyond doubt; that few gave a damn was just as certain. The one real constant during research in the 1960s and early 1970s was that the Establishment could not have cared less.

For the next five years, Pete Lowry (sometimes accompanied by me) conducted extensive fieldwork in northern Georgia and the Carolinas, mainly around Durham. The vast bulk of Lowry's recordings have yet to be heard. Some material was released on his own Trix label: Frank Edwards and Roy Dunn from Atlanta, Peg Leg Sam and Henry Johnson from South Carolina, Pernell Charity, Willie Trice, and Guitar Shorty from North Carolina. (Edwards and Trice recorded before World War II.) It is a veritable treasure trove, and if this is an example of where research *was* undertaken, albeit after persistent and unstinting effort, then an idea of what has been lost through apathy and obstinacy can easily be imagined.

Research in northern North Carolina continued through the efforts of Kip Lornell and Glenn Hinson, and both shrewdly garnered Establishment support. Hinson was one of a group of Chapel Hill enthusiasts who helped promote the Durham Blues Festival and instigated support from the state's Department of Cultural Resources. Thanks to Roddy Moore at the Blue Ridge Institute in Ferrum, Virginia, Lornell undertook a remarkable documentation on album of the music of the state. It is salutory to think, when today we have blues festivals in umpteen countries, let alone umpteen states in the United States, that in March 1973, the first *ever* blues festival was held in the South—if we exclude Fort Valley. Thanks to the student union at the University of North Carolina and Dan Patterson of the Folklore Department there, a most successful little festival was held over three days. People listened to blues from southeastern musicians when they had no idea there ever had been any such music! It really wasn't long ago, and yet the fabric has changed dramatically in the twenty years since then. The day that George Mitchell could go out on a Sunday and know he'd locate at least one person who could play blues in rural Georgia, or when I could drive from Chapel Hill and within thirty minutes talk to one of half a dozen blues guitarists, has long gone.

Understandably, blues in the Southeast continued to evolve and, like black music almost everywhere throughout the United States (with the exception of the zydeco belt), it fell into the national pattern. Regionalism, if it ever properly existed, was at an end. This is not to deny that a handful of practitioners remained, undertaking State Department tours or playing white festivals and gigs. John Jackson, who did record Willie Walker's "South Carolina Rag," John Cephus, and Archie Edwards embodied the spirit and style of the region, while Etta Baker and Algia Mae Hinton proved that women were just as capable of retaining the musical thread of their background. Somehow, Hinton's fame never spread far from her North Carolina home, but do try to hear her music.

Times change, and music follows. At the time of the death of the eccentric but undeniably brilliant Guitar Shorty from North Carolina, a friend remarked that she would be glad when she could no longer hear music like his, as it would mean that the social context that gave rise to it was gone. Perhaps that was simplistic, but it made me wonder why we had investigated it in the first place. I don't have an answer, but I'd like to think that one enduring truth is that music was recorded that will give lasting pleasure to people who could not hear it at the time, and to others who were unwilling to listen. Anyway, the people who made the music enjoyed doing so.

Jimmie Rodgers
America's Blue Yodeler
Victor Artist

A LIGHTER SHADE
OF BLUE

WHITE COUNTRY BLUES

CHARLES WOLFE

◆◆◆

It was a rainy Friday morning in early November, and at the temporary recording studio on Peachtree Street in downtown Atlanta, engineers were busy checking their equipment for another day's work. Frank Walker, who was in charge of Columbia's field recording unit, and his assistant Bill Brown, a small, sharp-tongued man who was Walker's liaison with the local talent, were looking over the list of performers scheduled for the 4th. The team had been in town for a week, and they had already recorded some fifty-five masters; today they hoped to get at least twenty more. Though the idea of taking a portable unit into various southern cities to get more authentic examples of blues, gospel, and hillbilly music was still new, it was already proving its worth. A couple of years before, Columbia, like most other major labels, had created a separate series of "race" recordings and another of "hillbilly" music. Columbia referred to the former as its 14000 series, and the latter as the 15000 series ("Old Familiar Tunes"). A couple of hundred records had been issued in each series, many of them selling surprisingly well. But, though the music was segregated when it came out on disk, in the field it was a different story. As Walker later recalled, "If you were recording in Texas, well, you might have a week in which you recorded your country music; cowboy music thrown in and a little Spanish music from across the border. . . . And the next week might be devoted to so-called 'race music,' because they both came from the same area, and with the same general ideas."

Today's schedule in Atlanta was even more varied. First up was a set of sweet string-band sides by McMichen's Melody Man; next came a set of blues by Charlie Lincoln (Laughing Charlie Hicks), the brother of "Barbecue Bob" Hicks, one of Columbia's more successful blues singers. Brown had approved six songs for Lincoln, including "Hard Luck Blues" and "Chain Gang Blues." After lunch came Riley

Jimmie Rodgers, "the Blue Yodeler"—single most influential artist in the history of country music. CHAPTER OPENER

Puckett, the blind yodeler and singer who had become the best-known country artist in the 15000 series. Finally, there were the Allen Brothers, Lee and Austin. They were something quite different.

Walker had recorded them the previous spring, and their release of "Salty Dog Blues," issued a couple of months earlier, was selling very well. (It would eventually sell around 18,000 copies, making it a modest hit by 1920s standards.) Although it was called a blues, and although it bore some relation to the version of "Salty Dog" recorded by the venerable bluesman Papa Charlie Jackson, it didn't sound much like the classic country blues Walker was familiar with. Buoyed by Austin's vocal solo, propelled by a tenor banjo, kazoo, and guitar, it bounced along at a brisk tempo, full of jivey patter, asides, and hey hey heys. Nonetheless, it was selling, and the Allens seemed to have a lot of other pieces like it. Today they were scheduled for four songs,

Riley Puckett was as much at home singing ballads and "heart" songs as he was playing guitar in a host of string bands. RIGHT

ELECTRICALLY RECORDED
LICENSED BY MANUFACTURER ONLY FOR
NON-COMMERCIAL USE ON PHONOGRAPHS
IN HOMES

IN A LITTLE GYPSY TEA ROOM
Riley Puckett
Singing with guitar and violin
M-4760-B

MONTGOMERY WARD

three of which were called blues: "Chattanooga Blues," "Coal Mine Blues," and "Laughin' and Cryin' Blues."

After lunch, the two young Allens appeared in the studio. They didn't fit the stereotype of blues singers. They looked like a couple of well-mannered college students, dressed in double-breasted suits, Austin's cowlick drooping over his left eye, instruments carefully tuned. And they were young. Lee was only twenty-one, Austin (who did most of the singing) twenty-six. They had been born on Monteagle Mountain, about fifty miles north of Chattanooga. Lee had even attended the prestigious St. Andrews prep school there, at about the same time as James Agee did—the famed writer who would produce the classic work on Depression America, *Let Us Now Praise Famous Men*. The Allens had grown up listening to the old ballads and sentimental songs their mother sang, but they heard little of the blues until they had grown up and moved on down to Chattanooga. That town was hardly a blues center—though it had produced Bessie Smith—but the Allens did get a chance to hear guitarist May Bell, who performed on riverboats in the area, and the busking team of Evans and McClain, who were later to record as the Two Poor Boys. They were fascinated and soon created their own particular style of the blues. Now, on November 4, 1927, they were ready for the next chapter of their recording career.

The Allen Brothers, Austin and Lee.

They waited for the engineer to turn on the little green light, and the Allens launched into take one of what they thought was their best new song, "Chattanooga Blues":

> Oh I thought I heard my baby cry,
> Wow wow wow-wow, wow wow wow-wow,
> Thought I heard my baby cry,
> Oh she cried like she never cried before.

The racist caricatures were par for the course in 1927, when Austin and Lee Allen cut "Laughin' and Cryin' Blues" for Columbia.

The lyrics were hardly original or even evocative, but Austin's strong, heavily accented voice carried them through. Lee took a break, forging a raggy, infectious kazoo solo. "Percolate, mama, percolate," urged Austin. There were a few more topical references to give the commonplace stanzas some sense of identity: references to Chattanooga's hospitality, and to the "lock and dam" of the Tennessee River. Then the yellow light went on in the studio, and the brothers wound down. That take was history.

After a couple of hours, the Allens finished their four recordings, and left the studio. On their way out, Walker gave them the monthly catalog supplement to the new Columbia releases, showing them that Columbia 15175, their "Salty Dog Blues," was featured on the new list. The Allens left pleased, their dreams of a record career a good deal stronger. They returned to their circuit of radio broadcasts and theater dates around Chattanooga, and to their work with rural medicine shows. Walker, for his part, didn't think much of two of the songs cut that day, but he judged that "Chattanooga Blues" had as much of a chance of hitting well as "Salty Dog." He packed the wax masters for shipment to New York and went on with his session.

Then something odd happened. Columbia's New York office, overwhelmed by the dozens of masters Walker was shipping up, familiar with neither southern accents nor music, listened to the Allens' sides and decided the pair was black. Accordingly, their next coupling, "Chattanooga Blues" and "Laughin' and Cryin' Blues," was issued on the 14000 Race series (14266). It was rushed out on December

Eck Robertson was country music's first recorded instrumentalist.

20, 1927, just six weeks after the session. Back in Chattanooga, the Allens were overjoyed at how soon their new record was out—until they noticed it was in what the local record dealer called the Race Series. They frantically wired Walker to ask him to correct the mistake before it went any further, but over six thousand records had already been pressed, and there was not much he could do. The brothers then contacted a local attorney, who initiated on their behalf a $250,000 lawsuit against Columbia for damaging their reputations.

The suit got Walker to thinking that he might be able to issue the record in the 15000 series as well as the 14000 series. The Allens decided to go to the spring sessions in Atlanta, which went off well enough, but, after a final talk with Walker, the brothers decided to sever their ties with Columbia. A few weeks later, they dropped the lawsuit and signed with Victor.

The Allens recorded a total of thirty-six releases (seventy-two songs) on Columbia, Victor, and Vocalion. They became known for their topical blues, such as "Chain Store Blues" (a diatribe against early supermarket chains), "Tiple Blues" (about a coal-mining camp in Lynch, Kentucky), "Roll Down the Line" (derived from the convict-lease system of the 1890s), "Price of Cotton Blues," and (for Victor in 1930) "Jake Walk Blues"—about an epidemic of palsy caused by drinking Jamaica Ginger during the height of Prohibition. The record sold over twenty thousand copies, making it one of Victor's best sellers for the year. Their version of "A New Salty Dog" also sold well, staying in print on Bluebird and Montgomery Ward reissues well into the 1930s. In the latter half of their career, which ended in 1934, the Allens also developed a taste for the rowdy, double-entendre blues similar to the kind of stuff turned out by groups like the Hokum Boys. These included "Slide, Daddy, Slide," "Pile-Drivin' Papa," "Shake It, Ida, Shake It," "Warm Knees Blues," and "Misbehavin' Mama." Their version of "(Mama Don't Allow) No Low Down Hanging Around" (1930), with its well-known line, "Come here mama, just look at Kate,/ She's doing her loving in a Cadillac Eight," sold well and was copied by other singers. But the peak of the Allens' creativity, 1930–32, happened to coincide with the worst years of the Depression, and their later records simply had no chance. "Shanghai Rooster Blues" sold only 3,500 copies in 1930, and "Price of Cotton Blues" sold a meager 2,700. Many of the later Victors sold fewer than 2,000 copies—no worse than other releases in the series, but not enough to support a career. After a stint in the theater, the brothers broke up, Austin staying in New York, Lee returning to Tennessee to work as an electrical contractor. After a final "reunion" session in 1934 for Vocalion-ARC in New York, in which they rerecorded some of their biggest hits, the brothers retired, never to perform together again.

The case of the Allen Brothers, while dramatic, was not all that unusual in the history of early country music. Just as white jazz bands eagerly tacked the label "blues" on almost any dance tune, early country artists were quick to add the "blues" suffix to a variety of songs of all type. Yet, although the major record companies maintained segregated series for blues and country recordings in the 1920s, and although racial dividing lines were generally well maintained, the field sessions that recorded the music were themselves quite integrated. Black songsters sat waiting next to white gospel quartets; black blues singers took their turns with white fiddle bands. The give and take between white and black music "in the field" was always greater than the segregated record series implied; what had upset the Allen brothers in their lawsuit was not so much that their music had been mistaken for the work of African-Americans, but that they themselves had been mistaken for blacks. "We were trying to get into vaudeville back then," recalled Lee Allen. "It would have hurt us in getting dates if people who didn't know us thought we were black." But the Allens were only one out of many hillbilly performers in the 1920s who knew what real blues was, who did not tack the label on to any song or tune, and though few of these performers tried to emulate authentic blues singers exactly (in the way, for instance, that white urban folksingers in the 1960s did), they found in the blues rich inspiration. As they adapted and reworked both material from the city blues and the more indigenous country blues, they soon forged their own version of the music: a genre called white blues. From 1925 to 1940, this genre defined itself as one of the most interesting—and most commercial—subtypes of early country music.

There were forms of blues in country music from its earliest days. Most historians agree that the first country instrumental was fiddler Eck Robertson's 1922 Victor cut of "Arkansas Traveler," and that the first real country vocal was Fiddlin' John

Fiddlin' John Carson, playing here with his daughter Rosa Lee (Moonshine Kate), did not record until he was fifty-five years old. Nevertheless, by the time his recording career was finished, he had more than 125 issued sides to his credit.

Henry Whitter

Carson's "Little Old Log Cabin in the Lane" for Okeh in 1923. We now know, however, that Virginia millhand Henry Whitter had recorded several sides for Okeh as early as March 1923, before Carson, and that one of these was "Lonesome Road Blues." The sides were issued only after Carson's sales had shown there was a market for such music, and "Lonesome Road Blues," coupled with "The Wreck on the Southern Old 97," was issued in March 1924, becoming one of the year's best-sellers. No one knows where Whitter learned "Lonesome Road Blues," with its famous opening line, "Going down the road feeling bad," or if, in fact, he had composed it himself. With its incessant guitar and high, nasal voice, Whitter's record sounded little like any black blues, but the song was in the standard blues form, and stanzas of it had apparently been circulating in black and white folk traditions. It became very popular, due in part to the success of "Old 97" on its flip side, and soon other singers like George Reneau were starting to cover it. (It remains a bluegrass standard even today.)

During the next couple of years, as record companies tried to get a handle on just what their new working-class southern audience wanted—and how the companies could find it—other pioneers of Whitter's generation included an occasional blues in their recorded repertoire. A few months after Whitter's first record was released, banjoist and singer Uncle Dave Macon traveled to New York to make his first sides for Vocalion. Macon was from rural middle Tennessee and had a huge repertoire that included a very large number of songs he had learned from black singers; in the middle of some of his later records (which were often designed as

Uncle Dave Macon, shown here broadcasting over radio station WSM with his son Dorris, was among the Grand Ole Opry's first generation of country music superstars. BELOW RIGHT

medleys in the vaudeville manner) he does passable imitations of a country blues
singer, a black preacher, and a gospel singer. But one of his earliest sides was "Hill
Billie Blues," a reworking of W. C. Handy's popular "Hesitation Blues." It was the
first song actually to use the word hillbilly in its title and was probably drawn from
the touring vaudeville act Macon had at the time, "Uncle Dave Macon and his
Hillbillies." Though he was to keep "Hesitation Blues" in his repertoire through his
later career and through his long stint as a star of the Grand Ole Opry, Macon later
dropped the references to "hillbilly" in the piece.

There were other isolated early blues hits by artists who never really tried to
specialize in the genre. One such was "Blue Ridge Mountain Blues," first recorded by
Riley Puckett, the Georgia singer, late in 1924; within a few months, all the major
companies rushed out cover versions by singers like Ernest Stoneman (Okeh),
Vernon Dalhart (Victor), and Uncle Dave Macon's back-up man, Sid Harkreader
(Vocalion). It, too, has survived into the modern era, a staple with bluegrass and
honky-tonk bands. There was Roba Stanley, a very young woman from north Georgia
who became the first woman soloist to sing on country records; in 1924 she had
done a surprisingly strong version of "All Night Long" for Okeh. Two members of the

*Ernest Stoneman, guitar, appears
in a sober pose with one of his
earlier groups, "The Dixie
Mountaineers."*

One of the very best of all white slide-guitar players, Frank Hutchison brought to his recordings a decidedly African-American approach to the blues.

popular radio string band the Hill Billies recorded an influential and moving instrumental called "Bristol Tennessee Blues" for Vocalion in 1926. Though issued under the name the Hill Billies, the disk featured the fiddling of Fred Roe, a native of upper east Tennessee. It resembles a country blues more than anything else recorded during this era, with its sharp, acerbic tone and brother Henry Roe's finger-picked guitar accompaniment. Unfortunately, Roe never followed up on this style of playing, and most of his later records were conventional, if well played, hoedowns and songs.

None of these early performers from the 1922–27 period specialized in blues, and few of them really sounded like blues singers. Most were using the term blues cavalierly, tacking it on to any jazzy song, or any song that had the suggestion of a lament or of double entendre. This all changed in the watershed year of 1927, a year that saw the apogee of old-time recorded music. By 1927, the major record companies were releasing dozens of new hillbilly records every week and sending their field-recording units into southern cities on a regular basis. The result was a series of dramatic recordings that celebrated everything from Cajun to gospel music, and that also celebrated white blues. In fact, the year saw the emergence of a number of singers who specialized, one way or another, in the blues, and whose intense popularity did much to define the genre we now call "white blues." In addition to the Allen Brothers, these included banjoist-singer Dock Boggs, slide guitarist and singer Frank Hutchison, Georgians Tom Darby and Jimmie Tarlton, and famed "blue yodeler" Jimmie Rodgers.

The first of these to record was a sometime West Virginia miner named Frank Hutchison. He was reared in Logan County, a rugged and isolated region near the border of West Virginia and eastern Kentucky. This Appalachian area was to become a fertile pocket for the developing genre of white blues, producing singers like Dock Boggs and Dick Justice, as well as Roy Harvey, the Shepherd Brothers, and, somewhat later, Roscoe Holcomb. Logan County itself, surrounded by mountains and dense hardwood forests, had become a center for coal mining by the turn of the century. When Hutchison was a teenager, several local residents were killed in what was called the Battle of Blair Mountain, a fight between federal troops and miners trying to unionize. It was a place where many of the miners, both black and white, living in company towns and doing some of the most dangerous work in the country, felt a sense of desperation and frustration akin to what black sharecroppers in the Mississippi Delta felt. It was a place that nurtured the blues.

Hutchison was born in 1897, and almost at once he was attracted to the black music in the area. When he was seven or eight he met one of the black railroad workers who were coming into the county to lay tracks for the mines. The man's name—as preserved by family folklore—was Henry Vaughn, and he could play the blues on the guitar. Frank soon picked some of this up, and soon was playing his guitar with a knife, sliding the strings the way he had seen Vaughn do. A little later he met a "crippled Negro living back in the hills" named Bill Hunt; Hunt was about fifty at the time and was apparently a songster as well as a bluesman. He taught young Frank dozens of songs from his repertoire of nineteenth-century traditional tunes that blacks and whites had shared before the blues became fashionable. By 1920, Hutchison's repertoire contained a bagful of rare old songs: rags, blues, traditional ballads, and novelties like "Coney Isle," about a giant amusement park, not in Brooklyn, New York, but near Cincinnati, Ohio.

By the early 1920s, Hutchison was good enough to eke out a living with his music, playing small stage shows he set up in mining camps, at political rallies, at pri-

The natural shyness of Dock Boggs crippled what might well have been a highly successful recording career.

vate parties, and at movie theaters to introduce and even accompany silent films. Though his few surviving publicity pictures show him as an intense, brooding young man, he was apparently pretty lively. Pioneer recording star Pop Stoneman remembered him as "a big red-headed Irishman," and one of his sidemen remembered mainly the kinds of jokes he would tell on his shows. (Much of the rural vaudeville aspect comes out in his records, which are full of asides and quips.) But all agreed with one of his banjo players that Frank "always specialized in the blues. Just blues of all kinds." He traveled often, but seldom left the West Virginia–Kentucky area, sensing that his blues style would be best received there.

Somehow, late in 1926, Hutchison got hold of Okeh Records and traveled to New York to record his first two sides, "Worried Blues" and "The Train That Carried My Girl from Town." Both featured Hutchison using his pocket knife as a guitar slide, the instrument tuned to D, which so impressed later mountain musicians. "Worried Blues" is a classic blues in its lyric form, with a number of stanzas that Hutchison could have borrowed from a variety of sources. Some stanzas, such as "When you got the blues you can't eat nor sleep/ You'll walk around like a police on his beat," and one that mentions him left "to sing my ragtime song," have a decidedly urban feel to them, a reference to a world far away from Logan County. Later songs, though, were more topical. As Okeh continued to call him back again and again for sessions that would eventually account for some thirty-two sides, he did songs like "Miner's Blues." Here Hutchison sings "Ain't gonna work on no tipple," and backs it with a series of distinctive runs in an E-natural tuning. His "Cannon Ball Blues" (1929) was probably based on Furry Lewis's Victor recording, and his odd narrative about the Titanic ("The Last Scene of the Titanic," 1927) might have been adapted from a black "toast" (an oral narrative poem) on the subject. (Miners both black and white knew and enjoyed these long, often bawdy, toasts.) Hutchison's records continued to sell well through the late 1920s (though almost half of them date from 1927), and most of them were blues of some sort, either vocals or guitar instrumentals. There was "Stackalee," "All Night Long," "The Deal" ("Don't Let Your Deal Go Down"), "Old Rachel," and a version of "John Henry" he called "K. C. Blues." He was popular enough that when Okeh decided to put together an all-star skit called "The Okeh Medicine Show" for a six-part record series, Hutchison was chosen to join the label's biggest stars: Fiddlin' John Carson, Narmour and Smith, Emmett Miller, and others. He told friends that he would have recorded more blues if the label had let him, but the A & R men at Okeh seemed to want him to diversify, and on one of his last sessions they insisted he join a fiddler for a series of breakdowns. Possibly for this reason, but more likely because of the Depression, Hutchison stopped recording after the "Medicine Show" skits, and stopped making music altogether. He spent his later life as a storekeeper, and eventually moved to Columbus, Ohio, where he died in 1945.

Some eighty miles southeast of Logan, at Norton, Virginia, was the home of the second major white blues figure to emerge in 1927, Dock Boggs. He did his first sides for Brunswick in March, and though there were only a handful of them, they proved about as influential as Hutchison's. In some ways, Boggs's background was typical of that of many mountain musicians: he first learned to play the old clawhammer banjo-style, to sing traditional ballads like "Poor Ellen Smith," and to sight-read old gospel songs. Yet the area where he was born (in 1898) was already a grimy coal mining and railroad center. Immigrants and blacks were moving into the area to work alongside white mountaineers, who were seeing their old ways of farming and logging give way to the newer world of unions, mining bosses, and company stores. There was more give and take between blacks and whites in this region than might be expected; both shared work in the mines, and both were exploited by mining companies. They shared music in a number of ways; ledgers that have survived from storekeepers who sold records in places like War and Richland show that country blues records, especially the Paramount label featuring singers like Blind Lemon Jefferson, sold as well as fiddle records and hillbilly songs.

Unlike Hutchison, who only occasionally worked in the mines, Boggs was working in the mines full-time by 1910. He was also trying to balance his love of music (which he considered a hobby) with his need to make a living. As a boy, he would occasionally escape from the mines and go to nearby black communities, such as Dorchester, to listen to the kind of string-band music that was played there. Shyly

On the road with Fiddlin' John Carson and Moonshine Kate.

standing on the edge of a crowd of dancers, he listened intently to the things the banjo player did. Years later, he recalled, "I heard this fellow play the banjo. . . . And I said to myself—I didn't tell anybody else—if I ever, I want to learn how to play the banjo kinda like that fellow does. I don't want to play like my sister and brother. I am going to learn how to pick with my fingers." Later he followed and learned from other black musicians in the area, one called Go Lightning, another named Jim White, and pillaged the large record collection of his brother-in-law. Soon he was creating a new style of banjo finger picking and an intense, moaning method of singing. He had a powerful voice and a keen sense for the kind of vocal embellishments he heard on the blues records.

In 1926, Boggs went to a Brunswick "talent audition" in Norton, Virginia, and was surprised to find that he was one of three acts chosen to record—out of a field of

Tom Darby, standing, appears here with Jimmie Tarlton, one of the most outstanding lap slide-guitar players.

seventy-five that even included A. P. Carter. One of Boggs's first releases was "Down South Blues," which he had adapted from a 1923 Vocalion disk by city blues singer Rosa Henderson. Boggs turned the regular, rather predictable rhythm of a mediocre city blues singer into a complex redaction of raw, urgent force—mountain blues as its best. Later in the same session he did "Sugar Baby," "Country Blues" (an old traditional song called "Hustling Gamblers"), "New Prisoner's Song," and "Sammie, Where Have You Been So Long." He cut eight sides in all. The Brunswick people, astounded by their luck in finding a white coal miner who could sing with such power, begged him to record more, but Boggs was afraid of being cheated by the company, and demurred. The songs he did do were not all blues, but most of them were at least stylistically close. "Country Blues" and "Down South Blues" were especially potent, and two generations of banjoists copied them as models of the "high, lonesome sound" that soon came to characterize mountain blues. Boggs knew exactly what he was doing with his music; he once commented that he wished he had been given the gift to play the guitar instead of the banjo, so he could copy the music of his favorite, Mississippi John Hurt. Another time he said, "I put so much of myself into some pieces that I very nearly broke down emotionally."

The Brunswick records were successful in every way, but for a variety of reasons Boggs was unable to capitalize on his success. Shortly after he returned from New York, he returned to his job in the mines. It was a hard life and, in the wake of the miners' struggles to unionize, a dangerous one. Dock saw many of his friends killed in the mines or shot to death in mining camps and on mountain trails. Yet he seemed unable to venture out on his own, to try to make it as a professional musician.

When he finally did try, it was too late. The Depression hit, devastating not only the mining economy but the record and entertainment industry. On one occasion, Boggs had lined up a new recording session for Victor in June 1931, but couldn't scrape up the money to get there. Another time he went to Atlanta to record for Okeh, but froze in front of the mike on a radio-show audition and lost out there as well. He signed to record for an independent West Virginia label called Lonesome Ace, but was forced to record compositions by the label's owner, a local lawyer named W. E. Myers; it made little difference, since the records, produced in 1929, didn't get out until after the stock market crashed. By the time Roosevelt was in the White House, Boggs had given up and was back at work in the mines. In the 1960s he was rediscovered by folklorists, did a series of albums for Folkways, and performed at festivals. He still played very well and still had a remarkable feel for the blues, but his shot at real fame was little more than a memory.

The mountain blues of Hutchison and Boggs was matched in the Deep South by a team who actually sold more records than both of them combined: Tom Darby and Jimmie Tarlton. They recorded over sixty sides for three major labels in the period from 1927 to 1933, making them among the most prolific of the early country artists who took their blues seriously. To casual fans, Darby and Tarlton were best known for their two-sided Columbia hit record of "Birmingham Jail" and "Columbus Stockade Blues," one of the biggest selling old-time records of the decade. Their style was built on Darby's soulful singing and Tarlton's superb slide guitar work, and it was one of the loosest, least formulaic sounds in classic country music. Their repertoire was equally quirky, eclectic, and vast, and in some ways summed up the best aspects of white blues.

Jimmie Tarlton, who seems to have been the dominant member of the duo, was born in Chesterfield County, South Carolina, in 1892. The son of sharecropper parents, he learned to play the fretless banjo from his father, and to sing old ballads from his mother. By the time he was twelve, he was playing the guitar in both the open tuning and in the slide style he had learned from black musicians in North and South Carolina, and in Georgia, where his family had traveled in search of work. When he was seventeen, he left home, determined to try to make a living as a musician. For a time he worked in the textile mills in the Piedmont, North Carolina, then took off "busking"—going around the country, playing on street corners, at fairs, in

The irascible Thomas Alva Edison complained in the audition notes he made on Rosa Henderson: "This is the limit. Can't stand this voice. I have heard needle machine blues with much better voices."

Hank Williams—seen at the height of his career.

bars, wherever he could find an audience. He got a lot farther than many of his contemporaries who went this route, getting to Oklahoma, to California, and back to New York. As he went, he picked up new songs and other musical styles. During World War I, in fact, he played his guitar in bars in New York and Hoboken. About 1922, on the West Coast, he met the famed Hawaiian guitarist Frank Ferera; this was during the height of Hawaiian music's popularity, and Ferera taught Jimmie how to use a better slide, a piece of highly polished steel that allowed him to note with more dexterity. He also taught him a lot about adapting old pop songs to the steel guitar's sound. By the mid 1920s, when Jimmie had returned to the South to settle near Columbus, Georgia, he had been exposed to a wider range of musical styles than most of his fellow old-time musicians. He quickly set about synthesizing what he had heard into his own unique style.

In 1927 he teamed up with another guitarist from Columbus, Tom Darby. Though Darby was the same age as Tarlton, he had traveled very little—stints to Georgia and Florida—and performed in public even less; his guitar playing and singing style were adopted almost completely from musicians he had heard in and around Columbus. Darby's singing featured a very strong blues component, replete with a harrowing falsetto, tendency to improvise around the melody, and a complex sense of rhythm. Darby's parents had come from the mountains in north Georgia, and he was second cousin to Skillet Lickers star Riley Puckett. His grandfather and some of his uncles were apparently full-blooded Cherokees, and he recalled hearing his uncles play fiddle music at family gatherings. A local talent scout persuaded Darby to team up with Tarlton and got them an audition for Columbia records. Their first Columbia release, a send-up of Florida land speculators called "Down on Florida on a Hog," coupled with "Birmingham Town," was cut on April 5, 1927 and sold well enough that Columbia's A & R man, Frank Walker, invited them back to the Atlanta sessions that fall.

Thus it was that on November 10, 1927, the pair once again recorded, this time doing "Birmingham Jail" and "Columbus Stockade Blues." Both had traditional roots, but both had been substantially reworked by the singers to the point where even today it is not clear how much they had created and how much they had borrowed. In later years, Tarlton liked to say that he wrote "Birmingham Jail" in 1925 when he had been given an eighty-five-day sentence in the Birmingham jail for moonshining. He was allowed to keep his guitar, he said, and as he sat in his cell thinking of his girlfriend Bessie, he created the song. The guards and warden were so impressed that they got a pardon for Jimmie, and in 1937, when the city dedicated a new jail, Tarlton was asked to return for the ceremonies. All of which showed, if nothing else, just how popular this first record had become. It sold almost two hundred thousand copies for Columbia, making it one of the best-selling entries in their Old Familiar Tunes catalog. Both singers would have been rich had they taken royalties on the song, but Darby talked Tarlton into accepting a flat fee for their work—a lump sum of $75 each.

Though "Columbus" became a country standard and was repopularized by Jimmie Davis (in the 1940s) and by Willie Nelson and Danny Davis (in the 1960s), in the 1920s Columbia thought "Birmingham Jail" was the bigger hit. They encouraged Tarlton to come up with two sequels, "Birmingham Jail No. 2" (in 1928) and "New Birmingham Jail" (in 1930). The former, backed by "Lonesome Railroad," became the team's second-best-selling record. Their other Columbia hits included two down-and-dirty country blues pieces, "Traveling Yodel Blues" and "Heavy

Jimmie Rodgers poses with his like-named friend, the humorist Will Rogers.

Hearted Blues"; a bizarre, uptempo version of the Victorian chestnut "After the Ball"; a Civil War song, "Rainbow Division"; an uptempo guitar instrumental called "Birmingham Rag"; and an intense, almost rhythm and blues "Sweet Sarah." These lesser hits sold between fifteen and forty thousand each. Other records, which did not sell as well but became favorites with later fans, included "My Little Blue Heaven" (derived from the Gene Austin hit), "Captain Won't Let Me Go Home," "Lowe Bonnie," "Ft. Benning Blues," and "The Weaver's Blues." By late 1929, the team was having contract disagreements with Columbia, and in April 1930 they did their last session for the firm. In the next few years, each man did separate sessions (Tarlton for Columbia, Darby for Victor), and got back together for two unsuccessful sessions in 1932 and 1933. But the magic was gone and the glory days were over.

The team had traveled with some of the best-known figures in the music—from the Skillet Lickers to the Delmore Brothers to the Dixon Brothers—but the new slick harmony sounds of the mid-1930s made the free-wheeling sound of Darby

A & R man Ralph Peer was responsible for finding and recording some of the best that both white and black vernacular music had to offer.

and Tarlton obsolete. By 1935 both men were retired. Then, in the 1960s, they were rediscovered by young enthusiasts of the folk revival movement. Tarlton was found in Phenix City, Alabama, and made a brief comeback that included stints at folk clubs around the country and a new solo LP on the Testament label. (It remains an astounding album even today, showing that Tarlton had lost little of his skill and creativity.) Soon after, Tom Darby was also "discovered," but only a few concerts were scheduled featuring the reunited team. It was learned that Tarlton had tried various comebacks before, even appearing for a time in a medicine show with Hank and Audrey Williams. The 1960s appeared to presage better things, and soon he was appearing at the Newport Folk Festival, and seeing a reissue of the original Darby and Tarlton sides on the Old Timey label. But it was, after all, late. Jimmie died in 1973, Darby in 1971, having barely tasted the fruits of their new careers.

On November 30, 1927, twenty days after Darby and Tarlton recorded "Columbus Stockade Blues" in Atlanta, the next chapter in white blues unfolded in the old Trinity Baptist Church in Camden, New Jersey. The old church, with its remarkable acoustics, had been converted into Studio #1 by the Victor Talking Machine Company, and on that afternoon it was hosting a session by a brash, hawk-faced young man named Jimmie Rodgers. He had been born in 1897 in southern Mississippi, had started working on the Mobile and Ohio Railroad when he was fourteen, contracted what was later diagnosed as tuberculosis a year later, and started out in music by doing black-face comedy in a tent show in 1923. During the next few years, he worked with a number of vaudeville and string-band groups, eventually winding up in Asheville, North Carolina, in the spring of 1927. That summer he auditioned for Victor's talent scout, Ralph Peer, who set up a field studio in the mountain town of Bristol, Tennessee. At this time Peer had just joined Victor, moving there from Okeh, where he had helped pioneer blues recording by releasing Mamie Smith's "Crazy Blues" in 1920. Blues had proved to be a bonanza for Peer, and now he was hoping to repeat his success by developing another genre of southern music, "hillbilly," or what the Victor publicists liked to call "Native American Melodies." He still recorded blues—usually going to Memphis for that—but he wasn't sure where to go for hillbilly material. He chose Bristol because, he told a newspaper writer at the time, "in no section of the South have the prewar melodies and old mountaineer songs been better preserved than in the mountains of east Tennessee and Southwest Virginia."

At first, it seemed, Rodgers was hardly doing that. Peer later recalled that "in order to earn a living in Asheville, he was singing mostly songs originated by New York publishers—the current hits." This Peer didn't want, in part because it was not "old-time" enough for his series, in part because he wanted original or public domain songs to which he could get publishing rights. Rodgers eventually came up with two sentimental songs that were passable; Peer paid him a hundred dollars on account and went on with the session. The record was issued in October and sold fairly well for a new artist, yet Peer did not call Rodgers back for more. So the singer took it upon himself to go to New York, check into a hotel (billing the room to Victor), and telephone Peer. Looking over the sales figures for the first disk, Peer shrugged and agreed to schedule a session at Camden. He soon found that Rodgers didn't really have much material ready to record; he chose three songs that seemed old-time enough, but for the fourth he reluctantly agreed to try something else. Peer recalled years later, "We did not have enough material and I decided to use [one] of his blues

Commemorative plaque honoring Jimmie Rodgers.

songs to 'fill in.'" Rodgers called this song "T for Texas," but it was eventually released by Victor as "Blue Yodel."

No one knows exactly where Rodgers got the set of blues stanzas he used for "T for Texas." Growing up in an area with a large black population, meeting numerous black musicians in his travels as a brakeman, he was certainly exposed to a wider range of black music than were people like Boggs and Hutchison. Some evidence suggests that he knew singers Ishman Bracey and Tommy Johnson, and stanzas that he used for this and his later "blue yodels" also show up in records by Peetie Wheatstraw, "Ma" Rainey, Bo Carter, Sadie McKinney, and other black singers. But the full extent of specific interaction between Rodgers and other bluesmen of the 1920s and 1930s will probably never be known. Rodgers quickly mastered the rhetoric of the country blues—catchphrases like "good gal," "sweet loving daddy,"

"whole wide world"—and used it to patch together lyrics that had the effect, if not the intensity, of blues. When "T for Texas" ("Blue Yodel") was issued, on February 3, 1928, publicity agents and reviewers were not sure what to call the new music. Victor ads described the release as "Popular Song for Comedian with Guitar" and praised Rodgers for his "grotesque style." Edward Abbe Niles, a Wall Street lawyer who wrote surprisingly hep reviews for The Bookman, called the song "engaging, melodious, and bloodthirsty"; a few months later he was describing Rodgers as

Emmett Miller in black face. Miller was quite unique in that he recorded with such popular jazz artists as Tommy Dorsey, Jimmy Dorsey, Eddie Lang, Jack Teagarden, and Gene Krupa as well as with the most rural of country musicians.

"White man gone black"—an epithet that would be used three decades later to describe Elvis Presley.

"Blue Yodel" (Victor 21142) became in many respects the seminal record for white blues. It almost certainly actually sold over a million copies—one of the very few early country discs to do so—and established Rodgers as the premier singer of early country music. The balance of 1928 saw Victor issue no fewer than seven more Rodgers records, though only six of the fourteen songs were actually in the vein of "Blue Yodel." (Rodgers's blues songs have fascinated modern historians and folklorists, but his sentimental songs and railroad ballads were about as popular in his own day.) He recorded until just a few days before he died in 1933, having laid down some 110 songs, of which 13 were in the "Blue Yodel" series, and 25 others were related blues pieces—about a third of this recorded repertoire. Peer himself was convinced, though, that the blues was the key to Rodgers' sales and insisted he record more and more blues. The most popular included "In the Jailhouse Now" (1928, similar to earlier songs by Blind Blake and radio singer Ernest Rogers); "Blue Yodel No. 4 (California Blues)" (released in early 1929 and selling 365,000 copies); "Brakeman's Blues" (1928, subtitled "Portland, Main Is Just the Same as Sunny Tennessee"); "Desert Blues" (1929, with sales of 200,000); and "Blue Yodel No. 8" ("Mule Skinner's Blues," 1931). As Peer realized that the Rodgers records were "crossing over"—appealing to a pop audience in addition to hillbilly and blues audiences—he began experimenting with a variety of studio back-up bands. While many of the biggest hits featured Rodgers alone with his guitar or with a small string band, starting in October 1928, Peer set him up with a small jazz band and by early 1929 was backing him with Victor studio orchestras. Genuine jazz and blues figures soon followed. Louis Armstrong and Lil Hardin Armstrong backed him on "Blues Yodel No. 9" (1930), though the newspaper ads failed to mention them, in spite of the fact that Armstrong was one of the biggest jazz names in the country. Clifford Hayes's Louisville Jug Band served as his band for "My Good Gal's Gone Blues" (1931), and the fine St. Louis guitarist Clifford Gibson backed him on "Let Me Be Your Side Track" (1931); the issued take of this number only featured Rodgers's own guitar, and for years it had been assumed that the Gibson takes were lost. Recently, however, they have been discovered and have been issued on the Rounder/Bear Family set of Rodgers's complete works. Sadly, some of Rodgers's best blues, in the most challenging settings, were done in the depths of the Depression and were hardly heard by anyone. "Let Me Be Your Side Track," for instance, sold only about thirteen thousand copies in its original edition.

Rodgers's biographer Nolan Porterfield has written, "While no one could seriously suggest that Jimmie Rodgers was another Blind Lemon Jefferson or Robert Johnson or even Furry Lewis, his performance of 'Blue Yodel,' insofar as it is a direct, serious, and authentic rendering of the material, is scarcely distinguishable from that heard on dozens of black blues recordings of the time." The most important thing Rodgers added to the blues conventions was his yodel; this is what held together most of his blues stanzas, and this was the thing that his imitators tried to emulate. No one really knows how Rodgers came up with it, but it was distinctly different from the pseudo-Alpine yodel that earlier singers like Riley Puckett adopted, and different, too, from the cowboy yodels. It might have borrowed something from the falsetto singing of certain Delta blues singers, or even from black field hollers and work songs. One source that might have been closer to Rodgers than any of these, however, was a well-defined tradition of black-face singing that had emerged on the vaudeville and

medicine show circuits shortly before World War I. Such singing was part black-face parody, part exaggeration, part vocal contortion, and part sincere imitation. One of its first stars was Lasses White, who recorded and featured a song called "Nigger Blues" about 1916, and who later starred on the Grand Ole Opry in the 1930s. But the singer who really developed the style on records and who influenced two generations of country singers was a man named Emmett Miller.

Though Miller seldom appeared on radio and confined much of his activity to the live vaudeville circuit, he left behind an impressive series of recordings, done between 1924 and 1936, which reveal him to be adept at the kind of falsetto singing and "blue yodeling" that Rodgers later did. Miller was born in Macon, Georgia, in 1903 and grew up mimicking the black dialects he heard there and in other southern towns. By 1919, when he was sixteen, he began doing black-face shows with Dan Fitch and within a few years was starring in the show at New York's Hippodrome along with Cliff Edwards and the team of Smith and Dale. By 1924, Billboard was referring to Miller's "trick singing stunt" that almost stopped the show and won him "encore after encore." The "trick singing" was in part Miller's ability to break into a falsetto in the middle of a word, and in 1924 he committed this technique to wax for the first time when he recorded "Anytime" for Okeh.

By 1925, Miller had relocated to Asheville, North Carolina, where he worked in clubs, and where he impressed local singers. A young duo named the Callahan Brothers heard him there and adopted his version of "St. Louis Blues," with an eerie falsetto chorus, to their duet style. In 1934 they recorded their version for ARC, giving that label its biggest hit of the decade and challenging all later harmony duet singers. Miller might also have met Rodgers in Asheville—his singing partner Turk McBee said he did—and there taught Rodgers some of the "trick singing." Miller also recorded again in Asheville, doing a version of a song that would become his trademark and a country standard, "Lovesick Blues." Soon he was touring again, with the Al G. Field show, the newspapers describing him as a "comedian unexcelled in the impersonation of the southern Negro."

During 1928, in a flurry of activity, Miller began recording in earnest for Okeh. Often backed by a studio band he called the Georgia Crackers and that sometimes included jazzmen Tommy Dorsey, Eddie Lang, and Gene Krupa, he rerecorded his two big hits, "Anytime" and "Lovesick Blues," in the new electrical process. He also did his version of "St. Louis Blues" and "I Ain't Got Nobody," with his famous descending yodel built on the syllable "I." The next year, 1929, he did three others that became standards, "Right or Wrong" (which western swing singers took over), "Big Bad Bill Is Sweet William Now," and "The Blues Singer from Alabam." Occasionally the Okeh producers tried to force him to record a ballad like "She's Funny That Way," but he resisted, complaining to his friends that the company was "trying to make another damned Gene Austin out of me." All told, Miller cut some twenty-eight sides featuring music (plus others done as skits and a set in "The Okeh Medicine Show").

It was a small body of work, but surprisingly powerful. Down in Fort Worth, young fiddler Bob Wills painstakingly copied into his notebook the words to many of Miller's records and added them to his repertoire. When he hired his famous singer Tommy Duncan a couple of years later, Wills tested him by asking him to do Miller's version of "I Ain't Got Nobody." Duncan passed with flying colors and shortly after recorded the piece with Wills. In Alabama, singer Rex Griffin watched Miller do a live show in a club, and then adapted "Lovesick Blues" to his own country style. He had a major hit with it on his own for Decca in 1935, which inspired Hank Williams to do his version in 1949. By the 1950s (when Miller, ironically, was doing his last attempt at vaudeville in a touring show called "Dixiana"), "Lovesick Blues," an old Tin Pan Alley song, had become the most famous white blues in modern country music. Later singers like Merle Haggard and Leon Redbone dedicated entire LPs to Miller and his work; and though none of his records were really designed either for the specific blues or old-time market, Miller's many fans found him, and appropriated his loose, sinuous, double-jointed vocal style for their own. Unfortunately, Miller saw little of this recognition, and until recently has been an enigma to both country and blues fans.

With the spectacular success of Rodgers's "Blue Yodel" and the surprising sales of Darby and Tarlton's "Columbus Stockade Blues," the major companies began a

Gene Autry began his career as a Jimmie Rodgers imitator doing Rodgers-style blues songs and yodels. His later work reflected very little of this.

Gene Autry: portrait of the Singing Cowboy as a young man.

feeding frenzy to find and record more white blues. Ralph Peer, seeing his own royalties from Rodgers's publishing roll in so fast he had to set up a dummy corporation to manage the profits, was especially eager. Some of his artists, such as the Allen Brothers, got upset with him because he began insisting they do blues to the exclusion of almost everything else. Other companies rushed to find Rodgers clones, and for the next ten years yodeling became almost synonymous with country music. Young Gene Autry, fresh from Oklahoma, started off doing superb Rodgers covers and pastiches for Gennett and Victor before he found his cowboy image. Howard Keesee (Gennett) and Bill Bruner (Okeh) came so close to Rodgers's style that their own careers lacked any real sense of identity. Dwight Butcher (Victor), Daddy John Love (Bluebird), Jerry Behrens (Okeh), and Jimmie's own cousin Jesse Rogers (Bluebird) all began their careers as serious Rodgers devotees. Ramblin' Red Lowery

(ARC), a native of west Tennessee who worked over Memphis radio, moved further away from the Rodgers style than did many, yet the handful of records he did in the mid-1930s, such as "Ramblin' Red's Memphis Yodel—No. 1" (Vocalion, 1934), showed how a singer could still merge some of Rodgers's mannerisms with a more authentic blues sensibility. Young Jimmie Davis, five years before he won national fame (and eventually a governorship) with the sentimental "Nobody's Darlin' But Mine," did a series of Rodgers sound-alikes for Victor. But he also did a set of racier

Jimmie Rodgers's cousin Jesse:
"R.C.A. Victor Recording &
Rodeo Artist."

255

Cliff Carlisle assumes his standard playing position.

titles, such as "Sewing Machine Blues" (1932), "Red Nightgown Blues" (1932), "Yo Yo Mama" (1932), and "She's a Hum Dum Dinger from Dingersville" (1930). On many of these he was accompanied by two well-known black musicians from Shreveport, Buddy Woods and Ed Schaffer, as well as Buddy Jones—all of whom had recorded on their own.

Another who built a career on the Rodgers style, but who successfully parlayed it into an extensive series of recordings, was West Virginia radio singer Bill Cox (1897–1968). Known as the Dixie Songbird, Cox started off as a worker in an axe factory in Charleston (West Virginia); he began singing over station WOBU in 1927 and soon had a local reputation as a good guitarist, harmonica player, and singer of rowdy songs. He began recording for Gennett in 1929, first doing many Rodgers covers and then recording some of his own pieces in the Rodgers style. At first, these included comedy songs like "Rollin' Pin Woman" and "Alimony Woman," but later he began to do more serious pieces like "East Cairo Street Blues." By 1933 he was recording for the American Record Company, becoming one of the first to do "Midnight Special" (1933) and having a real hit with "NRA Blues" (1933), a protest song from the early New Deal days. In 1934 he injured his hand, and Cox hired as a temporary sideman a teenager named Cliff Hobbs to help out. At the suggestion of A & R man Art Satherly, Cox taught Hobbs how to sing tenor, and the two started recording as a duet. From 1933 to 1941, Cox recorded over sixty solo sides for ARC, and seventy duets with Hobbs. These included such topical songs as "Franklin D. Roosevelt's Back Again" (1936), off-color pieces like "Sally, Let Your Bands Hang Down" (1936), later country standards like "Filipino Baby," and covers of "Didi Wa Didi" (1939). The only major hit from all these was a piece called "Sparkling Brown Eyes" (1937), and Cox, unable or unwilling to work the kind of live tours that would have made him a decent living, slowly faded into obscurity. In 1965 he was discov-

Bill Cox

Wilbur Ball and Cliff Carlisle

Woody Guthrie and Leadbelly rapt in song.

ered living in a tiny converted chickenhouse in the slums of Charleston, scarcely aware of the effect his old records had had on listeners, fans, and other singers.

As prolific a record maker as Cox was the Kentucky singer Cliff Carlisle (1904–83), who was not only a remarkable singer and composer but one of the first old-time artists to understand and feature the Hawaiian steel guitar. "My music," he once said, "is a cross between hillbilly and blues—even Hawaiian music has sort of blues to it." Unlike many early hillbilly guitarists, Carlisle started playing the steel from the very beginning, patterning his work on the records of Sol Hoopii and Frank Ferera, Hawaiian guitarists whose popularity was especially strong in the South. He won his first record contract (for Gennett) by doing Rodgers covers, but soon was producing his own Rodgers-like songs and billing himself as "The Yodeling Hobo." Like Cox, he moved over to the American Record Company in the early 1930s and began recording everything from murder ballads to a series of zany songs about domestic violence, such as "Pay Day Fight" (1937) and "Wildcat Woman and a Tomcat Man" (1936). Among his most popular, though, was a series of double-entendre pieces like "Shanghai Rooster Yodel" (1931) and "Tom Cat Blues" (1932). The latter featured the well-known lines:

Here comes a ring-tail tom,
He's boss around the town,
And if you got your heat turned up,
You better turn your damper down.

Chickens were favorite images, showing up in "Chicken Roost Blues" (1934) and "It Takes a Old Hen to Deliver the Goods" (1937); frogs were eulogized with "When I Feel Froggie, I'm Gonna Hop." Two 1933 songs, "Mouse's Ear Blues" and "Sal's Got a Meatskin," were about deflowering virgins. And pieces like "Copper Head Mama" and "Onion Eating Mama" (both 1934) went far to dispel the delicate, sentimental coun-

Brothers Kirk and Sam McGee,
two of white country music's best
blues-oriented artists.

A very young Sam McGee with his sometime mentor, country great Uncle Dave Macon.

try lass described in earlier country songs. Many of the gamier songs were released under a pseudonym ("Bob Clifford"), a practice that didn't seem to affect sales but allowed Carlisle also to release items like "Valley of Peace" and "Jesus My All."

Other varieties of white blues, though, took forms quite different from the Rodgers model. One that became ubiquitous among radio singers in the 1930s was the so-called talking blues. Though casual fans often associate it with folksinger Woody Guthrie, its roots were a generation deeper than that. In April 1926 a young mandolin player named Chris Bouchillon appeared with his brothers for a try-out at a Columbia field session; they were from Greenville, South Carolina, and all worked at a foundry there. Frank Walker was not overly impressed with them, and when Chris tried to sing what he called his "blues thing," Walker stopped him. "I thought his singing was the worst thing I had heard, but I liked his voice. I liked the way he talked to me. I said, 'Don't sing it. Just talk it. Tell them about the blues but don't sing it.'" Backed by his brother, guitarist Uris, Bouchillon did as he was told and created "Talking Blues," with its famous opening line, "If you want to get to Heaven, let me tell you how to do it." The record was issued in early 1927, and soon became one of the year's biggest hits. It would eventually sell over ninety thousand copies, and soon Chris was back in the studios doing a series of follow-ups: "Born in Hard Luck," "New Talking Blues," and "My Fat Girl." Several stanzas of Bouchillon's original "Talking Blues" had been collected previously by folklorists from black informants, and early recordings by Talking Billy Anderson and by Coley Jones suggest the genre may have been known in black tradition.

During the next decade, old-time performers added to their repertoires a wide variety of talking blues. Lonnie Glosson, Curly Fox, Buddy Jones, the Prairie Ramblers, and others all recorded forms of talking blues, but the performer who became best known for it was Robert Lunn, a fixture on Nashville's "Grand Ole Opry" through the 1930s and 1940s. Born in Franklin, Tennessee, in 1912, Lunn spent his youth in vaudeville, where he somehow picked up Bouchillon's "song." By 1935 he was on the Opry, performing his "Talking Blues" every Saturday night before a nationwide audience; he used Bouchillon's verses at first, then began adding new ones, including topical material, until he had over a hundred verses in his repertoire. Fans loved it, and in 1936 they voted Lunn the show's most popular performer. Seven extra clerks were hired just to take care of the mail he was receiving. Though he never got around to recording the piece until the 1950s, Lunn did publish in various songbooks and helped spread the talking blues across the country to other entertainers like young Woody Guthrie.

Another variety of white blues was centered on the fiddle. Though the fiddle was the primary instrument of nineteenth-century folk culture, both with whites and blacks, not all that many of the early country fiddlers from the late 1920s and 1930s specialized in blues. The one exception would probably be the distinctive Mississippi fiddler Willie T. Narmour (1889–1961). A native of rural Carroll County in north-central Mississippi (the same area John Hurt came from), Narmour and his guitarist Shellie Smith grew up learning a rich collection of unusual, bluesy fiddle tunes. Like many Mississippi fiddlers, Narmour preferred the more deliberate "long bow" technique to the "jiggy bow" (fast, choppy strokes) of mountain fiddlers. This gave his playing an unusual tone and allowed him to experiment with nuances of expression and rhythm that gave his music such a distinctive sound. He and Smith did thirty-one tunes for Okeh in 1928–30 (rerecording many of them for Bluebird in 1934), but the most famous were "Carroll County Blues" (1929) and "Charleston No. 1" (1929). The former was Narmour's adaptation of a tune he heard a black fieldhand humming; the latter was not a version of the dance step, but a local piece named after Charleston, Mississippi, a county seat to the north of Carroll County. Both became standards with southern fiddlers and bluegrass bands, and both are still heard in fiddle contests today.

There were other blues fiddle tunes that won fame in the 1930s, though many of them were from fiddlers not necessarily known for the blues. The "train piece" format, in which a song built slowly through a series of alternating drone and breakdown passages, came from two records by east Tennessee mountain fiddler G. B. Grayson. These were "Train 45" (Victor and Gennett, 1927) and "Going Down the Lee Highway" (Victor, 1929). Tommy Magness, a veteran north Georgia fiddler who later played with both Bill Monroe and Roy Acuff, popularized "Natural Bridge Blues" and "Polecat Blues" (both Victor, 1940) in records he made with Roy Hall and his Blue

Kokomo Arnold

Bill Monroe, one of country music's patriarchs, was steeped in the blues and profoundly influenced by Arnold Shultz, an African-American blues guitarist and fiddler.

Ridge Entertainers. Arthur Smith, probably the most famous fiddler in the 1930s through his work on the Opry and records for Bluebird, had a number of jazzy tunes (like "House of David Blues") that he called blues. He also made some more serious efforts, replete with his sliding notes and patented E-string double stops, including "Chittlin's Bookin' Time in Cheatham County" (Bluebird, 1936), his version of "St. James Infirmary," and "Florida Blues" (Bluebird, 1937), a driving, swinging workout that impressed two generations of fiddlers. Fellow Opry star Kirk McGee, who played all manner of music on guitar and banjo, reserved his fiddle work for blues and was judged by many critics to be the very finest of old-time blues fiddlers. His "Salt Lake City Blues" and "Salty Dog Blues" (both Vocalion, 1927) were both adapted directly from a Papa Charlie Jackson record, and "Milkcow Blues" he learned from Kokomo Arnold.

Early country music also produced a number of individual guitarists who, among their other accomplishments, recorded examples of country blues that were far more faithful to the original than anything Rodgers produced. Dick Justice (ca. 1900–ca. 1955), a friend of Frank Hutchison's from Logan County, West Virginia, recorded a version of "Cocaine" and a pastiche he called "Brown Skin Blues" (both Brunswick, 1929). The former was a redoing of Luke Jordan's 1927 record, while the latter seems to have been drawn from a Lemon Jefferson side. Unfortunately, Justice recorded only one session before dropping into obscurity. Larry Hensley (1912–73), the guitarist and mandolin player for the well-known southern Kentucky band Walker's Corbin Ramblers, recorded a version of "Match Box Blues" (ARC, 1934). It was derived from Lemon Jefferson's recording and elaborates not only on Jefferson's vocal, but also on his guitar style. Sam McGee (1894–1975), another early Opry star and long-time companion of Uncle Dave Macon, contributed his masterpiece with "Railroad Blues" (Gennett, 1934). Here, too, the guitar work overshadows the singing. The guitar choruses are full of pulls, bent notes, choked chords, and even a high falsetto vocal done in unison with the guitar, in the manner of Delta Bluesmen. McGee continued to play this and similar numbers well into the 1960s and 1970s, as he was discovered by the folk revival movement. By the mid-1930s some guitarists had gotten their hands on the dobro, and pioneers like Clell Summey were exploring its possibilities. Summey, from Knoxville, was a member of Roy Acuff's first band and was featured on some of Acuff's first releases, such as "Steel Guitar Chimes" and "Steel Guitar Blues" (both ARC, 1937).

As the 1930s drew to a close, the blues was assimilated into more and more forms of commercial country music. The "blue yodel" was gone, a victim of overexposure, and there were no longer many country artists who thought of themselves as blues specialists. Yet as the records and radio shows proliferated, taking country music far from the mountain mining camps or country vaudeville shows, the newer groups routinely added blues songs and styles to their repertoire. Milton Brown and then Bob Wills defined western swing in part through reworkings of "Sitting on Top of the World," "Joe Turner Blues," "Brain Cloudy Blues," and "Steel Guitar Rag" (the latter derived from Sylvester Weaver's 1923 "Guitar Rag"). Duet singing and blues were first merged by the Memphis team of Reece Fleming and Respers Townsend, and then by the more technically adept Delmore Brothers; their "Brown's Ferry Blues" (Bluebird 1933) had become one of Bluebird's best-selling records by 1935, and it anticipated the Delmores' even heavier involvement with blues after the war. October 1940 brought another taste of things to come, when Kentucky mandolin player Bill Monroe made his first recordings with a band he called the Blue

The Delmore Brothers

Grass Boys. At the Kimball Hotel in Atlanta, under the direction of veteran Frank Walker, Monroe did "Mule Skinner Blues," "Dog House Blues," and "Tennessee Blues," giving notice that "the taste of the blues," as he put it, would be a major part of the new music he was inventing. The notion of white blues was no longer novel, and producers no longer thought of it as an automatic ticket to big sales, but it was on its way to becoming a part of the deep fabric of country music. The universal appeal of the blues was merely being validated once again.

DON'T LEAVE
ME HERE

NON-COMMERCIAL BLUES:
THE FIELD TRIPS, 1924–60

JOHN H. COWLEY

◆◆◆

While the commercial recording of blues by black performers in the United States is recognized as having begun with a session by Mamie Smith for the General Phonograph Corporation (Okeh) in 1920, field recordings of black folk songs had begun earlier, in the first decade of the century. Most notable among these earliest projects are Howard W. Odum's pioneering studies in Mississippi and Georgia. Made with a cylinder machine, none of his originals appear to have survived, but song texts, both sacred and secular, were published in contemporary articles and, later, in book form. In the secular field, much of what Odum collected can be called "Proto Blues," to use a term recently adopted by Paul Oliver. Some ten or more years later, such songs stood beside and sometimes crossed over into the repertoire of recordings made specifically for black consumption, especially in the late 1920s. Later surviving field recordings, therefore, augment available evidence for black music in this period and continue to do so for the three and a half decades to 1960, when a growing popular enthusiasm raised the status of blues to a world music, alongside American jazz and other black musical styles from the Caribbean and South America.

The principal watershed in this era was World War II, which interrupted both commercial and field recordings. Despite the interruption, there was innovation in recording techniques. In addition, prior to the war, few, if any, field recordings could be heard, except at the institution or other location where they were housed. During the war, however, the Library of Congress began producing its large repository of pre-war field recordings in annotated 78-rpm albums. Later, these were converted into long-playing records. At the same time, improved portable recording equipment spurred independent investigation by enthusiasts and folklorists, and it became feasible for small specialist companies to release long-playing records of these recordings

Working for the Library of Congress, John Lomax and his son Alan ventured far afield to record a vast treasury of the nation's vernacular music, including non-commercial blues. ABOVE

Inmate Buddy Moss plays guitar in a Georgia prison, 1936. CHAPTER OPENER

for more general distribution. Noncommercial black music, therefore, was more readily accessible after the war. In consequence, this survey is divided into two distinct periods. The first dates from 1924—when the first available field recordings are supposed to have been made—to 1944—when no relevant recordings are known. The second dates from 1946—the commencement of new recordings—and ends in 1960—which marks a change in popular taste for blues.

For reasons explained, the status of field recordings made before World War II is more easily defined than that for recordings made in the period 1946–60. Recordings are included in this discussion based on their original purpose as documents of black—mostly rural—music.

Since the mid-1960s there has been a trickle of long-playing records featuring black music from the prewar holdings of the Library of Congress Archive of Folk Culture (formerly Archive of American Folk Song). A few have been produced by the Archive itself, but, more often, commercial record companies have made this material more generally available. Together with the Library's earlier publications and releases of relevant recordings made between 1946 and 1960 by specialist companies, these more recent releases provide the basis for this analysis. In addition, occasional reference will be made to unreleased items held by the Archive or other organizations.

The repertoire of songsters in the early twentieth century—and before—has yet to be established on a firm basis, little comparative work having been undertaken on black music from this period. Such songsters performed a variety of styles, reflecting rural, and sometimes urban, black experience, both sacred and secular. In turn, these kinds of music represent components in the evolution of blues, which became a particularly influential vocal genre among blacks, following the advent of specialized "race" recordings in 1920.

As has been implied, the interest of the folk-song collector was not necessarily the same as that of the commercial record producer, although it should be remembered that in the early part of this century a worldwide technique for encouraging the purchase of phonographs was for manufacturers to record and release music from a particular locality. Inevitably this included music from oral traditions and styles that in other circumstances would not have been considered commercial. This probably accounts for the secular black ballads, songs from road shows, and ragtime pieces (from an earlier era) that were recorded together with blues from troubadour songsters in the 1920s. By the late 1930s, however, such music was much less apparent in record company lists. Black singers of this type concentrated in their recordings almost exclusively on stylized blues for sale to rural and urban purchasers (many of the latter having recently moved to northern cities). Field recordings made throughout the first and second periods of this survey nevertheless continued to reflect the broader base of black musical tradition and have, therefore, to be considered in this wider context.

With this in mind, it is necessary to establish a general guide to the kinds of music performed in southern black rural and urban communities in these two eras and to point out that songs relating to occupation and religious worship form part of the overall pattern. It must also be remembered that some black entertainers played for both black and white audiences and, where necessary, adjusted aspects of their repertoire accordingly.

Using categories defined by contemporary studies of black folk songs published in the 1920s and 1930s, as well as evidence from field recordings from this period, we can say that black vernacular music comprises:

ballads (and "outlaw" songs)
barrelhouse songs (bawdy, jazz, minstrel, popular, and ragtime)
blues (and blues narratives)
calls and hollers (some of which might be categorized as work songs)
game songs (play party, ring play, etc.)
hymns (from the white tradition)
spirituals
square dances (or breakdowns, including reels and jigs)
topical and protest songs
work songs (for individual or gang work)

For entertainment, most of this music was performed by songsters, string bands, jug and washboard bands, fife and drum bands and, occasionally, brass bands. Religious music was sometimes included in this repertoire, which was played by local amateurs as well as touring professionals, with medicine shows, carnivals, circuses, and the like.

FIELD RECORDINGS, 1924–44: FROM "NEGRO SONGS OF PROTEST" TO ROOSEVELT AND HITLER

On the basis of a somewhat doubtful dating, the first recordings in this survey were made by Lawrence Gellert in Greenville, South Carolina, in 1924. They comprise four guitar-accompanied blues on the theme of black protest, relating to imprisonment. In this, they form part of Gellert's remarkable, almost unique, collection of this type of music—principally unaccompanied hollers and group work songs— on the evidence of available recordings. While Gellert undoubtedly began making field recordings in 1924, like others during this period, he first used a wax-cylinder

The rear of John and Alan Lomax's automobile, showing some of the recording equipment they used on their many field trips. Note the disk cutter on the left.

Alan Lomax

acoustic machine. Aural and other evidence indicates, however, that all items actually issued from his collection were recorded electrically, using a semiprofessional portable disk cutter. Reliable versions of the latter were first developed in the early 1930s, and it is likely that Gellert's surviving recordings date from that time. They will be discussed subsequently in this context.

Robert W. Gordon also used wax cylinders in his extensive and methodical research into the origins of the American folk song. Although Gordon apparently recorded no blues, in 1925 (or perhaps 1928) he captured on cylinder the ragtime composer Ben Harney singing a version of his "You've Been a Good Old Wagon" (published in sheet music in 1895). The lyrics of this relate to dummy line, or small construction and logging-camp railroads. Such songs formed part of the repertoire of turn-of-the-century musicians—whether piano players or string instrumentalists— who performed for workers in such camps and became one element in the development of blues. Another constituent in this evolution was work songs, of which Gordon recorded many examples from blacks at Darien in the Georgia Sea Islands. Two of them, made in 1926, are currently available: "Finger Ring," by Mary C. Mann, a rowing song, and "Blow Boys Blow," by J. A. S. Spencer, a sea shanty.

In 1928, Gordon was appointed to head the new Archive of American Folk Song at the Library of Congress, a position he would hold until 1933, when funding ran out. Gordon was particularly interested in the interplay between black and white oral traditions and the influence of commercial culture on that of the vernacular. This, however, was not Lawrence Gellert's purpose; he saw black protest songs as a way to document otherwise hidden reactions to injustice. In this he skillfully gained

John Lomax recorded Leadbelly at Angola State Penitentiary, Louisiana, in 1934.

the confidence of his informants—who remained anonymous—on chain gangs, prison farms, and in other penal institutions in North and South Carolina and Georgia.

While the texts to most of the songs he obtained are unique, a few show some relation to commercial recordings by black performers (many of which, however, might be classified as vernacular). As has been noted, Gellert recorded some guitar-accompanied blues, such as "Mr. Tyree" (a song about the warden at Bellwood Prison Camp, Atlanta, Georgia); ballads, like "Delia"; an unaccompanied variant of the "John Henry–Nine Pound Hammer" ballad/work-song cycle, "Come Get Your Money"; and work songs proper, including "Cap'n Got a Pistol" (known otherwise as "Muley on the Mountain"). Songs available that relate directly to commercial recordings include the unaccompanied holler "Annie Lee" (similar to Texas Alexander's 1928 recording "Penitentiary Moan Blues," Okeh 8640), the unaccompanied blues "Cap'n What Is On Your mind" (related to Blind Lemon Jefferson's "Prison Cell Blues," Paramount 12622, also recorded in 1928), "Standin' on the Streets in Birmingham" (a variant of Jefferson's "One Dime Blues," Paramount 12578, recorded in 1927), and the guitar-accompanied "Prison Bound Blues" (some verses from which are in Leroy Carr's 1928 recording with the same title, Vocalion 1241). Inadvertently, therefore, these serve a purpose similar to Gordon's objective of documenting the relationship of commercial culture to that of oral traditions. In addition, evidence from other 1930s field recordings also contributes to Gordon's aims.

About the time that Gordon's luck ran out with his Archive of American Folk Song appointment, John A. Lomax, another collector of folk songs, suggested to his New York publisher an anthology of "American ballads and folk songs." To his surprise, the idea was accepted. This was in 1932, and Lomax, his fortunes at a very low ebb, was galvanized by the good news. He set to work at once and made an arrangement with the Library of Congress to provide apparatus (including recording blanks) for a field-recording expedition. Like Gordon, Lomax was seeking novel "American" material in an age when conservative scholars believed ballads of European origin to be the only folk songs. Secular black music, associated with what was seen as the tarnished world of minstrelsy, ragtime, and jazz, was treated as worthless. The Lomaxes—John A. and his son Alan—succeeded in sweeping such views aside, establishing popular acceptance of American vernacular song.

Alan Lomax was seventeen when he set out with his father in mid-June 1933, equipped with an Edison cylinder machine to make recordings of "the secular songs of the Negroes." He described these in 1934 as "work songs, barrel-house ditties, bad-man ballads [and] corn songs." In addition, he noted that the "singers classed all these songs to distinguish them from recorded music and from written-out songs in general as 'made up songs.'" They were also referred to as "'sinful' songs or 'reels,'" John A. Lomax reported. These kinds of music were "sought from particular locations—the plantation, the lumber camp, and the barrelhouse"—were grouped in one general category, "prison farms" provided a second.

Starting from their Texas home, the Lomaxes recorded at locations across the spectrum of their interest. Prison-farm work songs, reels, blues, ballads, and barrel-house songs were obtained from James "Iron Head" Baker, Mose "Clear Rock" Platt, "Lightnin'" Washington, and Ernest (Mexico) Williams, among others. A similar repertoire was recorded—in places other than penitentiaries—from K. C. Gallaway, Willie "Bubba" Grimes, "Ivory Joe" Hunter, and Henry Trevellian (Truvillion), again among others. None of the Texas cylinders, however, has ever been released,

James Baker, also known as Iron Head, in Sugarland, Texas, June 1934.

although songs from most of these performers were published in *American Ballads and Folk Songs* (New York, 1934).

The disk recording machine provided by the Library of Congress reached the Lomaxes on July 15, when they were in Baton Rouge, Louisiana. They first put it to use during the next four days when they visited the Louisiana State Penitentiary at Angola.

John A. Lomax with Uncle Rich Brown, whom he recorded near Sumterville, Alabama, 1940.

After their success in obtaining material in Texas, the Lomaxes had become convinced that the penitentiaries of Louisiana and Mississippi would yield many songs. They were, however, somewhat disappointed at Angola. "The officials of the Louisiana prison in their wisdom," reported Alan, "had decided all history to the contrary, that Negroes work better when they are not singing." Their consolation was a singer named "Lead Belly," Huddie Leadbetter, later to be known as Leadbelly, who claimed he was "King of the 12-string-guitar players of de worl'." He proved to be a highly skilled songster with a very wide repertoire, but he was serving his second term in prison for a violent crime.

Leadbelly provided the Lomaxes with recordings of several songs they printed in *American Ballads and Folk Songs:* the ballads "Ella Speed" and "Frankie and Albert"; the barrelhouse song "Honey Take a Whiff on Me"; the cowboy song "Western Cowboy"; and a reel that also served as a work song, "Julie Ann Johnson."

After the discovery of Leadbelly at Angola, the Lomaxes pursued disk recordings of black music at prisons in Mississippi and Tennessee. Most of these were not blues, however. The Lomaxes concluded their expedition at Washington, D.C., in September, and immediately began the compilation of *American Ballads and Folk Songs* at the Library of Congress.

On the successful completion of this manuscript and with the encouragement of the Library, the Lomaxes were able to negotiate sponsorship for the continuation of their folk-song collecting in the field. In December, they made new recordings of their most productive Texas prison-farm singers, this time on disk. The following April, they began a series of additional recordings, gaining access to the State Penitentiary at Huntsville for the first time. Here they obtained a version of the bawdy ballad "Stavin' Chain" from Tricky Sam (Homer Rober[t]son) and, from a singer-guitarist named "Little Brother," a very fine blues entitled "Up And Down Building K. C. Line."

In May, at Richmond, the Lomaxes discovered and recorded their second significant black songster, Pete Harris. A singer-guitarist, Harris had a repertoire that paralleled Leadbelly's, including reels, cowboy songs, barrelhouse songs, and blues. One of his barrelhouse pieces was the bawdy "Jack and Betsy," another was the popular "Alabama Bound." The latter, particularly representative of songsters, is part of a cycle that includes "Don't Leave Me Here," "Elder Green's in Town," "On the Road Again," "Another Man Done Gone,"and "Baby Please Don't Go." Over several decades, songsters, bluesmen, and other performers made commercial and field recordings of these interrelated songs.

Some of Harris's songs were associated with the recorded repertoire of the famous Texas bluesman-songster Blind Lemon Jefferson. Leadbelly had played with Jefferson on the streets of Dallas, when he had lived in Texas. Another blues performed by Harris had been first recorded the previous year at a commercial session by three different Alabama singers, Bessie Jackson (Lucille Bogan), Walter Roland, and Sonny Scott. This was "Red Cross Store," which Leadbelly later recorded for the Lomaxes and which Gellert collected as a black protest song in the Carolinas and Georgia.

During June, July, and August, the Lomaxes were in Louisiana; for part of this period, Alan and Irene Thérèse Whitfield took charge of the recordings. In June fine renditions of ballads and reels were obtained at Lafayette from the songster Wilson Jones (Stavin' Chain). Performed in string-band setting—guitar, banjo, and fiddle— the ballads were "Stavin' Chain" and "Batson." Ellis Evans at Lloyd sang an excellent

Prison Compound Number 1, Angola, Louisiana, July 1934. Leadbelly is hatless in the foreground, left.

blues, "When I Leave You Baby," to the accompaniment of his own harmonica, with washboard by Jimmy Lewis. The most important finds in this month, however, were secular and religious *juré*—circular dances to polyrhythmic vocals by a leader and chorus (call and response) with clapping and (reportedly) washboard accompaniment. Recorded at Jennings, lead singers were Joe Washington Brown, Austin Coleman, and Jimmy Peters. Like the Georgia Sea Island shouts documented by Robert W. Gordon, *juré* have direct African-Creole antecedents and parallels in the Caribbean.

On July 1, the Lomaxes paid a return visit to the Louisiana State Penitentiary at Angola and recorded Leadbelly again. They rerecorded his 1933 pieces and explored further facets of his repertoire, notably his blues, including two associated with Blind Lemon Jefferson. They also recorded a scintillating guitar-accompanied blues, "Baby, Low Dow, Oh Low Down Dirty Dog," by Ernest Rogers. Most important to Leadbelly and the Lomaxes, however, was Leadbelly's pardon song (the second in his lifetime), addressed to the governor of Louisiana, O. K. Allen. Allowing him to select the recording on the other side—he chose "Irene," a popular song in waltz time—the Lomaxes promised to deliver a copy of this disk to the governor.

They were true to their word, although whether Leadbelly was pardoned as a result of it remains a matter of dispute.

Three days later, John Lomax recorded a group of seven "boys," led by Curtis Harton, singing two blues to the accompaniment of homemade instruments at Oscar Post Office, Pointe Coupée Parish. This level of variety in their recordings of black music at this time continued through the beginning of the next month when, on August 1 (the day of Leadbelly's pardon), Alan obtained blues sung in French Creole by Joseph Jones—"Blues de la prison"—and Cleveland Benoit and Darby Hicks—"Là-bas chez Moreau."

On his release, Leadbelly went to Shreveport, Louisiana, where he had been living prior to his incarceration. On September 16, however, he arrived in the lobby of the hotel in Marshall, Texas, where John A. Lomax was staying, and offered to be the driver for Lomax's next field-recording expedition. Lomax took him on, and Leadbelly became his assistant, singing (and sometimes recording) songs to demonstrate the type of material Lomax was interested in obtaining from black convicts at state prison farms. This expedition took them to Arkansas, where, at Little Rock, on September 27, Lomax recorded ballads, blues, and reels from the black fiddle player Blind Pete, accompanied by George Ryan on guitar. They were street singers with a repertoire of twenty-nine blues (according to Lomax's field notes), although only two appear to have been recorded. One, entitled "Banty Rooster," is similar to the song recorded in 1929 by Mississippian Charley Patton (Paramount 12792).

Early in October, after calls at prisons in Pine Bluff and Tucker, Lomax made recordings at the Cumins State Farm, Gould. Here Leadbelly witnessed the performance of "Rock Island Line" by Kelly Pace and group, a work song with which he was later to become associated. Martha, Leadbelly's new girlfriend, "had not seen his new

This ad for a Leadbelly concert in lower Manhattan reveals the nature of the singer's audience. The Irving Plaza venue was convenient to New York University and Greenwich Village. For most of his career, Leadbelly was thought of less as a blues singer than as a very authentic folk singer.

Leadbelly at a New York nightclub, about 1936.

clothes," and the singer became restless for Shreveport. He also wanted to reestablish his reputation there by driving Lomax's car "down Fannin Street" (the main black thoroughfare and notorious red-light district). This indulgence was allowed and, if Library of Congress dates are correct, Lomax then doubled back to Texas, making recordings of work songs at the Central State Farm, Sugarland, on October 14. He and Leadbelly returned to Louisiana, en route to Alabama; near Morgan City, on October 17, the singer-guitarist John Bray was recorded performing "Trench Blues," a fascinating topical song about World War I.

In Alabama, at Birmingham on October 25, Lomax obtained a travel blues to knife- or bottleneck-style accompaniment, entitled "Going North," noting that "the singer," Tom Bradford, "was half higher than pine on corn whiskey." Three days later, at Kilby Prison, Montgomery, Lomax recorded a fine "Boll Weevil Rag" sung and played on the guitar by Charles Griffin. This is based on the "Boll Weevil" ballad and is related to a 1926 commercial recording, "Devil and My Brown Blues," by Sam Butler (Bo Weevil Jackson), scheduled for issue by Vocalion (1055), but apparently never released.

By November, Leadbelly was back in Shreveport, and Lomax had returned to Texas, where he again visited the State Penitentiary at Huntsville. Here he obtained further black ballads from Tricky Sam and well-performed traditional blues and hollers from Augustus "Track Horse" Haggerty and his guitarist "Black" Jack Johnson.

John A. Lomax had intended his September–October field trip to be the only one that he undertook with Leadbelly in 1934. He had told him that his next expedition would be to New York and that with his son in the car there would be no room for another passenger. Lomax, however, was invited to present Leadbelly and his songs at a meeting of the Modern Language Association in Philadelphia, on December 30 and, urged by Alan, decided to accept. An extra passenger seat was squeezed into the car (into which the recording machine had been built), and, early in December, the Lomaxes arrived in Shreveport to collect Leadbelly for the long drive north. Their route took them through Georgia and South and North Carolina; in each state they called at prisons to make recordings. At Bellwood Prison Camp

Huddie Ledbetter, NYPD mug shot, 1939.

PRISONER'S CRIMINAL RECORD D.O. 24 (Rev. 8-58)	POLICE DEPARTMENT CITY OF NEW YORK	BUREAU OF CRIMINAL IDENTIFICATION

NAME   Huddie Ledbetter   B # 1 7 7 8 7 6

ALIAS   "Ledbelly"   E #

This certifies that the finger impressions of the above named person have been compared and the following is a true copy of the records of this bureau.

D.C.I. #

F.B.I. #

Date of Arrest	NAME	Borough or City	CHARGE	Arresting Officer	Date, Disposition, Judge and Court
6/7/18	Huddie Ledbetter	Dekalb, Tex.	Homicide	P.S.	
1/15/30	Huddie Ledbetter	Louisana	Asslt. with Intend to Murder	P.S.	2/26/30 - 6 to 10 Yrs. State Prison - Baton Rouge, La. #19469
3/5/39	Huddie Ledbetter	Manh. 1816-18	Fel. Asslt.	Hammond 18 Sqd.	Gen. Sess. 5/4/39 - Fin. Chg. Asslt. 3rd. (Conv. by Jury.)

Record prepared on   6/2/67
by   P. SAMUEL   Date
CIVILIAN TYPIST   Signature

Rank   Shield No.   Command   I.U.

X represents notations unsupported by fingerprints in Bureau of Criminal Identification files.
"This record is furnished solely for the official use of law enforcement agencies. Unauthorized use of this information is in violation of sections 554 and 2050, penal law."

NYPD rap sheet on one Huddie Ledbetter.

near Atlanta they obtained "Alabama Prison Blues," on the theme of arrest and incarceration, from Jesse Wadley (accompanying himself on guitar), and at the State Prison Farm, Milledgeville, another personalized blues, "Trouble," in which the vocals were shared by "Cool Breeze" and Reese Crenshaw, the latter playing guitar. At Columbia, South Carolina, prison authorities refused them access for recording, but at the State Penitentiary, Raleigh, North Carolina, they obtained two superlative guitar-accompanied blues from "Blind Joe," "When I Lie Down Last Night" and "In Trouble." The latter took up the theme of arrest and imprisonment and suggests that the Lomaxes asked for songs on this subject. The party arrived at Washington, D.C., on Christmas Eve and spent the festive season in that city.

At the end of the month, Leadbelly's performances for the Modern Language Association were a great success. This was followed by further accolades when Leadbelly and the Lomaxes reached New York at the beginning of the new year. From the middle of January, arrangements were made for them to stay at a cottage belonging to the folklorist Mary Elizabeth Barnicle in nearby Wilton, Connecticut. It was here that Leadbelly recorded most of his repertoire of ballads, barrelhouse songs, blues, hollers, square dances, and work songs for a book on his life and music being prepared by the Lomaxes. As with all their recordings, the originals were deposited at the Library of Congress.

Commencing June 15, at Brunswick, Georgia, Alan Lomax, accompanied by Mary Elizabeth Barnicle and the noted black folklorist Zora Neale Hurston, embarked on a field trip that took them to the Georgia Sea Island (Frederica, on St. Simon's Island) and Hurston's native Florida. Lomax and Barnicle then went on to the Bahamas. At Frederica they obtained spirituals and shouts similar to those

Novelist Zora Neale Hurston (left), Rochelle French, and Gabriel Brown (playing guitar) relax at Eatonville, Florida, June 1935.

recorded by Robert W. Gordon at nearby Darien. Secular repertoire included ballads, breakdowns (or jooking), and even a "fandango." Examples of the latter, played on the guitar by John Davis, Robert Davis, and Bill Tatnall, have been made available on LP, as have selections of subsequent recordings made in Florida under Hurston's expert guidance. Lomax later wrote that "she had been almost entirely responsible for the success of our trip and for our going to the Bahamas."

At Eatonville, Florida, her hometown, Hurston introduced Lomax and Barnicle to the singer-guitarists Gabriel Brown and Rochelle French, together with vocalist John French. They obtained excellent recordings of ballads, barrelhouse songs, and religious repertoire from these performers. Some of the blues were original, but others were almost certainly based on commercial releases.

Moving further south to Belle Glade, the party encountered an especially exciting "jook" band comprising Booker T. Sapps (vocals, harmonica), Roger Matthews (vocals, harmonica), and Willy Flowers (vocals, guitar). Along with individual harmonica pieces from Sapps and Matthews (demonstrating instrumental dexterity), this band recorded ballads, blues, a holler (by Flowers, accompanying himself on guitar), and one religious song.

In 1936 John A. Lomax continued his tour of southern prison farms, where he occasionally recorded blues. These locations included the State Farm, Raiford, Florida, the State Penitentiary, Parchman, Mississippi, and in Virginia the State Farm, Lynn, and State Penitentiary, Richmond. Among others, for example in Mississippi, Frank Evans and an unidentified singer-guitarist performed blues in styles associated with that region. In Virginia, Jimmie Strothers (an important songster) was recorded at Lynn, and a number of fine guitar-accompanied blues performances were obtained from convicts at Richmond.

John A. Lomax first visited a community of blacks living in or near Livingston, Alabama, in 1937. Here he obtained religious pieces, some hollers, and a few blues.

He also recorded several important proto-blues from Blind Jesse Harris, who accompanied himself on accordion, an instrument popular with blacks in the late nineteenth and early twentieth centuries but little represented in either commercial or field recordings of vernacular black music.

Demonstrating the relationship between vernacular and more commercial culture, Alan Lomax undertook, in 1938, recordings of great importance to the history of blues, ragtime, and jazz. As he wrote in the *Report of the Librarian of Congress* for that year, "W. C. Handy, the composer of the 'St. Louis Blues' and others told his story of the origin of the 'blues' before the 'mike.' Later 'Jelly Roll' Morton, one of the early jazz composers, filled fifty-one disks with the social and cultural background of New Orleans jazz—a sort of folk preface to modern popular music on record."

Brown and French, Eatonville, Florida, 1935.

Handy sang solo or to the accompaniment of his guitar, examples of proto-blues he told Lomax he had learned in the early 1890s. These included river songs, work songs, and hollers, as well as versions of "Joe Turner" (about a prison transfer official) together with the familiar "Careless Love" and "I Walked All the Way from East St. Louis" (or "One Dime Blues"). His "Olius Brown" is a variant of a vernacular song recorded commercially in 1927 by Ollis Martin as "Police and High Sheriff Come Ridin' Down" (Gennett 6306).

In May, the same month that Handy made his recordings, Jelly Roll Morton began his extraordinary biographical reminiscences to the accompaniment of his own piano. While Morton is recognized as a very prominent musician in the history of jazz, less significance has been given to his wanderings as a barrelhouse pianist. Morton's descriptions and music from the early 1900s (as given to Lomax) provide an unparalleled glimpse at the development of ragtime and blues piano by a principal exponent. His barrelhouse repertoire included "Alabama Bound," "Salty Dog,"

Jelly Roll Morton, about 1939, when he recorded for Alan Lomax and the Library of Congress.

*Roger Matthews, harmonica,
Willie Flowers, guitar, and Booker
T. Sapps, harmonica, play at Belle
Glade, Florida, June 1935.*

"Hesitation Blues" (recorded as "If I Was Whiskey and You Was a Duck"), and
"C. C. Rider," all of which Leadbelly had performed for the Lomaxes in 1935. In
addition Morton recorded bawdy material such as "The Dirty Dozens," "The
Winding Boy," "Make Me a Pallet on the Floor," and "The Murder Ballad." His
monologues and dialogues with musical illustrations throw light on "early blues
and Buddy Bolden" in New Orleans, "saloons and piano players of Beale Street,
Memphis," and the relationship between "jazz and blues." He also recorded a number of blues proper, such as "Levee Rambler Blues," "Low Down Blues," "Game Kid
Blues" and "Mamie Desdoumes' Blues."

During October and November, in Detroit, Alan Lomax discovered Sampson
Pittman and the Frazier family, black migrants from Memphis, Tennessee, who were
skilled musicians. From Pittman and Calvin Frazier, he obtained significant record-
ings of blues and barrelhouse music from the Arkansas side of the Mississippi River.
A contemporary of the better-known bluesmen Johnny Shines (his cousin) and
Robert Johnson, Calvin Frazier wrote songs that were representative of the younger
generation of blues singer-guitarists. Based on aural evidence, we can conclude that
Pittman was an older musician. His most important song was "I Ain't No Stranger
I've Been Down in the Circle Before," about the cabal of contractors who operated a
system of peonage in Mississippi River levee-maintenance camps. He also contributed "Cotton Farmer Blues," based on the boll weevil ballad; a blues in praise of
the boxer Joe Louis; and "Welfare Blues," critical of conditions in Detroit. Frazier
recorded a similar song, as well as tunes akin to commercial recordings by Robert
Johnson, and a version of "The Dirty Dozens" closer to earlier commercial recordings
than the song Lomax had obtained from Jelly Roll Morton.

In the *Report of the Librarian of Congress* for 1939, Alan Lomax noted how he
had obtained another significant group of blues-oriented recordings for the Archive
of American Folk Song in December 1938. He stated that "with the help of John

Boogie-woogie pianist Albert Ammons with two unidentified friends.

Hammond, organizer and mainspring of the *New Masses* swing concert at Carnegie Hall, and the Allied Recording Company, who lent their machine for two days, I was able to make for the Library recordings of five of the most remarkable Negroes in American music: Albert Ammons, Meade "Lux" Lewis, and Jimmie [*sic*] Johnson, the 'boogie boogie' pianists; Jimmie Johnson, the blues [*sic*] pianist and composer;

and Saunders Terry, the blind harmonica player from North Carolina." The Johnsons were, in fact, Pete (boogie woogie specialist) and James P. (best known as a jazz stylist, although he principally performed blues for Lomax).

As with his pioneering interviews with Handy and Morton, Lomax pursued unusual aspects of the repertoire of these musicians and paid attention to the origin of their styles. Sonny Terry (Saunders Terrell) played traditional harmonica virtuoso pieces and sang blues from his recent partnership with the Durham, North Carolina, bluesman Blind Boy Fuller. None of the pianists specialized in vocals, although each occasionally sang during these recordings. James P. Johnson described his early life, working with the vaudeville blues singer Ethel Waters, and played blues and bawdy sporting house pieces, together with a version of the rag "Pork and Beans." Meade "Lux" Lewis explained the background to his "Honky Tonk Train Blues" while Albert Ammons and Pete Johnson demonstrated blues and boogie-woogie styles. Ammons, for example, played "Sweet Patootie Blues," which he had learned from the St. Louis pianist Doug Suggs. Lomax also recorded further aspects of Leadbelly's repertoire at this time.

Early in March 1939, Charles Seeger visited South Carolina, where he made unusual recordings. These included the local black ballad "The McKenzie Case" (sung by Belton Reese to the accompaniment of his own banjo) and others such as the minstrel piece "Bile Dem Cabbages Down" (sung by Israel Alston, accompanied by Reese on banjo and Thaddeus Goodson playing bones.) The year 1939 also saw John A. Lomax and his wife (Ruby T.) making an extended field trip through the South. Commencing in Texas on March 31, they visited Louisiana, Arkansas, Mississippi, Florida, South Carolina, Georgia, and Virginia. The expedition ended in Washington, D.C., on June 14. Recording of blues performances was not a primary objective of this trip, although they did locate and record the superlative bluesman-songster Smith Casey at the Clemens State Farm, Brazoria, Texas. Like Pete Harris, he had a guitar-accompanied repertoire that included pieces associated with the commercially recorded legacy of Blind Lemon Jefferson. They also recorded "Ella

Meade "Lux" Lewis strikes a pensive pose.

Speed," a black ballad from Texas, and two blues at the Ramsey State Farm, Otey, Texas, performed by Wallace Chains and Sylvester Jones. In addition, at the State Penitentiary, Parchman, Mississippi, the celebrated bluesman Washington "Barrelhouse" White, who had made commercial records as Bukka White, contributed "Sic 'Em Dogs On" and "Po' Boy" to Lomax's collection.

A separate field expedition conducted by folklorist Herbert Halpert visited the Mississippi State Penitentiary in the same May–June period. Halpert obtained a series of recordings of blues, hollers, game songs, and religious pieces sung a cappella by black women prisoners. One blues, "Shake 'Em on Down," performed by Lucille Walker, was a version of Bukka White's influential 1937 commercial recording (Vocalion 03711). Halpert also secured valuable recordings of work calls and hollers during this tour of Mississippi.

In August 1940, Alan Lomax obtained an important series of recordings from Leadbelly in New York. Using the interview technique he had developed earlier with Jelly Roll Morton, he encouraged songs and descriptions revolving around specific

Leadbelly plays for youngsters in New York City. He enjoyed playing for children more than for any other audience.

subjects: tuberculosis, square dances, blues, and "the mourner's bench." The latter were the most significant in that they represented Leadbelly's religious repertoire and were based principally on recollections of his youth. He also recorded ballads, topical and protest songs, and a work song.

Commencing in late September, and again starting from Texas, John A. Lomax and his wife made another journey through the southern states. As in the 1939 Texas trip, they obtained work songs from Henry Truvillion (the same singer recorded in 1933), and they collected ballads and barrelhouse songs from the songster Finous Rockmore. A guitarist, Rockmore ran a small string band called the Lufkin Boosters, although the group did not perform for the Lomaxes. Rockmore had once played with Coley Jones, a Dallas-based songster who also ran a string band, and claimed he had made commercial recordings—the latter possibly with Jones, who recorded for Columbia in 1927, 1928, and 1929.

At Shreveport, Louisiana, on October 8, the Lomaxes encountered three more musicians who had made commercial recordings: Oscar Woods, Joe Harris, and Kid West. Although they usually performed together, Woods was recorded separately. A specialist in playing open-tuned slide guitar, with the slider laid across the strings, he contributed barrelhouse songs and one blues, "Sometimes I Get to Thinking." Joe Harris (guitar) and Kid West (mandolin) were recorded the following day and performed ragtime and other barrelhouse material, as well as one ballad ("Bully of the Town") and four blues.

One purpose of John A. Lomax's field recordings of black music in this area in 1940 was almost certainly to discover something of the background to Leadbelly's repertoire. To this end he and his wife drove north from Shreveport on October 10 to Oil City, where they recorded Bob Ledbetter (Leadbelly's uncle) and Noah Moore (Leadbelly's cousin). Uncle Bob Ledbetter had suffered a stroke and was unable to sing much for the Lomaxes, although he managed a version of "Irene" (to Noah's guitar accompaniment). He explained how his brother, Terrell, had taught Leadbelly this song. Noah was a man of his time, and blues predominated in his repertoire, including "Jerry's Saloon Blues" to slide-guitar accompaniment. He also performed barrelhouse songs and reels.

After making further recordings in Louisiana, the Lomaxes drove to Natchez, Mississippi, where, on October 19, they discovered three singer-guitarists, two of whom, Lucious Curtis and Willie Ford, made several recordings of blues, barrelhouse songs, and one ballad, "Stagolee" (variously spelled "Stagolee, "Stagger Lee," "Stacker Lee," and "Stack O'Lee," this ballad appears to have been widely distributed early in the century, as Odum collected versions in Mississippi and Georgia at that time). The Lomaxes' third bluesman, George Boldwin, recorded a hesitant "Country Girl Blues." But it was Curtis who made most of the recordings. He earned his living from small-time entertaining at dance halls and, like Ford, was a highly proficient performer. He claimed he had "made some commercial records" with Bo Carter, of the famous Chatmon family string band, also from Mississippi.

Traveling north to the Mississippi State Penitentiary at Parchman, Lomax, who was not carrying his customary letter from the governor granting permission to record songs from the inmates, was turned away by the new warden. This setback was made up for by a large selection of recordings gleaned at Livingston, Alabama, which the Lomaxes reached at the end of October. The performances they obtained included hollers, ballads, and work songs from Rich Amerson, as well as fine versions of "Another Man Done Gone" and "Boll Weevil Blues" by Vera Hall. On October 3

Leadbelly's uncle, Bob Ledbetter, at home in Shreveport, Louisiana, 1940.

they recorded excellent guitar-accompanied blues and dance tunes from Tom Bell. One day later, in Atlanta, Ruby T. Lomax spotted "a negro man with a guitar" stationed by a "'Little Pig' (barbecue) stand." This was the celebrated bluesman-songster Blind Willie McTell, veteran of many commercial recording sessions. The following day, McTell made records for the Library of Congress, including a selection of ballads, barrelhouse songs, blues, and religious performances, together with monologues on blues, his life, his recording career, and old-time (i.e., religious) songs. There was a regional, East Coast emphasis in his repertoire, which included the ballads "Will Fox" and "Delia," and a blues work song, "Murderer's Home Blues." The latter two songs had been recorded earlier by Gellert in the same area—"Murderer's Home Blues" being a song he identified as "Chain Gang Blues," or "Down in the Chain Gang." Odum had collected a version of "Delia" in Newton County, Georgia, about 1906–1908.

A group of recordings supervised by John W. Work of Fisk University, at Fort Valley State College in Georgia, was probably made during the College's annual folk festival in March 1941. Many highly proficient local musicians competed at this event, and guitar-accompanied blues and ballads were a prominent feature. Harmonica players and string bands also participated, and one blues-piano performance is known, "My Big Fat Hipted Mama," by Charles Ellis. The emphasis in the repertoire of the participants was generally traditional. Also active in research in the eastern seaboard states in 1941 was Roscoe Lewis of the Hampton Institute, Virginia, who recorded a fine singer-guitarist known only as "Big Boy," performing a repertoire that included blues and ballads. In July of the same year, Robert Sonkin made a survey of music played in Gee's Bend, Alabama. Most of the repertoire was religious, but at nearby Selma, on July 17, he obtained two blues played by a "Washboard Trio," one of which was another version of "Red Cross Store."

The most significant recordings in 1941 were those made in Mississippi by Alan Lomax, John W. Work, and Lewis Jones, which form part of a collaboration between the Library of Congress and Fisk University to document "the musical habits of a single Negro community in the [Mississippi] Delta." The region selected was "Coahoma and Bolivar Counties, one hundred miles south of Memphis," where the black population was significantly high. During an exploratory recording trip in late August, Lomax and his party located the blues singer-guitarist McKinley Morganfield—better known as Muddy Waters—from whom they obtained superlative performances. Waters had learned his bottleneck guitar-playing techniques from the eminent Delta bluesman Son House. On being told this, Lomax immediately searched for House and found him. Like Son Sims, who played guitar for Waters and also fiddle, House had made commercial recordings for Paramount a decade before, as had one of his companions, Willie Brown. Lomax recorded blues from House and his compatriots playing in a small combo (House, vocal-guitar; Brown, guitar; Fiddlin' Joe Martin, mandolin; Leroy Williams, harmonica). Martin also recorded two vocals, a blues and a minstrel-type piece, leading this group. House, Brown, and Martin all participated in "Camp Hollers," which was unaccompanied, while Brown contributed a vocal-guitar rendition of the barrelhouse song "Make Me a Pallet on the Floor." Odum had collected a version of the latter from a singer in Lafayette County, Mississippi, early in the century. Williams's harmonica-accompanied "Uncle Sam Done Called" has lyrics that related to the draft prior to entry into World War II.

The spring of 1942 saw Lewis Jones undertaking a further exploratory survey for the Fisk University–Library of Congress project. Jones supervised a few recordings at

Blind Willie McTell in an Atlanta hotel room, November 1940.

this time, such as those by Thomas "Jaybird" Jones, a pianist who had made commercial blues recordings in 1928. This laid the ground for more extensive field work in the summer.

In March of the same year, John W. Work was responsible for recording songster repertoire in Nashville from a street-corner musician and busker named Ned (or Nathan) Frazier, a highly proficient banjoist who was accompanied by an equally skilled fiddle player, Frank Patterson. Their repertoire consisted of one blues, barrelhouse songs, and reels, played in a highly distinctive manner. Work was especially interested in this under-documented repertoire, and, before setting out with Alan Lomax on their summer expedition to the Mississippi Delta, they recorded the Nashville Washboard Band at Work's home on July 15. This small group consisted of James Kelly (mandolin), Frank Dalton (guitar), Tom Carrol (tin can, bull fiddle), and Theopolis Stokes (washboard). Vocals appear to have been shared among band members, and their repertoire, like Frazier's ranged from blues to minstrel pieces and reels.

Traveling via Memphis the following day, Lomax encountered Willie "61" Blackwell, a blues singer-guitarist who composed highly original lyrics and had

Stavin' Chain (Wilson Jones) sings for the Library of Congress at Lafayette, Louisiana, June 1934.

recorded commercially for Bluebird the previous year. Blackwell sang a version of one of his 1941 pieces, together with a wartime song, "Junior, a Jap's Girl Christmas For His Santa Claus." He was supported on second guitar by another bluesman, William Brown, who also recorded three blues, including a version of "I Walked All the Way From East St. Louis."

At Robinsonville, Mississippi, on July 17, Lomax again recorded the doyen of Delta bluesmen, Son House, exploring his repertoire in depth. House explained how he had learned one of his songs, "Pony Blues," from Willie Brown (not to be confused with William Brown). His earliest repertoire came from Willie Williams (or Wilson)—"Special Rider Blues" and "Depot Blues" (melody only). The guitar accompaniment to his "Jinx Blues" is in a style associated with Drew, Mississippi, in which Willie Brown was schooled, and which is best represented in commercial recordings by the work of Charley Patton.

Blues and religious pieces played on the harmonica were obtained on July 19 from Turner "Junior" Johnson, while on July 20 and 22 the blues guitarist David "Honeyboy" Edwards was recorded. His repertoire included a ballad, barrelhouse songs, blues, a game song, and a work song, all to his own accompaniment. Many of Edwards's blues were based on earlier commercial recordings, although his contemporary "Army Blues" (on which he also played harmonica) was an original composition.

On July 24, Muddy Waters was again recorded, playing with the Son Sims Four, of which he was a member. He recorded on his own as well, and with Sims, or his brother-in-law Charley Berry, on second guitar. Berry also recorded several unaccompanied hollers. The Son Sims Four was a string band, with Waters playing guitar, Sims fiddle, Percy Thomas guitar, and Louis Ford mandolin. Ford, like Sims, had played with Charley Patton, and, in this respect, they were of an older generation than Waters. Ford sang "Joe Turner," the same song recalled by W. C. Handy and which Odum had collected in Mississippi prior to 1906. The band played blues and breakdowns, while Waters principally performed blues, such as the second version of his "Country Blues," a song he had also recorded in 1941. This piece, accompanied on bottleneck guitar, is in the style Son House taught Waters and Robert Johnson (who had been murdered four years before).

A songster named Will Storks was recorded on July 25 at Clarksdale, Mississippi, the locale for all the field work since July 19. Again, on July 26, Thomas "Jaybird" Jones contributed to the meager documentation of piano blues in the Archive of American Folk Song. He also accompanied Minnie Lee Whitehead, one of the few female blues singers recorded by the Archive, singing a version of Big Maceo's popular "Worried Life Blues" (Bluebird B8827, recorded in 1941). Further ballads and barrelhouse songs were obtained from Will Storks on August 9.

The other important group of secular recordings in this expedition, by Sid Hemphill and his band, were made on August 15 at Sledge, Mississippi, as Lomax was returning north. Hemphill, the son of a slave fiddle player, was skilled in playing many instruments and ran a string band that doubled as a fife and drum band. Lomax recorded examples of both aspects of this band's music and Hemphill's playing of the ten-hole quill, as well as his associate Alex Askew playing the four-hole quill.

Buster Brown

The string band (in which Hemphill led on fiddle) played for both white and black dances. Accordingly, they had a mixed repertoire of old-time fiddle pieces (principally reels) and blues ballads. Some of the latter were traditional, such as "The Boll Weevil" and "John Henry," and some were Hemphill's local compositions, such as "The Carrier Railroad" and the "Strayhorn Mob." The band rarely played blues.

The repertoire of the fife and drum band (in which Hemphill played fife) was generally late nineteenth- and early twentieth-century popular music. They performed at picnics.

Willis James and Lewis Jones again made recordings at the Fort Valley State College Folk Festival in March 1943. With the United States engaged in World War II, there were songs on this theme, such as Buster Brown's harmonica-accompanied "War Song" (a blues) and Buster "Buzz" Ezell's guitar-accompanied "Roosevelt and Hitler." Ezell made another recording of the latter, together with similar patriotic ballads later in the year. They signal the end of one era and the opening of another.

FIELD RECORDINGS AND QUASI-FIELD RECORDINGS 1946–60: FROM "STOMP DE LOWDOWN" TO "TOMORROW GONNA BE MY TRYING DAY"

"Stomp de Lowdown" was the first of four tunes recorded by Ollie "Dink" Johnson in March 1946, accompanied by his own piano, with guitar and bass. The brother-in-law of Jelly Roll Morton, Johnson, who also played clarinet and drums, was discovered by the jazz historian William Russell in Los Angeles. He recorded for American Music, Russell's small private label devoted to the documentation of New Orleans jazz. Like many of Morton's performances for the Library of Congress, however, Johnson's piano repertoire reflected the blues and ragtime of prewar barrelhouses, as well as music of more ornate jazz ensembles.

Johnson's recordings pinpoint one area of blues development researchers (whether folklorists or enthusiasts) pursued infrequently. An equally important and similarly neglected aspect of black musical evolution was the black string band, including tub, jug, and washboard bands. Little attention was paid to the crucial role of these ensembles in bridging the gap between nineteenth- and twentieth-century black and white repertoire, the audiences for which were often segregated. An exception to the neglect was the joint studies by Alan Lomax and John W. Work in 1941–42, and further important evidence in this area was gathered about September 1946 for the Library of Congress in Campaign, Tennessee, by Margot Mayo, Stuart Jamieson, and Freyda Simon, who obtained recordings by a black string band led by fiddler John Lusk. Other members of the band were Albert York, guitar, and the celebrated banjo player Murph Gribble, who, like a number of blues and jazz performers was part black, part Native American. While this band's repertoire is remembered as "strictly old-time breakdown music," and the recorded material reflects this, Gribble recalled in 1949 that they also played tunes such as "C. C. Rider," which he categorized as "some of that ole black country music, you know, a sukey jump"—a term Leadbelly also used for his repertoire of square dances.

In 1947, Alan Lomax (no longer working for the Library of Congress) made a further series of evocative recordings at the Mississippi State Penitentiary, Parchman, which included work songs, hollers, ballads, and blues. He also coaxed music and reminiscences of segregated southern experiences from three important blues performers based in Chicago, whose roots were in the Mississippi River basin. These were the singer-guitarist Big Bill Broonzy (as Natchez), the singer-pianist Memphis Slim (as Leroy), and the singer–harmonica player John Lee "Sonny Boy" Williamson (as Sib). Broonzy sang unaccompanied work songs. To his own piano, Memphis Slim performed a similar work and prison-oriented repertoire together with the ballad "Stackerlee" (Lomax had also obtained a version of the latter from Bama, at Parchman Farm). Williamson sang "My Black Name." He had performed this, based on a holler, for Bluebird in 1941 (B8992), but it had been recorded first by the Texas blues woman Bessie Tucker, as "Black Name Moan," in 1928 (Victor 21692). Likewise, 1920s commercial recordings by bluesman-songsters of the ballad "Stackerlee" are "Billy Lyons and Stack O'Lee" (Furry Lewis, 1928, Vocalion 1132) and "Stack O'Lee Blues" (Mississippi John Hurt, 1928, Okeh 8654).

On October 6, William Russell recorded more prewar ragtime pieces and piano blues sung by Dink Johnson in Los Angeles. These included Dink's version of Jelly Roll Morton's "Jelly Roll Blues" (American Music 525), as well as his own "Dink's Blues" (American Music 526).

In addition to further Dink Johnson recordings in California (by Cecil Charles), 1948 saw sessions with Leadbelly, conducted by another jazz historian, Frederic Ramsey, Jr., in New York during September and October. Although he obtained ninety-four performances (with some duplications), Ramsey's unfulfilled purpose was to record Leadbelly's complete repertoire. He did succeed, however, in adding to the stock of songs Leadbelly had recorded in the pre- and postwar periods, including familiar as well as unfamiliar ballads, blues, hollers, reels, religious songs, and work songs. One of his miscellaneous songs, which might be categorized as a protest song, serves to demonstrate the process of assimilation adopted by songsters. "Nobody in the World Is Better Than Us" was originally a calypso composed by Lord Pretender (Alric Farrell). Highly popular in Trinidad calypso tents during the 1943 Carnival season, the song had been brought from the West Indies to New York by Lord Invader (Rupert Grant, another Trinidad calypsonian), a successful performer in Trinidad as well as the United States, when he made visits to New York in 1945, 1946, and 1947. Invader recorded the song there as "God Made Us All" in 1947 (Disc 5080). Leadbelly, who also recorded commercially for Disc in this period, almost certainly learned the song at the same time.

In the spring of 1949, the Library of Congress made more recordings of the John Lusk string band at Rocky Island, Tennessee. Fortuitously, Leadbelly was also recorded, at a concert at the University of Texas, Austin, on June 15, six months

Leadbelly at home in New York City, 1949—one of his last known photographs.

before he died, on December 6, at Bellevue Hospital, New York City. Both Lusk's band and Leadbelly performed familiar repertoire. In late July, William Russell located another string band called the Mobile Strugglers. Based in Mobile, they recorded two songs to the accompaniment of violins, mandolin, guitar, and bass: "Memphis Blues" and "Fattenin' Frogs" (American Music 104). "Memphis Blues" was W. C. Handy's melody (published 1912) sung to George A. Norton's lyrics (added 1913).

Harold Courlander, who, before the war, had conducted extensive research into the black music of Haiti and Cuba, visited Livingston, Alabama, in January and February 1950. His recordings constitute an extension of the work done there by John A. Lomax in 1937, 1939, and 1940.

Several personalities who had performed for Lomax were recorded anew, including Rich Amerson, Enoch Brown, Peelee Hatcher (Emanuel Jones), Doc Reed, and Vera Hall (Ward). Among his secular performances, Amerson sang a blueslike "Black Woman," a work-song-like "Railroad," and, with his sister providing a closely harmonized second vocal, the ballad "John Henry" as a *cante fable* (which Leadbelly had recorded as a reel for Frederic Ramsey, Jr. in 1948).

A younger man, Joe Brown, recorded a harmonica blues and also led a vocal quartet. "Red" Willie Smith provided guitar-accompanied songster material, such as "Kansas City" and "Salty Dog," and also had a repertoire of blues. "Now Your Man Done Gone, (described as a work song, and part of the "Alabama Bound" cycle), "Captain Holler Hurry" (a work song), and "John Henry" (as a ballad) were performed by Willie Turner. Like Amerson's "John Henry," these unaccompanied songs again featured unusual closely harmonized second vocals in a tradition Courlander seems to have considered African. Peelee Hatcher contributed a work-song blues, "I'm Going to Have a Talk with the Chief of Police."

While their function sometimes changes with the circumstances of their performance, most of these songs can be identified with prewar commercial recordings by bluesmen and/or songsters. This is true similarly of "Meet Me in the Bottoms" by Davie Lee (another song performed unaccompanied with closely harmonized second vocal), which Courlander recorded in Mississippi.

Pink Anderson was a songster from Spartanburg, South Carolina, who spent much of his life working in medicine shows and had made commercial recordings for Columbia in 1928. He was at the state fair in Charlottesville, Virginia, when he was recorded by Paul Clayton on May 29. His guitar-accompanied repertoire comprised black ballads like "John Henry" and "The Ship Titanic," together with barrelhouse-minstrel pieces such as "Everyday in the Week" (a song he had recorded in 1928), "Greasy Greens," and "I've Got Mine." He also performed a version of the celebrated white train-disaster ballad, "The Wreck of the Old 97." Odum had collected both "Greasy Greens" (in Mississippi) and "I Got Mine" (in Georgia) during the first decade of the century.

Black prison inmates were recorded again in Texas in March 1951, at the Ramsey State Farm, Otey, and Retrieve State Farm, Snipe, by a group interested in black folklore, including Pete Seeger and John Lomax, Jr., an elder brother of Alan Lomax. At least one blues, "Lowdown Dirty Shame," performed by the Ramsey prison band (Ray Schuler, vocal, accompanied by trombone, two saxophones, piano, bass, and drums) can be identified among these recordings, although most are generally call-and-response work songs or performances of a religious nature.

The popularity of New Orleans jazz among aficionados in this period led to a number of investigative recordings by enthusiasts in the Crescent City. On August

30, a band led by Emile Barnes and (on some performances) Lawrence Tocca was recorded playing creole songs, blues, and so on, including "Shake It and Break It," with piano and vocal by Billie Pierce. This prewar bawdy barrelhouse song was widely performed in different styles; for example, it was in the repertoire of the Mississippi songster Charley Patton, who recorded a vocal-guitar version in 1929 (Paramount 12869); a year later, the Mississippi blues pianist and vocalist Louise Johnson also recorded it. Using the melody of "Cow Cow Blues" (a famous piano theme), she called her version "On the Wall" (Paramount 13008). There was a swinging, solo-oriented jazz-band version of "Shake It and Break It" in 1933, performed by Joe

Scott Dunbar at his home in Old River Lake, Mississippi.

Robichaux and his New Orleans Rhythm Boys (Vocalion 2592), with vocal by Walter Williams, the band's guitarist.

Jazz dance-band vocal blues and barrelhouse music has been little studied, although the same team who recorded Barnes in 1951 (Alden Ashforth, Dave Wycoff, and Jim McGarrell) made similar recordings in 1952. On August 20, Jimmy "Kid" Clayton's band contributed "Jimmy's Blues" (with vocal by Clayton) and the traditional "Corrine Corrina" (with vocal by Clayton and George Guesnon). Emile Barnes (clarinet) and Charlie Love (cornet), with banjo, drums, and bass, recorded "Blues," an instrumental version of "Careless Love," for Wycoff and McGarrell on September 8.

While recordings by enthusiasts provide one means by which certain styles have been preserved, another source is radio stations. WBLT Bedford (Bedford County), Virginia, recorded a local bluesman, James Lowry, singing three guitar-accompanied blues for them in 1953. One was "Tampa Blues" (well known in the area), another "Caro Blues" (based on Blind Lemon Jefferson's "One Dime Blues"), and the third, "Early Morning Blues" (using traditional stanzas).

Billie Pierce (vocal, piano) and her husband Dee Dee (trumpet) recorded a version of one of the earliest of proto-blues, "Careless Love," for Samuel B. Charters

Jesse Fuller, "The Lone Cat." His invention, the fotdella, is at his left and is played with his right foot.

and Bert Stanleigh in New Orleans on March 27, 1954. Their "Married Man Blues," from the same session, represents the style of vaudeville blues singing especially popular in theaters in the 1920s.

In contrast, Frederic Ramsey, Jr.'s survey of southern black music, which commenced in April, set out to trace what could be discovered of earlier rural styles. One of his endeavors was to look at the effect of such styles on the musical environment of New Orleans and the development of jazz in that city. Certain rules were established for this field trip. Performers were sought by word of mouth and, generally, in "remote rural regions"—Alabama, Louisiana, and Mississippi. No specific location had been visited by researchers previously, and all performers were amateurs playing everyday music. None had recorded before. One exception was allowed, in that recordings were made in New Orleans.

Starting in Alabama, Ramsey obtained proto-blues and blues from Horace Sprott, a singer-harmonica player in his late sixties, whom he first recorded on April 10. Although a somewhat uninteresting performer, Sprott had a varied songsters' repertoire comprising ballads, barrelhouse songs, blues, hollers, religious songs, and work songs. One of the latter was "Take This Hammer" (in the "John Henry"/"Nine Pound Hammer" ballad/work-song cycle). Several of Sprott's blues can be traced to earlier commercial recordings. He also performed buck dances and hoedowns with younger musicians such as guitarist Philip Ramsey. Together, they recorded a version of Little Junior Parker's 1953 hit "Feelin' Good" (Sun 187) entitled "I Feel Good Now Baby." (Ultimately, this derives from Big Bill Broonzy's "I Feel So Good," Okeh 6688, recorded in 1941.)

Also discovered in Alabama were two country brass bands, the Laneville–Johnson Union Brass Band and the Lapsley Band. Blues and minstrel tunes formed part of their repertoire, which was recorded respectively on May 6 and 15.

The most exciting singer-guitarist found by Frederic Ramsey, Jr., on this field trip was Scott Dunbar, who lived at Old River Lake, southwestern Mississippi, almost opposite the Louisiana State Penitentiary, Angola, on the other side of the Mississippi River. His percussive, exuberant guitar playing provided just the right accompaniment for buck dances and other stomps, such as the instrumental "Memphis Mail," or "Easy Rider" (on which he shares the vocal with his wife, Rose). His "Forty Four Blues" and "Going Back to Vicksburg" (on which Rose also sings) are taken at different tempos on the guitar. They have, however, lyrical affinities to traditional songs with similar titles and are usually linked by the same accompaniment on the piano, known generally as the "44s."

On June 29, some four days after recording Dunbar, Ramsey managed to persuade some old-time black string-band members to record for him in Vicksburg, Mississippi. Tom Johnson and John Copeland, both of whom doubled on guitar and mandolin, performed a ragtime dance ("Hootchie Kootchie"), a reel, and two blues, as the Mississippi String Band. In this, Johnson sang two familiar prewar songs, "It's Tight Like That" (the reel) and "See See Mama" (or C. C. Rider), an early blues. Samuel B. Charters also visited Alabama in July, searching for the Mobile Strugglers. While he didn't find the band recorded by William Russell, he located three musicians who appear to have played with the group on other occasions: Ollie Crenshaw (kazoo, guitar, vocal), Moochie Reeves (guitar, vocal), and Tyler Jackson (washtub bass, vocal). They had a varied repertoire of popular and minstrel songs, as well as blues. Their most evocative piece in the latter style was "Trouble Trouble's Followed Me All My Days," in which Ollie Crenshaw sang the vocal alone, eschewing his kazoo.

A one-man band entertainer was likewise recorded in 1954, Jesse Fuller, a wanderer who had been born in Georgia but eventually settled in Oakland, California. Exuberantly, he performed six songs for Margaret Goldsmith accompanied by his own twelve-string guitar, harmonica, kazoo, and fotdella (a self-made, foot-operated double bass, to which he later added a high-hat cymbal). The songs admirably demonstrate the secular repertoire of songsters and the way in which they merged a variety of styles. His "Railroad Worksong" belongs to the "John Henry"/"Nine Pound Hammer" ballad/work-song cycle, while his "Lining Up the Tracks" (sung to fotdella alone) is a work song proper. His gambling song "Hanging Round a Skin Game" incorporates barrelhouse and work-song elements related to the "Olius Brown"/"Police and High Sheriff" song cycle. "Railroad Blues" is, of course, a blues, but his celebrated "San Francisco Bay Blues" is essentially a barrelhouse ragtime song. Jesse also performed a ballad version of "John Henry" to a guitar accompaniment he had learned about 1913 in the country near Atlanta, Georgia.

Fuller recorded similar material (without duplication) and religious songs for Tom Spinosa, James Salemi, and Norman Pierce in April 1955. Later in the year, on the trail of former members of the Mobile Strugglers, Sam Charters tracked down Virgil Perkins, a washboard player who occasionally sang vocals, in Houston. He recorded him there on November 6, accompanied by a twelve-string guitarist named Jack Sims. They performed the barrelhouse/minstrel song "Goin' Around the Mountain," the ballad "John Henry," and the well-known prewar blues "Trouble in Mind."

While it was still possible to track down and record street entertainers in the mid-1950s, generally they were no longer performing at roadsides. Black string bands, as Frederic Ramsey, Jr., had found, now performed only infrequently for dances, black or white, throughout the South. The repertoire of such aggregations and songsters, however, was still maintained in homesteads, such as those of the Reid family and their relatives, of mixed black, white, and Native American ancestry. In the summer of 1956, Diane Hamilton, Liam Clancy, and Paul Clayton visited Caudwell County, North Carolina, where the family lived. There they recorded Etta Baker (guitar), her father Boone Reid (banjo), and his son-in-law (Theopolis) Lacy Phillips (banjo), each playing instrumentals. Both Phillips and Reid—the latter was seventy-nine at the time of these recordings—performed tunes on the banjo associated with old-time white string-band dances. Etta Baker's guitar solos, however, consisted of blues and ballads from the black tradition. The former included the well-known "One Dime Blues," while lyrics to two of the ballads, "Bully of the Town" and "Railroad Bill," had been collected by Odum in Mississippi and Georgia before 1910.

On September 2 in St. Louis the veteran blues piano player Speckled Red (Rufus Perryman) recorded for the first time since his session for Bluebird in 1938. Supervised by piano blues aficionado Erwin Helfer, these new recordings explored Red's past repertoire. There was, for example, "Dad's Piece," an instrumental named after an old-time Detroit pianist called "Dad" (and known also as Fishtail), who had greatly influenced him. He also remade "The Dirty Dozens," the bawdy barrelhouse song he had been first to put on record in 1929 (Brunswick 7116). These and other songs and instrumentals from the two decades before World War II were performed with good-humored panache.

Some time in 1956, Helfer also recorded two superlative piano instrumentals by Doug Suggs, who, as has been noted, had greatly impressed Albert Ammons when they had performed together at Chicago rent parties in the 1920s. One of his pieces

Speckled Red at work.

was "Sweet Patootie," the tune Ammons played and attributed to Suggs in 1938. In turn, Suggs had learned this from Claude Brown in St. Louis, where he lived before moving to Chicago. His 1956 version is closer to "Sweet Petunia," a related bawdy barrelhouse song, first sung on record by Lucille Bogan (with piano by Alex Channey) in 1927 (Paramount 12459).

By chance, Ed Rhodes, an Atlanta record-store owner, recorded Blind Willie McTell in the fall of 1956. McTell performed songs from his wide-ranging street repertoire, principally barrelhouse material such as "Salty Dog," as well as Tin Pan Alley songs. Blues were hardly featured, but this may reflect Rhodes's lack of interest rather than McTell's intentions.

In California, Sam Eskin recorded a younger singer-guitarist, K. C. Douglas, who had been taught by the archetypal Mississippi bluesman Tommy Johnson. He featured blues, including Johnson's influential "Big Road Blues," the railroad ballad "Casey Jones," and the barrelhouse song "Kansas City." The latter was also sung and played by veteran banjo stylist Gus Cannon when he was recorded by Samuel B. Charters in Memphis, on December 5, 1956. At the same time, Cannon, a songster who had recorded with his own jug band for Victor in the late 1920s, took part in a recreation of the Memphis Jug Band with two of its ex-members: Will Shade (harmonica, guitar, vocal) and Charlie Burse (guitar, vocal). Cannon blew into the jug, producing a resonant burr, for "Take Your Finger Off It," a barrelhouse song the

Memphis Jug Band had recorded in 1934 (Vocalion 03175). However, they also had performed the majority of their blues and barrelhouse songs for Victor in the late 1920s. Shade (vocal, guitar) recreated one of the latter for Charters, "I Can't Stand It" (originally recorded in 1929, Victor V38551).

In New York, during June 1957, a usually reticent Reverend Blind Gary Davis was persuaded by folklorist Kenneth S. Goldstein to record guitar instrumentals and one vocal from his preconversion repertoire. (He had made commercial recordings for ARC in 1935 and subsequent religious recordings). Davis sang an expurgated "Candy Man" and played a version of the "Hesitating Blues," together with a "Buck Dance" and other barrelhouse titles.

Erwin Helfer made further recordings of Speckled Red's piano playing in St. Louis on June 4. He also recorded two other St. Louis–based pianists at unknown dates during the same year. These were James Crutchfield and James Robinson. The

A 1950s photograph of Blind Willie McTell taken at his home.

McTell at a family function in Georgia during the 1950s.

latter, known also as "Bat the Hummingbird," had made commercial recordings for Champion in 1931. On June 6, 1957 and early in September (again in St. Louis), Helfer played piano on sessions with the Mississippi blues singer-guitarist Big Joe Williams, who went to make vocal-guitar recordings for Robert Koester in January 1958. Like his sessions with Helfer, Big Joe concentrated on the blues repertoire with which he had made his reputation as a popular recording artist before and immediately after World War II. Jesse Fuller recorded further samples of his songster material for Lester Koenig in the same month, including interpretations of the ballad "Stagolee" ("Stack O'Lee") and the barrelhouse song "Hesitating Blues," better known as "Hesitation Blues."

February 8, 1958, saw Big Joe Williams make further recordings for Robert Koester, in the company of J. D. Short, another singer-guitarist who had made prewar commercial recordings. Short contributed a version of the bawdy barrelhouse ballad "Stavin' Chain." Williams recorded on his own on February 19, performing his celebrated "Baby Please Don't Go." He had done much to maintain the popularity of this "Alabama Bound" song-cycle variant, from his earliest recording of it in 1935 (Bluebird B6200).

Beginning in January, a young blind New Orleans street singer named Snooks Eaglin was recorded by Harry Oster, a folklorist then working at Louisiana State University, Baton Rouge. Unlike the old-time performers who had often been the focus of attention for the field recordings assessed in this survey, Eaglin was only twenty-two years old when Oster discovered him. In this he provides an especially good example of one of the means by which repertoire was passed from generation to generation from the time that mass marketing of records to black consumers began in 1920. Blind since early childhood, Eaglin had learned his considerable repertoire from records and radio transmissions, adapting accompaniments to his felicitous guitar playing. Many were blues, but he also sang gospel songs and used popular tunes as instrumental showcases to demonstrate his guitar-playing technique.

Another singer-guitarist of considerable technique was "rediscovered" in Indianapolis in 1958. This was Scrapper Blackwell, who from 1928 to 1935 had made commercial recordings, most notably in a celebrated partnership accompanying the pianist Leroy Carr. Art Rosenbaum supervised Blackwell's first recordings since then on June 4, 1958, comprising "Little Girl Blues" and an instrumental entitled "Cherry." Blackwell made further recordings in the same month, including "Little Boy Blue," with its first stanza taken from the nursery rhyme of the same name.

Songster material was obtained from two other singer-guitarists at undetermined dates in this year. Frederick Ramsey, Jr., traced a singer called Cat-Iron (William Carradine), who lived in Buckner's Alley, Natchez Bottom, a segregated "no man's land" in Natchez, Mississippi. Carradine's repertoire was a mixture of religious songs and old-time barrelhouse material, including two variants of the "Alabama Bound" song cycle: "Jimmy Bell" and "I'm Goin' to Walk Your Log." His "Got a Girl in Ferriday, One in Greenwood Town" is lyrically related to "Vicksburg Blues," although he uses a different melody than the "44s" usually employed by blues pianists singing this theme.

Guitarist-singer K. C. Douglas, Oakland, California, about 1960.

In Washington, D.C., Elizabeth Cotten performed songster material for Mike Seeger, singing to her own guitar or banjo accompaniment. These recordings included her famous "Freight Train" and various rags and blues played on the guitar. One, for example, was an instrumental version of "Ain't Got No Honey Baby Now," a song recorded by the North Carolina bluesman Blind Boy Fuller as "Lost Lover Blues" in 1940 (Okeh 05756). Cotten was also from North Carolina, and her three vocal-banjo pieces were old-time regional dance tunes: "Here Old Rattler Here" (known otherwise as a work song), "Sent For My Fiddle, Sent For My Bow," and "George Buck" (or "Georgia Buck").

Two pianists were recorded in 1958; one was George Coleman (better known for chanting to his own oil-drum playing), whom John Bryan recorded playing a version of the popular "After Hours Improvisation" in Houston. The other was Robert McCoy, recorded in Birmingham, Alabama, by Pat Cather, on December 25. An accomplished stylist in the local tradition, he had made commercial recordings as an accompanist in 1937.

There was intense activity by field researchers in 1959, most diligent among whom were Mack McCormick in Texas and Harry Oster in Louisiana, who made significant recordings of black folk music from January to December. In addition, Alan Lomax returned to the United States from Britain, where he had been making field recordings and broadcasting. Accompanied by Shirley Collins, a British revival folk singer, Lomax spent two months traveling through the South, obtaining high-quality recordings by both black and white folk musicians. Their tour probably took place in July and August.

In September two French researchers, Jacques Demêtre and Marcel Chauvard, visited the United States. Although they did not record music, their pioneering interviews with active and retired blues musicians in New York, Detroit, and Chicago paved the way for more transatlantic field trips and added impetus to similar research by U.S. enthusiasts such as Duncan Scheidt and Art Rosenbaum, in Indianapolis, Indiana, and Chris Strachwitz in Oakland, California, who made recordings in the latter part of the year. The year opened, however, with Sam Charters (following a lead from Mack McCormick) locating and recording Lightnin' Hopkins in Houston on January 16. The discovery of this singer-guitarist, who had made many commercial recordings in the postwar period, contributed greatly to awareness among white "folk" enthusiasts of black blues as a folk-art form in the United States, in the light of Hopkins's improvisational skills as a folk poet, as well as his romantic status as a wandering troubadour. McCormick carefully recorded his repertoire in a series of sessions.

For Charters, Hopkins recorded contemporary songs and two associated with Blind Lemon Jefferson. The first, "Penitentiary Blues," incorporates Texas prison work-song stanzas and elements from Jefferson's blues of the same title (Paramount 12666, recorded in 1928). Hopkins had originally recorded this theme in the 1940s (unissued at that time) and had similarly recorded versions of "See That My Grave Is Kept Clean" (also made by Jefferson in 1928, Paramount 12608). The Lomaxes obtained performances of the latter from Pete Harris in 1934 and Smith Casey in 1939 for the Library of Congress.

In his sixty-five recordings for McCormick, Hopkins demonstrated the range of his talents, showing off his improvisational skills in such songs as "Get Off My Toe" and "Mama and Papa Hopkins." He performed impressionistic and autobiographical vignettes, such as "Beggin' Up and Down the Streets." He contributed further ver-

Snooks Eaglin

Scrapper Blackwell, photographed shortly after his rediscovery in Indianapolis, 1958.

sions of traditional themes (ballads, barrelhouse songs, blues, reels, and work songs) and played blues standards in his repertoire, many from his previous commercial releases. His bawdy repertoire included "The Dirty Dozens."

These sessions, commencing February 16, were held throughout the year. During the same period McCormick recorded several other aspects of black music in Texas, including blues accompanied by guitar and harmonica from R. C. Forrest and Gozy Kilpatrick; a barrelhouse minstrel piece from Dennis Gainus (vocal-guitar); and other barrelhouse material from Andrew Everett (another singer-guitarist). Dudley Alexander sang a zydeco version of "Baby Please Don't Go," in French Creole and English, to his own accordion, with violin and washboard. In the open air, George Coleman performed an evocative and arresting *cante fable*, "This Old World's in a Terrible Condition," to the accompaniment of his own drumming on the head of a steel oil barrel. Jealous James Stanchell recorded his novel "Anything From a Footrace to a Resting Place," to his own guitar.

Complementing his recordings of Lightnin' Hopkins, however, McCormick's most important supervisions were two sessions he undertook with Lightnin's second-eldest brother, Joel Hopkins, on June 12 and October 31. Sung, almost declaimed, to a percussive guitar accompaniment, Joel Hopkins performed songs such as "Matchbox Blues," which reflected the influence of Blind Lemon Jefferson. This was his favorite and a theme that Leadbelly had also learned from Jefferson; he recorded it for the Lomaxes in 1934 and 1935. Other aspects of Joel's repertoire were guitar-accompanied renditions of nonthematic plantation and prison-gang work songs and individual hollers. These included "Accused Me of Forgin', Can't Even Write My Name" and "I Ain't Gonna Roll For the Big Hat Man No More." His tour de force, however, was an eight-minute performance of floating stanzas that begins with one probably dating from World War I: "Thunder in Germany, Red Cross on My Own."

Four years older than Joel Hopkins (born in 1904) was the medicine-show song-ster Furry Lewis, whom Sam Charters recorded in Memphis, Tennessee, in February and October. Lewis had made commercial recordings of ballads, blues, and barrel-house songs in 1927 (for Vocalion), 1928 (for Victor), and 1929 (for Vocalion again). He remade some of these songs for Charters, such as "John Henry" and "Casey Jones" (ballads), "I Will Turn Your Money Green" and "Pearlee" (barrelhouse songs). He also contributed his version of "East St. Louis Blues" (the "One Dime" theme).

In January 1959, Harry Oster commenced making recordings of black music at the Louisiana State Penitentiary, Angola, where the Lomaxes had discovered Leadbelly in 1933. Oster visited Angola throughout 1959 and found several blues-singing guitarists, in particular Robert "Guitar" Welch, Matthew "Hogman" Maxey, and the outstanding Robert Pete Williams. Williams was remarkable for his free-flowing improvisational songs, as well as his equally creative and individualistic guitar accompaniments. Many of his songs were performed in this manner, such as his *cante fable* masterpiece "Prisoner Talking Blues," but he also sang interpretations of earlier commercial recordings. The latter include "Mississippi Heavy Water Blues" (with Welch on second guitar), based on Barbecue Bob's 1927 recording of the same title (Columbia 14222-D). He likewise performed traditional barrelhouse songs such as "Make Me a Pallet on the Floor" and, with Welch and Maxey, sang the ballad "John Henry" as an a cappella work song. Another work song (from the associated "John Henry"/"Nine Pound Hammer" cycle) was "Take This Hammer," performed by Welch, Maxey, and Andy Mosely. Maxey contributed a guitar-accompanied ver-sion of the ballad "Stagolee" as well as blues. Welch sang "Boll Weevil Blues" (relat-ed thematically to the "Boll Weevil" ballad) and other blues to his own guitar.

"Dig My Grave with a Silver Spade" by Tom Dutson (with Robert Pete Williams on guitar) was another version of Blind Lemon Jefferson's influential "See That My Grave Is Kept Clean." A woman inmate, Odea Matthews, sang "Five Long Years For One Man" a cappella. This, like Lightnin' Hopkins's "If You Ever Been Mistreated" (one of the songs collected by Mack McCormick) was based on Eddie Boyd's popular "Five Long Years" (JOB 1007, 1952; Oriole, no number, 1958). Both variants serve to demonstrate contemporary interplay between a commercial record and improvisational singers.

Outside the confines of Angola, Oster made further recordings by Snooks Eaglin, who continued to concentrate his considerable inventive skills in guitar play-ing while singing standardized lyrics. In addition to individual guitar-accompanied blues, Eaglin recorded a few gospel and old-time songs, instrumentals, and hokum (or good-time barrelhouse music). The latter was with a small combo (harmonica, washboard, tom-tom).

A similar combination (guitar and percussion) was intended to be used in new recordings by Billie and Dee Dee Pierce, supervised by Oster, but Eaglin never came to the session. On October 4, Billie sang several standard blues, including a bawdy version of "Jelly Roll Blues," Morton's composition, in which she accompanied herself on piano, with Dee Dee on trumpet and Percy Randolph on washboard. Lucius Bridges sang a version of "John Henry" to his own tom-tom, with Billie and Dee Dee playing their respective instruments. Earlier, Bridges had recorded this ballad to his own washboard and Eaglin's guitar.

String-band music was also recorded by Oster, who discovered an old-time black fiddle player, James "Butch" Cage (born in 1894), living at Zachary, Louisiana. Cage's regular guitar-playing partner was Willie B. Thomas, but he accompanied other guitarists with facility. At a session of October 27 there were two young guitarists, Clarence and Cornelius Edwards, whom Oster encouraged to play acoustic instruments. Clarence sang. The resulting performances produced versions of songs derived principally from pre- and postwar commercial recordings that had the feel of an old-time string band. They also, however, had an intensity in presentation that was entirely contemporary. Thus, for example, "I Can't Quit You Babe," recorded by the premier modern Chicago blues singer-guitarist Otis Rush in 1956

Lightnin' Hopkins—carrying on the rich blues tradition of Texas.

Robert Pete Williams, songster and bluesman.

(Cobra 5000), was interpreted in a fresh new setting. Edwards recorded one ballad, "Stagalee."

Alan Lomax began his 1959 field recording expedition in Virginia and made recordings of old-time music performed by whites in several states crossed by the Appalachian mountain range. He then moved to the Ozark Mountains and collected parallel regional traditions. His recordings in Virginia are of some interest in that, for example, he recorded Hobart Smith playing "Banging Breakdown" on the banjo in a style Smith had learned from blacks; the "banging" refers to knocking the banjo head while playing. Smith also sang a guitar-accompanied version of "See That My Grave Is Kept Clean," which had become well known in white tradition, as had "John Henry." Lomax recorded a bluegrass-style rendition of this ballad by the Mountain Ramblers.

If, in remote mountain regions, segregated traditions sometimes mixed and sustained different musical identities, continuity and change were also reflected in the repertoire of black music Lomax recorded in the South. At Hughes, Arkansas, he found a group of black juke joint entertainers led by harmonica player Joe B. Pugh— Forest City Joe. Their repertoire was the music popular for dances in the area south of Memphis, on the Arkansas side of the Mississippi River. Joe was a skilled harmonica player, and, accompanied by guitar and drums, he performed—with drive and vivacity—four songs derived from the commercial recordings of John Lee "Sonny Boy" Williamson, whom he idolized. He also sang two magnificent work-song-like pieces, "Levee Camp Reminiscence" and "Train Time," in which he excelled on harmonica and was otherwise unaccompanied. "Red Cross Store" was sung to his own piano. Two other musicians in this group, harmonica player Roy Blue (Roland Hayes) and guitarist Willie Jones, performed with accompaniment similar to Forest City Joe's combo. Their songs were based on commercial recordings by John Lee Hooker, the popular postwar blues singer-guitarist.

Probably after making recordings of black church services in the vicinity of Memphis, Lomax traveled to northern Mississippi and obtained significant examples

John Jackson of Virginia and Mance Lipscomb from Texas get together backstage at a folk blues festival during the 1960s.

of black music in this region. His recordings were centered on Senatobia, Como, and Parchman Farm—the Mississippi State Penitentiary, possibly the main unit, and certainly at Camp B, Lambert.

At Senatobia he visited the aged Sid Hemphill and recorded several more examples of his quill playing, accompanied by Lucius Smith on drums. The tunes appear to have been from his 1942 repertoire. Lomax also recorded two sensitive guitar-accompanied blues performed by Hemphill's daughter, Rosalie Hill. Further south, at Como, a variety of music was documented, including lively reels and barrelhouse songs played by a small family string band—Miles Pratcher (vocal-guitar) and Bob Pratcher (vocal-fiddle). There was exciting and compulsive fife and drum music played by another family unit, Lonnie Young (vocal-bass drum), Ed Young (cane fife), and Lonnie Young, Jr. (snare drum). There was superlative blues and religious music sung and played on the guitar by Fred McDowell. Religious services and children's game songs were also recorded.

The Pratchers' repertoire seems to date from the turn of the century and included a variant of the well-known "Take Me Back" (which they called "Buttermilk"). Published by Bert McMahon in 1898, the song was recorded by Leadbelly for the

Lomaxes in 1935, and Lightnin' Hopkins was to perform it for Mack McCormick later in 1959. The Youngs' music, which was a feature of local picnics and parties, comprised lively interpretations of old and recent tunes, as well as one religious accompaniment. Fred McDowell's secular performances, to his sonorous slide-guitar playing, included Bukka White's "Shake 'Em On Down" and versions of other blues recorded commercially in the 1930s, together with less well-known themes.

Like Harry Oster at Angola, Alan Lomax found that the collective work-song tradition had become almost moribund at the Mississippi State Penitentiary. He obtained a few examples of call-and-response hoeing songs at Lambert, some of which he described as ballads. One, "Po' Lazus," performed by James Carter and group, is more generally recognized in this light. Others, such as Floyd Batts's "Dangerous Blues," might equally be called a blues or a holler and demonstrates the links between these kinds of music. Further individual unaccompanied performances of this nature were also recorded, such as "Levee Camp Holler" by Johnny Lee Moore, who also sang lead in two collective work songs. At the Dairy Camp, Lomax discovered a sixty-year-old blues singer-guitarist named John Dudley. He performed sensitive renditions of "Cool Water Blues" (first recorded by Tommy Johnson in 1928, Victor 21279, as "Cool Drink of Water Blues") and "Po' Boy Blues" (first recorded by Ramblin' Thomas in the same year, Paramount 12722). Cat-Iron had performed a version of the latter song for Frederic Ramsey, Jr., in 1958. This explored a theme of very long standing, Howard Odum having collected yet another version of it from a visiting singer in Lafayette County, Mississippi, sometime during the early 1900s.

Moving on to Alabama, Lomax and his party visited Livingston and recorded Vera Hall once more, singing unaccompanied "Wild Ox Moan" (the same song as Rich Amerson's "Black Woman") and other secular and sacred repertoire.

Lomax's final recording location was the Georgia Sea Islands, the first time he had been there since 1935. Here he obtained many examples of a cappella group game songs, shouts, spirituals, and work songs. There was also some individual unaccompanied singing.

In Indianapolis, Duncan Scheidt recorded Scrapper Blackwell's piano playing at a concert in September. Blackwell performed Leroy Carr's "How Long Blues," on which, thirty-one years before, he had played guitar accompaniment to Carr's piano and singing. This was the first of their many commercial recordings as a duo (Vocalion 1191). In December 1959, Blackwell reverted to the role of accompanist again, in recordings supervised by Art Rosenbaum. To the sensitive singing of Brooks Berry, Scrapper played superb guitar (or, on one occasion, piano), and, in the finest of her blues, "Sun Burnt All My Cotton," they played an emotive guitar duet. At about the same time, Chris Strachwitz recorded the veteran blues singer-guitarist Big Joe Williams in California.

The pattern of recording established the year before was sustained in 1960. Melvin "Jack" Jackson was recorded in Houston, late in January, playing "The Slop," a piano duet with Lightnin' Hopkins, by Mack McCormick. The Lone Star State had a strong blues piano tradition, which set the scene for subsequent recordings in the summer by Texas pianists of different regional styles. Early in February, Harry Oster discovered and recorded the fine singer-guitarist Smoky Babe (Robert Brown) in Scotlandville, Louisiana. Among other performances he collected in the same month was an emotionally intense and moving "Almost Dead Blues" from the recently paroled Robert Pete Williams. The song reflected illness and, indirectly, Williams's

Roosevelt Sykes

conditional release from prison in December 1959. The parole was so stringent that it was to keep him in virtual peonage on a farm in Denham Springs, Louisiana, until 1964.

Also in February, Frederick Usher, Jr., obtained extraordinary field recordings in Los Angeles, California, from an itinerant named Eddie "One String" Jones. Jones, who also called himself "Mr. String" and went by the name "Jessie Marshall," constructed his own one-string instruments, using a metal wire stretched along a block of wood, raised at both ends, one higher than the other; this was covered at the lower end by a tin can, to form a sound-box. Jones beat the string with a shaped stick and stroked it with an empty whiskey bottle to change the tension and provide different notes. He recited and sang adaptations of blues (some based on commercial recordings) and a bawdy "Dirty Dozens." At the same time, Usher located another wanderer, an introspective blues singer and harmonica player named Edward Hazelton, whom he also recorded.

Alan Lomax undertook a spring field trip to Georgia and Virginia, where he made further recordings of a cappella black secular and religious music (including quartet singing), and similar styles with instrumental accompaniment. At the end of March and in the second week of April, Duncan Scheidt again supervised blues recordings by Scrapper Blackwell in Indianapolis, which featured Blackwell's solo virtuosity on the guitar, together with songs from his commercially recorded repertoire and that of his old partner, Leroy Carr. K. C. Douglas was recorded by Chris Strachwitz in California during April, and Harry Oster continued his work in documenting black music in Louisiana as he had since the beginning of the year.

In mid-1960, Chris Strachwitz traveled from California and joined Mack McCormick in Texas, where they searched for performers. After diligent enquiries, on June 30 they discovered Mance Lipscomb, a Texas songster of great talent who, like Leadbelly, had a wide repertoire of songs. Aged sixty-five, Mance was a fine guitarist who had entertained at dances since his youth. At this first encounter Strachwitz and McCormick recorded twenty-three items, ranging from ballads and barrelhouse songs to blues, reels, and one religious performance. Among the ballads was a Texas standard called "Ella Speed," which Mance played as a breakdown, and a previously unreported song of this type, "Freddie." Barrelhouse songs Mance recorded include "Baby Please Don't Go" (the "Alabama Bound" song-cycle variant) and "Jack O' Diamonds Is a Hard Card to Play," Texas versions of which include Blind Lemon Jefferson's 1926 recording (Paramount 12373) and recordings by Pete Harris and Smith Casey for the Library of Congress. Lipscomb also recorded the bawdy "Stavin' Chain" and a song entitled "Ain't It Hard," which incorporated elements of "See That My Grave Is Kept Clean." There were two versions of the Texas protest blues "Tom Moore's Farm," which had been recorded commercially by Lightnin' Hopkins in the 1940s (Gold Star 640) and by Hopkins for McCormick in 1959. Other blues were "One Thin Dime," the Texas version of "I Walked All the Way From East St. Louis," and "Going Down Slow," composed and recorded by St. Louis Jimmy in 1941 (Bluebird B8889). An early dance piece Mance had learned at age twelve or thirteen was "Sugar Babe."

At about the same time that Strachwitz and McCormick pooled their resources in Texas, British researcher Paul Oliver traveled to the U.S. with his wife, Valerie, to conduct extensive enquiries into blues. This work was sponsored by a Foreign Specialist Grant under the provisions of the Foreign Specialist Program of the Bureau of Education and Cultural Affairs of the United States Department of State.

The British Broadcasting Corporation provided a midget tape recorder, and funds were raised by enthusiasts for a number of recording sessions with musicians.

Oliver visited Detroit and Chicago in the first week of July, and one strand of his research was piano blues. In this respect, Boogie Woogie Red was recorded in Detroit, while in Chicago important documentary interviews and demonstrations of piano styles were obtained from the influential prewar pianists Eurreal "Little Brother" Montgomery and Roosevelt Sykes. Postwar stylists Sunnyland Slim and Otis Spann contributed similar material. The encounters with Montgomery and Sykes were particularly important in that they explored the origins of the related "Vicksburg Blues"/"44 Blues" theme. Both performers had made influential prewar commercial recordings of this musical strain, a piece that was used competitively in barrelhouses to test the competence of blues pianists. The lyrics to their songs, as mentioned previously, were completely different.

Blind James Brewer and Blind Arvella Gray, guitarists who earned money from playing and singing on Chicago's Maxwell Street, were also recorded by Oliver. Gray performed the old-time barrelhouse theme "Corinne Corinna" and two versions of "Have Mercy Mr. Percy," a blues providing continuous commentary on his life. His "Railroad Work Songs and John Henry" places stanzas from the "John Henry"/"Nine Pound Hammer" ballad/work-song cycle alongside a performance of the "John Henry" ballad proper.

Two other singer-guitarists Oliver recorded were active performers in Chicago clubland. Stepson of the now-famous Mississippi blues singer-guitarist Robert Johnson, Robert "Junior" Lockwood had originally recorded his "Take a Little Walk with Me" for Bluebird in 1941 (B 8820). He performed this again for Oliver, with Sunnyland Slim on piano. Lockwood's postwar recording career was generally as an accompanist, while J. B. Lenoir, the other singer-guitarist, had an established reputation as a solo performer. He composed original lyrics to both uptempo and introspective blues such as "I've Been Down So Long," a song he had first recorded in 1956 (Checker 856).

Paul Oliver and Chris Strachwitz had arranged to meet in the lobby of the Peabody Hotel, Memphis, Tennessee, and from there to search for and record bluesmen in the South. En route to Memphis, on July 10, Strachwitz recorded singer-guitarist L'il Son Jackson in Dallas. Jackson had made commercial recordings in the late 1940s through the early 1950s and performed new versions of several of his songs, such as "Cairo Blues," "Roberta Blues," and "Gambling Blues." He also sang traditional themes such as "Turn Your Lamp Down Low" (another variant of the "Alabama Bound" cycle) and "Rolling Mill Went Down" (a song Odum collected in Georgia early in the 1900s). "Charley Cherry" reflected childhood experiences of discrimination, while "I Walked from Dallas" was based on Blind Lemon Jefferson's "Long Lonesome Blues" (Paramount 12354, recorded 1926).

Reaching Clarksdale, Mississippi, on July 17, 1960, the same day Paul Oliver recorded J. B. Lenoir in Chicago, Chris Strachwitz found Wade Walton. Wade ran the Big Six Barbershop, where he also organized vocal quartets and was a civil rights activist. He was recorded singing "Rooster Blues" to his own guitar and the crowing of a cockerel.

Having joined forces with Paul and Valerie Oliver in Memphis, where Will Shade was recorded once more (on July 20), the party returned to Clarksdale (July 23–24). Several local performers made recordings, and pianist Jasper Love contributed a traditionally based "Santa Fe Blues" and other songs and instrumentals.

Blind Arvella Gray plays on Chicago's lively Maxwell Street.

Tractor driver Robert Curtis Smith played and sang to his own guitar a moving "I Hope One Day My Luck Will Change" and other blues. Wade Walton, with Smith playing guitar, stropped his razor in time, playing "Barbershop Rhythm" while cutting Paul Oliver's hair!

Further south, at Hollandale, Mississippi, Sam Chatmon was recorded on July 25. Born in 1899 and a member of the Carter/Chatmon family of musicians who played for blacks and whites in a string band, Sam's repertoire was based on this heritage. He and his brothers had recorded before World War II as the Mississippi Sheiks as well as in other family-based combinations. To his own guitar he performed songs from these prewar recordings and others such as "I Have to Paint My Face," which protests racial discrimination. His "God Don't Like Ugly" is another bawdy

Downhome in Clarksdale, Mississippi, 1960: Wade Walton and Robert Curtis Smith.

variation on the "Dirty Dozens" while stanzas of "You Shall Be Free" have been traced to the mid-nineteenth century.

Traveling to Dallas, Strachwitz and Oliver recorded L'il Son Jackson once more and, on July 30, found and recorded pianist Whistlin' Alex Moore. Like Sam Chatmon, Moore was born in 1899. In 1929, 1937, and 1951, he had made commercial recordings remarkable for the poetic imagery of his lyrics in addition to his skills as a blues pianist. Neither of these attributes had been lost in the interim. He performed old songs, new creations, instrumentals, and recorded his reminiscences of Dallas as a center of black music during its heyday before World War II.

In Chicago at about the same time, Donald R. Hill and Bjorn Englund made recordings of two more Maxwell Street entertainers—blues harmonica player and singer "King David" and an old-timer named Daddy Stovepipe (Johnny Watson), who performed as a one-man band (vocal, guitar, harmonica). Daddy Stovepipe had made commercial recordings before World War II, but by 1960 his repertoire hardly indicated that he had ever recorded blues.

At the suggestion of Harry Oster, Chris Strachwitz and Paul and Valerie Oliver visited James "Butch" Cage and Willie B. Thomas at Zachary, Louisiana, on August 7. Here they recorded blues, ballads, barrelhouse songs, religious music, and songs from white traditions. Cage sang and played guitar in the narrative blues " 'Tween Midnight and Day." This appears to have been the only time he was recorded playing this instrument rather than the fiddle. He performed on the latter in the slavery song "Kill That Nigger Dead," learned from his mother, in which he was accompanied by Willie B. Thomas on guitar. Thomas sang the chorus and shared the vocals in their versions of "One Dime Blues" and "Forty Four Blues," two themes popular among many musicians.

The Oliver–Strachwitz party then traveled to Houston, where, with Mack McCormick, they recorded the "Santa Fe" school blues pianist Edwin "Buster" Pickens, who had a repertoire of blues and barrelhouse songs reflecting this Texas tradition. About a hundred pianists had made up this group, centered on a triangle of railroad tracks connecting Houston with Richmond, to the north, and the Gulf Coast port of Galveston, to the south. Not surprisingly, many of Pickens's songs had railroads as their subjects, but he also performed other traditional themes, such as the ballad "Stagolee" and bawdy barrelhouse pieces including "Ma Grinder," "Raise Your Windows," and "Stavin' Chain" (the latter two recorded at a second session Mack McCormick conducted on August 17). "Hattie Green," about a legendary West Texas madam in Abilene, was a familiar regional theme. Augustus "Track Horse" Haggerty had sung it for the Lomaxes in 1934. Pickens's "Santa Fe Blues" had been recorded by Lightnin' Hopkins in the late 1940s (RPM 398), and in 1959 for Mack McCormick, while L'il Son Jackson recorded a version for Chris Strachwitz on July 10 in Dallas. Other songs based on earlier recordings included "Back Door Blues" (Paramount 12509, by Elzadie Robinson, recorded 1927) and "Ain't Nobody's Business If I Do," taken from Jimmy Witherspoon's 1947 version (Supreme 1506). In the early 1900s, Odum had collected two songs that used the lyric motif of the latter in Mississippi and Georgia.

McCormick and Strachwitz took the Olivers to meet and make further recordings with Mance Lipscomb at Navasota, on August 12 and 13. Mance performed many more songs from his wide-ranging repertoire. Also on August 13, at Sealy, they recorded another songster, Jewell Long, who played both guitar and piano and sang blues and ballads, including "Frankie and Albert" and "Ella Speed."

A chance remark in Forth Worth led Chris Strachwitz and Paul Oliver to B. K. Turner, who recorded commercially as Black Ace in 1937. Like his mentor, Oscar Woods, he was a specialist in playing the guitar, tuned to an open chord, laid flat in the lap, while stroking the strings with a bottle slider in one hand and plucking them with the other. After being convinced that there were still people interested in this type of blues performance, he was recorded anew on August 14 and September 10, playing songs from his past repertoire.

Paul Oliver visited St. Louis at the end of August and there traced another important prewar piano stylist, Henry Brown. Not a singer, although he recited monologues to his piano playing, Brown was an excellent performer. He recorded piano instrumentals named after local places, events, and personalities, much as he had done for Brunswick and Paramount in 1929 commercial recordings.

Little Brother Montgomery appears to have visited Britain twice in 1960 for club engagements. At the end of June and the end of August, he recorded a series of sessions for piano blues connoisseur Francis Smith. These were to be the most thorough exploration of Montgomery's wide repertoire. Instrumentals included "Trembling Blues," learned from Cooney Vaughan, and "Old Louisiana Blues" (or "Bob Martin Blues"), pieces that reflected early influences on his playing technique. He also recorded both of them for Paul Oliver in Chicago. Some of Montgomery's vocal blues were based on commercial recordings by vaudeville blues singers in the 1920s, as well as more traditional themes.

In late September, Francis Smith made similar recordings in Britain exploring the repertoire of another visiting blues pianist, Champion Jack Dupree. On the other side of the Atlantic, Art Rosenbaum recorded the singer-guitarist J. T. Adams and Shirley Griffith in Indianapolis. Griffith contributed "Big Road Blues" and "Maggie Campbell Blues," both learned from the prewar repertoire of Mississippi bluesman Tommy Johnson. Early in October, back in California, Chris Strachwitz again recorded the peripatetic Mississippi bluesman Big Joe Williams. He obtained some of this singer-guitarist's best performances, several based on Williams's pre- and postwar commercial recordings.

Harry Oster made field recordings in Louisiana throughout the year. In September he obtained a series of individualistic songs from Robert Pete Williams, which expressed the singer's feelings about the restrictive conditions of his parole. These included "Hay Cutting Song" (October 10) and "Death Blues" (October 18). "Butch" Cage and Willie B. Thomas performed another version of "44 Blues" for Oster on October 10 and accompanied Charles Henderson singing the old-time barrelhouse song "Corinna." Another performer whom Oster continued to record was Smoky Babe. Recited and sung to percussive guitar playing, his "Goin' Downtown Boogie" was made on November 3.

Oster held a long session with the gifted blues poet Roosevelt Charles at the Louisiana State Penitentiary, Angola, on November 19. Accompanied by Otis Webster on guitar, his songs ranged from the near work song "Pick 'Em Up Higher" to introspective songs such as "Mean Trouble Blues" and wry comments on sharecrop farming, such as "Mule Blues" and "The Boll Weevil an' the Bale Weevil."

The concentrated effort in documenting older styles of individualistic black music during 1959 and 1960 was to lead to a changed perception among white people in the U.S., Europe, and elsewhere of the evolution of black vernacular culture in North America. As has been shown, however, field research in these two years was the culmination of a pattern established by Howard W. Odum in the first years of the

Champion Jack Dupree, longtime European resident by way of New Orleans, Louisiana.

century. From that time, field recordings had existed in parallel to commercial music interests—first sheet music, then phonograph records. As Robert Gordon had been aware in the late 1920s, however, vernacular culture is intertwined with commercial culture more often than realized. This continued to be the case after 1960, as mass interest in black blues grew among white enthusiasts, even as it declined among the black population.

The epitome of such criss-cross relationships is "Tomorrow Gonna Be My Trying Day," recorded by "Butch" Cage and Willie B. Thomas for Harry Oster on December 5, 1960. Oster has shown that this is part of a cycle of songs, including "Alberta," "Corinna" (or "Corinne Corinna"), and "C. C. Rider." These occur in collections by folklorists from early in the century and are also represented in many commercial recordings. Without field research and related documentation, however, the historical understanding of cultural developments such as these—and others traced in this survey—would not have been possible.

JUMP
STEADY

THE ROOTS OF R & B

BARRY PEARSON

◆◆◆

Down home in South Carolina Bobby Ferguson preferred blues and boogie-woogie to the religious music his preacher father forced on him. After several confrontations over musical issues, he moved in with his sister. When Cat Anderson's band played the local theater, young Ferguson conned his way backstage, then talked his way onstage. It was a smart business move to give the hometown talent a token showcase, but the band leader got more than he'd bargained for. Two years later, Ferguson traded high school for the road, becoming a blues shouter called the Cobra Kid, a show-business name foisted on him by his manager, and he cut several records for two small East Coast labels, Atlas and Prestige. In 1951 he was approached by a talent scout, A & R man Lee Magid, who worked for Savoy Records, a Newark, New Jersey, company that had been producing African-American blues and gospel records since 1942. Ferguson recalled the meeting:

> He said, "I'm with Savoy Record Company." They were big like King, Syd Nathan in Cincinnati.
> He said, "The stuff you do, it's all right, but they didn't go all over the country. I'm with an international record company. We put records all over the United States."
> I said, "I've heard of you. Savoy Records."
> He said, "Well, we have to sign you up. Three years and add on one. You got any tunes?"
> I said, "Yeah, I got five."
> Now here's the catch. Lee Magid said he didn't like the Cobra name.

H-Bomb Ferguson.

I said, "Here we go again." I said, "That other guy I had that passed away, Mister Chet, now he named me."

He said, "I know it. I saw it on them little two record labels you were on." He said, "I got a name for you, gonna knock you out."

At that time the H-Bomb was hot.

He said, "We're gonna keep your last name, and I'm gonna call you H-Bomb Ferguson.

I said, "Man, you're talking about that bomb they're dropping. That's a bomb!"

He said, "Do you know, that name means something. From years to come people will remember the H-Bomb."

I said, "Yeah, but that don't sound right. H-Bomb Ferguson. That's not human."

He said, "You're not, when you open your mouth, believe it or not. I've sat in the audience many a night, and I heard you. You don't weigh nothing, but when you open your mouth you sound like a cat that weighs 300 pounds. You just explode. Your voice starts breaking out. So we're gonna call you H-Bomb Ferguson. And I already got the contract made up as such, and that's what's gonna be on the record."

I said, "I don't know if I'll get used to that name. You all keep changing my name."

Two years earlier, in 1949, the term "rhythm and blues" appeared in Billboard magazine, the music-industry publication that, among other things, lists current hit records. Jerry Wexler, an editor who would become an integral part of Atlantic Records, selected "rhythm and blues" as a heading for the top fifteen records projected for African-American consumers. While Wexler's source for the term remains obscure, a year earlier, in 1948, RCA/Victor used it in its catalog to designate recordings in black style. Those who worked in the record business at that time and current music historians concur that "rhythm and blues" was an industry name imposed on the music or, as Eileen Southern notes in The Music of Black Americans, was applied first to recordings and then, by extension, to the type of music that was being recorded.

Rhythm and blues, a name imposed from outside the black community, replaced the much-maligned label "race," the earlier industry designation that had initially come from within the black community itself. "Race" had been around since the beginning of black commercial recording in 1920 and covered all jazz, blues, gospel, pop, string-band, and what-not apparently by and for blacks. While designed to facilitate segregation, the term had been chosen with some care for its positive connotation current among African-Americans. By 1949, after more than twenty-five years of use, "race" had begun to smack of racism. While color-derived euphemisms such as "sepia" and "ebony" failed to catch on, "rhythm and blues," an artificial musical hybrid, was not overtly racial.

Perhaps more important, the category "race" was old-fashioned, an obsolete prewar term that no longer fit in a more positive postwar world. More than anything, the name change represents a broader acceptance of the value of African-American music. As an umbrella term invented for industry convenience, "rhythm and blues" embraced all black music, except classical music (a very small category) and religious music, unless, of course, a gospel song sold enough to break into the charts. As an

Little Richard at his height in the 1950s. CHAPTER OPENER

expansion of blues, R & B, unlike "race," couldn't include gospel as a matter of principle, since blues and religious song had been consciously kept apart as socially separate, though musically similar categories. "R & B" held sway for twenty years before giving way to the overtly political term "soul music," a name the black community imposed on the industry. A little more than a decade later, however, "rhythm and blues" made a comeback, and so it stands today. It's relevant to note that it means current African-American popular music, the stuff that sells, like funk, rap, and go-go. Ironically, what used to be called rhythm and blues, the music that was happening in the late 1940s and early 1950s, is currently named "blues" and marketed as such.

Back in 1949, when R & B meant something new, and artists like Ruth Brown were expressing a distaste for "blues," the industry's willingness to change names

Charles Brown: a gentler approach to the blues.

Amos Milburn: boogie-woogie, blues, and ballads.

stemmed more from economic than altruistic motives. More than anything, it indicates a response to African-American consumer power and a new respect for the companies that catered to the black musical tastes. By 1949 black popular music had become a strong enough force in the music business to warrant consumer-related considerations. Like its white double-genre industry counterpart, "country and western," the term "rhythm and blues" was primarily a marketing tool, designed to stop offending potential customers with what had become a "derogatory" musical category.

As far as specific meaning, one could argue that R & B is far too broad to be a useful musical genre or even a complex of genres. On the other hand, it logically designates blues and something more, call it rhythm music, dance music, or simply up-to-date dance blues. Blues, of course, was dance music from the turn of the century, but during the 1930s faster styles came to the fore, double-time blues and blues propelled by an aggressive shuffle beat. The multiple origins of the heavier dance beat—piano boogie, swing bands, Kansas City riff jazz, Mississippi or North Carolina juke joint blues—make it impossible to date when the beat started to change. But change it did. At the same time, it reflects the accelerated tempo of black life during and after the urban migration as well as an upbeat sense of expanded possibility. The beat changed, attitudes changed, and, in 1949, the name of the music did, too.

THE SETTING

Fifty years ago America was embroiled in a global conflict that commanded all its resources and energy. Everyone was supposed to do their part, in uniform, at work, on the homefront. Defense production created unparalleled employment opportunities, and wartime tension created a need for morale-building entertainment. The record industry looked to do its part, but the scarcity of shellac (a key ingredient in record production), lack of access to production machinery, and an ill-conceived 1942 ban on recording all limited the opportunity to supply the demand for records. By 1943 record buyers turned in old records in order to purchase new ones, and the industry as a whole scrambled to find recyclable records to make enough stock to press new recordings. Then they had to vie for time at the few available presses to get their disks produced. The companies best able to solve wartime production and distribution problems found a ready market for their wares, especially among the relatively neglected consumers whose tastes ran outside the mainstream of pop music. Thanks to the skills of a handful of businessmen, who, like their African-American customers, happened to be good at improvising, a small segment of the recording industry at the edges of the pop market managed to get its foot in the door and even expanded operations as the war came to an end. The companies that focused on African-American consumers produced records that would eventually be called rhythm and blues.

Looking back, it's a wonder it took so long for wartime and postwar "race" music to generate a name change. Change had been percolating throughout the 1940s. Black life-styles had changed and record buyers wanted music that would reflect the changes in their lives. Although some down-home blues continued to sell to southerners and recently urbanized former southerners, the R & B era witnessed an ongoing rejection of older blues styles along with their connotations of down-home life, mules and a plow, and limited expectations. Hipsters and youngbloods of the late 1940s wanted their own thing, not the music that had served their parents. Urban and newly urbanized blacks sought sounds that spoke to their own experience and reiterated the sounds happening on the street. Of course, the interplay of music and daily life was not unique to the postwar 1940s, and the connection of music to social change and as a commentary on community life stretches back to African antecedents.

Looking back fifty years to songs now perceived as "oldies" makes it hard to imagine the immediacy of tunes blasting out of the corner record store, the jukebox, and the radio. Despite the obvious musical connections to older traditions, which we will explore later, rhythm and blues was the soundtrack of a new world of opportunity, the product of wartime jobs, urban migration, and confidence bolstered by the prowess of athletic heroes like Jesse Owens, Jackie Robinson, and Joe Louis—the latter two commemorated in R & B songs.

Though not exclusive to the city, R & B was folk music that captured urban ethnic attitudes and mores. Successfully marketed to urban consumers (and rural folk who wished to be), R & B embodied the latest fads in language and dance; it spoke of heroes and even the consumer goods now within the reach of postwar

blacks—automobiles, clothing, popular beverages. An index of African-American popular culture, R & B presaged a consumer mentality concerned with this week's current hits, in contrast to the popular music of the 1920s and 1930s, when a record might sell for five years or more.

Music historians Nelson George (*The Death of Rhythm and Blues*) and Arnold Shaw (*Honkers and Shouters: The Golden Age of Rhythm and Blues*), authors of two of the best books on the subject, agree that R & B reflected the spirit of the times and African-American urban community life. At the same time, R & B connects with its rural taproots: regional blues and gospel traditions, carried north, east, and west by rural southerners on the move from the Piedmont, the Delta, or Texas. Rhythm and blues artists can themselves serve as representatives of the ongoing movement away from these most commonly cited blues regions. For example, Virginian Ruth Brown and North Carolinian Clyde McPhatter went to New York. Delta artists Arthur "Big Boy" Crudup, Sonny Boy Williamson, and Muddy Waters went to Chicago, and Texans T-Bone Walker, Charles Brown, and Amos Milburn recorded in Los Angeles. Such regional considerations colored the texture of early R & B as musicians from down home took a little bit of down-home with them into the city. In 1945 conditions were right for the growth of R & B. Urban workers had the money for leisure activities and for buying records. A burgeoning club scene developed on Central Avenue in Los Angeles, Hasting Street in Detroit, and on Chicago's South Side. Although the era of the swing bands was drawing to a close, smaller bands found ample club work and musicians flourished, learned from each other, and competed in a friendly manner, some times playing just across the street from each other.

In 1945 Delta blues artist David "Honeyboy" Edwards came to Chicago with his traveling partner Little Walter Jacobs. His recollections of the mixed ghetto called Maxwell Street Market capture the excitement of the boom years:

The biggest stars of R & B went uptown to the Rockland for an eight-hour, all-night "Breakfast Dance Spectacular."

> "At that time all the steel mills was open. There was so many people. People come from the south everywhere to get a job. That's right after war time. And all the stockyards was open, slaughter pens, all that was open and people were working. Like people didn't have no where to stay then. All they had was like, I rent this room here. Sometimes two or three shifts would sleep in this one bed. I'd get up go to work, there's a shift getting off and the landlady would change linens for them to sleep. Next shift, she'd pick up for them and change linens again. And when they come in from work, they wouldn't go right to bed. They come out there get some breakfast or get them a good drink walk the street and listen to us play the blues. And like Friday, Saturday, Sunday, all the people that live out of town would be down on Maxwell Street. They, there were just so many people you couldn't walk the streets. You had to turn sideways.*

Two years later, in 1947, Maxwell Street merchant Bernard Abrams decided he could make and sell records. He asked several street musicians, including Edwards's former partner Little Walter Jacobs, if they were interested in trying to make a record. Walter and Othum Brown went into the back of the store and, using Abrams's slapdash recording machine, cut "Ora Nelle Blues," issued on the Ora Nelle label, named in honor of Abrams's wife. It wasn't big business, and the endeavor soon folded, but it exemplifies the community base of R & B companies. Other entrepreneurs, many of them Jewish immigrants, also worked in the ghetto or in open-air

markets like Maxwell Street, and tried to make money from the street music, jukebox play, and club scene they witnessed firsthand.

As Arnold Shaw points out, the proliferation of the jukebox and the wartime scarcity of African-American music on record fueled the early R & B industry. While some form of coin-operated music machine had been around since the turn of the century, Prohibition, then its repeal, spawned speakeasys, then legal roadhouses, juke joints and taverns, all of which were likely sites for Seeburgs, Wurlitzers, Rockolas, and "piccolos." Jukeboxes, which took their name from the juke joints they were placed in, provided cheap entertainment and sometimes even a small profit for the house. By the 1940s, it is estimated that more than three hundred thousand were in operation, and, according to jukebox historian Ian Dove, at the end of World War II Chicago's Wurlitzer Company shipped more than 56,000 of one model—the 1015—in 1946 and 1947.

Charles Brown, vocal and piano, with guitarist Johnny Moore and bass player Eddie Williams in their first appearance at Harlem's famed Apollo Theatre, October 25, 1946.

These machines wore out the most popular 78s and had to be frequently restocked, ideally with the latest and most popular recordings, but demand far outstripped supply. Joe Bihari, one of the Bihari brothers who founded the Modern label of Los Angeles in 1945, told Arnold Shaw that his brother Jules operated a jukebox

Memphis's gift to the music world: Rufus Thomas—sometime disk jockey, blues singer, comic, and "Funky Chicken."

chain that served black neighborhoods. Frustrated by his inability to secure records, he decided to make the records himself. The first artist the Biharis cut was a local piano player, but they later went on to the likes of B. B. King and John Lee Hooker.

Rhythm and blues was even more a creature of the air waves than of the jukebox. Given the incentive and a halfway decent product, powerful disk jockeys could make or break a record. A few black-oriented stations employed live musicians paid for by a local sponsor, and a number of R & B artists—Doctor Isaiah Ross, Robert Nighthawk, Junior Parker, Sonny Boy Williamson, and B. B. King among them—worked this medium. The major stations, however, shifted more and more to an all-record and deejay format. Black radio was a collaborative effort among stations, sponsors, deejays, and record suppliers and promoters. To the local communities, star disk jockeys were often greater celebrities than the recording artists themselves. In fact, some R & B artists spent time as deejays, including Muddy Waters, Rufus Thomas, Elmore James, and Lavada Durst, a piano-playing deejay known as Dr. Hepcat. Part and parcel of the R & B business, disk jockeys doubled as songwriters, A & R men, promoters (like Chicago's Big Bill Hill, who also owned a popular blues nightclub), or even record company owners (like Chicago's Al Benson).

Rhythm and blues flowered as a commercial product and a racial ethnic art form during the postwar boom. Major record companies could not keep pace with the changing tastes of an ethnic audience. The lag had begun in the Depression, which contracted the industry as a whole, then was exacerbated by the wartime slowdown. These conditions created a postwar market that the smaller independent labels were anxious to supply. These new labels had a greater sense of the direction the music had taken over the past half-dozen years because most of the early companies were located in—or connected to—the black community.

Unlike the major companies, which stockpiled or recycled older styles of blues, or simply lost interest in anything but mainstream popular music, the independents often knew very little about the music business. Free of preconceptions, they saw and heard what was happening in the black community around them. In Chicago, the Chess brothers ran a liquor store and a club featuring live entertainment. Don Robey, in Houston, Texas, one of several black entrepreneurs, also ran a nightclub and a booking agency. They were in a position to see who was hot, who got jukebox play, and who was or was not under contract. Even with limited capital, when they got down to the business of recording R & B, they had the advantage of laying down what was happening at the street level. Awareness of traditional aesthetics and cutting-edge style characterized many independents. Even if the owners were square, someone in the organization, A & R men like Jesse Stone or Ralph Bass, would be alert for a new sound, a new gimmick, or a new artist to keep the money coming in.

While some companies, Atlantic Records for instance, created a sound, many of the earliest attempts simply involved locating and recording local artists. Contemporary blues legend John Lee Hooker's account of his journey to Detroit and subsequent discovery sheds light on the connection between the postwar boom years, urban migration, and the way in which the independent record companies found their talent within the community:

> In about two weeks I got a job and went to work. By that time I was old enough to get into bars, used to play around for local bars and things like that for a long time. I was the hottest thing in Detroit, and still I had no name. Except in Detroit.

Willie Dixon was one of the greatest of blues composers. His list of hits is endless, and virtually every artist of significance during the 1950s and 1960s recorded at least one of his songs.

And everybody would come around and say, "This kid"—I was just a boy—"has a different style." Everywhere I played, it was packed full of people. And I had a little small combo, and I had a great long cord, and I would walk the floor and play. It would be all over town you'd hear it: "John Lee Hooker, John Lee Hooker."

And so I went down, it was about 1948, to a little club called The Apex Bar, and this record company came to see me, a guy from Modern Records. He had heard of me. Word had got around. There was a guy named Elmer Barbee told them "you ought to go out and take a listen to this kid."

So he come around to this little old bar. Weren't nobody there. And these two guys come in there with suits of clothes on, and ties and shined shoes. I looked at them and said "Is this the police?"

Elmer Barbee said, "Naw, this is the Bihari brothers. Said they want to talk to you."

They sat there and listened for a while and then called me over to their table said, "We're very interested in maybe talking with you about signing up with us."

I laughed and said, "Well, how many times I been told that and nobody'd do nothing but talk." Barbee was sitting there with them, and a guy that had a record shop. He says "Do you drink?" "Well, yeah." Well, he bought me a beer and said, "Look, what are you doing on Wednesday?" I said, "Anything that you want me to be doing." Said, "Aren't you working?" I said, "I don't have to go in. If they fire me I can get another job." The jobs were plentiful then. You could get a job anywhere. They could fire you from this job; you could go right across the street and get another job. It ain't like it is now. So then Barbee took me down on Woodward Avenue to the office. We talked, and they made me a proposal, and they signed me up. I had never had that much money in my life. They give me a thousand dollars to sign.

So I showed it to everybody. I told all the fellows that I got a record deal. "You ain't got nothin."

I showed them my money and contract, and a week later I went down and recorded a number called "Boogie Children," then "Hobo Blues," "Crawling King Snake," and "My First Wife Left Me," on and on. I recorded a bunch of tunes I had.

And when "Boogie Children" came out it was a natural born hit— record charts, Billboard, Number one.

Allegedly, the session at Bernard Bessman's studio was a big party, carrying the tavern, so to speak, into the studio. Everybody got drunk, and toward the end of the session Bessman requested an up-tempo song. Hooker complied with "Boogie Children," a best-seller then and a rock 'n' roll staple to the present day.

Parallel with the early commercial field recording of blues and hillbilly music in the 1920s, the independent labels recorded a cross section of urbanized African-American folk music. They hoped they would make money, and some did. If they didn't know what they were doing, so much the better. Forced to rely on their perceptions, as well as those of A & R men like Willie Dixon, they were quick to learn what satisfied changing public taste. In this sense, the independents far outstripped the major labels, who had a greater investment in the way things used to work and were committed to their tried-and-true formulas for producing hits—even when the formulas were hopelessly out of date.

Competition forced the independent labels to be daring. Theirs was a cut-throat business, with its share of gangsters, and everyone appeared to be cheating everyone else. Yet, remarkably, the whole thing worked. From the mid-1940s to the mid-1950s, an unlikely confederation of artists, managers, record makers, jukebox distributors, disk jockeys, and tour promoters kept the enterprise afloat.

AN EXCLUSIVE MUSIC

Back in the 1960s, Amiri Baraka, then writing under the name of LeRoi Jones, discussed rhythm and blues in his influential book *Blues People*. Looking to the decade

1945 to 1955, prior to the advent of rock 'n' roll, Baraka noted: "Rhythm and blues was still an exclusive music. It was performed almost exclusively for and had to satisfy a Negro audience. Rhythm and blues may have been a business collaboration between immigrants like the Chess brothers and recent arrivals like Delta-born Muddy Waters, but the product was understood to be black music for black consumers. Baraka's choice of the word "exclusive" implies this sense of proprietorship. It was also the name Leon Rene chose for his label, Exclusive Records (changed from Excelsior in 1944), which produced the major hit of 1945, Joe Liggins's "The Honeydripper." Exclusive also signed Texan Charles Brown, who played a piano and sang the blues with Johnny Moore's Three Blazers. Unfortunately for brothers Leon and Otis Rene, Charles Brown did not record for them exclusively, and his three number-one rhythm and blues hits—"Drifting Blues" in 1946, "Trouble Blues" in 1949, and "Black Night" in 1951—were cut for another West Coast label, Aladdin, owned by the Mesner brothers.

Ed and Leo Mesner began their label, originally called Philco-Aladdin, in 1945. The artists they recorded during their first two years reveal the era's incredible pool of ready and willing talent, artists who represent a cross section of African-American musical styles and who, considered together, provide a fair survey of the component parts of rhythm and blues. They include big-band jazz blues artists Jay McShann, jazz vocalist Helen Humes, saxophone players Lester Young and Illinois Jacquet, Texas piano blues singer Charles Brown, New Orleans–to–New York piano bluesman Cousin Joe, Texas down-home bluesman Lightnin' Hopkins, Texas urban blues guitar stylist Gatemouth Brown, blues shouter Wynonie Harris, gospel great Sallie Martin, and the legendary Texas gospel quartet the Soul Stirrers. Aladdin's provocative mix of big-band jazz, down-home guitar blues, urban guitar blues, urban piano blues, blues shouters, and gospel illustrates the tremendous and intensely exciting diversity of rhythm and blues in its early days.

A combination of dance music and the voice of the streets, R & B was a commercial product tempered by consumer demand. Production was geared to sales and, by extension, to how well a specific record suited African-American aesthetic expectations. From the industry perspective, the records were product, not art or political statement, yet songs like Percy Mayfield's number-one hit in 1950, "Please Send Me Someone to Love," were both great art and moving political statements. Mayfield came from Louisiana to Texas and then on to California, where his skills as a vocalist, piano player, and songwriter landed him a contract with Specialty and then Imperial. An exponent of a relatively cool, jazz-inflected style, Mayfield had a productive career as a recording artist and songwriter. Music historian Charlie Gillett refers to his music as "club blues," in contrast to the less urbane, harder-edged stylings of Chicago and Memphis blues artists.

In spite of their initial usefulness, regional differences should not be overemphasized, because, as labels expanded beyond regional distribution, they also expanded their search for recording talent. For example, Art Rupes's Specialty label and Lew Chudd's Imperial label, both California companies, also recorded New Orleans rhythm and blues. Imperial signed Smiley Lewis, Archibald, Cousin Joe, and Fats Domino, who had fourteen hits between 1950 and 1955, including two number-one songs. Specialty recorded Lloyd Price, whose "Lawdy Miss Clawdy" was number one in 1952, and Larry Williams and Georgian Richard Penniman, who, as secular gospel shouter Little Richard, scored multiple hits. In 1955, Specialty also recorded zydeco legend Clifton Chenier, who had several marginal hits. While rhythm and blues is

Studio publicity shot of Percy Mayfield

not a regional style, it opened the door to national distribution for regional or ethnic records like those of Chenier.

Rhythm and blues was a music of change and movement, too much so to remain committed to one single style. Labels changed names and bought and sold artists. Artists changed labels or, like John Lee Hooker, recorded for several at the same time. Despite initial regional influences—of Texas blues in California, Delta blues in Chicago, southeast gospel in New York—rhythm and blues thrived on change, always responsive to consumers and ever alert for a new fad or gimmick.

Still, some artists who had successfully recorded before the war went back into the studios after it. Relying on their ability to change with the times or come up with the right song at the right time, they enjoyed varying and unpredictable degrees of success. Count Basie, with vocalists Helen Humes and "Mr. Five by Five," Jimmy Rushing, had continued success through the 1940s and 1950s, scoring a number-two hit in 1955 with the standard "Every Day I Have the Blues." Jazz-blues veteran Lonnie Johnson changed labels, moving to Sid Nathan's Cincinnati-based King Records. A masterful prewar guitarist, vocalist, and songwriter, he surprisingly came out with 1945's runaway number-one song, "Tomorrow Night." Another prewar star, Memphis Minnie, found it harder to keep pace with changing trends. A true guitar hero who would have been perfectly suited to the 1990s, she played too hard and too

Two bona-fide legends: Jimmy (Mister 5 by 5) Rushing at the far left and the bandleader with whom he most often worked, Count Basie, at the far right.

Blind John Davis accompanies the legendary Lonnie Johnson at a recording session for Disc.

down-home for the rhythm and blues era, moving to progressively smaller labels, from Columbia, to Regal, to Checker, and, finally, to J.O.B.

As the partial listing of Aladdin artists shows, West Coast rhythm and blues drew heavily on Texas and on Kansas City, Missouri, a center for the territory bands. Kansas City jazz historian Nathan W. Pearson, Jr., commented on the Kansas City roots of rhythm and blues: "Much of the early power of rhythm and blues came from the same strong rhythm and riff foundation that powered the greatest K.C. bands of the thirties. Jay McShann, Walter Brown, Wynonie Harris and particularly Big Joe Turner brought the K.C. drive to rhythm and blues."

While McShann and Brown were fine blues artists, the latter two, Wynonie Harris and Big Joe Turner, truly epitomize the rhythm and blues shouter. Big Joe, a Kansas City native and former singing waiter, worked with numerous bands, includ-

ing those of Benny Moton, Andy Kirk, and Count Basie, as well as with pianist Pete Johnson. In December 1938, he appeared with Johnson in John Hammond's first Carnegie Hall From Spirituals to Swing concert. A week later, he was in the studio with Johnson recording the masterful stomp-down classic "Roll 'Em Pete" for Vocalion. Even without drums, the shouting boogie could be called rhythm and blues—or, for that matter, rock 'n' roll. Turner switched labels in 1951, beginning the second stage of his career in collaboration with New York–based Atlantic Records. During the next four years he placed eight songs in the charts, including Jesse Stone's classic composition "Flip Flop and Fly" and Charles Calhoun's "Shake Rattle and Roll," which would also become a cover hit for country singer turned rock 'n' roller, Bill Haley.

Omaha-born Wynonie Harris, if not the finest shouter of the era, was certainly the most flamboyant. Comedian, dancer, drummer, singer, he toured with Lucky Millinder, Johnny Otis, Illinois Jacquet, Jack McVea, and Lionel Hampton. Although he made some early records for Aladdin, his biggest hits, "Good Rockin' Tonight" in 1948 and "All She Wants to Do Is Rock" in 1949, were for the King label. He also had many other songs on the charts, and is remembered as a superb, if somewhat eccentric, showman.

Harris's sense of personal style and his flair for theatrics typified the spirit of rhythm and blues, which placed a high premium on showmanship. The great artists of the era, showstoppers or house wreckers like Harris, utilized whatever choreography or instrumental highjinx it took to work their audience and beat out their competitors. Blow-top sax players fell out, lying on their backs kicking at the air. T-Bone Walker and Guitar Slim played their guitars behind their backs or leaped in the air and landed in splits. Sometimes, they walked out into the crowd or out onto the street, blasting out lead solos. Vocal groups and small jump bands put together frantic stage routines with all manner of synchronized moves, fancy footwork, dramatic stops, and extended grooves. Like athletes, rhythm and blues artists Don and Dewey, the Treniers, Screaming Jay Hawkins, Muddy Waters, and Little Richard gave their all, leaving the stage exhausted. In turn the audiences appreciated the effort, responding in kind, feeding energy back to the on-stage stars.

Not all showstoppers had to be frantic. In 1941, vocalist, saxophone player, and comic showman Louis Jordan put out a two-sided hit for Decca, "Knock Me a Kiss," backed by "I'm Gonna Move to the Outskirts of Town." The record sold half a million copies, primarily within the black community. Jordan came from a musical family in Arkansas some fifty miles outside of Memphis. After working with several bands, he ended up in Harlem working with Chick Webb's group. Eventually, he came out front as a saxophone player and vocalist. In 1939 he formed the Tympany Five, and during the 1940s recorded a string of hits, including "Caledonia," "Choo-Choo Ch' Boogie," "Let the Good Times Roll," and "Saturday Night Fish Fry." Jordan took advantage of his residency in Harlem, the center of African-American style; his work reflects a streetwise hipness. A remarkable showman, Jordan even made movies, including a rhythm and blues western.

The recordings of Joe Turner, Wynonie Harris, and Louis Jordan all radiate terrific energy and a deep racial humor, which endeared them to their audiences, except for a few, who found their narratives of black life and love too ethnic for middle class comfort. Nat King Cole offered a cooler alternative. Cole started out as a jazz pianist with little interest in becoming a vocalist. But toward the end of the 1930s, the role of the singer, traditionally just another member of the band, was becoming more important. In response to audience demand, Cole became the exponent of a jazz-inflected, cool club blues style. Although he was never completely a rhythm and blues artist, he recorded some R & B songs, including a 1943 version of an African-American animal tale, "Straighten Up and Fly Right," and the blues/jazz standard "Route Sixty Six." Unlike Jordan and Harris, who addressed themselves primarily to a black audience, Nat King Cole, along with groups like the Mills Brothers and the Ink Spots, moved away from rhythm and blues and into mainstream pop. Eventually, Cole became one of America's best-loved artists, with his own TV show and a number of movie parts, including that of W. C. Handy in *St. Louis Blues*.

Instrumentalists Louis Jordan, Cole, and trombone player Clyde Bernhardt began to sing, only to find themselves suddenly stars. As the vocalist stepped out front, other changes came in the musical pecking order. The saxophone and the guitar evolved from section or rhythm team players to lead voices. The saxophone, with its amazing emotional and tonal range, approaching that of the human voice, and its potential for screaming rhythmic leads, shed its soft melodic contour for a harsher, vocalized sound. Sax players were the stars of rhythm and blues bands, firing off barrages of riff-based pyrotechnics. Cutting contests became possession rituals, and artists like Sil Austin, Red Prysock, Illinois Jacquet, Willis Jackson, Eddie Davis, and Big Jay McNeely served as high priests of the art.

Clarence Gatemouth Brown

The development of the electric guitar in the late 1930s, first associated with southwestern jazz or western swing, provided another new lead instrument with an equally expressive voice. The guitar as a folk instrument and the blues as a folk form were married from the start. Amplification, however, allowed it a much broader range, both as a rhythm instrument drawing its repertoire from piano boogie riffs, and as a lead voice able to sustain notes and cut through a band sound. Capable of emotionally expressive, vocally derived tonalities, the guitar became crucial to the racial ethnic sound of African-American music. Using the instrument, pioneers T-Bone Walker and Gatemouth Brown evolved a Texas urban blues sound. B. B. King developed his own version of the single-string style while he was a disk jockey in Memphis, and went on to become the most influential guitarist of his generation. Fellow guitar heroes include Johnny "Guitar" Watson, Guitar Slim, Mickey Baker, Albert King, Eddie Taylor, and the more down-home stylists Elmore James, Muddy Waters, and John Lee Hooker.

Later still in the 1950s, the amplified Fender bass guitar changed the role of the bass forever, further augmenting the power of the rhythm section. By the 1960s the bass had become such a dominant instrument that a number of Motown groups used the bass player as the band leader. Rhythm and blues piano players included Count Basie, Amos Milburn, Charles Brown, Percy Mayfield, Ray Charles, Cousin Joe, Fats Domino, Professor Longhair, Smiley Lewis, Roosevelt Sykes, Memphis Slim, Floyd Dixon, H-Bomb Ferguson, and Little Richard. Styles ran the gamut from jazz, to boogie, to gospel, to down-home blues. Even the drums had to work harder in response to amplified guitar and bass rhythm-section mates. Shuffle rhythm and back beats clarified, if at times simplified, the drum's role as an indicator of dance rhythm. Musicians, engineers, and studio technicians also searched for new sounds or novelty effects that would make the public sit up and take notice. Yet, for all of the change and newness, rhythm and blues kept in touch with its roots. Despite commercial goals, corporate manipulation, and changes in instrument and recording technology, R & B remained folk music, the urban vernacular music of African-Americans.

FROM OUT OF THE CHURCH

In 1955, twenty-four-year-old Napoleon Brown left his home in Charlotte, North Carolina, to record for Herman Lubinsky's Savoy label. His father was an elder in the Baptist Church and Nappy, as he was called, sang with several important gospel quartets, including the Golden Bells and the renowned Selah Jubilee Singers. Looking back from the vantage point of the 1990 Chicago Blues Festival, he told me:

> *I got into the music business about 1951. I went to Savoy in Newark, New Jersey, to make a spiritual record, a gospel record, and they captured me from there. I come out of gospel into music, into the blues. When I was younger, I was strictly in the gospel field but, well, I would sing a little blues. I would stand by the side of the Piccolo in little juke joints, liquor*

Big Joe Turner with disk jockey and rock 'n' roll promoter extraordinaire Alan Freed. ABOVE

Wynonie Harris, New York publicity shot. LEFT

clubs, and people would walk up, give me a dollar or two. But I would never let my mother and them know it because they didn't want all that. They felt if you do blues, you were doing the devil's work, but they were highly mistaken, because the blues is nothing but a living, a job like anything else.

Actually, Mr. Brown bears some responsibility for his metamorphosis. He entered a local talent show with his self-composed and anything but religious "Lemon Squeezing Daddy," which earned him second prize. He also caught the eye of Savoy's Fred Mendelsohn, who was in the market for a rhythm and blues vocalist. Brown came through with several hits, including a number-two hit in 1955, "Don't Be Angry," which coincidentally was covered by the Crew Cuts.

Nappy Brown. ABOVE

Albert King with his famed Flying V guitar. RIGHT

Other R & B artists tell similar stories. Clyde McPhatter, from up the road in Durham, started out singing in the Baptist church as well. Moving to New York, as North Carolinians and Virginians often did, he continued gospel singing, eventually joining up with Billy Ward, who also worked the gospel side of the fence. In 1950 they switched over to blues and, as the Dominoes, put out 1951's number-one song, "Sixty Minute Man," on King Records' subsidiary Federal, under the direction of A & R man Ralph Bass. Several Federal hits later, including "Have Mercy Baby" and "The Bells," McPhatter jumped labels to Atlantic, forming the Drifters, who cranked out hits like Jesse Stone's finance-romance saga "Money Honey," which later also worked for Elvis Presley.

The great women vocalists, both "big" and "little," followed similar paths. Big Maybelle, born Mabel Smith in Jackson, Tennessee, in 1924, started out playing piano in the Sanctified church, where she honed her powerful vocal style. After winning first prize in a Memphis talent show in 1932, she hit the road with several bands, eventually hooking up with Tiny Bradshaw's outfit. From 1947 on, she record-ed for King, Okeh, Savoy, and Rojac, placing a half-dozen songs on the rhythm and blues charts. Big Mama Thornton, born Willie Mae in Montgomery, Alabama, came from a religious home, where her father was a minister. On stage by sixteen, she worked the southern club circuit, including Houston's Bronze Peacock, where she

Big Joe Turner in an NBC tele-vision appearance.

caught owner Don Robey's eye. Signing with Robey's Peacock label in 1951, she enjoyed several minor hits, and in 1953 hit number one with "Hound Dog," later an even bigger hit for Elvis Presley. After some years of relative obscurity, she returned to prominence during the blues revival of the 1960s.

Little Esther Phillips moved from Texas to California and also sang in the Sanctified church. After winning a talent contest, she signed up at the age of thirteen with band leader and R & B godfather Johnny Otis. In 1950, she had two number-one hits for Savoy, "Double Crossing Blues" and "Mistrusting Blues."

Sister Rosetta Tharpe stuck with gospel. After touring with her mother, singing in the Sanctified style, she scored some rather unusual crossover hits, this time crossing from gospel to the rhythm and blues charts with material like "Shout Sister Shout," "That's All," and even "Silent Night," which hit number six in 1949.

Big Maybelle. ABOVE

Johnny Otis (left), Little Esther Phillips, and Billy Eckstine captured during a light moment. RIGHT

Billy Ward and the Dominoes

Although her repertoire remained religious, at least in subject matter, she took her act into secular venues, working with Cab Calloway and Lucky Millinder.

Dinah Washington also worked the church circuit with her mother, won her "amateur" contest at fifteen, worked with Lionel Hampton's band, signed with Mercury, and hit number one in 1949 with "Baby Get Lost." Sarah Vaughan performed in church, won a talent show at the Apollo in New York, worked with band leader Earl Hines, and recorded for Mercury as well. LaVern Baker cut her teeth in the Baptist church and hit the club circuit in Chicago as "Little Miss Sharecropper" before she signed with Atlantic.

Other women—Savoy's Varetta Dilliard and Tiny Topsy, Regal's Annie Laurie, Mercury's Ella Johnson—recorded hits, but the most representative and the most visible rhythm and blues vocalist was Ruth Brown, who was on the charts 129 weeks, from 1949 to 1955. Born in Portsmouth, Virginia, in 1928, she grew up in a steadfastly religious family, performing religious music early on. Nevertheless, Brown dabbled in secular song on the sly. Disdaining down-home blues, she performed the more sophisticated stylings of Billie Holiday. Flying in the face of her parents' wishes, she landed a job with Lucky Millinder, who subsequently fired her in Washington, D.C., where she was then "discovered" by Cab Calloway's sister Blanche. With Blanche Calloway as her agent, she signed with Atlantic, which hoped to loosen her up a bit after she stated she didn't like "blues." Named "Little Miss Rhythm," she had five number-one hits from 1950 to 1954. Ironically, in 1991, she was popularly dubbed

Queen Mother of the blues, and this time she was gracious enough to accept the title. Today she is once again a bright star, not simply a survivor but a powerful presence in the music business.

Of all the categories of rhythm and blues, church traditions most immediately affected the doo-wop or vocal group style. From 1946 through 1951, several East Coast groups, the Ravens in New York, Sonny Til and the Orioles in Baltimore, and the Clovers in Washington, D.C., began to experiment with their sound, progressively adding vocal stylings traditionally associated with gospel song and religious ritual. Atlantic Records' Jerry Wexler tied the proliferation of gospel-tinged doo wop in the eastern cities to the migration of African-Americans from Virginia and the Carolinas, traditional breeding grounds for gospel quartet singing. Quartet singing in the Norfolk–Hampton Roads region of Virginia was especially rich, producing the Norfolk Jubilee Quartet and the Golden Gate Jubilee Quartet, which performed both

The Golden Gate Quartet were giants by any standard.

*Dinah Washington (Ruth Jones)
went on to fame as a jazz vocalist,
but she started her career as a
gospel singer.*

sacred and secular material on radio and record throughout the 1930s and 1940s, before moving to Europe. Gospel stars of the late 1940s and early 1950s, like the Swan Silvertones and the Dixie Hummingbirds, trace their roots to a southeastern quartet tradition that extends back into the nineteenth century. Professional quartets were active in show business at the end of the nineteenth century, and several Virginia groups, including the Standard Quartette, the Southern Negro Quartette, the Dinwiddie Colored Quartet, and the Old South Quartette, recorded by 1910. Similar ensembles were to be found throughout the country, and some of the major figures in America's music history could be found in their ranks. Scott Joplin, for example, worked with the Texas Medley Quartette, and W. C. Handy, stepfather of the blues, worked with the Lauzetta Quartet, performing songs like "I'm Gonna Chop 'Em in the Head with a Golden Axe." Such quartets were more at home in saloons than church and included in their repertories religious parodies, sentimental favorites, and, later on, blues. This early merger of the stylings of university-based jubilee singers with African-American barbershop harmony produced a popular commercial sound. Later groups, such as the Palmetto Jazz Quartet and the Monarch Jazz Quartet, should be credited with first performing vocal group blues tinged with gospel flavor. The Monarchs changed their name from Jazz Quartet to Jubilee Quartet when they recorded their religious records. Similar repertoire and name changes took place in the rhythm and blues decade. The North Carolina gospel group the Royal Sons Quintet became New York's R & B Five Royales. In Detroit, Tommy Evans's group, the Unity Baptist Five, became the Carols. This type of shift occurred throughout black America, because the street-corner vocal group tradition was very much grassroots folk music, as contemporary Piedmont blues artist Bowling Green John Cephas recalls: "We had one of those corner groups [in Washington,

D.C.] back in the late forties. It was a corner group, like the boys harmonizing together, and we would sing pop songs, rhythm and blues and doo wop." The same group worked with the then-current gospel sound modeled on the Dixie Hummingbirds, and before long Cephas was touring with a gospel quartet called the Capitol Harmonizers. All his life he had been singing gospel and spirituals with the rest of his family at social get-togethers, and he was equally skilled in gospel and blues. Performing religious songs in pop style—and vice versa—continued into the 1940s, and in 1947 the Delta Rhythm Boys had a hit on RCA/Victor with the old folk spiritual "Dry Bones."

Besides the gospel quartets, the other models for group singing were such "popular" crossover vocal acts, as the Mills Brothers and the Ink Spots. Initially, the music of these acts drew on an earlier street-corner style, in which makeshift bands used novelty instruments like jugs, kazoos, and ukuleles and blended dance, vocal harmonies, and even vocal imitations of instrumental sounds in an upbeat, jazz-inflected potpourri of blues and pop songs. At first, the Mills Brothers thrived on their novelty vocal imitations of a jazz band, but they later opted for a smoother, cleaner pop sound accessible to a mainstream audience.

Philip Groia lists the Mills Brothers, the Ink Spots, the Charioteers, the Choclateers, the Red Caps, and the Delta Rhythm Boys as successful early black groups in his study of doo wop, They All Sang On the Corner. Former Ink Spot Jerry Daniels's story confirms the aptness of Groia's title:

> We started in Indianapolis as a coffee-pot band on the street, and we ended up in Cincinnati on WLUK; at that time, that was the world's largest station. A coffee-pot band is, well, fellows used to get kazoos or little tin horns, you put some tissue on it, and improvise on it, and it sounds like an instrument, and that's the part the guys would stick in the coffee pot and play the coffee pot. And the rhythm section was washboards. Everybody played or danced. We were known as King Jack and the Jesters when we were at Cincinnati. We got to New York, and there was another group called the King's Jesters. So, as we were deciding to change our name, our manager, Mr. Moe Gale, had his pen and was signing a contract, and some ink fell on the page, and he said, well, that's the name, The Ink Spots.

The Delta Rhythm Boys onstage.

The anecdote points up the street-corner folk roots of even the most commercial crossover groups. Still other street-corner jazz or jive outfits—New York's Spirits of Rhythm and Chicago's Cats and the Fiddle, for example—worked a novelty string-band format and cut records. In the gradual evolution of the rhythm and blues vocal group sound, many ensembles can be credited with their own specific combinations of gospel, pop, blues, jazz, and vocal harmonies. Vicksburg, Mississippi, native Willie Dixon moved to Chicago, where he teamed up with another ex-Mississippian, Leonard "Baby Doo" Caston, in the Five Breezes. Typically, Dixon had gospel quartet experience singing with the Union Jubilee Singers. As Caston recalls it, the Five Breezes "were kind of on an Ink Spot kick—we all worked one microphone, get the heads together. You had to do your balance."

Perhaps because of their lack of originality—their similarity to the Ink Spots' sound—the Five Breezes didn't make it. Later, however, after the war, Dixon, Caston, and Ollie Crawford teamed up as the Big Three Trio, which, according to Caston, used the gimmick of singing blues in three-part harmony:

The Mills Brothers onstage—plus Father Mills at the right.

Well, the Mills Brothers was the first to sing pop tunes together, but I'm talking about the blues. The Ink Spots was doing pop tunes, see, but we were singing the blues together. In harmony. So after that, it's been the Midnighters and the Clovers and the Moonglows. After my singing, everybody jumped on it, so now, as of this day, all these groups get together, and they sing the blues together now. See, the Orioles, they varied between the Big Three and the Ink Spots."

While Caston's history is limited to his immediate era and is, admittedly, self-serving, his references to a stylistic continuum from the Ink Spots, to the Orioles, to the Big Three, and the dependence of the Midnighters, Clovers, and Moonglows on blues influence rather than gospel, deserves attention, as does the impact of the group itself. The Big Three signed with Columbia in 1947 and recorded several hits, including a version of the folk narrative "The Signifying Monkey," which Dixon claimed as his own. Dixon went on to work with various blues greats, including

Memphis Slim and Chuck Berry. A great studio musician, he is best remembered as a powerful Chicago A & R man and, with Jessie Mae Robinson and Jesse Stone, one of the finest writers of R & B songs.

Looking back from today's vantage point of urban violence, it is hard to resist the appeal of a group of teenagers harmonizing under an inner-city streetlight one day, scoring a hit the next, and (of course) living happily ever after. Unfortunately, this nugget of urban Americana doesn't present the whole truth. Rags-to-riches seldom happened, and even when it did, it was more likely to read rags-to-riches-to-rags. On the up side, a remarkably large number of groups got to record—though few had hits, and fewer still several hits. Nevertheless, through the collaboration of vocal groups, coaches, managers, and businessmen and women, a true American art form developed. The rhythm and blues doo-wop tradition represents one of the few undeniable urban grassroots—or, better yet, street-corner—folk-song styles unselfconsciously documented by independent rhythm and blues record labels.

Rhythm and blues was a most natural extension of the related bedrock folk traditions of spirituals or gospel and the blues; yet it remained controversial. During the R & B decade, 1945–55, not all African-Americans thought positively about rhythm and blues. To the middle class, it was vulgar; to the intelligentsia, who preferred

The Big Three Trio consisted of (left to right) guitarist Ollie Crawford, pianist-guitarist Leonard "Baby Doo" Caston, and Willie Dixon on bass. The group bridged the substantial gap separating country blues from R & B.

Willie Dixon and Champion Jack Dupree, California, 1991

more cerebral forms of jazz, it was simplistic and commercial; and to the staid church folk, it remained the devil's music—uptown though it was. Parents and preachers decried rhythm and blues on the jukebox with the same energy they used to decry down-home blues in the juke joint.

But in spite of ongoing attempts to keep church music and dance music separate—and performers on one side of the fence or the other—the merger of religious and worldly music became tighter during the decade 1945 to 1955, culminating in the development of soul music in the 1960s. Historically, it is clear that both forms of expression drew from the same wellspring, and even the institutions of the church and the secular weekend dance were not antithetical. As far back as the early nineteenth century, the African-American folk church in the South compromised religious injunctions banning dance. Houses of praise allowed rhythmic body motion if it adhered to certain arbitrary rules: if the feet never crossed and were seldom lifted, it wasn't dance, but a "shout" or "ring shout." Ironically, the Isley Brothers' 1959 "Shout" was an obvious church song sinfully tailored to secular rather than sacred ecstasy. Back in the 1930s, gospel pioneer Thomas A. Dorsey applied to his religious compositions the skills he learned as bluesman Georgia Tom. Early blues artists Charley Patton in the Delta, Blind Lemon Jefferson in Texas, and Blind Boy Fuller in the Piedmont also recorded religious songs under assumed names, as a token concession to the religious scruples of potential consumers.

Which rhythm and blues artists came out of the church? It would be easier to list those who didn't. It is difficult to overestimate the strength of the church as a primary institution in African-American life, especially in the 1930s and 1940s, and as a means of easing the transition from rural to urban life. At the same time, we shouldn't sell the secular institutions short. Country house parties, fish fries, juke joints and roadhouses, urban rent parties, beer gardens, after-hours joints, taverns, and show clubs all served similar community needs, softening the aches of the work week and healing the trauma of urban migration. That the major performers in black music should have had experience in both Saturday night and Sunday morning ritual should come as no surprise. After all, if you showed musical aptitude, these, along with school, were the major performance and learning venues.

As Ralph Ellison wrote in his tribute to rhythm and blues shouter Jimmy Rushing, blues and the Saturday night dance were more than mere entertainment: "Jazz and the blues did not fit into the scheme of things as spelled out by our two main institutions, the church and the school, but they gave expression to attitudes which found no place in these and helped to give our lives some semblance of wholeness. Jazz and the public dance was a third institution in our lives."

Both Jimmy Rushing and Count Basie, with whose band he sang, were the kind of workmates musicians particularly admired, because their wit and humor made the road that much more bearable. Other band leaders were less popular, however—quick to hire and quick to fire. Even if you played by the rules, life on the road was grueling, dangerous, and only briefly glamorous, with hundreds of miles between venues. As H-Bomb Ferguson recalls, making it as an R & B vocalist meant you earned the right to a seemingly endless series of one-night stands:

> We used to get five dollars a night, and you sing three times three songs, nine songs. First start, band played two. They take a break, maybe sometimes three, they come back and play one or two more and then put you on. You sing three. They play two more. Break. They come back, they play two, you come out, you sing three more. Then play three songs. Break. They come back, they play one, you come up and sing three, they play the rest of it.

Little Esther Phillips, glimpsed in a quiet moment.

That's every night. Nine to ten songs a night. When they get through, the man hands you five dollars. That was money then, see?

We all used to travel in station wagons. And that station wagon had a rack on top. They used to put canvas over it and tie the instruments on. Get what you can on the top and the back, and everybody ride in one car. We keep stepping. Next stop is so-and-so, 185 miles or 200 miles. We get there like three hours before the gig. You be tired.

You wash yourself, you stop, we sleep in the dressing room. "All right. Show time. Show time. You all got fifteen minutes."

I said, "God Dog."

You look out at the audience. It be jam packed. And they want you to perform like you ain't never went nowhere before. And entertainers probably still do that. We done drove two or three hundred miles; they expect you to jump out there and go crazy. And this every night.

We played an eighteen one-nighter, and we worked every night, and every time you get there they want you to act like you're fresh. 'Course, the people don't give a damn. They paid their money."

These conditions were exacerbated by segregation throughout most of the circuit and were even harder on female vocalists, who had to cope with sexual harassment and who were generally excluded from the comraderie of the male musicians' in-group. No wonder trading church and home for blues and the road generated family showdowns. Show people have traditionally been typecast as morally loose and irresponsible. Whether or not this reputation is deserved, the road was laced with temptation. The conditions H-Bomb describes, the need to be up for each night's performance, let alone having to cope with day-to-day racism, generated numerous road casualties, especially victims of alcohol and (to a much lesser degree) heroin, the drug of choice during the 1940s and 1950s.

Besides the dangers of alcohol and drugs, musicians had to survive random audience violence, the Ku Klux Klan, and agents of organized crime. Big Maybelle and Little Esther became addicts. Johnny Ace blew his brains out backstage. Sam Cooke was killed in a motel room dispute. Nevertheless, musicians needed the road. Working with touring bands and package shows promoted records. They needed to keep in the public eye and to earn their daily bread.

STILL ANOTHER NAME CHANGE

Rhythm and blues started as a loose, homespun colaboration, but, by 1955, economic forces were at work that would split R & B into two camps, bringing yet another name change. H-Bomb Ferguson was part of these changes:

They had a tour that took you through Charleston, West Virginia; Wheeling; Charleston, South Carolina; certain parts of Florida; Jacksonville. This is the tour that B. B. King, Tiny Bradshaw, and me made. This guy's name was Weinberger. He was a promoter. He start you out in West Virginia. It was Charleston, Wheeling. We went from there to Jacksonville, Miami, Savannah, Georgia, Mobile, Alabama. Man, this cat had them lined up. Just like every other night we was at different places.

When I was doing this, they used to rope off the dance hall. The white was over there, and the black was over here. I ain't gonna never forget none of it. And sometimes when we played, we had a half hour to get the hell out of there, 'cause the sheriff came up and told us. "You all get the hell out of here when you get through." And they'd be dancing. But you know one thing, people are funny. I don't care if it was prejudicial then. Do you know, a lot of white people would cross the line and come on to the colored side of the dance. I used to be able to tell in a second just looking at them. The sheriff would grab them and push them back but they'd still do it. The blacks wouldn't do it, because they know they'd go to jail. They would break the rope line. They had police lined up. You dance on your side, and everybody dance on their side. And they would come over.

By the 1950s, rhythm and blues steadily attracted more whites, who turned out for shows in venues that attempted to maintain conventions of segregation. But because of the participatory nature of the music, when the house was rocking certain barriers fell. Whites crossed the line into black dancing space. More important for the rhythm and blues industry, the same thing was happening at the record store.

Initially, the business people who ran rhythm and blues—record makers, record sellers, club owners, jukebox distributors—welcomed the influx of white teenagers. Rhythm and blues had always shown a keener interest in the color green than in black or white. The economic stability that had initially led to the rise of rhythm and blues likewise affected the postwar baby boomers, producing a potentially huge market of teenagers with money in their jeans. In the past, music—black, white, country, or pop—was directed at an adult market, because only adults could afford to buy records. But now the industry was confronted by teenagers with the buying power to carve out part of the rhythm and blues pie. In retrospect, it is easy to see why R & B attracted youth culture. Early 1950s pop music seemed to serve the older generation; teenagers, like the first rhythm and blues audience, wanted something different from their parents' music, which they could appropriate as their own. Initially, black R & B served this purpose.

By 1955, rhythm and blues was in full bloom, inexorably expanding into the popular market. In 1956, *Billboard*, which had given the music its name in the first place, editorialized that it was R & B's greatest era.

In a way it was. A quick look at the charts shows that they were dominated by major stars Fats Domino, Little Richard, and Elvis Presley. These figures, rhythm and blues artists all, had the crossover power to usher in a new era, which called for a new name.

Rock 'n' roll, a tried-and-true African-American folk term that meant different things to churchgoers than it did to the juke joint crowd, took on still another meaning as a musical category. Conventional wisdom has it that rock 'n' roll resulted from the union of rhythm and blues and country and western music. Artists like Bill Haley of Chester, Pennsylvania, or Elvis Presley of Memphis support this contention, but, in fact, black blues and white country had been involved in an incestuous relationship on and off throughout the history of American music. This time around, the difference lay in the age variable. The independent labels, which often produced both rhythm and blues and country and western, ever on the alert for a new trend, zeroed in on the youth market.

*Joe Hill Louis at radio station
WDIA, Memphis.*

As the Mills Brothers, the Ink Spots, and Nat King Cole proved, there were more white Americans to buy pop records than black Americans to buy rhythm and blues. The potential revenue generated by the youth culture market and a national rock 'n' roll fad led label after label to focus on developing rock 'n' roll hits at the expense of their R & B artists and R & B audience. A brief look at Chicago's Chess Records and Memphis's Sun Records illustrates this mid-1950s schism. Chess shifted away from its Delta stalwarts Muddy Waters, Howlin' Wolf, and Sonny Boy Williamson in order to promote the purveyors of a new sound—Mississippi-born (but Chicago-raised) Bo Diddley and the best writer of youth culture hits, Missourian Chuck Berry.

Doctor Isaiah Ross performed some excellent down-home blues for Sam Phillips's Sun label. According to Ross, Phillips told him if he could find a white man who could play and sing as good as a black man, he would make him a million dollars. Sun found its star in Elvis Presley, and, as Doctor Ross recalls it, "The next time I went back, Elvis Presley had come through . . . so they took my promotion off of my record and they put it on him. . . . I was probably one of the first ones. Me, Joe Hill Louis, and Willie Nix. There was a bunch of us there that was on that thing. But we were the ones who really started it."

The shift in priorities from the artists who established the labels to the new teen idols made good business sense. Though the process didn't happen overnight, by 1956 there was a new set of rules that changed the game, as had happened earlier, in 1945. From 1956 on, R & B coexisted with its red-headed stepchild, rock 'n' roll, and many records were plainly both. Unfortunately for rhythm and blues and its first audience, the idea of finding a white man who could sing like a black man persisted.

◆ 343

Lil Green was a popular blues and R & B artist. RIGHT

Peggy Lee, best known as a stylish jazz vocalist, also sang the blues. BELOW

Fifty years ago in 1941, Mississippi-born Lil Green recorded a minor-key semi-blues oddity entitled "Why Don't You Do Right?" An intriguing transitional artist spanning prewar and postwar blues, Green was a popular rhythm and blues artist whose music stretched from her Mississippi church and juke joint roots to New York's Apollo Theatre. After moving to Chicago, as so many other Mississippians and Mississippi musicians had, she worked with Big Bill Broonzy, bassist Ransom Knowling, and pianist Henry Simeon, writing "Romance in the Dark," a substantial hit in 1940. After "Do Right," however, she moved on to bigger things, touring with Luis Russell, Clyde Bernhardt, and, later, Tiny Bradshaw. During her career she recorded for RCA/Victor, Aladdin, and Atlantic. According to gospel legend R. H. Harris of the Soul Stirrers, somewhere along the line she did time for her involvement in a juke joint killing. Broonzy remembered her as a friend, a good-natured, deeply religious woman, who neither smoked nor drank. She died in Chicago in 1954 at age thirty-five, and few people outside the black community remember her. Her 1941 record "Why Don't You Do Right?" made pop music history when it was successfully covered by Peggy Lee.

"Covering" a record meant recording someone else's hit, either for a different market or to compete with the original. Part of the music business since the 1920s, covers took several forms. Historically, the same companies that recorded blues also recorded so-called hillbilly music, and big hits like "Sitting on Top of the World" were recorded by both blues and country artists. This practice continued, as several independent labels, like King, Imperial, and Sun, worked both the rhythm and blues and the country and western market. It wasn't uncommon for a label to put out a country version of a rhythm and blues hit, or vice versa.

For the other type of cover, a pop artist redid a country or rhythm and blues hit. R & B and country songs, as performed by Lil Green or Hank Williams, could be recut in a diluted pop format and then sold to a market unlikely to have purchased the original. By the mid 1950s, the practice of covering became more problematic as the previously segregated divisions among black music, country, and pop began to break down, and rhythm and blues labels were in a stronger position to compete with the majors. The competition became especially fierce in response to the interests of white youths in rhythm and blues. Suddenly there was much more money to be made.

While Peggy Lee's covers of Lil Green's hit and of Little Willie John's 1958 classic, "Fever," didn't take away their air play or cut into their original market, by the mid-1950s, covers did begin to compete for the same market. For example, in 1954 the Crew Cuts covered the Chords' rhythm and blues hit "Sh-Boom." In 1957, the Diamonds, a notorious cover group, copied the remarkably innovative "Little Darlin" by the Gladiolas, led by Maurice Williams. In both cases, the slicker cover versions promoted by stronger labels eclipsed the R & B originals. In some cases—such as Pat Boone's, attempt to cover Little Richard's gospel-inspired classic "Long Tall Sally,"—the results were artistically hilarious. Nevertheless, Boone hit the charts with a half-dozen or so cover hits for cover specialist Dot Records. One could joke that the label didn't contain a single "dot" of soul, but humor glosses over the unfairness of the competitive cover phenomenon. One could also argue that the cover phenomenon remains with us to the present day, if we extend it to mean white artists working in an essentially black idiom and making more money out of it than their African-American peers. But, then, that's the history of American music.

Rhythm and blues and rock 'n' roll draw on similar sources and remain musically akin, yet each has taken its own path. Today the music industry recognizes them as separate categories. As in the late 1940s, "rhythm and blues" now denotes music that was at first exclusive to the black community and includes rap, funk, go-go, hip-hop, and whatever else percolates up from the ever creative streets. Yet, as we have seen time and again, the music seldom stays exclusive for long. What was once called "race music" was renamed rhythm and blues, then rock 'n' roll, then soul, and today is back to rhythm and blues again. Through all the changes you can hear the echo of H-Bomb Ferguson's words: "You all keep changing my name."

During the dark early days of World War II, Charlie Glenn took it upon himself to keep his countrymen smiling with something he called Rhumboogie.

I ONCE WAS LOST, BUT NOW I'M FOUND

THE BLUES REVIVAL

OF THE 1960s

JIM O'NEAL

◆◆◆

The year 1960 began somewhere over the Atlantic Ocean for Willie Dixon and Memphis Slim, who had left from Chicago on New Year's Eve en route to their debut appearances in Europe and the Middle East. This very trip was a crucial link in a chain of events during the 1960s that changed the world's view of the blues, and the bluesman's view of the world. Back home, other events that were bringing social change to the United States set yet other courses for the blues, and all the while, a good many bluesmen simply kept on playing the music they and their people had grown up with in their own neighborhoods and hometowns, regardless of what was happening in Birmingham, England, or Birmingham, Alabama. For the media it was the "re" decade of the blues—revival, rebirth, rediscovery. It was a decade of expansion and exploration for the music and its audiences—a phenomenon that was multidimensional, multidirectional, and multinational.

Social and political countercurrents of the era led many of the sixties generation to embrace the blues as an honest, direct, and earthy people's alternative to Establishment culture. Yet in some quarters it was disparaged as too earthy—low-class, old-fashioned, and unenlightened—while still other listeners latched onto the blues simply for love of the music, regardless of political connotations one way or the other. By the end of the decade several distinct audiences had developed for the blues, each with its own venues and own tastes in blues styles; the more adaptable performers often learned to move from one circuit to another. If it was a time of rejuvenation for some, it was also a time when many bluesmen had to readjust, regroup, and redefine their approach to cope with changing tastes among blacks and with new listeners among whites.

John Lee Hooker plays on Detroit's Hastings Street.

The blues took hold among college students, coffeehouse folkies, festival crowds, psychedelic ballroom trippers, and rock 'n' rollers; it was played and sung for the youth counterculture, for white southern fraternity parties, and for its traditional black audiences at blues bars, juke joints, dance halls, and theaters; it was categorized, analyzed, transcribed, and critiqued by professors, folklorists, collectors, and writers. In a decade of causes, the blues not only found itself allied with one front or another but also emerged as a cause in itself. The blues magazine, the blues book, the blues album, and the blues festival began finally to establish a public perception of the blues not only as a legitimate art form, but one worthy of an identity discrete from (rather than merely a subgenre or root of) folk, jazz, or rock.

Folk, jazz, and rock did, however, play major roles in bringing new listeners to the blues in the 1960s. White audiences were often introduced to the blues by white performers, first in the folk music boom that began in the late 1950s (and the similar skiffle fad in England), and then during the British blues-rock invasion of the mid- and late 1960s (joined by American groups like the Butterfield Blues Band). It was a jazz connection that led to the "folk blues" festivals that first brought John Lee Hooker, Sonny Boy Williamson, Howlin' Wolf, and others to Europe; there, British bands like the Rolling Stones learned the music of their idols and in turn brought the blues back home to American audiences via rock radio, records, and tours.

European jazz critics had been writing about blues records since the 1940s, although they'd had little personal contact with many of the artists. In his autobiography, *I Am the Blues*, Willie Dixon said, "Big Bill Broonzy had been going over to

Rice Miller—far better known as Sonny Boy Williamson II—affects a typically devilish pose.
CHAPTER OPENER

348

Europe and telling people he was the last of the blues artists in America." Dixon was determined to bring the blues to light, and on the 1960s tour he began plans with German promoter Horst Lippmann. In 1962, with Dixon's guidance, the Lippmann & Rau organization booked the first American Folk Blues Festival tour of Europe. The all-star package featured John Lee Hooker, T-Bone Walker, Sonny Terry, Brownie McGhee, Helen Humes, Shakey Jake, Jump Jackson, Memphis Slim, and Dixon. In the years that followed, AFBF stars included Muddy Waters, Sonny Boy Williamson, Howlin' Wolf, Big Joe Williams, Otis Rush, Buddy Guy, and many more. European audiences embraced the bluesmen with a passion; Memphis Slim ended up moving to Paris, and Sonny Boy made plans to become a British citizen but never made it back to Europe after he came home from a final tour in 1964. In retrospect, Dixon's forthright comment was, "I wouldn't have gone over there in the first place had I been doing all right here, you know."

"There was not much enthusiasm in Europe when we came up with the idea," Lippmann told Dixon's coauthor Don Snowden. "Only Paris right away liked it . . . England was the last country to pick it up." Once in England, however, the blues roared like thunder. French producer-promoter Philippe Rault recalled: "Those shows had a really big impact. There was a bunch of English bands that put the fuse to the dynamite—like Alexis Korner and Cyril Davies—who really inspired all those groups like the Stones, but they were always the second-hand product. When those

Helen Humes in her glory, singing with the Count Basie Band. She started her professional career at age sixteen, singing the blues to the accompaniment of guitarist Sylvester Weaver in Louisville, Kentucky.

shows came over, there was a lot of attention, not only from the blues fans going to the shows but from all of the English pop stars of the time. It was a major influence on spreading the blues in Europe at the time. . . . This was really a pivotal period, 1962–64—people were so starved for those shows because it was the real thing finally happening."

"There were about forty blues fans in London that had collected some records and had been looking towards the blues for regenerating the entire music scene, which was dying on its feet at the time," producer Giorgio Gomelsky told Snowden. "We didn't have access to records. If somebody found a Howlin' Wolf album, we would all sit around listening for hours. . . . When the blues musicians came to London, they would come to my house. We became kind of a link between Chicago blues and British R & B, which is fundamentally blues-based music. . . . Jimmy Page came often, the Yardbirds, Brian Jones, John Mayall came when Sonny Boy was there. . . . The first time the American Folk Blues Festival came over, I got the Stones tickets. They were all broke so I got about twenty of these blues musicians tickets in the first rows and they were sitting there worshipping these wonderful people."

The fact that the Rolling Stones, the Yardbirds, and other British groups ended up recording so many of Willie Dixon's songs was part of the plan. When in England, Dixon often sang, wrote, or taped his songs for his young admirers, hoping that one or another of them would record his material. Long John Baldry recalled that he didn't speak with Giorgio Gomelsky for a year after Gomelsky intercepted a tape Dixon had left for Baldry and gave it to the Yardbirds instead.

Meanwhile, blues source material was becoming steadily more plentiful thanks to a transatlantic exchange that developed between American and British collectors, writers, record producers, and musicians. Reissue labels like Origin Jazz Library revived the songs from the 1920s and 1930s. New York writer-producer Larry Cohn recalled, "The things that came out on Origin were really revelatory. I mean, they were things that were really never available commercially since the beginning of LP in '48, so it was a whole new kind of thing, and really kind of invited a new audience. And then I think you can trace a lot of the blues revival directly to the English people, you know, right from those Origin records. That would include Clapton, Jimmy Page, Beck, and, even before that, Alex Korner, Baldry, and the guys who were playing blues in England." It was the 1950s Chicago sound of Muddy Waters, Howlin' Wolf, Sonny Boy, and the rest, however, that really took hold in England.

"The Rolling Stones came out named after my song, you know, and recorded 'Just Make Love to Me,' and the next I knew they were out there. And that's how people in the States really got to know who Muddy Waters was," Muddy said in Bossmen. Muddy's manager Bob Messinger added: "One of the first things the Beatles said when they got here was that they wanted to go see Muddy Waters and Bo Diddley. Some reporter said, 'Where's that?'"

The influence of events in Europe was potent, but it took time for the blues to complete its transatlantic cycle via the British bands. It was not until Beatlemania hit the U.S. in 1963 that America paid much attention to British pop music, and the accompanying first wave of English groups was on the whole more pop-oriented than blues-based (with the likes of the Dave Clark Five, the Searchers, Gerry & the Pacemakers, and Herman's Hermits outnumbering their bluesier counterparts such as the Rolling Stones, Animals, and Yardbirds). Nor were American teens deemed ready for a straight dose even of Anglicized blues. The Stones' 1964 cover of "Little Red Rooster" was a number-one single in the U.K., but London Records would not release it on a U.S. 45. The Stones countered by bringing Howlin' Wolf (whose "Smokestack Lightning," then nearly ten years old, had hit the Top 50 in England) with them for a TV appearance on "Shindig" in 1965. But the heavy British blues influence didn't strike until the arrival of another musical wave led by Eric Clapton (with John Mayall and then with Cream), Fleetwood Mac, and Jimi Hendrix (returning to the U.S. as an imported act). Through the songwriters' credits on their albums, and from the credit they gave to the blues originators in their interviews, the Englishmen turned on thousands of young American (and European) rock fans to Muddy Waters, Howlin' Wolf, Robert Johnson, B. B. King, John Lee Hooker, Freddy King, Otis Rush, and many more. The hardcore audience for the originals never equaled the mass audience for the rock versions, but a new base of support for the blues had been created nonetheless.

Howlin' Wolf with an unidentified admirer.

England was not only the bedrock of blues-rock, it was the source of much of the blues scholarship and literature of the 1960s. But the English were hardly the only channel to the blues for the sixties generation in America. Listeners had been tuning into the blues through a variety of sources, and for most blacks and some (mostly southern) whites, the blues was nothing new.

Among blacks, many heard it first at home, on the radio or the family record player, or from an older relative or neighbor who played the music; for those reared in nonblues households, discovery might be made peering in the window of the neighborhood juke joint or tavern, or listening to music with friends. Most came to the blues through either its popular practitioners like B. B. King, Bobby "Blue" Bland, and Muddy Waters, or through local musicians, but a few who did not grow up in working-class blues environments went back to the roots the same way many white kids did, via Paul Butterfield, Jimi Hendrix, or John Mayall's Bluesbreakers, and a larger number got into it from the soul end of the spectrum through blues like Aretha Franklin's "Today I Sing the Blues," Jackie Wilson's "Doggin' Around," or Jimmy Hughes's "Steal Away."

Whites were, of course, far less likely to be exposed to the blues at home, but a number did happen upon the blues in the 1950s and 1960s by simply hearing it on the radio, and the music was in the environment of some who had been raised in or near black neighborhoods. Growing up in Farrell, Mississippi, writer Andy McWilliams heard the blues all around him; so did Chicago Blues Festival organizer Barry Dolins, who grew up on Maxwell Street. But producer Patricia Johnson's first encounter with the blues came at Disneyland; author Paul Garon heard a Brownie McGhee record by accident in a Louisville record shop. At southern universities, blues bands were commonly hired for fraternity parties, and in Mississippi Delta towns like Helena, Greenville, and Clarksdale, for private parties and occasional high school dances as well. Just as many rock 'n' roll fans backtracked to the blues from the composers' names on rock albums, folk records provided a similar path earlier in the decade. Rock 'n' roll hits by Chuck Berry or Bo Diddley led some to investigate

Otis Rush: southpaw guitarist.

In a genre that has produced more than its share of living legends, B. B. King is one of the best known, most successful, and most active. He was one of the sparks that ignited the blues revival of the 1960s.

the label roster of Chess and Checker Records and learn of Muddy, Wolf, and Little Walter. The local bookstore or library might be the beginning of the blues trail for readers who found copies of Samuel B. Charters's *The Country Blues* or Paul Oliver's *Blues Fell This Morning*, or later, LeRoi Jones's *Blues People: Negro Music in White America* or Charles Keil's *Urban Blues*. A plug on the back of a Canned Heat album for Blues Unlimited hipped American blues-rock fans to the existence of an all-blues periodical published in England.

Most white kids who became blues converts did not head for the nearest ghetto bar or country juke joint in their quest to hear the music. Usually, the music had to come to them, at their clubs or colleges or festivals. The first way it came to many was on the radio, which gave millions of listeners free access to blues. In their homes or in their cars, listeners could immerse themselves in the sounds of the blues, if not the in-person experience of it. At the University of Mississippi, wide-eyed fraternity kids who partied to the bands of Muddy and the Wolf had already heard the music on the radio, recalled photographer D. Gorton, a member of the Kappa Alpha house in 1959–62. There were more blues records in the pop music charts and on pop radio in the 1960s than in any decade before or since. At the same time, the number of rhythm and blues stations was growing; black music took over more and more spots on the radio dial, and even if the proportion of hardcore blues on the R & B hit lists had decreased from the previous decade, there were still some vital strongholds that developed faithful listenerships among both blacks and whites.

Most prominent was WLAC, continuing a tradition begun in the 1940s of broadcasting late-night blues via its 50,000-watt clear-channel signal from Nashville to a vast audience that extended from the Caribbean to Canada. Moreover, its black-sounding crew of white deejays, most notably John R. (Richbourg), was always hawking mail-order blues specials from sponsors like Ernie's, Randy's, and Buckley's (all retail record operations in the Nashville area) in addition to baby chicks, hair pomades, and various tonics. Listeners could have a package of the latest blues hits

Record buyers have made Jimmy Reed one of the most successful blues artists of all time.

Fats Domino—caught singing without his trademark piano.

delivered straight to their door for only $3.99 plus postage. With a blues 45, as Louisiana record producer Floyd Soileau put it, "If you don't make it on WLAC, you're nowheresville!" Other stations around the country, from WROX in Clarksdale, Mississippi, and WDIA in Memphis, to WOPA and WVON in the Chicago area, put the blues on the air for anyone who cared to tune in. The performers and listeners may have had their boundaries and restrictions, but the airwaves did not.

Already something sounded familiar when the Rolling Stones and the Animals came along doing Jimmy Reed and John Lee Hooker; even if the young rock 'n' roll audience hadn't been paying close attention to the names on the radio, they knew they'd heard the music somewhere before.

The majority of radio listeners were tuned into the pop stations and not the R & B programs, but even those listeners were getting tastes of blues from crossover hits by Jimmy Reed and hit parade artists like Ray Charles, Fats Domino, and Bobby Bland, most of whose 1960s hits showed on the pop charts as well as the R & B.

The out-and-out blues artist with the most widespread appeal and influence during the 1960s—at least the first part of the decade—was Jimmy Reed, then based in Chicago, but no longer closely associated with the local blues scene due to a touring schedule that took him around the country to colleges, nightclubs, dance halls, and concerts with his own revue or with rock 'n' roll package shows. Reed's music and lyrics made him the most accessible of all bluesmen; he sang in plain language, not about mojos, killing floors, or prison cells, but mostly about basic male-female relationships. "Jimmy Reed's lyrics were singalong lyrics," said D. Gorton, "and everybody knew the songs." This blues was not of the sad, mournful sort. In fact, Reed said, "I never did name one of my records the blues after all. Everybody else called my sounds what I made 'the blues.' But I always felt good behind 'em; I didn't feel like I was playin' no blues." And yet, as blues music, it was the form honed to its basics, played with such relaxed ease and in such uncomplicated patterns that his songs were easy for bands to learn and made musicians out of countless listeners, black and white, who thought "I can play that!" Bluesman Lonnie Brooks recalled, "This is what made him so popular, because everybody could play his music. It's so simple." Louisiana record dealer Eddie Shuler marveled, "Jimmy Reed sold a lot of guitars." Beginning harmonicists were likewise pointed in Reed's direction by the first blues harmonica instruction book, Tony Glover's Blues Harp (1965), which noted: "[Reed] works with a very basic rhythm pattern—and almost all of his numbers are variations of the same bass line. You can hear the progressions and changes very easily—and for this reason Reed is probably one of the best recording bluesmen to learn from." Reed's manager-producer Al Smith even gave Jimmy credit for showing white folks how to dance: "See, the white kids never learned how to slow dance with each other . . . but with that slow off-beat Jimmy Reed had, they began to hug up and learn how to really dance close together like black people."

To this day, Jimmy Reed stands as the most successful down-home bluesman ever to "cross over" into the pop market. In 1960 and 1961, six consecutive Reed 45s, from "Baby What You Want Me to Do" through "Bright Lights Big City," all on the Vee-Jay label, hit both the Top 20 of the rhythm and blues charts and the Top 100 of the pop charts in Billboard magazine. His music earned him a permanent niche with black audiences and musicians, and he was also the first bluesman from the postwar Chicago scene to attract a large white audience, particularly among southern high school and college kids. "Jimmy Reed, he was like a president down there in Texas," his reputed half-brother and soundalike A. C. Reed recalled. Jimmy Reed's songs entered the repertoire of rock (both American and British) and country and western; his blues also formed the core element of the "swamp blues" style of south Louisiana artists Lightnin' Slim, Slim Harpo, and others. Quite probably it was the proven sales potential of Jimmy Reed's blues that led companies to record artists like Frank Frost, Smokey Smothers, Willie Cobbs, and Sam Myers in the early 1960s. In 1967, comedian Bill Cosby even devoted half an album to Jimmy Reed songs. Had it not been for problems with alcohol, epilepsy, and money management, there is no telling how far Reed could have gone; but within a few short years both his health and career were cascading downhill. He died in 1976, and the blues movement he preceded went on without him.

Until the blues gained respect as the blues, promoters usually tried to fit it into some already popular or acceptable format such as folk, jazz, rock 'n' roll, rhythm and blues, or, in later years, the roots of rock. Jimmy Reed was in essence marketed as a rock 'n' roll act like Chuck Berry and Fats Domino. Rock 'n' rollers had been developing a taste for the blues since the 1950s, not just on radio and record, but also at dances and rhythm and blues extravaganzas that featured Domino, Berry, Big Joe Turner, Little Richard, LaVern Baker, Bo Diddley, and Jimmy Reed—and, of course, the blues also traveled via Elvis, Bill Haley, Carl Perkins and the like. Record companies faced a hard sell marketing blues as teen dance music, but King/Federal went all out with the Freddy King instrumental boom of the early 1960s, when "Hide Away" and "San-Ho-Zay" both hit the Top 100, and the company raced to think up titles for Freddy's blues guitar workouts such as "Surf Monkey," "The Stumble," and "Bossa Nova Watusi Twist." When Chubby Checker proved that a black dance record could create a nationwide sensation in 1960, all of a sudden Crown threw together some sides from the vaults and was inviting teens to "Twist With" B. B. King, Etta James, and Jimmy McCracklin. Atlantic's entry was Do the Twist With Ray Charles, actually an excellent blues album that, like the Crowns, came complete with dance instructions on the back cover. The Checker label came up with Bo Diddley Is a Twister, and Chess even issued a "Muddy Waters Twist" single in 1962. A few years down the line, when the alternative rock culture was tripping to Big Brother & the Holding Company, the Electric Flag, Canned Heat, and the Blues Project, the root music was recycled again: *Turn On with B. B. King, Underground Blues, Heavy Heads, Switched On Blues.*

Chess Records struggled to get Muddy Waters's singles back onto the rhythm and blues charts and at the same time packaged his albums as folk music before tak-

Intensely active on the folk blues circuit: the legendary team of Sonny Terry on harmonica and Brownie McGhee on guitar.

ing cues from the underground rock phenomenon and recording "supersession" albums, psychedelic LPs, and Muddy-as-godfather-of-rock sessions. Chess's black attorney John Burton recalled, "Some people wanted Muddy to change. When the folk record idiom became popular we tried to sell Muddy as a folk artist." (Following Muddy's *Folk Singer* LP of 1964, Chess released an entire series of *The Real Folk Blues* and *More Real Folk Blues* albums by Muddy, Howlin' Wolf, Sonny Boy Williamson, Memphis Slim, and John Lee Hooker, consisting mainly of reissued singles originally targeted for the R & B audience. A live recording done at a black West Side nightclub was released as *Folk Festival of the Blues*; when reissued in the 1970s, after the folk boom had passed, it was retitled *Blues from Big Bill's Copa Cabana*. Hooker, Wolf, Elmore James, Smokey Hogg, Lightnin' Hopkins, and others were also featured on Kent Records' *Original Folk Blues* series of LPs assembled from singles and previously unissued tracks or retitled from earlier albums.) Burton tried in vain to get Muddy to prepare a forty-minute act in which the folk bluesman would "relate [each] song to a period and weave into that program artfully the story of a people or a story of a concept so that he'd become identified with a movement—with something. You know, like Joan Baez . . . she stands for something." In the end, though Muddy's records never made the charts in the 1960s, the entree into the worlds of folk and rock—and jazz, via a 1958 British tour and a groundbreaking live LP from the 1960 Newport Jazz Festival—did build a huge new audience for Muddy. But fans kept flocking to him, not because of folk, rock, or jazz, or any polished stage routine, but because of Muddy's own movement, which was the blues, played and presented the way he'd been doing for years. As Muddy put it: "They tried to put me over in another bag but I just don't fit no other bag. Exactly I fits one shoe, and that is the blues."

Blind Reverend Gary Davis spent a lifetime playing on the streets before he finally reaped the financial rewards of recognition during the blues revival of the 1960s.

Mississippi Fred McDowell is seen here with Bonnie Raitt during the mid-1960s, long before she achieved her phenomenal popular success.

While Muddy Waters never really transformed his electric Chicago ensemble act into that of a "folk singer," there were other bluesmen ready and able to fill the bill for the traditional styles in vogue with the folk audiences of the 1960s. Some took a stylistic step back in time as they traded their amplifiers for acoustic guitars. Brownie McGhee (who'd been heading in the direction of electric R & B prior to the folk revival) and his partner Sonny Terry were among the most successful and prolific artists on the folk-blues circuit. Josh White was another folk favorite, performing everywhere from Disneyland to ABC-TV's "Hootenanny," while California's one-man band, Jesse Fuller, was hailed in both folk and traditional jazz circles. Reverend Gary Davis and Mississippi John Hurt awed and inspired a whole new generation of acoustic guitar pickers. Just as rock bands of the 1960s helped bring new fame to the blues veterans, so did many white folk and folk-rock acts, including Bob Dylan, Koerner, Ray & Glover, Eric von Schmidt, Dave van Ronk, Barbara Dane, John Fahey, Geoff & Maria Muldaur, the Lovin' Spoonful, and the Youngbloods. When the Rooftop Singers scored a number-one pop hit in 1963 with Gus Cannon's "Walk Right In," Stax Records made one of its rare ventures into traditional blues by recording an entire LP by Cannon in Memphis. (Copies of the LP were, however, as rare as the experiment.)

Festivals—in particular the Newport Folk Festival and the touring American Folk Blues Festivals in Europe—played a major role in bringing traditional blues artists into public view. It was at such events that many bluesmen first played before large concert audiences. The Newport festival produced a historic series of albums that featured not only by-then seasoned veterans of the folk circuit like McGhee, Terry, and Davis, plus the ever-adaptable John Lee Hooker and Lightnin' Hopkins in their folk-blues guises, but also an exciting roster of country bluesmen, whose careers truly characterized the term "blues revival." This group included some legendary fig-

Mance Lipscomb

Arthur "Big Boy" Crudup performs at a 1960s folk blues festival.

ures who had recorded back in the 1920s and 1930s, including Hurt, Son House, Skip James, Reverend Robert Wilkins, Sleepy John Estes, as well as some veteran musicians who had only recently started to tour and record thanks to the new interest in authentic blues: Mississippi Fred McDowell, Robert Pete Williams (just released from the penitentiary), and Mance Lipscomb. The unfortunate term applied to these bluesmen (and others, such as Booker "Bukka" White, Big Joe Williams, and Furry Lewis) was "rediscovered." More than one blues veteran is known to have said or thought, "I wasn't lost, I've been here all along," upon his "rediscovery" by white civilization. Despite its terminology, the process by which researchers, collectors, and enthusiasts sought out and met the artists whose names they knew only from old records, was an exciting one for the developing new blues audience. John Fahey, Sam Charters, Bob Koester, Dick Waterman, Chris Strachwitz, Paul Oliver, Tom Hoskins and others earned special mention in blues history for their efforts in renewing the careers of some of the greatest performers of the blues.

According to many, the most unforgettable of the country blues legends were Mississippi John Hurt, the gentle songster ("the patriarch hippie"—Dick Waterman; "the nicest person I ever met"—Larry Cohn), and Son House, the preaching bluesman. Cohn remembered: "I saw Son House's first performance when he was rediscovered, in New York City, and I thought I'd have a heart attack. I had never seen or imagined that anyone could sing with such intensity and not drop dead on the spot. Because every song was like a complete catharsis. I mean it was so emotional, you know, he'd just throw his head back, and I used to wonder, my God, this is 1965— what was he like in 1930? I mean it was just absolutely incredible."

Dick Waterman became the major booking representative for traditional blues artists in the sixties, and eventually expanded his roster to include Chicago acts such as Junior Wells, Buddy Guy, Magic Sam, and J. B. Hutto. In a 1969 letter he wrote:

> *The audience for traditional blues seems to run in cycles. The best was 1962–64 with what I call "Folk/Blues" and that featured Mississippi John Hurt and an added push to the careers of Josh White, Brownie & Sonny, Jesse Fuller, etc. It was a poor time for the traditionalists like Son House, Skip James, Booker White (he is more commercial than the first two), John Estes, Robert Pete Williams, etc. It is only in the recent year or two of Black re-awakening (is that what we shall call it?) that Black Arts festivals have booked older musicians. The outstanding artistic success of the [1969] Ann Arbor Blues Festival seems to have sparked added interest. . . . The uniqueness of AA is that it paid a commercial price to the artists. Others such as Newport, Berkeley, UCLA, Mariposa (Toronto), et al insist on $50-a-day-plus-travel which is fine for an act that is making a regular living—Baez, Dylan, PP&M [Peter, Paul & Mary], St. Marie, Paxton—but hard on the bluesman who needs the festival for exposure but also needs it for actual living money. I recently have invoked a $400–450 concert minimum for my older artists. For the ones living in the rural South (McDowell, Estes, [Arthur] Crudup), the $650–700 left after two concerts (less travel) can last for a long time at home.*

Skip James, Waterman noted, "lived (and died) in the frustrating period between the Folk/Blues craze and the Black Arts comeback. His second career of 1964–68 was in the middle and he had the smallest audience available to him. He worked very little, but he was a bluesman's bluesman and I think that time will show that he will be considered one of the greatest of all time."

The blues revival did not translate into prosperity for traditional bluesmen, either in performing fees or in recording income, though a few did reap royalties from rock band versions of their songs (Skip James for Cream's cover of "I'm So Glad," and Robert Wilkins for the Rolling Stones' rendition of "Prodigal Son," for instance). Traditional records of folk-blues and country blues never sold in great numbers, but a great many were released by labels like Delmark, Arhoolie, Testament, Folkways, Vanguard, Storyville, and Prestige/Bluesville for a faithful listenership whose format of choice was now the LP, not the 45. The January 1964 issue of Blues Unlimited reported that "several of Bluesville's 72 LPs have only sold a few hundred." Sleepy John Estes and Big Joe Williams albums dominated the early blues output on Bob Koester's Delmark label in Chicago. In a January 1966 article, the *Chicago Daily News* noted: "Koester's first Estes LP remains his biggest seller. It sold 1,200 copies in the first year, close to 2,000 all totaled. But he expects his latest release—Junior Wells' Hoodoo Man Blues—to outsell it." Indeed, the Wells LP did just that, going on to become (along with Magic Sam's West Side Soul) one of Delmark's two

Mississippi John Hurt at Ontario Place Coffee House, Washington, D.C., in 1963.

Skip James in the studio.

Reverend Robert Wilkins performs in Washington, D.C., some time during the early 1960s.

"desert island discs" among blues aficionados worldwide, as Delmark and other specialist labels initiated a shift toward urban blues. However, traditional blues certainly came out of the 1960s well documented. Big Joe Williams, Lonnie Johnson, Lightnin' Hopkins, John Lee Hooker, Memphis Slim, Sonny & Brownie, Fred McDowell, Mance Lipscomb, Roosevelt Sykes, Sunnyland Slim, and Champion Jack Dupree recorded prolifically (some of them in Europe more than in America), and many lesser known singers entered recording studios for the first (and sometimes only) time. Even the major labels took a few shots, and Columbia came up with one of the most emotionally compelling recordings of the decade in Son House's Father of Folk Blues, plus the most influential reissue album, Robert Johnson's King of the Delta Blues Singers. In general, the majors left the reissues to their European affiliates or to the collectors' labels: OJL showed the way early on with its two Charley Patton volumes and assorted country blues collections, while Yazoo and the Austrian-based Roots labels built the most impressive catalogs, mined from the world's leading collections of vintage blues 78s. It was the work of the reissue companies, which also included Blues Classics, RBF, Historical, Flyright, Riverside, and many limited-edition labels, that focused renewed interest on the blues stylists of old and reintroduced the classic songs of the prewar era into the repertoire of the 1960s revivalists.

Piano players benefited less than guitarists from the revival in America. One by one, a small but significant group of pianists—including Memphis Slim, Eddie Boyd, and Curtis Jones, all following the lead of Jack Dupree, who had moved by 1959—undertook a gradual exodus to Europe, where demand for their talents was greater, and where they seemed either more able or more inclined to adapt to continental living than their guitar- and harmonica-playing counterparts who opted to remain in the U.S. even after experiencing tremendous European welcomes on tour. The expatriate bluesmen also tended to be outspokenly critical of race relations in their home country. By blues standards, Memphis Slim lived like a king in Paris for the rest of his life (at least he made sure to give that impression), but European residency was no guarantee of success: Curtis Jones was buried in an unmarked pauper's grave in Germany.

The revival clearly applied primarily to reviving prewar down-home blues and to that genre's direct descendants—for example, practitioners of the Chicago blues. The Chicago stars included not only Muddy Waters, Howlin' Wolf, Junior Wells, Otis Rush, Magic Sam, Buddy Guy, and Sonny Boy Williamson, but also top sidemen such as Otis Spann and James Cotton from Muddy's band, for instance, who were able to begin solo recording careers and cut album after album, becoming among the first of the modern bluesmen to succeed without having established a substantial prior base of commercial support among blacks. The legendary reputations of Willie Dixon and Earl Hooker likewise enabled them to step out front by the

MEMPHIS SLIM
*Premium
Recording Artist*

Peter Chatman—better known as Memphis Slim—is seen in a Premium Records publicity shot many years before he moved to Paris.

John Lee Hooker's cousin, Earl Hooker, considered by many of his peers to have been the best of all blues guitarists.

late 1960s, as Hooker recorded a slew of albums shortly before his death in 1970 and Dixon began taking his Chicago Blues All Stars on the road. New names such as Luther Allison, Johnny Littlejohn, and Jimmy Dawkins created a stir with their debut albums; Koko Taylor's "Wang Dang Doodle" was one of the big blues hits of the decade; and many names recognizable from records of the 1950s were back in the studio again: Robert Nighthawk, Johnny Shines, J. B. Hutto, Homesick James, Sunnyland Slim, Eddie Taylor, Big Walter Horton, Billy Boy Arnold, and Johnny Young, now doing albums for many of the same labels that had been recording the country bluesmen. But Elmore James died in 1963, having never played the white blues revival circuit; Sonny Boy died back home in Helena, Arkansas, in 1965, Nighthawk in 1967; and between 1968 and 1970 Chicago lost Little Walter, Magic Sam, Spann, and Hooker, all dead by the age of forty. If recording opportunities were more plentiful, the music was rarely commercial, and money from album sessions and club work didn't go far. Only a few of the best-known acts could count on consistent paying jobs, and in the local black clubs, harmonica players whose wailing had been in vogue when the Muddy Waters/Little Walter sound was hot often took up bass or drums to keep gigs. Some bluesmen gave up performing altogether.

James Cotton poses with his harp.

Although Muddy was still the king, and Wolf was just as powerful, if not more, it was the newer styles of guitarists like Otis Rush, Buddy Guy, Freddy King, and Magic Sam that took the fore. Rush's band was often cited by fellow Chicago musicians as the best of the era. Yet for Otis it was a frustrating period, one of many that would plague his career after an initial success with Cobra Records in the late 1950s. His early 1960s tenure with Chess yielded another classic in "So Many Roads," but no hit records, and a contract with the Duke label served only to get one 45 on the market and mainly, from Otis's perspective, to tie him and up and keep him out of the way of Duke's established blues stars Bobby Bland and Junior Parker. The best-selling Chicago album of the era was by Paul Butterfield, who was also the first to take a band to the Newport Folk Festival, an irony duly noted by the blues community. The benefits of Butterfield's popularity were substantial for other Chicago acts.

However, by the end of the decade Butterfield and the other major white Chicago players—notably Elvin Bishop, Mike Bloomfield, and Charlie Musselwhite—had all relocated to the West Coast, along with some of the black musicians (Shakey Jake, Luther Tucker, and Freddie Roulette). Chicago remained the blues capital, but as such it also gave added credentials to Windy City musicians who chose to reestablish themselves elsewhere. The black South and West Side clubs were becoming internationally famous among blues aficionados, in addition to white clubs and coffeehouses in the Old Town area. Active blues scenes existed in the 1960s in other urban centers—St. Louis, Houston, Detroit, Oakland—but, unlike in Chicago, news rarely filtered out of the ghetto.

The jazz audience formed another part of the support system for blues in the 1960s. But most blues artists didn't work the jazz circuit, and the jazzier blues stylists generally didn't work the blues revival, which seemed to want its music either folksy or electrified. However, the early American Folk Blues Festivals did feature some blues artists with jazz credentials, especially Lonnie Johnson, Big Joe Turner, T-Bone Walker, and Helen Humes; the Newport Jazz Festival did book Muddy Waters, John Lee Hooker, Little Brother Montgomery, and others; and similar festivals at Monterey and elsewhere also featured a few blues acts. The jazz fraternity respected traditional blues as a root, and blues was allotted its spot in much the same way that many books on jazz included the obligatory chapter on blues. Blues partisans might also turn to jazz for credentials: Delmark Records' blues series was called the Roots of Jazz, and the most important of the early blues reissue labels was initially named Origin Jazz Library. Record stores like Bob Koester's Jazz Record Mart were instrumental in making newly recorded and reissued blues albums available. Jazz magazines, television specials, and radio programs in Europe and America all gave space to the blues. Down Beat's better-late-than-never jazz critics voted for Jimmy Witherspoon as best New Star, Male Vocalist in 1961 and for Lightnin' Hopkins in 1962; their nods for "Talent Deserving Wider Recognition" went to Muddy Waters

Like a number of his contemporaries, Curtis Jones, writer of the successful "Lonesome Bedroom Blues," went to live in Europe.

John Littlejohn, slide guitarist.

J. B. Hutto in concert. ABOVE

Robert Johnson's traveling companion Johnny Shines compares notes with Fred McDowell. RIGHT

in 1964 and Junior Wells in 1968. The jazz buff, however, was not necessarily a staunch blues lover, as AFBF organizer Horst Lippmann found out. Lippmann told Don Snowden, "When we started the blues festivals, we did it from the aspect of a jazz lover. We like blues because we liked jazz and always thought that the blues was the foundation of jazz. We thought a lot of jazz fans would come, but they didn't show up at all. We found a new audience that was very enthusiastic, young people who started to learn a little about rock and really had sort of a feeling about folk music, rock music, and jazz."

The time had not yet come back around for California/Texas urban blues, 1940s-style jump blues/R & B, and most jazz-oriented blues. A few of the top vocalists, such as Big Joe Turner, Jimmy Rushing, Jimmy Witherspoon, and Joe Williams, continued to work mostly jazz venues. But times were leaner for former headline

Slide guitarist Elmore James (at right) is accompanied by Sunnyland Slim on piano and Homesick James Williamson.

artists like Louis Jordan, Cleanhead Vinson, and Amos Milburn; in Sheldon Harris's *Blues Who's Who*, time and again phrases like "worked mostly outside music" crop up for at least some portion of the 1960s in the West Coast artist entries (including Charles Brown, Roy Brown, Roy Milton, Wynonie Harris, Floyd Dixon, and Pee Wee Crayton). And the surviving blues divas of the classic/vaudeville period were all but absent from the blues performing circuit of the 1960s, as indeed were women in general, with a few exceptions like Big Mama Thornton, Victoria Spivey, Etta James, Elizabeth Cotten, and newcomer Koko Taylor. Alberta Hunter, Helen Humes, Sippie Wallace, Edith Wilson, and Viola Wells performed only occasionally or not at all; for the women, and the uptown men, the blues revival did not occur until the 1970s, when, by most perceptions, there was no revival equivalent to that of the 1960s.

Only a small percentage of active blues performers were pulled into the revival of the 1960s, although more would feel its effect in later years. The only artists who enjoyed any degree of steady revival work were some of those who'd made legendary records years earlier or who were now cutting albums for the new, predominantly white market. At first the main beneficiaries were older musicians whose styles had become passé with the mainstream black audience. Attention then turned toward a small group of great modern guitarists—notably, B. B., Albert, and Freddy King, Otis Rush, and Buddy Guy—whose music had inspired the late-1960s blues-rock explosion. By the time most whites discovered the leading contemporary black bluesman—B. B. King—he had been acknowledged as King of the Blues by black America for an entire generation. In Phyl Garland's 1969 book, *The Sound of Soul*, B. B. commented: "I played a place, not long ago, where I saw a notice in the paper the next day that say, 'B. B. King—New Blues Discovery,' after 21 years. But this is what's been happenin'. And another thing. We're beginnin' to be treated among them as stars, with respect, the same as they would give any other artist."

*Eddie "Cleanhead" Vinson
achieved success in the realms of
blues as well as jazz.* ABOVE

*Pee Wee Crayton has yet to receive
the recognition he deserves.* RIGHT

Blues that made the news (which, as always in America, was reported primarily by and to the white majority) was blues that had come to be played for whites, in white venues. The other side of blues at the Avalon Ballroom, the Ash Grove, Club 47, Mother Blues, and the Village Gate was blues at Smitty's Corner, the Club Paradise, the Moonlight Lounge, the Harlem Inn, and places in Mississippi with no name posted other than "Colored Cafe." Contemporary blues within the black community was barely acknowledged by the mass media; if so, it was likely to be pronounced dead, dying, or disowned. But blacks did constitute a huge segment of the blues audience of the 1960s, an audience that was not a part of the blues revival as such. In the home territory of the blues, the music didn't need to be revived or rediscovered; it was there, in countless local bars, juke joints, and nightclubs. There were modern blues artists reworking their styles to keep up with changing times and tastes,

in the way that blues artists had always progressed from one stylistic period to the next throughout the music's history, and there were many others playing less commercial styles or covering the popular blues hits and oldies that neighborhood listeners or townsfolk still wanted to hear.

Blues, at least what most listeners defined as blues, was no longer commercially dominant on the rhythm and blues charts as it had been up through mid-1950s. In the increasingly competitive, teen-directed and mass hit-oriented marketplace, newer forms of black popular music (notably soul) took the fore, though some would argue that all that music was the blues, too. But the 1960s produced twenty-seven Billboard chart entries by B. B. King, eleven by Junior Parker, several apiece by Jimmy Reed, Albert King, Jimmy McCracklin, and Freddy King, and a few by Sonny Boy Williamson, Elmore James, Tommy Tucker, Slim Harpo, Lowell Fulson, Bo Diddley, Buster Brown, Junior Wells, John Lee Hooker, and others. An ever-heftier share went to records on the soul-blues side by Ray Charles, Bobby Bland, Little Milton, Etta James, Johnnie Taylor, Little Johnny Taylor, Syl Johnson, O. V. Wright, and Ike and Tina Turner. A "modest hit," according to Charles Keil, might mean sixty thousand to one hundred thousand sales of a blues 45. This kind of blues record obviously sold in far greater quantities than that produced for the white blues collector. Record companies like Chess, Duke, Stax, King/Federal, ABC, Mercury, Excello, Kent, Jewel, and Fire were not about to write off or overlook the black commercial market for blues in the 1960s.

Victoria Spivey: rediscovered in the blues revival of the 1960s.

The black audience still bought blues records. What B. B. King and others emphasized was that their music needed to be respected. The blues suffered image problems among blacks in the 1960s, as Charles Keil described it, due to "growing class-consciousness on the part of Negroes and a corresponding reluctance to be identified with that 'nasty,' 'gutbucket,' 'bottom,' 'in-the-alley' music 'from slavery days.'" John Burton explained: "In the 1950s and early 1960s you had a black person known as a striver. He worked two jobs, he went to college and whatever—he was going to make it. And then you had some others who took what was given to them. That is, one job, forty-hour week, a transplant, and he had brought with him a semi-agrarian culture, which was wholesome for him. That is, he worked his forty hours; Friday night through Saturday and through Sunday evening was his time. Now, he was a blues buyer. That striver bought a more contemporary sound, because the blues sound reached back into the twenties and thirties. It was not progressive in the sense that this so-called progressive person was." In this context, the blues-buying individual was sometimes referred to as a "slacker." Many blues artists maintained, justifiably, that significant numbers of black people—strivers included—did buy their records and listen to their music, but were embarrassed to admit to it in public.

Junior Parker

"The middle-class black or the upper-class black used to frown upon it and would not play the record because that was a record from across the track," Burton said. "It represented the barrelhouse, it represented the sporting house. . . . He liked it all the time—he just didn't want to be identified with it. I mean he might get the record and play it in the closet but he didn't want it to go in the front door—he wanted that damn record across the counter 'cause he didn't want to be associated with that kind of person." That private tastes were subordinate to public voices in the black community (as well as to purely commercial forces) was evident. Chess owned two R & B radio stations, WVON ("Voice of the Negro") in Chicago and WNOV in Milwaukee, and could presumably have commanded more airplay for Muddy Waters and its other blues veterans, but the older style blues records were

369

*Riley—B. B.—King during the
1960s.*

way down on the playlists. In Bossmen, Buddy Guy lamented: "The black people are
kept from this style of blues. They don't hear Muddy today on the radio or see him
on television. And what you can't hear you'll never like."

Chess continued to record Muddy, said John "Lawyer" Burton, "in days when
we knew that the records weren't going to sell, not because the buyers weren't there,
it's just that relatively speaking, it was the other acts that were selling." Chess
Records' top hitmakers of the era were Little Milton and Etta James. From 1960 to
1969 Chess and its subsidiary labels had twenty-one chart hits by Etta and fourteen
by Milton; between Muddy, Wolf, Little Walter and Sonny Boy, they had a total of
two. Soul/blues singers' records by and large far outsold those of the more straight-
ahead blues artists, but in general made few inroads into the white market—a situation that remains basically unchanged today. Ray Charles's celebrity elevated him to
a different sphere of show business, but most fairly successful soul/blues artists—
Milton, Etta, Bobby Bland, Johnnie Taylor, et al.—toured the "chitlin circuit" of
black nightclubs, dance halls, and theaters. The rawer blues styles were played by
bands in bars and juke joints; to get to a higher-paying stratum among a black clien-
tele, blues either had to travel the soul avenue or needed to be cleaned and polished.
That approach was polished to perfection by B. B. King. Its tremendous appeal with
black listeners—especially women—was superbly documented in 1964 on the classic
ABC album *Live at the Regal.*

In *Urban Blues* (published in 1966), Charles Keil observed, "B. B. King is the
only straight blues singer in America with a large, adult, nationwide, and almost
entirely Negro audience." And: "I doubt that more than a few thousand white
Americans outside the Deep South have ever heard B. B. King's music." John Lee
Hooker, meanwhile, was busy playing all sorts of venues, for several different, mostly
white, audience groups. "With Hooker's example in mind," Keil wrote, "it is astounding that B. B. King has never been to Europe, has never done a college concert or

appeared at a folk club; he has never been on a jazz festival stage and, aside from a few obscure records with strings and trimmings, he has never directed his efforts toward a pop or teenage market. In other words, he is still singing to the same audience he has always had—that is, the people who know best what the blues are about."

That same year, B. B. King's following began to change dramatically. In The Arrival of B. B. King, Charles Sawyer gave Keil's book credit for blowing away "the mysterious cloud that obscured urban blues from the sight of Middle Americans," but the mass impetus was the new guitar hero phenomenon with rock audiences. Some of those guitar heroes, notably Eric Clapton and Mike Bloomfield, stated bluntly that the master was B. B. King. Soon B. B. was booked at the Fillmore Auditorium, the Cafe Au-Go-Go, the Monterey Jazz Festival, on European tours, and on national TV. His records scaled new heights on the pop charts, and his new audience found him to be much more than a superb guitar player. They, too, discovered that he sang with a message, from the heart, and that he was an eloquent spokesman for the blues.

A few years later, Chicago deejay and blues impresario Pervis Spann would publicly bemoan the fact that he and other black promoters who had booked B. B. for years could no longer afford him, though black audiences still bought his records and still wanted to see him. The perceived shift in the blues audience from black to white was, some would say, actually only a move from a low-income base of support to the lure of more well-endowed audiences who could pay (by black blues standards) lucrative fees to have the music brought to their doorsteps. As Bob Koester told Jerry De Muth of the Chicago Daily News in 1967: "The basic problem is that blues appeals to people who don't have any money." B. B. King, however, became so much of a public figure that his original audience regained some access to him via television. His shining star set an example, proving that blues could be both lucrative and respectable, and he continued to be a preeminent influence among the blues artists who followed.

The B. B. King–inspired school of lead-guitar-dominated electric blues bands and the gospel-influenced singing of the soul-blues singers set to tight studio arrangements were the major trends in contemporary black blues of the 1960s. The soul influence took the form of the commercial soul-blues hybrid music popular on black radio, and it also manifested itself in the incorporation of soul songs into the repertoire of most younger black blues bands. Some observers made definite distinctions between blues and soul, asserting that the blues idiom had in essence been supplanted by the more progressive and contemporary sounds and attitudes of soul music. Others viewed soul as a natural extension of blues or as part of the same whole: to Keil, soul music meant "blues, gospel, and some of the many popular and jazz styles derived therefrom." Phyl Garland's book treated B. B. King as equally integral to soul as Aretha Franklin and Otis Redding (B. B.'s calling card read: "Blues Is King—King Is Soul"). Yazoo Records founder Nick Perls, whose specialty was 1920s and 1930s blues, was of the opinion that "Blues is dance music whether it's Charley Patton or Otis Redding or Blind Lemon or James Brown. It's all dance music and it's all blues, the only difference is stylistic 'cause styles always change."

Shows billed as blues events that were sponsored by black organizations commonly came to include singers who by some definitions sang soul music and not blues, at least not in the strict twelve-bar sense. Aretha Franklin was simultaneously the Queen of Soul and the Queen of the Blues to many listeners, who regarded her domain not as two different kinds of music, but as just one. On ghetto bandstands, musicians often gave little thought to following a B. B. King song with a James Brown

Bobby "Blue" Bland

workout, or to working both approaches into the same night's music, perhaps starting with the hot dance numbers and saving the deep blues for the late set. The bluesmen usually stopped short of incorporating too much of the slicker, more pop-oriented rhythm and blues peddled by the major recording studios in favor of funkier rhythms and deep soul. The songs of James Brown, and later of Tyrone Davis, were much more popular with Chicago blues musicians, for instance, than were hits by the Four Tops or Temptations.

It has been said that no major stylistic developments occurred in the blues after the 1960s. True, the basic musical structures have not changed, but rather than marking the end of the line for the blues, the 1960s saw blues reach a new level of maturity. Just as country music continued to grow within an established framework, the blues likewise provided a continuing foundation of expression for the old and the new. Its messages, performances, and emotions continued to be delivered with the same relevance and same power.

As part of the maturation process, blues became fully certified as adult black music, a music that dealt with life experiences young listeners might not appreciate, but would by the time they reached middle age. With the exception of big shows at theaters and halls, in African-American communities blues was presented almost exclusively at adult venues: bars, lounges, taverns, social clubs. Of course blues had always to some extent been viewed as old folks' music. As record charts became more youth-oriented, reflecting the new buying power of baby boomers, blues slipped down the list, since it not only was adult music but was also becoming more of a listener's music than a dancer's. Blues and black dance music were once synonymous (and still are, by some definitions), but different terms have been applied to the prevailing trends in black dance since the sixties: soul, funk, disco, hip-hop, rap. Though blues always retained some functions down South as good "jookin'" music, its developing attraction as a sit-and-listen phenomenon caused frustration among those blues musicians who judged the impact of their performance by the number of people they inspired to get up, move, and signify.

Black society's perceptions of the blues gradually began to improve as the stigma of the music's lower-class origins was replaced by a sense of pride in the blues as a cultural heritage during what Dick Waterman called the "Black reawakening." The new, young, educated middle class that took up the music in the 1960s did include blacks as well as whites. "There was a whole movement, and not just white musicians, but also it was a class thing," noted Worth Long. "'Cause people like Taj Mahal, I saw him when he was just beginning to hit some blues. He was playing some spoons out on Harvard Yacht in 1964. He was up at the University of Massachusetts. And the Chambers Brothers played in that area, came through, in '63, '64. I also saw 'em at Newport. And they legitimized some aspects of blues. They played some gospel, they played some pop, and they played some blues. The Chambers Brothers—a Mississippi group."

As blues secured its maturity and legitimacy, and its King B. B. was crowned for all to honor, it was publicly endowed with its own identity, promoted at last from subcategory status. At first, only folk and jazz festivals booked blues; only folk, jazz, and rhythm and blues magazines covered blues. The 1960s finally brought the blues its own specialized festivals and workshops, magazines and books, historians, pundits and ideologists, esoterica and collectibilia. "Blues Power!" became the believer's cry after its proclamation by Albert King on his influential live album from the Fillmore West in 1968.

B. B. King in an elegant interlude.

*Artists of substance—and girth—
Roosevelt Sykes and Big Mama
Thornton.*

The three-day Ann Arbor Blues Festival of 1969 was generally regarded as the
first major national all-blues festival, bringing together a host of the leading contemporary and traditional figures (all black except for Charlie Musselwhite) for a com-
munal summertime crowd of several thousand mostly young white enthusiasts (the
blues' own mini-Woodstock, some opined). A University of Michigan group sponsored the Ann Arbor fest in (and only in) its first year, and the University of
Wisconsin also presented a blues festival in 1969. That year the City of Chicago held
a free blues festival in Grant Park, and a black organization proffered the Operation
Breadbasket Blues Festival to benefit the needy. The eclectic Memphis Country
Blues Festival ran from 1966 to 1969 under the auspices of the Memphis Country
Blues Society, a nonprofit coalition that included New York blues cognoscenti,
Memphians and Mississippians who were scouring the hills and the Delta for the
blues, and performer-enthusiasts who were members of the Insect Trust band. By
1966 the Berkeley Blues Festival was putting Texas and California blues artists on
stage. The Europeans were, of course, ahead of their white American brethren: in
addition to the American Folk Blues Festival (sometimes called the American Negro
Blues Festival), events billed as blues festivals were held in Paris and Hamburg as
early as 1962, followed by the London National Jazz and Blues Festival in 1964.
What may have been the first blues festival of the decade, however, was a black event
in Maryland Heights, Missouri, on July 31, 1960: the St. Louis Blues Festival (hot on
the heels of the Newport Jazz Festival earlier that month) was advertised in a local
black newspaper as "A Gigantic Outdoor Show Starring 3 Great Bands in Person." The
supporting acts were Howlin' Wolf and E. Rodney Jones (then a bandleader, later a
Chicago deejay); the headliner was Elmore James. Advance admission was one dollar.

Blues coverage in periodicals such as *Jazz Journal, Down Beat, Sing Out!* and
Rhythm and Blues helped develop a core readership for blues magazines launched in

Bukka White: one of the great Mississippi slide guitarists.

Belgium, England, Holland, New Zealand, Australia, and elsewhere during the 1960s. In America, Len Kunstadt—who ran the Spivey record label with Victoria Spivey— was publishing the discographical periodicals *Record Research* and *Blues Research*, and both Bob Koester at Delmark/Jazz Record Mart and Chris Strachwitz at Arhoolie put together occasional blues newsletters. Blues made its way into the pages of publications ranging from *Saturday Review* (which in the early 1960s could boast of Larry Cohn, Stanley Dance, and Martin Williams in its corps of critics) to *Ebony* (which might chronicle the occasional "success story" of a popular bluesman) to *Rolling Stone*, along with more esoteric periodicals such as the *American Folk Music Occasional* and *78 Quarterly*. In 1969 the lack of a full-fledged U.S. journal devoted exclusively to blues led to discussions among blues enthusiasts in Chicago, and the following year *Living Blues* was founded. The number-one blues magazine of the 1960s was the internationally read *Blues Unlimited*, which like much of blues literature, emanated from England. The pioneering work of editors Simon Napier and Mike Leadbitter was fed by a network of collectors, researchers and musicians; new-generation Chicago bluesman Jimmy Dawkins was once a regular columnist. The first book on the blues revival was written by the editor of a smaller British journal, Bob Groom of *Blues World*. In general, it was the British writers who told readers about the wealth of blues artists and records whose names weren't likely to crop up in other pages. French and Belgian chroniclers were on the case just as early, but French-language works did not circulate to the same extent. This group included Georges Adins, Marcel Chauvard, Jacques Demetre, Yannick Bruynoghe, and Serge Tonneau, whose *R&B Panorama* was cited by Bob Groom in *The Blues Revival* as "the first blues periodical in Europe (and probably the world)."

British scholar Paul Oliver, whose books included *Blues Fell This Morning* (1960), *Conversation with the Blues* (1965), *Screening the Blues* (1968), and the comprehensive *The Story of the Blues* (1969), emerged as the most prolific and generally most respected blues author. Oliver also edited the November Books/Studio Vista series, which featured the work of several other writers, published in 1970–71 but mostly written in the 1960s. Like his American counterpart Samuel B. Charters, Oliver conducted extensive field research and recording in the South and in Chicago. Charters authored *The Country Blues* (1959), *The Poetry of the Blues* (1963), and *The Bluesmen* (1967), and produced a number of historic records of traditional and urban blues (the *Vanguard Chicago/The BluesToday!* set introduced new listeners to the tough ghetto blues sounds of several important bands at once, just as earlier Charters reissue compilations on RBF enabled listeners to sample some of the best in country blues). It was, in fact, Charters's first book and the accompanying RBF and Lightnin' Hopkins Folkways albums that launched the blues revival in the United States, according to Jeff Titon. Books more reflective of the blues in contemporary black society were LeRoi Jones's *Blues People: Negro Music in White America* (1963), Charles Keil's *Urban Blues* (1966), and Phyl Garland's *The Sound of Soul* (1969). Blues discography became a science with its own literature, notably *Blues and Gospel Records, 1902–1942*, by John Godrich and Robert M. W. Dixon, and *Blues Records, 1943–1966*, by Mike Leadbitter and Neil Slaven (both books published in England). Blues guitar instruction manuals by Stefan Grossman, Happy Traum, Jerry Silverman, Mickey Baker, and others appeared. Audio-visual documentation came from Europe (where the AFBF footage was especially historic) and from various independent filmmakers and producers in the U.S., including Charters, Les Blank, Harry Oster, Bill Ferris, Gene Rosenthal, and occasional network or local TV crews. Of special note were the performances filmed at the University of Washington and the Newport festivals.

The caveat attached to blues literature, scholarship, and documentation of the 1960s is that chunks of it were peppered with false history and outright fiction, some attributable to a lack of existing reference material in a new field of study, some to faults of the writers, but much to the blues artists themselves. For some, the blues interview became a performance art form of its own. Bluesmen may have concocted

Sleepy John Estes sang a most soulful brand of the blues.

tales to amuse themselves, please questioners (or fool them, or both), or elevate their own position in the blues history that was obviously of such importance to interviewers. One veteran told of participating in lying contests with a group of artists on a European tour. In 1963 Chess producer Ralph Bass wrote: "A college student asked me to help him write a thesis on the blues. I asked him why come to me when he could go to the source by questioning various singers he had access to. His answer was, 'One day they will give me one answer, the next day another.'" Dick Waterman's advice was: "In talking to older bluesmen, you must be well aware that they are going to tell you what they think that you want to hear."

Among the newly developing American community of collectors, writers, and devotees, much of the serious study and appreciation of blues began in the Northeast—Boston, Philadelphia, Washington, D.C., but most of all, New York. Larry Cohn recalled,

> We had a thing in New York called the Blues Mafia. We would have meetings at a different person's house every week. They were very loose, and the purpose was just to play records and really just have dialogue. Bernie Klatzko and Nick Perls and Charters for a period of time, Don Kent, most of the New York East Coast collectors. Pete Whelan, Steve Calt. I learned a lot from Pete Whelan certainly about country blues, and there was a guy named Jim McKune who was murdered who was like a grand doyen, if you will, and he was a real mentor. I mean he was listening to the Charley Pattons before any of us even knew who Brownie McGhee was. And then Washington had its own collectors' contingent, guys like Dick Spottswood, Bill Givens, a whole bunch of people. It was great fun.

From this circle of collectors came reissue companies (OJL, Yazoo, Herwin, Melodeon, Mamlish), new productions, liner notes, books, and bookings for the blues artists. In California, Chris Strachwitz played a pivotal role in the revival, and there was one circle of enthusiasts that had a hit record of its own: Canned Heat band members Bob Hite, Al Wilson, and Henry Vestine were all avid record collectors. The westward wave of the 1960s also brought a new contingent to the Coast, including John Fahey, Bill Givens, Pete Welding, and David Evans. The OJL, Testament and Takoma labels all ended up with California addresses.

In Chicago, the new blues subculture centered around Koester's Jazz Record Mart, where the ranks of employees during this period counted a succession of clerks who were or would become writers, editors, producers, and musicians, including Don Kent, Charlie Musselwhite, Paul Garon, Amy van Singel, and Bruce Iglauer; Big Joe Williams was also a frequent resident in the basement. Down South, there was the Memphis Country Blues Society, which included Robert Palmer, Steve LaVere, Bill Barth, and the occasional visiting New York mafioso, but the southern scene was fairly dispersed, with aficionados and researchers such as Gayle Dean Wardlow, Bill Ferris, Bobby Ray Watson, Worth Long, George Mitchell, and Mack McCormick canvassing the countryside along with visiting colleagues from the east and west coasts and Europe.

Obviously, people were coming to the blues from every angle and through all kinds of musical and literary channels in the 1960s. But why? Why, beyond mere musical attraction to the sounds and the rhythms; beyond appreciation of blues as the root form of so much popular music; beyond the pastime it provided discographers, collectors, and historians; beyond just enjoying the music for partying and dancing? Why were young whites so taken with the music of a culture so alien to their own upbringing? Just what was it about the blues?

First of all, it must be admitted that many listeners said they listened to blues for no deeper reasons than those mentioned. It sounded good. It was just music, for listening, dancing, playing, or whatever. It was hip to dig the blues. Enjoyment did not have to be related to any political or sociocultural awareness, or to any philosophical or psychological mindset. Subconscious connections might prove otherwise, however. For the blues exerted tremendous powers, and there were plenty of followers who openly proclaimed the messages they found within the twelve-bar code.

In *Urban Blues*, Charles Keil wrote, "Not long after the rock-and-roll craze had begun, white intellectuals, college students, liberals, cognoscenti, and later the

Big Joe Williams readies his fabled nine-string guitar.

beatnik-folknik crowd rediscovered the blues in their quest for 'truth,' 'vitality,' and 'authentic ethnicity.'" He also noted: "Although Negro musical styles seem to match or reflect current life styles, the demand for Negro-like music on the part of whites, usually of the younger generation, as in the eras of swing and rock and roll, seems to indicate a perceived or felt deficiency of some sort in the American mainstream that the recurrent adoption of Negro or Negro-derived musical expression helps to remedy. The needs of young white Americans to reject and rebel, to blow off steam, have often been cited."

The 1960s counterculture of alienated American youth adopted more than just the music of the blues as part of its own expression. Many saw in the blues a value system, a life-style, a way of dealing with the world. The blues represented an "alternative" culture itself, and one that seemed unbelievably exotic and romantic as well. It was already the voice of an alienated and oppressed people, misunderstood and denied by Middle America. And it was as authentic and "natural" as any American music could be. Not just artistically, but physically. It was uninhibited and down to earth. It was erotic, sweaty, hypnotic; it dealt on the level with the battle of the sexes. (Thus, according to folklorist Ray Allen, the blues revival was directly connected both to the sexual revolution and the feminist movement; the tension inherent in the blues gave voice to the tension produced by social change.) In the eyes of the rebel youth, blues was sung by guitar-slinging outlaws and macho antiheroes. In his chapter on the blues revival in Transforming Tradition, ethnomusicologist Jeff Titon noted: "Rejecting conformity to middle-class values, blues revivalists embraced the music of people who seemed unbound by conventions of work, family, sexual propriety, worship and so forth. The blues revival was a white, middle-class love affair with the music and lifestyle of marginal blacks."

The romance of the older bluesman could also be based not on rebellion, but on rustic imagery and a fascination with the inhabitants and artifacts of an exotic time and place. Larry Cohn explained: "You know, it's the sharecropper, the black man suffering in the noonday sun and moaning and singing and that kind of thing. I think there was tremendous visual romance that came out of this thing. Plus the romance of the recordings. These things were in their own ways little mysteries . . . the Gennetts in 1929 or '30 or Paramount or Black Patti, I mean, they really were quite mysterious, I think. And the thrill of discovery, I guess. To find these people was unbelievable."

Rhythm and Blues magazine wrote of Lightnin' Hopkins in 1963: "He's suspicious of the new white audience that calls him an 'Artist.' . . . Lightnin' doesn't think the audience will understand what he's singing about so he does fast songs avoiding those that are harsh and poignant. To the audience he is an exotic and in return he only gives a small part of himself."

The blues revival was nothing if not full of romanticisms and stereotypes. Those who lived the blues, however, were not heard to describe their world as romantic, exotic, or carefree. The blues, Willie Dixon said, was the facts of life, a heritage of the black race and "a thousand generations of poverty and starvation." In the 1960s, the blues heroes and their families still lived under discrimination and often in dire poverty, unable to enjoy the basic rights and comforts that their white listeners took for granted. Even the most successful bluesman, B. B. King, told Phyl Garland in 1969, "I bought an apartment building in Memphis . . . in a white area. . . . But I can't live in my apartment buildin' because if I do I'm likely to lose my tenants there. So, therefore, I have to still live in motels and hotels, wherever I happen to be."

"Today's youth," wrote Jeff Titon in *Blues Unlimited* in 1969, "may share the alienation of the black man; but not the cultural heritage!"

Blues stood as a definite statement from "outside the system," but was it true protest music? On the surface, most of its lyrics seemed not to address political, racial, and social issues—not even, in Titon's words, in "the era of civil rights and black power, when interpretive voices from the black community spoke loudly on racism and exploitation in music as in all aspects of American life." The folk singers, they sang protest songs. Some of the rock and soul singers, too. Spirituals and gospel were viewed as music of the black political struggle. Modern jazz had a decidedly militant element. But blues? Not so, many thought. Those who sought out the politics of the blues could be confused even by a young bluesman like Junior Wells who recorded songs with such topical titles as "Vietcong Blues" and "The Hippies Are Trying." In 1968, Wells returned home from a State Department–sponsored tour of Africa and told a Newsweek correspondent, "We got to one place and they had banners saying 'Welcome Home, Junior.' I told 'em, man, I said, this ain't my home, I live one block north of the Loop. Then they asked me what I thought of black power. I said black power is me making it with Aretha Franklin."

"I see the blues as an eminent example of protest tradition within African-American song style," said black folklorist Worth Long. "It's a question how they felt they were able to express it, whether it was direct or indirect, hidden or just straight out. . . . a lot of it was double entendre and hidden. When Jimmy Reed put out 'Big Boss Man'—man, now, everybody wanted to hear that. They understood it. He didn't have to say anything more. He's just philosophic: 'you ain't so big, you're tall.' So that's a freedom song as far as I'm concerned, and it is of course blues. In India they would have said it different: 'Behold the mighty Englishman, he rules the Indian small, because being a meat eater, he's so many cubits tall.' That's a

Sleepy John Estes in concert with his longtime companion, mouth harp player Hammie Nixon.

379

folk saying in India. 'Cause being a meat eater, that's the same as Big Boss Man as far as I'm concerned."

"Kind of reimbedding oneself in the blues in the 1960s was a natural political move, even though everybody else thought it was as nonpolitical as could be," recalled Paul Garon, author of Blues and the Poetic Spirit:

> To me it didn't seem nonpolitical at all. . . . I had always thought of blues as protest music. . . . Everybody was willing to admit that spirituals were hidden cryptic messages of revolt, and then when you said that about blues, they'd act like you'd said something defamatory.
>
> I will say that except for surrealist circles, it doesn't seem like 1960s people saw the blues as having a radical message. I mean it was certainly a message many people identified with. But I don't think they thought it was a radical movement. Obviously a lot of people didn't think about it either, they may have just enjoyed it as a part of the whole movement.

While the hidden politics and protests of the blues remained hidden to many, the message was overt from Chicago bluesman J. B. Lenoir. His songs have been quoted widely and in depth in literature on the subject, but finding a listening public in the 1960s was not so easy. Lenoir's landmark blues protest album *Alabama Blues*, dealing with racial violence, civil rights, and Vietnam, was released only in Europe. German producer Horst Lippmann told Don Snowden, "At the time, no one was willing to release [it] in America because of the political content." Lippmann wrote, "I made arrangements that J. B. Lenoir finally should get his chance—without any limitation—to sing and play what ever comes through his mind, whatever he might think was and is wrong in the United states toward Black People. Since I had to leave Chicago before the recording date, I asked Willie Dixon to take over supervision and have no fear that J. B. Lenoir records everything he wants to record regardless if this would cause problems in the United States in the year of 1965." No LPs of Lenoir's music were released in America until after his death in a 1967 auto accident.

The civil rights movement coincided with the folk-blues boom and the blues revival years. But spirituals, gospel, and folk songs, not blues, were popularized as the "freedom songs" of the movement. Worth Long, a Student Non-Violent Coordinating Committee (SNCC) organizer, recalled a movement festival in Greenwood, Mississippi: "Julius Lester came in with a music caravan. Bob Dylan was there, Pete Seeger, Theodore Bikel. But what they forgot about was that for about 100 miles around, [they] had some of the best traditional music ever. And we didn't have the consciousness then to pull that together, you know, to pull in those living legends of blues men and women who were right there." Yet all along Long had been simultaneously seeking out blues artists in the South and marching (or going to jail) for their rights as citizens: "I would ask people to vote and I'd also ask, 'Hey, you know anybody that play music?'"

Long's experiences in southern jails gave him a closer perspective on the blues as freedom song: "You could sing a freedom song that was straight blues. The freedom singers would sing spirituals, gospel, and then they had some work song and blues element. The fact that it happened in jail for your freedom meant that it became sacred in a sense, no matter how you sang it. In jail, people sang a lot of blues, man, a lot of blues. Made-up songs that I would consider blues."

In the blues and civil rights movements there were parallels, there was interaction, there were contributions, conflicts, and controversy. For some believers, working on behalf of the blues was equivalent to civil rights work. Just as blues was, for some whites, their first window on the black experience, it provided some blacks their first opportunity for nonsubservient entrée into white society. When Mississippi John Hurt, Son House, and others began to perform at folk festivals, Jeff Titon noted, the festivals "were making a statement that the media, reporting about

Bukka White: Mississippi bluesman, slide guitarist nonpareil, piano player, and poet.

Lightnin' Hopkins and Muddy Waters with an unidentified admirer backstage at a blues festival.

the civil rights movement and looking for heroes, could not ignore." Charles Keil drew a comparison in Urban Blues between Dr. Martin Luther King, Jr., and B. B. King, noting that the preacher and the bluesman shared a "stylistic common denominator that binds the sacred and secular realms of the two Kings into one cultural unit." The two gave their followings "much the same kind of emotional lift." In his autobiography, Willie Dixon recalled that he once started to join a peaceful march with Dr. King, but thought better of it when he realized he couldn't stop himself from striking back if he were attacked.

Several blues singers recorded tributes to King after his assassination. Johnny Otis wrote a book, Listen to the Lambs, that dealt with the Watts riots of 1965, white prejudice, black violence, and the problems of integration. Paul Oliver, writing of his first trip to America in Blues off the Record, recalled checking into a Memphis hotel in 1960 and learning it was being picketed for discrimination. When he and Chris Strachwitz went to Clarksdale, they visited with bluesman Wade Walton and pharmacist Aaron Henry, the NAACP's "leader of the Mississippi battlefront." "Some weeks after we left," Oliver reported, "his [Henry's] shop was bombed and I always feared that my visit may have led to the violence." Clarksdale's bluesmen represented no unified front on civil rights (though all agreed with its goals). Walton became local NAACP vice president, but young harmonica player Arthneice Jones left for Chicago, returning only years later when things had calmed down. When civil rights workers were in town, Jones said, all of a sudden black and white people who had gotten along with each other all of their lives were quarreling. In Chicago, white blues freaks on their way to a blues bar like Pepper's or Theresa's in the black South Side ghetto could expect to be discouraged by white police doing their duty to maintain urban segregation: "Don't you know you're not supposed to be in this neighborhood?"

Blues record companies had no set approach. On the one hand, Leonard Chess was praised by WVON's Roy Wood as "the world's best humanitarian." He was the Urban League's "top money raiser and contributor" and a supporter of Martin Luther King and the Southern Christian Leadership Conference. "He supported the poor people's campaign . . . the March to Montgomery . . . the Birmingham Demonstration." On the other hand, one Louisiana record man's stock-in-trade not only included some of the finest southern blues of the era but also under-the-counter antiblack and anticivil rights records with titles like "Nigger Hatin' Me."

Blues may have, in a small and strange way, opened some doors for civil rights; at least it did for D. Gorton, who said his eyes and mind were opened by the interaction between the all-black blues bands and the all-white fraternity and sorority groups at the University of Mississippi. Ironically, Gorton added, it was civil rights that closed some doors on the blues after James Meredith became the first black student to enroll at Ole Miss and the campus became a focus of integration efforts. "I think the civil rights movement scared a lot of people." Bluesmen like Muddy, Wolf, Lightnin' Slim, and Sam Myers didn't make it back to southern campuses much after that, though a rhythm and blues era at Ole Miss continued through the mid-1960s while future Malaco Records president Tommy Couch was booking the acts. Finally, though, the white reaction to integration pushed the blues artists and their southern white audiences further apart for the rest of the decade and some time afterward.

Gayle Dean Wardlow, a white collector and native Mississippian, traversed the state looking for blues singers and blues records. He was always worried that his visits into black neighborhoods might lead to an arrest (or worse) as a suspected Yankee agitator. White skin might also signal police! to black residents. In 1963, when Tom Hoskins showed up at Mississippi John Hurt's door exclaiming, "We've been looking for you for years," Hurt's first reaction (as quoted in a 1964 UPI story) was, "I thought he must be an FBI man. I said, 'You got the wrong man! I ain't done nothing mean.'" The truth is that just as there were political activists, surrealist subversives, and civil rights organizers involved in the blues, there were in fact, federal agents, undercover operatives, policemen, and detectives squarely in the midst of the blues revival, producing albums, writing articles, and promoting the artists. There were also bluesmen who were lawmen and bluesmen who were outlaws. The politics of the blues world was never cut and dried.

Neither were the philosophies. Along with the increased visibility of the blues and the broadening of its audiences came the great debates, particularly among whites, usually from perspectives wholly outside the African-American culture that produced the blues. Disputes over blues did not surface between whites and blacks nearly as much as they did on an intraracial level: the black community split over the morality, social status, and contemporary relevance of the blues, while among themselves whites contested its history, aesthetics, and authenticity. For blacks, the issues concerned living the blues; for whites, the interpretation of the art, whether as observers or performers.

In the United States and Great Britain, feuds developed among the emerging white blues cognoscenti over the ultimate truth and artistic value of blues. In California, Steve LaVere recalled when a blues-rock musician broke a chair over the head of a budding folklorist in a dispute over the merits of John Lee Hooker's music. At a Blues Mafia meeting, according to Larry Cohn, "You'd play Blind Boy Fuller or you'd play some midperiod Lonnie Johnson, and they didn't want to hear it. You know, 'We don't want to hear that city shit. Nothing beyond Charley Patton.' And it was hysterical. God forbid you'd try to play something like Bill Monroe to show some blues aspect of country music. They'd be ready to kill." Devotees of raw country blues might disdain the folk blues crowd, and both of them might frown on electric blues. A blues record with organ or horns, but especially with background vocalists, was guaranteed to horrify certain reviewers, just as the magic words harp and slide guitar were sure to certify a record as instantly collectible. And there were always debates over the definition of the blues. In the literature of the 1960s, observed Paul Garon, "There was a sociological school, of which I was a part, and a debunking school . . . and the condescension school." The debunkers, Garon said, were intent on refuting commonly accepted interpretations and definitions of blues (notably Paul Oliver's), while the condescenders were great admirers of the blues but not of the blues singers (a "real anti-blues thing: it was very pro–their music, but it was very much against them"). The issue most frequently debated concerned the growing white participation in the music.

When the Butterfield Blues Band debuted at the 1965 Newport Folk Festival, Charles Sawyer reported, America's preeminent folklorist Alan Lomax so questioned the group's blues credibility in his introduction that he was confronted backstage by Butterfield's manager Albert Grossman: "The two had words, and in a flash they were on each other, rolling in the dirt." But the Butterfield set at Newport came to be regarded as a turning point and prelude to wider acceptance of the whole Chicago blues genre. In 1966, the Jazz Record Mart/Delmark Records newsletter *Blues News* appraised Butterfield's success: "Let's face it—the folkies seem to find it easier to associate their personal problems with a young fay more easily than a middle-aged Negro, and perhaps we're lucky it wasn't the Hammond, Jr., record that crashed the electronic barrier." Chicago was the fountainhead of the white urban blues movement of the 1960s and at the same time headquarters of the opposition. The Surrealist Movement later declared its "unalterable hostility to so-called 'white' blues, in which we see nothing more than a cowardly attempt to appropriate black music for ends wholly inimical to its living essence." Proponents of blues as black music might in turn be attacked as reverse racists by those seeking to authenticate the white performers. Some musicians chose to remain identified as rock or folk performers, or took stances as blues interpreters, whose music should be differentiated from blues per se; others would not be satisfied unless they were recognized as bluesmen, whose blues were as valid and as colorless as any other music in the professed new dawn of integration, brotherhood, and equality. But blues was more than music, some might reply, it was the voice and life-style of a specific ethnic group; therefore, merely playing blues music didn't make one a bluesman any more than playing Cajun music made one a Cajun. From one perspective, one of the great strengths of the blues, its universal appeal, was also the great source of its dilution when it led to the music's being played by (or for) whites who did not share the cultural background of the black experience. White performers could play the music, sing the lyrics, and express personal emotions within a blues framework with all degrees of talent and sincerity; but only those born to the blues culture could deliver the blues as defined by B. B. King's Why I Sing the Blues or Willie Dixon's I Am the Blues. Muddy Waters's oft-stated view, as told to Robert Palmer, was "They got all these white kids now. Some of them can play good blues. They play so much, run a ring around you playin' guitar. But they cannot vocal like the black man." None other than Mike Bloomfield—who once told Paul Garon "I can play rings around him" when asked his opinion of one blues veteran—wrote in a 1964 issue of *Rhythm and*

John Lee Hooker was among those who found an entirely new audience during the 1960s.

Blues, "For while most young Negro musicians want to become famous jazz, rock 'n' roll or out-and-out 'pop' singers, to be where the 'real bread' is, it is still these youngsters who hold the future of the blues in their hands. It is only they, at this point, who have the spontaneous 'feel' for the blues in their blood, the marrow in their bones, and the bitter background that spawned the blues in the first place."

The blues journals and books of the decade, most of them emanating from England and all of them written or edited by whites—with the rare exception of a work like LeRoi Jones's *Blues People*—dealt with blues as almost exclusively black. *Blues Unlimited*, "The Journal of 'The Blues Appreciation Society,'" set the tone from its first issues in 1963, when irate readers protested the magazine's dismissal of the likes of Cyril Davies as "musical midgets" whose place, the editors felt, was, like Alexis Korner's, "that of a mere copyist, an English one, and a very poor one at that." It became a sensitive emotional issue and a question with answers that could only dissatisfy one faction or another. In the end, musicians almost always decided simply to play what they wanted to play, audiences paid for music played the way they wanted to hear it, and only a few white musicians declined to play blues out of respect for its black identity. Rather than get wrought up in the rhetoric, some, like John Fahey, gave the matter a comical twist. Bob Groom wrote that Fahey "had some recordings of his playing circulated, giving the impression that they were by an unknown negro. They were sufficiently skilled to fool at least one blues authority, and Fahey had his laugh." On another occasion, Fahey reversed the procedure: he dubbed some obscure blues 78s and put them out of his own recordings on one of his albums. Only the collector elite knew the difference.

Regardless of how the blues was defined and how its authenticity was judged, many of the black artists who were perfectly willing to share the music with whites still felt that their music never received its due in the marketplace. As Buddy Guy

Pianist Roosevelt Sykes appears uncharacteristically playing guitar.

said in *Bossmen*, "I want to hear Muddy and John Lee Hooker and Lightnin' Hopkins on the radio too so we can all make a living like these English cats." *Bossmen* author James Rooney commented on rock bands that had popularized Muddy's songs: "By the late '60s many of the groups were getting $10,000 or more per performance." Muddy was paid "nowhere near what the white groups were getting." When *Newsweek* touted "The Rebirth of the Blues" in 1969, Janis Joplin's photo graced the cover, and the big financial news of the decade was Johnny Winter's $300,000 contract with Columbia Records. By contrast, Willie Dixon, whose songs and promotional efforts had played an incalculable role in spreading the blues, said, "I wasn't making but $150 a week against my royalties when the Chess company stopped." In 1969, Dick Waterman's top traditional blues draw, Son House, was raking in $500–600 a show, but most blues bands were lucky to make $100 a night in a Chicago tavern. Lightnin' Hopkins's film biographer Les Blank noted that

Lightnin' had been offered $2,000 a week for a European tour, but he wouldn't fly, choosing instead to stay in Houston and play barbecue joints, pool halls, and beer bars for $17 a night. Lightnin' made most of his money as a gambler, and all but a small percentage of the most successful bluesmen were still working day jobs to make a living. If they were ever realized at all, the rewards of the blues revival were very hard earned indeed.

A final topic of blues discussion and literature in the 1960s revolved around the notion that, revival or no, the blues was on its way out. The jazz editor of the *Chicago Sun-Times* took a trip to the South Side and wrote in a 1961 issue of *Roque*, "They're still singing the blues in Chicago—but only on weekends. . . . The blues are dying." A few years later, Vee-Jay Records' Calvin Carter told Charles Keil, "If a young B. B. King with talent to burn walked in here today I'd have to show him the door because there's no future in it." Others asserted that no young blacks were playing the blues, or that they had no more reason to play the blues, and that the music would either expire or become an all-white idiom. In the 1966 edition of *Urban Blues*, Keil cited one line of reasoning in which "The inevitable conclusion is that a decade or so hence, when slums, bigotry and poverty are largely a thing of the past, the blues will die a natural death along with the environment that produced them."

Within the same paragraph, however, Keil reflected

> But I wonder, first, whether the poverty and prejudice that have nurtured Negro culture will be removed or intensified in the future, and second, whether a substantial increase in prosperity and tolerance will erase the culture or strengthen it. A rich man can still be a soul brother, and a blues man like B. B. King can adhere to some basic middle-class values without diminishing his authenticity one iota. Whatever the future holds, I suspect that men and women will have little trouble in finding excuses to fuss and fight. These basic conditions of friction are enough to ensure the continued existence of the blues for many generations to come, if only because no form of music yet evolved has been able to express so simply and directly the frustrations, satisfactions, and reversals of the mating game.

"Those who suspect that the driving force behind the blues will disappear in the harmonious and fully integrated society that the Reverend King envisions are probably mistaken," Keil continued, "because it is the conflict between the sexes more than conflict between cultures that motivates the blues artist to bring his troubles before a sympathetic audience." In a note prefacing a later edition of the book, he added: "All but a few paragraphs of this book were written before Watts and before our war against the Vietnamese. Any optimistic passages may be forgiven, laughed off, or cried over accordingly."

The blues no doubt owes its present state of wide acceptance to many seeds that were planted in the 1960s. As the sixties generation has come to positions of power and influence in the media, entertainment, and business worlds, the blues has risen with it. The revival has come full cycle. Dire predictions of the demise of the blues proved as errant as the promises of a utopian society and as shortsighted as the dismissal of the upcoming generation of blues musicians. The blues and its timeless message continue to defy the doomsayers.

STANDING AT THE CROSSROADS

THE BLUES TODAY

MARY KATHERINE ALDIN

◆◆◆

The flourishing blues scene we know today began in the early 1970s with the creation of two of the genre's most important driving forces. *Living Blues* magazine was started in February 1970 in Bruce Iglauer's Chicago living room by a group of young white blues enthusiasts, including Iglauer, Jim and Amy O'Neal, Paul Garon, Tim Zorn, and Diane Allman. Inspired by England's *Blues Unlimited* magazine, and full of confidence, excitement, and energy, they assigned themselves stories and produced and printed five thousand copies of Volume 1, Number 1. It took them seven years to sell them all. Shortly thereafter, Iglauer, then a full-time employee of Delmark Records, decided to leave that company to start his own blues label, Alligator Records, to cut an album by his recent discovery, the raw, exciting singer-guitarist Hound Dog Taylor. He pressed one thousand copies of Hound Dog's first album, which was released in August 1971, and ended up giving most of them away as promotional copies. In this chapter we'll look at how *Living Blues*, Alligator Records, and the blues world itself have changed in the two decades since these events took place.

HOW TECHNOLOGY HAS CHANGED THE BLUES

In an earlier chapter, we read of the progress that's been made during the past five decades or so in recording the blues. The earliest recordings were made in studios, after talent scouts had first held local auditions. The difficulties inherent in flying an itinerant blues musician out of his or her own familiar environment into a big city often produced stilted, uncomfortable blues recordings tailored to the artificial environment in which the musician found him- or herself. The primitive, field-recording equipment that followed shortly thereafter made it possible to record the performer more comfortably, but the sound quality left much to be desired and therefore limited the audience for such recordings.

The 1990s have seen the advent of CDs, DATs, multitracking, and other benefits of modern technology; production costs have soared accordingly, eliminating the rough edges and rendering the music slicker and more approachable by virtue of the more frequent rehearsals the producer insists on before that expensive studio clock begins to tick. Likewise, because it costs so much more to produce contemporary blues records, fewer get made, since even the independent record labels must be certain a blues artist has enough popular appeal at least to make back the costs of recording. Factor in the costs of advertising and promoting the recordings, which nowadays often include a promotional video, and it's easy to see how the good old days of producing on a shoestring and selling records at gigs have all but disappeared.

There are several "major independent" labels devoted almost exclusively to recording today's blues: Bruce Iglauer's Alligator label in Chicago; Malaco Records, based in Jackson, Mississippi; Antone's Records of Austin, Texas; HighTone Records, located in California; and a handful of others. Each of these companies has staff producers (sometimes one or more of the label's owners), and each has an identifiable "sound," just as Sun and Chess did during the 1950s. Their continued growth and success is a testimonial to the current good health of the blues; how long it will last is anybody's guess, but blues was here long before its present wave of popularity, and it's safe to assume that it will continue long after this particular wave passes.

In addition to the new recordings being made on independents, the major labels have also contributed to a resurgence of awareness. Recognizing that they have gold mines in their back-list catalogs, savvy companies like Capitol, MCA, BMG, Sony/Legacy, and PolyGram, among others, are suddenly discovering that hitherto obscure artists, recorded as long ago as the 1920s and 1930s, are salable commodities. For years the only access avid collectors had to this older music was via "bootlegs"—illegal recordings, often dubbed from rare 78s, with resulting terrible sound quality—issued by tiny independent labels during the 1960s and 1970s. With the CD revolution, major labels are now reissuing such recordings with extensive liner notes and superb sound, making traditional blues music accessible to a whole new generation. A great deal of major-label attention is a direct result of the success of Sony/Legacy's Robert Johnson box set, *Complete Recordings* (46222). Produced by Larry Cohn, this package of recordings from the 1930s performed by one of the most legendary and mysterious blues figures of all time, went to number 80 on the *Billboard* pop charts and had sold over half a million copies by 1992.

Billboard magazine, in a February 23, 1991, article entitled "Labels Panning for Gold to Reissue," noted the phenomenal chart success of the Johnson package and other blues and R & B reissue sets. In *Billboard*'s April 27, 1991, issue, music editor Chris Morris wrote a front-page story focusing on the upswing in "the blues business," mentioning that both record sales and ticket sales for blues artists have soared in the past few years.

Recording isn't the only aspect of blues that's undergone drastic modernization. Long gone is the romantic picture of Robert Johnson and Johnny Shines hopping that Greyhound bus to ride to the next gig in the next town. Booking and routing blues artists has become as complex as planning a rock star's tour. In the 1930s and 1940s, "package tours" sent caravans of blues and R & B artists out on the road under the toughest conditions imaginable. Usually, they had to drive all night to get

Johnny Winter—the guitarist whose virtuosity never ceases to amaze. CHAPTER OPENER

One of the contemporary scene's most formidable trios: Johnny Copeland, Robert Cray, and the venerable Albert Collins.

from one show to the next, they were restricted to black hotels in the poorer quarters of town, and the places they played were often real dumps. As recently as the 1960s, a solo acoustic artist like Mance Lipscomb would take a Greyhound out of his home in Navasota, Texas, to play at a loosely organized series of college and coffeehouse gigs across the country, and Delta bluesmen Son House and Bukka White often did the same. Until the advent of Manny Greenhills' Folklore Productions and Dick Waterman's Avalon Productions, the musicians had little or no formal management, and gigs were (as often as not) set up directly by the simple method of a club owner calling the artist at home. In this way, the performers crisscrossed the country, eking out a sparse living by the sale of their records after each show or by playing "pickup dates" and parties at private homes.

A far different picture prevails today. Agent Patrick Day, of Day & Night Productions in Silver Spring, Maryland, told *Billboard* magazine recently that "bookings for the blues artists [he represents] have pretty much doubled in a year overall," and Rosebud Agency's Mike Kappus of San Francisco finds the same true for his artists, Robert Cray, John Hammond, and others. With bookings more frequent and the whole world as an arena, bluesmen like Robert Cray and B. B. King forego the

Greyhound; now they take the Concorde. Higher touring costs, which today include expensive, state-of-the-art sound and band equipment, and the roadies to tend to it, means blues has moved up the economic ladder and that higher band fees are balanced by bookings in larger arenas. The juke joints of the 1930s and even the folk clubs of the 1960s have been replaced by blues festivals that draw tens of thousands.

And the festivals, too, mirror the growth enjoyed by all of the blues community. Small festivals are getting bigger, and big ones are getting unmanageable. The Chicago Blues Festival, probably the largest in America, drew seven hundred thousand people in 1990. It must, of course, be remembered that the Chicago festival is free. Of the ticketed events, the Long Beach Blues Festival in California drew seven hundred people to its first, one-day show back in 1980; twenty thousand each day was realized for the two-day 1991 festival. The longest-running blues event is the San Francisco Blues Festival, which began in 1973 and attracted about two thousand people that year. Producer Tom Mazzolini had twenty-three thousand at the 1991 event. He has built the festival from the ground up by a creative, ongoing booking process of putting a number of lesser-known artists on the same bill as the established headliners, thereby creating a festival that holds the interest of committed blues fans while it attracts newcomers to the genre. Other cities have yearly blues festivals as well, from Iowa to Alaska, and longtime blues aficionados are both delighted and disgusted by the music's newfound popularity. While it's great that so many people are jumping on the blues bandwagon, they say, waiting an hour in line to use a bathroom and another hour in another line to get food is nobody's idea of a good time. And watching Otis Rush from a quarter of a mile back doesn't make for an intimate musical experience, no matter how avid a fan you may be.

LADIES SING THE BLUES

The interesting thing about the present-day emancipation of women is that, while the movement is reflected in microcosm in the blues world, there are fewer women singers than at any time in the history of music. Women dominated the genre in the 1920s, when the likes of Bessie Smith, Ida Cox, Mamie Smith, "Ma" Rainey, and Clara Smith accounted for a substantial portion of "race" record sales. They were, however, "kept in their place" both personally and professionally, and with rare exceptions stayed that way until the late 1940s and early 1950s, when Memphis Minnie and Sister Rosetta Tharpe made it okay for their sisters to be tough, outspoken, and play a mean lead guitar. In today's Chicago blues scene, KoKo Taylor and Etta James bandy the title "Queen of the Blues" back and forth between them. James, with her R & B edge, seems to have enjoyed greater commercial success, while Taylor has received a more enthusiastic critical reception. In addition to these two performers, there are Margie Evans, expatriated, of late, to Switzerland, where she spends most of her recording and performing time, and Valerie Wellington, recently deceased, whose great talent has yet to be properly appreciated. Country blues is represented by Jessie Mae Hemphill, a scion of the Hemphill fife and drum family, who has been described with some accuracy as a female John Lee Hooker. The Malaco label's Denise LaSalle has made her name writing and singing funky, earthy, and often x-rated lyrics, while the contemporary interracial trio Saffire, who combine a feminist sensibility with their blues, have been recognized with a W. C. Handy Award for the Blues Song of the Year for their 1990 composition "Middle Aged Boogie Blues."

Etta James sings one.

While these are by no means all the women blues singers presently performing—Lynn White and Barbara Carr are two others that should be mentioned, and
Debbie Davies is one of the finest lead guitarists working in the field—compared to
male artists, they are few. Why this should be so, in an era of greater freedom of
expression for women, is a question for sociologists; the small number of women who
are active have reaped the benefits of a greater opportunity to control their own
careers, to write and sing their own material, and to make a contribution to the ongoing vitality of blues.

Valerie Wellington poses with her Blues Band in Chicago. This singer's recent untimely death was a great loss to the blues.

BLUES AS A MEDIA TOOL

The increasing popularity of blues music has inevitably led to its "discovery" as a
means of attracting both the buying public, through its use in commercials, and an
even wider audience, through its use in films and television. Columbia Pictures
released a short-lived film in 1986, purportedly about Robert Johnson's friend Willie
Brown, called *Crossroads*. Several years earlier, Huddie Ledbetter, better known as
Leadbelly, was the subject of an equally inaccurate biographical film portrayal, and
there are at present several production companies interested in making a movie
about the life of Robert Johnson. Blues singers have also had roles in films, playing

variations on themselves. KoKo Taylor appeared in David Lynch's *Wild at Heart*, and Valerie Wellington played blues singer Big Maybelle in *Great Balls of Fire*.

Television has recently opened up to blues music as well. Some of the cable networks, including Showtime and CineMax, produce occasional blues specials, though usually with white headliners like Eric Clapton. Sitcoms and dramatic series have also done episodes either about blues itself or with blues artists in leading roles. "The Trials of Rosie O'Neill," "Doogie Howser M.D.," and "The Bill Cosby Show" have all featured episodes with a blues singer as a central character. Unfortunately, with rare exceptions, the singer is usually portrayed as a down-and-outer; in one case, Joe Seneca, the fine actor who had starred in the movie *Crossroads*, was cast as an alcoholic street singer. Cosby also once used KoKo Taylor's recording of "I'm A Woman" in a scene of his show, though lip-synced by a four-year-old girl, and an episode of the TV series "Thirtysomething" used Taylor's "Let the Good Times Roll" as background music.

William Clarke—with shades and harp.

Willie Dixon takes a break from the blues on a strong-backed camel.

Advertising agencies have discovered blues in a big way. Again, stereotypes persist, as most of the commercials using blues music or musicians are for alcohol-related products. A partial listing of radio and television spots featuring blues music includes Albert Collins for Seagrams Wine Coolers (with Bruce Willis on harmonica); the William Clarke Band for the Shearson, Lehman brokerage firm (the band was not seen on-screen); Son Seals for Olympia Beer; Willie Dixon for Blues Berries; Valerie Wellington for the *Chicago Tribune*, a spot which led directly to her role in the movie *Great Balls of Fire*; Kenny Neal for Busch Beer; John Lee Hooker for Burger King (USA), Martel Cognac (USA), and ICI Pharmaceuticals (UK); Little Charlie and the Night Cats for Taco Bell; Lonnie Brooks for Miller Beer (USA) and Heineken (UK); Robert Cray for Michelob Beer (playing the music track only, not seen on-screen); Lonnie Mack for Dutch Boy Paints; Lil' Ed and the Blues Imperials for Tower Records of Japan (music track only, not seen on-screen); B. B. King for Kentucky Fried Chicken and Frito-Lay; and Muddy Waters for Busch Beer.

And what of the moral question raised by the specter of blues music being supported, even subsidized, by the tobacco and alcohol industries? Major blues festivals around the country are being funded and sponsored by Benson & Hedges cigarettes, Miller Beer, and similar companies, corporations that also make generous donations to nonprofit, blues-related organizations. Individual artists can, of course, make the decision not to appear on shows so sponsored, but, often, the smaller, nonprofit orga-

Little Charlie and The Night Cats.

nizations urgently need whatever funding they can get. Jay Sheffield, former director of the Blues Foundation, says, "Well, obviously as a nonprofit organization, fundraising is a big part of the events and activities we are able to do; we do get grants from the Memphis Arts Council, city government, state government, things like that—but we've got to be out there competing to get the money we need to operate. I'm a little concerned about the influence that the type of corporate money that is showing up now promoting blues activities—obviously that kind of thing does tend to have a corrupting influence. While we are out there looking for the money—and let's face it, the big corporations have more money than anybody—we do live in the real world, and things aren't always the way we'd like them to be. I don't know exactly how ideological you can afford to be when you start talking about corporate sponsorships."

The Blues Foundation, headquartered in Memphis, came together in 1980, with, as its stated goal, "the preservation and perpetuation of America's original indigenous musical art form, the blues." It presently has a national membership of over fifteen hundred, a thirty-member board of directors, and a fifteen-member advisory board. Jay Sheffield feels that, in the past five years, there has been more nationwide attention focused on the foundation and the W. C. Handy Awards than ever before; he credits the 1980 general upsurge of blues popularity for a great deal of the organization's increased visibility.

The Blues Foundation pays tribute to its past and present through the W. C. Handy Awards and the Keeping the Blues Alive Awards, created by the board of directors as a blues answer to the Grammy Awards. Members vote in several categories, similar to those used in the Grammys: Record of the Year, Male Blues Singer, Female Blues Singer, and so on. There is also an award for Blues Reissue of the Year, bringing the blues community long-overdue recognition. The future of the music is supported through the National Blues Amateur Talent Contest, held each Labor Day weekend on Beale Street. Would-be artists from all over North America travel to Memphis to compete for the Lucille Award, named after foundation board member B. B. King's celebrated guitar. Past winners have appeared on such high-profile media outlets as "The David Letterman Show," "The Johnny Carson Show," and various regional TV programs, and have received recording contracts from several well-known labels.

THE ROLE OF BLUES SOCIETIES

There are many blues aficionados today who feel, perhaps rightly, that it was the blues societies across America, and to some extent the "local white bands," who kept the music alive during the lean 1970s and 1980s. "Disco destroyed a whole generation of potential black blues players," says a southern California radio show host, and it was during the decade when most clubs weren't even bothering to book live music at all (why should they, when a turntable and one deejay worked so much cheaper?) that the blues societies came into their own. Founded, organized, and staffed by often inexperienced volunteers, they nevertheless managed to keep the flame burning long enough to ignite today's five-alarmer. They'd rent a club or small hall, print and sell just enough tickets to break even, and provide traveling blues artists with stops along the often rocky road where they could make just enough in a night's work to carry them on to the next town. These gigs, especially in smaller cities, were often the only blues shows in town. Local white bands were sometimes both opening act and accompanying band to the solo headliner, getting their experience as they went along. With the changes wrought by today's increasing awareness of the music, some blues societies have folded. When blues artists can get gigs at three or four major venues in a city, they no longer need "work for the door," which was all most societies could offer. Also, with two or three different blues shows every weekend in most cities, the societies can no longer count, as before, on the full house that resulted from being the only game in town. But in the outlying towns and cities they're still going strong, many with regular newsletters and bulletins that provide area blues fans with both news and reviews of current interest. And some of those "local white bands," once the object of derision from fans of "real"—i.e., black—blues artists, have gone on to surprise us all. Such is the case with Eric Clapton, Johnny Winter, Stevie Ray Vaughan, Paul Butterfield, Charlie Musselwhite, and Bonnie Raitt (who learned to play slide from Mississippi Fred McDowell).

L'il Ed Williams

HAS SUCCESS SPOILED THE BLUES?

Or, now that we've got what we worked so hard for, what are we going to do with it? In the face of success, record sales, chart recognition, and blues festivals raking in huge gate receipts, can there possibly be a downside? Some think so. Up until about ten years ago, a small core of loyal blues fans paid a low cover charge to crowd into tiny, smoky clubs all over the country to stand five feet in front of the stage and boogie all night in support of their heroes. Today, while some of these older bands still struggle in undeserved obscurity, others are now playing major arenas, festivals, and concert halls at around $25 per ticket. The audience usually cannot get closer than binocular distance, and the sense of immediacy, urgency, and intimate communication so essential to the blues experience has all but disappeared. While no one can begrudge the musicians their hard-won success, the music itself seems to be changing. It's nowhere near the terrible point of all sounding alike, but it is clear that certain of the older musical forms are dying and have yet to be replaced by anything that promises to be of lasting significance. A quick check of the current issue of *Living Blues* will show you a roster of countless electric blues bands, pouring out everything from exciting, creative original material to hackneyed renditions of old Jimmy Reed tunes, but not a single young artist is carrying on the tradition of, say, John Lee Hooker or Son House. Mike Kappus of the Rosebud Agency points out correctly that one reason is that the young people growing up today come from a differ-

John Lee Hooker—still doing it after all these years.

398

David "Honeyboy" Edwards, a slightly younger contemporary of Robert Johnson, is still active and still on the road.

ent background. They don't learn field hollers, don't pick cotton, aren't sharecrop-pers. They work city jobs, even in the small towns, and the music of the auto mechanic or car-wash operator is, by its very nature, going to be a more urbanized sound, so that what David Evans called "the solo work song that for years provided blues with its basic vocal and melodic material" no longer exists. Conditions change, and it is the essence of the blues to reflect the conditions surrounding it; yet it will be a shame if this seminal element of the blues tradition isn't picked up and carried on by some of the younger generation.

STANDING AT THE CROSSROADS

The first generation of country blues musicians (Robert Johnson, Charley Patton, Blind Boy Fuller, Son House, and their peers) is long gone, leaving a legacy of faded names on treasured old 78 labels, references in blues encyclopedias, and now—thank-fully—some fine CD reissues as well. Except for recorded survivals, their music has almost totally disappeared from the blues sound we know today. Charley Patton can-

Clarence "Gatemouth" Brown is not only a superb guitarist, but a highly sought-after fiddler.

not be heard in the musical stylings of Robert Cray; nor can Son House's influence be traced in the recordings of the Kinsey Report.

The second generation, the Chicago–Texas connection, is also nearly gone. Still with us and performing, though less often, are some names to conjure with: B. B. King, Sunnyland Slim, Lowell Fulson, Robert Lockwood Jr., David "Honeyboy" Edwards, John Lee Hooker, Henry Townsend, and too few more. The obituary columns of *Living Blues* grow longer each year; the list of survivors, shorter. Recently deceased are Willie Dixon and Johnny Shines.

The third generation now comprises the elder statesmen, albeit to their own surprise: Johnny Copeland, Clarence "Gatemouth" Brown, Joe "Guitar" Hughes, James Cotton, Buddy Guy, Junior Wells, KoKo Taylor, and Larry Davis are all over fifty, and some are over sixty. While they're still going strong, and it's to be hoped

will continue in this way for many years to come, it's to the youngsters, those whom
Alligator Records so aptly nicknamed "The New Bluebloods," that we must look to
preserve the future of the music.

Blues-festival rosters are full to overflowing with the names of the new generation. Seventy years after the earliest blues 78s were waxed, Robert Cray, Magic Slim,
Taj Mahal, Kenny Neal, Lil' Ed Williams, Bobby Rush, C. J. Chenier, Lucky
Peterson, Roosevelt "Booba" Barnes, Joe Louis Walker, Vasti Jackson, Larry McCray,
Lonnie Pitchford, Son Seals, and many others are recording, touring, and finding
full-time work within the blues tradition. They have already paid their dues, learning,
in some cases, directly from the older blues artists. Joe Louis Walker learned to play
from (and often opened for) Fred McDowell, and Taj Mahal shared the bill with
many of the older Delta bluesmen at Los Angeles's famed Ash Grove club during the
late 1960s. In other cases, these younger players came by their blues talent through
their bloodlines. Kenny Neal, who along with Taj Mahal was featured on Broadway in
the Zora Neale Hurston–Langston Hughes play *Mule Bone*, is the son of Baton Rouge
bluesman Raful Neal. Zydeco artist C. J. Chenier is the son of the late, great zydeco
king, Clifton Chenier. Guitarist Lil' Ed Williams, of Lil' Ed and the Blues Imperials,
is the nephew of Chicago slide veteran J. B. Hutto, and Chris Thomas is the son of
Baton Rouge's Tabby Thomas. John Watkins is the nephew of Jimmy Johnson, while
the group the Kinsey Report includes three sons of Ed "Big Daddy" Kinsey. Lurrie
Bell is a scion of Chicago's Bell–Harrington clan, which includes father Carey Bell
Harrington as well as cousin Eddie Clearwater Harrington. Guitar Slim, Jr. is, of
course, the son of the late Eddie "Guitar Slim" Jones. Whether they fall into the category of "the young traditionalists," as do Magic Slim, Booba Barnes, and Joe Louis
Walker, or are "modernizers," like Robert Cray and Kenny Neal, the blues artists of
today and tomorrow are not slavish imitators of older styles; they write their own
songs, bend their own notes. They create a new sound from a respected tradition and
know that only in this way can the music survive.

*Guitar Shorty was one of the
most unusual blues artists on the
contemporary scene.*

Muddy Waters takes a break—Big Joe Williams's nine-string guitar in the background to the right.

In addition, regional pockets of blues musicians thrive all over the country. The Mississippi Delta remains fertile ground; *Living Blues* founder Jim O'Neal continues to discover and record new young talent for his Rooster Blues label in the area around Clarksdale. Southern California has produced a whole crop of white blues singers and harp players, from the William Clarke Band to the Mighty Flyers, the James Harman Band, and more. This situation is being repeated from coast to coast. In cities as unlikely as Minneapolis there's a blues society with over a thousand members, and up in the Pacific Northwest a core of blues players churns out high-energy sounds every weekend.

The real key to the survival of the music, as Willie Dixon would tell anyone who'd listen, is education. "Blues is the ROOTS of all music," he thundered. "And you know you can't have no fruits without first you have the roots!" His nonprofit Blues Heaven Foundation, based in southern California, has as its first priority educating young people, not only about the history of the blues, but about its business aspects as well. While he donated musical instruments to inner-city public schools and funded the annual Muddy Waters Scholarship, he also pushed another kind of musical education, remembering the bad times when blues artists were exploited by paternalistic white promoters and record companies. "They can't rip you off if you understand the contracts, understand the paperwork, take CARE of your business. Learn to do copyrights, learn to protect yourself, know what you're getting into," he told music history students when he lectured to their classes. Other committed musicians, like writer/singer Margie Evans and bluesman Billy Branch, work within such institutions of public education as the Chicago public school system and an organization called Urban Gateways to bring live blues music and history to young students. Far from being a dying tradition, as some feared it was in the 1970s, blues seems stronger and its future more secure than ever before as it enters the final decade of the century.

This photograph of Taj Mahal dates from the 1960s, but Taj hasn't changed much. He has been a blues spokesman and standard bearer for more than thirty years.

IN CONCLUSION

Twenty-one years after its inception, *Living Blues* magazine has long since left the confines of Bruce Iglauer's small Chicago apartment. After spending several years headquartered in the basement of Jim and Amy O'Neal's Chicago house, it was sold by them to the University of Mississippi. Shortly thereafter, Jim O'Neal resigned from the magazine to run his own operations, Rooster Blues Records and Stackhouse Record Mart in Clarksdale. In late 1991 the circulation of *Living Blues* was fifteen thousand, and its subscriber base is still growing. Alligator Records now has over 120 blues recordings in its catalog, enjoys worldwide distribution, has won two Grammys (and twenty-four nominations) and forty-four W. C. Handy Awards, and provides a musical home to artists like Kenny Neal, KoKo Taylor, Son Seals, Fenton Robinson, and many others. Bruce Iglauer told *Billboard* that he anticipated that Alligator would gross a million dollars more in 1991 than it did in 1990. *Living Blues* and Alligator are still connected, though tenuously, through the free plug for *Living Blues* that has appeared on the back of every Alligator recording ever issued.

THE NEW GENERATION: A SHORT LIST

LURRIE BELL

The son of veteran harmonica player Carey Bell, Lurrie Bell was born December 13, 1958, in Chicago. At the age of fourteen he took up the guitar and numbers among his influences artists like Fenton Robinson, Albert Collins, B. B. King, and Magic Sam. Bell's performing career took off after a well-received stint in Berlin in 1977 with the New Generation of Chicago Blues Band, a group that later became the Sons of Blues. He played with KoKo Taylor's band in 1978 and has recorded with his cousin Eddie Clearwater and with Eddie C. Campbell, among others. In the 1980s he cut two albums with his father, and he has a solo CD out on the British label JSP.

Magic Sam

BILLY BRANCH

Billy Branch, one of the best known harmonica players on the contemporary Chicago blues scene, was born in that city on October 3, 1952. His professional career began in the late 1960s, when he played in a group with blues pianist Jimmy Walker. He credits his later association with Willie Dixon for tightening and polishing his musical ability; in fact, he made his recording debut with Dixon on a McKinley Mitchell session, which produced the Hank Aaron tribute "The Last Home Run."

His first recordings under his own name were released on a blues anthology for the Barrelhouse label entitled *Bring Me Another Half a Pint*. In addition, he appeared on volume three of Alligator's *Living Chicago Blues* series. His band, the Sons of Blues, is on the forefront of the Chicago club scene, as well as doing regular tours. The group began the 1990s with a month-long tour of Canada. Branch is also deeply committed to the principal of educating young people about the blues; to this end he does a series of programs through a Chicago-based organization called Urban Gateways, bringing live blues music instruction and history to inner-city public school students.

The name of the band is Harp Attack! Personnel (left to right) are Carey Bell, James Cotton, Junior Wells, and Billy Branch.

BARBARA CARR

Barbara Carr was born and raised in St. Louis and, like many other singers, got her initial musical experiences in church. She started performing professionally as a dancer while still in school and began to develop a serious interest in rhythm and blues singing shortly thereafter. Her first band, the Comets Combo, performed regularly at a local club, the Dyna-Flow, and in 1963 she cut her first record for the Teck label with a group called the Petites.

In 1965 Oliver Sain, well known on the St. Louis scene as a producer and songwriter, discovered Carr while looking for a replacement for Fontella Bass. The two worked together for seven years, and in February and July 1966 Sain produced sessions for Carr on Chess, which remain unreleased. Additional sessions throughout the 1970s produced by Sain and others fared no better, and it was not until she formed her own label, Bar-Car, that she was able to take control of her own record production. A guest appearance on Johnnie Johnson's 1988 Pulsar LP, *Blue Hand Johnnie*, and a steady stream of club and festival dates stirred up a great deal of attention for Carr, and the late 1989 release of her Bar-Car album, *Good Woman Go Bad*, has earned her critical acclaim across the country. Formerly St. Louis's best-kept secret, she is now touring widely and joining the ranks of the better-known women blues and R & B singers.

C. J. CHENIER

Unlike other bluesmen's children who grew up listening to their father's music, C. J. Chenier was raised by his mother in Port Arthur, Texas, several hundred miles from where his famous father, Clifton Chenier, was establishing the zydeco sounds of Louisiana as a major American roots music form.

C. J. was born on September 28, 1957, and although he gravitated toward playing music at an early age, it was not until adulthood that he reunited with his father and became a member of the Red Hot Louisiana Band. He played trumpet and, occasionally, accordion, fronting the band for several years toward the end of the elder Chenier's long and illustrious career. When Clifton passed away, he left his famous personalized accordion to C. J., who still uses it onstage. The New Red Hot Louisiana Band continues, with some personnel changes, to tour and record with Chenier, and their first album on Arhoolie, *Let Me in Your Heart*, showcases not only the ongoing zydeco tradition that C. J. is carrying on, but also his own abilities as an original songwriter. A song he wrote in tribute to his father, called *Check out the Zydeco*, leads off the LP and is both a loving accolade and a bouncy dance tune.

ROBERT CRAY

Robert Cray was born in 1953 in Columbus, Georgia, where his Army father was stationed at the time. His family moved frequently during Cray's childhood as his father was transferred from one base to another. Among the places they lived were California, Germany, and Virginia, before the family settled permanently in Tacoma, Washington, in 1968. Cray got his first guitar in 1965–66 and joined a band called One Way Street, which played music he described as half psychedelic and half soul. As Cray sharpened his skills during his late teens he was greatly influenced by Albert Collins's guitar style. Shortly after graduating from high school, Cray and a friend, Richard Cousins, moved to Eugene, Oregon.

He recorded his first album, with Cousins on bass, in 1978 for Tomato Records (*Who's Been Talking*, produced by Bruce Bromberg and released in 1980). His first HighTone album, *Bad Influence* (1983), brought him nationwide recognition, a couple of W. C. Handy Awards, and launched his career. Today he remains one of the most recognizable and most visible of the young blues stars, and he is one of the few whose videos are played regularly on MTV and VH-1. His records chart, his concerts sell out, and he tours with major rock stars; in short, he's hot. Many consider that his success has opened doors for other young bluesmen and women.

VASTI JACKSON

Guitarist, songwriter, producer, drummer, arranger—Vasti Jackson is all of these and more. He was born into a musical family on October 20, 1959, in McComb, Mississippi. His grandmother and grandfather both played guitar, and his aunts and uncles played a variety of instruments and sang, so he grew up with music as a primary influence. He learned guitar by ear at age fourteen and at fifteen was playing with a local band called Tower of Soul, which later changed its name to Black Cotton. He was a percussion major at Jackson State University and played with its jazz band during college. He moved to Jackson and worked with local artists and writers there, including Tommy Tate and McKinley Mitchell. This led to his association with Malaco Records, where he was the musical director for Z. Z. Hill and Johnny Taylor during their Malaco years. Currently, he tours and records with Katie Webster, the Swamp Boogie Queen. He coproduced her *Two Fisted Mama* and *No Foolin'* albums for Alligator and played guitar and arranged the horn sections on both sets. He also works frequently with Bobby Rush, and tours and records in Los Angeles, Memphis, Chicago, and the San Francisco Bay area.

THE KINSEY REPORT

The Kinsey Report is a family that hails from Gary, Indiana, where Ralph, Donald, and Kenneth Kinsey were born to traditional Delta bluesman Lester "Big Daddy" Kinsey. Donald Kinsey, a guitarist since age four, was a child prodigy who, at eighteen, went on the road with Albert King. Brother Ralph learned drums at age six, and the boys began performing at local clubs with their father even before they reached their teens. In 1972 the family band broke up when Donald went on tour with Albert King's road band and then to work with reggae superstars Bob Marley & the Wailers and Peter Tosh. By 1984 they were back together, featuring Donald, Ralph, and youngest brother Kenneth on bass, along with Ron Price on guitar. Their first album, *Bad Situation*, was released on Rooster Records in 1985, and their next, *Can't Let Go* on Blind Pig, came out in the summer of 1989. All their most recent recordings are on Alligator.

KENNY NEAL

Kenny Neal is the son of Baton Rouge, Louisiana, bluesman Raful Neal and has been playing music almost all his life. He grew up listening to and learning from his father's friends Slim Harpo and Lazy Lester, among others, and was already a professional musician, playing bass in his father's band, by age thirteen. A talented multi-instrumentalist, he plays guitar, bass drums, trumpet, piano, and harmonica. At eighteen he joined Buddy Guy's band as a bassist and later moved to Canada, where he formed a group with some of his brothers, called the Neal Brothers Band. Bob Greenlee signed him to his Florida-based Kingsnake Records label after hearing Kenny do an opening set for his father. His first album for Kingsnake, *Bio of the Bayou*, was released in 1987 and caused such an immediate stir in the blues world that Alligator Records' Bruce Iglauer made an arrangement to lease it from Kingsnake. It was remixed and reissued on Alligator in 1988, retitled *Big News from Baton Rouge*, and was the first in a series of highly successful albums for the label. In 1990, Neal made his Broadway acting debut in the musical *Mule Bone*; for the role, in which he played a guitarist who fights for the love of a woman, Neal performed several songs from the score. He won a Theater World Award for Outstanding New Talent of the 1990–1991 season. His live blues shows are highly charged and entertaining, and he is one of the brightest young stars on the blues horizon.

Kenny Neal at ease

Lucky Peterson, whose first hit came at age five, still plays the blues.

LUCKY PETERSON

Judge Kenneth "Lucky" Peterson was born in 1963 in Buffalo, New York. His father was a blues singer and owned a nightclub, and, as a small child, Lucky began playing organ. He was discovered by blues legend Willie Dixon, who produced his first album for the Chicago-based label Today Records, featuring a single called "1-2-3-4," when Lucky was only five years old. The novelty of the child prodigy attracted nationwide attention, and appearances on "The Ed Sullivan Show," "The Tonight Show," and others made him famous.

When Peterson was seventeen he was asked to sit in at his father's club with Little Milton, whose own organ player didn't show. Milton was so impressed that he immediately asked Lucky to join the band on a permanent basis. He spent the next three years as Milton's bandleader before moving over to perform the same duties for Bobby Bland. He toured Europe on his own in 1986, recording an album for France's Isabel Records.

He left Bland in 1988 and moved with his family to Florida, where Kingsnake Records used him as a session player with Kenny Neal, Rufus Thomas, and Lazy Lester. His first solo album for Alligator Records, *Lucky Strikes*, found him playing both keyboards and guitar, and he has a strong repertoire of original blues.

JOE LOUIS WALKER

Joe Louis Walker was born on Christmas Day, 1949, in San Francisco. Both his mother and his father owned blues 78s, giving Joe exposure to the music of Howlin' Wolf, Roscoe Gordon, and Amos Milburn at an early age. He learned to play music from his cousins, and grew up in the Bay Area blues scene of the 1960s. Walker left home at sixteen and sharpened his skills playing as an opening act for Earl Hooker, Fred McDowell, and Lightnin' Hopkins at clubs like the Matrix on Fillmore Street. Roommate Mike Bloomfield set up a recording session for Walker to cut a demo for Buddah Records in the late 1960s or early 1970s, but nothing from that session was released.

In 1985, things really began to come together for Walker. Saxophone player Nancy Wright, who was playing with him at the time, recorded one of the band's gigs, and Walker sent the tape to several record labels. Larry Slaven at HighTone liked what he heard and signed Walker to a contract. His first album, *Cold Is The Night*, was released in 1986, and his second, *The Gift*, in 1988, both produced by Bruce Bromberg. Other HighTone albums followed, most recently the exciting set, *Live At Slim's: Volume One*.

Although sometimes compared to Robert Cray, largely because they shared both a label and a producer for several years, Walker has his own style that is quite different from that of Cray, both as a vocalist and a guitarist. Walker is much the tougher of the two and writes almost all his own material. He has achieved enormous popularity in Europe, particularly in England, where he has appeared on the covers of blues magazines and toured widely to great critical acclaim. He was the subject of an extensive profile in *Living Blues* in August 1989.

DISCOGRAPHY

The following is neither presented as nor meant to be an exhaustive listing. Its purpose is to provide an overview of recordings that are essential to any blues collection, that best typify the genre, and that are reasonably easy to obtain. In a few cases, we have provided information concerning out-of-print items that would be well worth the trouble entailed in acquiring them.

The question aside of who owns the rights to a given recording (laws vary from country to country), a number of companies offer reissues of rare and out-of-print items and publish excellent catalogs. For the blues completist, Johnny Parth's Document Records (Eipeldauerstr. 23/42/5, A-1220, Vienna, Austria) is far and away the best. A cursory glance at this company's catalog will suggest an abundance of musical riches.

For those interested in "Best of . . ." compilations and other collections short of Complete Works, Yazoo Records (at 37 East Clinton Street, Newton, NJ 07860) is an excellent place to start. Also, in recent years, Sony Music/Legacy, MCA/Chess and Duke-Peacock, BMG/Bluebird and EMI/Capitol have mounted fine reissue programs. Indeed, much of the material they are issuing is previously unreleased.

A number of small, independent companies have acquired the assets of other small, independent, defunct companies and have embarked on admirable reissue programs. The reader will find some of their best offerings among the items listed below.

In the following listings, we have noted availability on CD. Most CDs are also available on cassette, though we have made no special note of this. Where no CD indication is given, the recording was originally issued as an LP and is not yet available on CD.

African-American Blues and Game Songs. Library of Congress AFS L4

African Journey Vols. 1 and 2. Sonet SNTF 666/667

Alexander, Alger "Texas," *Texas Troublesome Blues.* Agram Blues AB 2009 (Netherlands)

Alligator Records, *20th Anniversary Collection.* Alligator 105/6 CD

Altamont: Black String Band Music. Rounder 0238

American Skiffle Bands. Folkways FA 2610

Ammons, Albert, Pete Johnson, and Meade "Lux" Lewis. Jazz Piano JP 5003

Are You from Dixie? Great Brother Teams of the 1930s. RCA 8417 CD

Atlanta Blues, 1933. JEMF 106

Beale St. Sheiks, *Stokes and Sane.* Document 5012 CD (Austria)

The Best of the American Folk Blues Festivals 1963–67. L+R 42.066. CD (Germany)

Better Boot That Thing: Great Women Blues Singers of the 1920s. BMG/Bluebird 66065-2 CD

Big Maybelle, *Blues Candy.* Savoy Jazz ZDS 1165

Black Diamond Express to Hell. Matchbox SDX 207/208 (UK)

Blake, Blind, *Ragtime Guitar's Foremost Picker.* Yazoo 1068 CD

Bland, Bobby Blue, *I Pity the Fool: The Duke Recordings, Volume One.* MCA 10665. 2 CDs

Blues Masters Volume 7: Blues Revival. Rhino 71128 CD

Blues Masters Volume 10: Blues Roots. Rhino 71135 CD

Blues 'n' Trouble. Arhoolie F1006

Blues Roots. Tomato 2696181

Bluesville, Volume 1: Folk Blues. Ace 247 (UK)

Bob, Barbecue, 1927–30. Matchbox MSE 1009 (UK)

Bogan, Lucille, *Complete Recordings, Volumes I and II.*

Blues Document 6036, 6037 CD

Boggs, Dock, *His Twelve Original Recordings.* Smithsonian-Folkways RBF 654

Bradford, Alex, and the Abyssinian Baptist Choir, *Shakin' the Rafters.* Sony/Legacy 47335 CD

Broonzy, Big Bill, *Good Time Tonight.* Sony/Legacy 46219 CD

Brown, Charles, *Let's Have a Ball.* Route 66 KIX-34

Canned Heat Blues, *Masters of the Delta Blues.* BMG/Bluebird 61047-2 CD

Cannon's Jug Stompers (1927–30). Yazoo 1082/3 CD

Carlisle, Cliff, *Cliff Carlisle, Volumes 1 and 2.* Old Timey LP 103, 104

Carr, Leroy, *Blues Before Sunrise.* Sony/Portrait 44122 CD

Chess Blues Box. MCA/Chess 9340. 4 CDs

Chess Rhythm and Blues, *Best of Chess Rhythm and Blues, Volume I.* MCA 3137 CD

Chicago: The Blues Today! Vanguard 79216, 79217, 79218. 3 CDs

Collins, Albert, Robert Cray, Johnny Copeland, *Showdown!* Alligator 4743 CD

Conversation with the Blues. Decca LK4644

Cooke, Sam, *With the Soul Stirrers.* Specialty 7009-2 CD

Country Negro Jam Session. Folk Lyric FL111

Crudup, Arthur, *That's All Right Mama.* BMG/Bluebird 61043-2 CD

Davis, Jimmie, *Barnyard Stomp.* Bear Family BFX 15285 (Germany)

Davis, Rev. Gary, *Pure Religion and Bad Company.* Smithsonian-Folkways SF 40035 CD

Dixon, Willie, and The Big Three Trio. Sony/Legacy 46216 CD

Dorsey, Thomas A., *Say Amen, Somebody: Original Soundtrack.* DRG 12584

East Coast Blues: 1926–35. Yazoo 1013 CD

Eight-Hand Sets & Holy Steps: Traditional Black Music of North Carolina. Longleaf 001

Estes, Sleepy John, *Sleepy John Estes, Volumes I and II.* Document 5015, 5016 CD (Austria)

Fuller, Blind Boy, *East Coast Piedmont Style.* Sony/Legacy 46777 CD

Fuller, Jesse, *Frisco Bound.* Arhoolie 360 CD

Georgia Blues (1960s). Rounder 2008

Golden Gate Quartet, *Swing Down, Chariot.* Sony/Legacy 47131 CD

Golden Gate Quartet, *Travelin' Shoes.* BMG/Bluebird 66063-2 CD

Good Time Blues: Harmonicas, Kazoos, Washboards, and Cowbells. Sony/Legacy 46780 CD

Gospel Tradition: Roots and Branches. Sony/Legacy 47333 CD

Grace, Daddy, *A Night with Daddy Grace.* Harlequin 702

Great Blues Guitarists: String Dazzlers. Sony/Legacy 47060 CD

Great Bluesmen/Newport. Vanguard 77/78 CD

Honkers and Screamers: Roots of Rock and Roll, Volume VI. Savoy 2234 CD

Hooker, Earl, *2 Bugs & a Roach.* Arhoolie 324 CD

Hooker, John Lee, *The Vee-Jay Years 1955–64.* Chess Box 6. 6 CDs (UK)

Hooker, John Lee, *No Friend Around.* Red Lightnin' RL 003 (UK)

Hopkins, Lightnin', *Gold Star Sessions, Volumes I and II.* Arhoolie 330, 337 CD

Hopkins, Lightnin'. Folkways SF40019

House, Son. Folkways FA 2467

House, Son, *Complete 1965 Sessions.* Sony/Legacy 48867. 2 CDs

Howell, Peg Leg, and His Gang, 1927–30. OJL-22

Howlin Wolf, *Memphis Days, Volumes I and II.* Bear Family 15460, 15500. 2 CDs (Germany)

Howlin' Wolf, *The Chess Box.* MCA/Chess 9332. 3 CDs

Hurt, Mississippi John, *1928 Sessions.* Yazoo 1065 CD

Hutchinson, Frank, *The Train That Carried My Girl from Town.* Rounder 1007

Jackson, Mahalia, *Gospels, Spirituals, and Hymns, Volumes I and II.* Sony/Legacy 47083; 2 CDs. 48924; 2 CDs

Jailhouse Blues. Rosetta RR1316

James, Elmore, *Complete Chess, Chief, Fire Sessions.* Chess Box 4. 4 CDs (UK)

James, Skip, *Devil Got My Woman.* Vanguard VMD-79273

James, Skip, *The Complete 1931 Session.* Document 5005 CD (Austria)

Jefferson, Blind Lemon, *Complete Recordings, Volumes I–IV.* Document 5717-5020 CD (Austria)

Jefferson, Blind Lemon, *King of the Country Blues.* Yazoo 1069

Jerry's Saloon Blues. Flyright-Matchbox FLY LP260 (UK)

Johnson, Blind Willie, *Complete Recordings.* Sony/Legacy 52835. 2 CDs

Johnson, Henry, *Union County Flash.* Trix 3304

Johnson, Lonnie, *He's a Jelly Roll Baker.* BMG/Bluebird 66064-2 CD

Johnson, Lonnie, *Steppin' on the Blues.* Sony/Legacy 46221 CD

Johnson, Robert, *The Complete Recordings.* Sony/Legacy 46222. 2 CDs

Johnson, Tommy, 1928-30. Document 5001 CD (Austria)

Jordan, Louis, *Complete Decca Recordings.* Bear Family 15557. 8 CDs (Germany)

Kelly, Jack, and The South Memphis Jug Band. Blues Document 6001 CD (Austria)

King, Albert, *Laundromat Blues.* Edsel 130 (UK)

King, B. B., *Live at the Regal.* MCA 27006

King, B. B., *King of the Blues.* MCA 10677. 4 CDs

Leadbelly, *Complete Library of Congress Recordings.* Document 601-612 (Austria)

Leadbelly, *King of the 12-String Guitar.* Sony/Legacy 46776 CD

Legends of the Blues, Volume I. Sony/Legacy 46215 CD

Legends of the Blues, Volume II. Sony/Legacy 47467 CD

Lenoir, J. B., *Alabama Blues.* L+R 42.001 CD (Germany)

Lewis, Furry, 1927–28. Document 5004 CD (Austria)

Louis, Joe Hill, *The Be-Bop Boy.* Bear Family 15524 CD (Germany)

Lipscomb, Mance, *Texas Songster.* Arhoolie 306 CD

Liggins, Joe, *Honeydrippers.* Specialty 7006

Little Walter, *Complete Chess Recordings.* Chess Box 5. 4 CDs (UK)

Little Richard, *The Specialty Sessions.* ACC ABOXCD-1. 6 CDs (UK). (*See also* Penniman, Little Richard)

McDowell, Fred, *Mississippi Delta Blues.* Arhoolie 304 CD

McGhee, Brownie, *Complete Okeh Recordings, 1940.* Sony/Legacy 52933. 2 CDs

McGhee, Brownie. *Brownie McGhee and His Buddies: Let's Have a Ball 1944–55.* Travelin' Man (UK) TM CD 04

McGee, Rev. F. W., *Reverend F. W. McGee, 1927–30: Sermons with Congregational Singing and Jazz Band Accompaniment.* Eden ELE 1-200 (Austria)

McTell, Blind Willie, *Atlanta Twelve String.* Atlantic 82366 CD

McTell, Blind Willie, *Library of Congress Recordings.* Blues Document 6001 CD (Austria)

McTell, Blind Willie, *Complete Columbia, Vocalion, and ARC Recordings.* Sony/Legacy 53234. 2 CDs

Memphis Blues. Document 5014 CD (Austria)

Memphis Jug Band. Yazoo 1067 CD

Memphis Minnie, *I Ain't No Bad Gal.* Sony/Portrait 44072 CD

Memphis Minnie, *Hoodoo Lady.* Sony/Legacy 46775 CD

Memphis Minnie, *Volume 2: Early Recordings with "Kansas Joe" McCoy.* Blues Classics 13

Mississippi Sheiks, 1930: Volume 1. Matchbox MSE 1005 (UK)

Mister Charlie's Blues. Yazoo-L-1924

Monroe, Bill. *The Essential Blue Grass Boys.* Sony/Legacy 52478. 2 CDs

Moss, Buddy, 1930–41. Travelin' Man (UK) TM CD 05

Mountain Blues. County 511

Music from the South, Volume 5. Folkways FA2654

Negro Blues and Hollers. Library of Congress AFS L59

Negro Folk Music of Alabama, Volume 1. Folkways FE4417

Negro Prison Camp Worksongs. Folkways FE4475

Negro Songs of Protest. Rounder 4004

Nobody Knows My Name (Gellert Recordings). Heritage (UK) HT 304

Okeh Rhythm & Blues Box. Sony/Legacy 48912. 3CDs

Patton, Charley, *Complete Recordings, Volumes I–III.* Document 5009-5011. 3 CDs (Austria)

Penitentiary Blues (John Lomax Recordings for the Library of Congress). Travelin' Man (UK) TM CD 08

Penniman, Little Richard, *Gospel.* Pickwick SPC-3258. (*See also* Little Richard)

Phillips, Washington, *I Am Born to Preach the Gospel.* Yazoo 2003 CD

Preachin' the Gospel: Holy Blues. Sony/Legacy 46779 CD

Primitive Piano. Tone LP1

Professor Longhair, *New Orleans Piano.* Atlantic 7255-2

Rainey, Ma, *Complete 1928 Sessions.* Document 5156 CD

Raunchy Business: Hot Nuts and Lollypops. Sony/Legacy 46783

RCA Victor Blues and Rhythm Revue. RCA 86279

Red River Blues. Travelin' Man (UK) TM CD 08

Reed, Jimmy, *The Best of Jimmy Reed.* Vee-Jay 1039

Religious Recordings from Black New Orleans, 1924–31. 504 LP 20

Rock Me All Night Long: Aladdin Records, 1945–58. EMI ST-201

Rodgers, Jimmie, *Complete Recordings.* Bear Family 15540. 6 CDs (Germany)

Roland, Walter, *The Piano Blues, 1933–35, Volume Six.* Magpie PY 4406 (UK)

Roland, Walter, *Complete Recordings, Volumes I and II.* Document 5144, 5145. 2 CDs (Austria)

Roots 'n' Blues: The Retrospective, 1925–50. Columbia/Legacy 47911. 4 CDs

Rush, Otis, *Right Place, Wrong Time.* High Tone 8007 CD

Sam, Magic, *West Side Soul.* Delmark DD-615 CD

Shouters, The, *Roots of Rock and Roll, Volume IX.* Savoy STL 2244

Slide Guitar: Bottles, Knives & Steel, Volumes I and II. Sony/Legacy 46218 CD, 52725 CD

Smith, Bessie, *Bessie Smith: Empress of the Blues: Complete Recordings, Volumes I–IV.* Sony/Legacy 47091; 2 CDs. 47431; 2 CDs. 47474; 2 CDs. 52838; 2 CDs

Staple Singers, *Pray On.* New Cross Gospel Series GNC

Stokes, Frank. Document 5013 CD (Austria)

Straighten Up and Fly Right: R & B from the Close of the Swing Era to the Dawn of Rock and Roll. New World Records 261

Strutting at the Bronze Peacock. Ace 223 CD (UK)

Suso, Jali Nyama, *Songs from the Gambia.* Sonet, SNTF 729

Sykes, Roosevelt, 1929–35. Matchbox MSE 1011 (UK)

Taj Mahal, *Taj's Blues.* Sony/Legacy 52465

Tampa Red, *The Guitar Wizard 1932–34.* Sony/Legacy 53235 CD

Tampa Red, *Bottleneck Guitar, 1928–37.* Yazoo 1029 CD

Texas Blues, *Gold Star Recordings.* Arhoolie 360 CD

Thomas, Henry, *Ragtime Texas.* Yazoo 1080/81 CD

Thornton, Big Mama, *Peacock Recordings.* MCA Peacock 10668 CD

Toure, Ali Farka, *African Blues.* Shanachie 65002

Treasury of Field Recordings, Volume 1. 77-LA-12-2 (UK)

Turner, Big Joe, *R & B Years.* Atlantic 781663 CD

Turner, Big Joe, *Greatest Recordings.* ATCO SD 33-376

Turner, Big Joe, *I've Been to Kansas City, Volume 1.* MCA/Decca/MCA 42351 CD

Virginia Traditions: Western Piedmont Blues. Blue Ridge Institute BRI 003

Southwest Virginia Blues. Blue Ridge Institute BRI 008

Walker, T-Bone, *T-Bone Blues.* Atlantic 8020-2

Walker, T-Bone, *The Complete Imperial Recordings, 1950–54.* EMI E4-96739. 2 CDs

Waters, Muddy, *At Newport 1960.* MCA Chess 31269 CD

Waters, Muddy. *The Chess Box.* MCA Chess 80002. 3 CDs

Washboard Sam, *Rockin' My Blues Away.* BMG/Bluebird 61042-2 CD

Wells, Junior, *Hoodoo Man Blues.* Delmark DD-612 CD

Wheatstraw, Peetie. Old Tramp OT 1200 (Netherlands)

White, Bukka, *Complete Vocalion Recordings.* Sony/Legacy 52782 CD

White Country Blues, 1926–38, A *Lighter Shade of Blue.* Sony/Legacy 47446. 2 CDs

Williams, Big Joe, *Early Recordings 1935–41.* Mamlish S-3810

Williamson, Sonny Boy, *The Chess Years.* Chess Red Box 1. 3 CDs (UK)

Winter, Johnny, *Scorchin' Blues.* Sony/Legacy 52466 CD

BIBLIOGRAPHY

◆◆◆

The number of books devoted to the blues has increased enormously over the last three decades. Before 1960, blues scholarship was limited to rather few specialist publications. To cite everything presently available would require an extended study, which, it is to be hoped, some qualified individual will undertake very soon.

The following listings are catholic in approach and treat-ment of subject. It is sincerely hoped that they will serve as the impetus to further research.

Albertson, Chris. *Bessie.* New York: Stein & Day, 1972.

Bastin, Bruce. *Never Sell A Copyright: Joe Davis and His Role in the New York Music Scene, 1916-1978.* Chigwell, Essex, England: Storyville Publications, 1990.

Bastin, Bruce. *Red River Blues: The Blues Tradition in the Southeast.* Urbana & Chicago: University of Illinois Press, 1986.

Berry, Jason, Foose, Jonathan and Jones, Tad. *Up from the Cradle of Jazz: New Orleans Music since World War II.* Athens: University of Georgia Press, 1986.

Broonzy, Big Bill, and Yannick Bruynoghe. *Big Bill Blues.* New York: Oak Publications, 1964.

Broughton, Viv. *An Illustrated History of Black Gospel.* New York: Blandford Press, 1985.

Broven, John. *Rhythm and Blues in New Orleans.* Gretna, Louisiana: Pelican Publishing, 1978.

Burton, Thomas G., ed. *Tennessee Traditional Singers: Tom Ashley, Sam McGee, Bukka White.* Knoxville: University of Tennessee Press, 1981.

Calt, Stephen, and Gayle Dean Wardlow. *King of the Delta Blues: The Life and Music of Charlie Patton.* Newton, New Jersey: Rock Chapel Press, 1988.

Cantor, Louis. *Wheelin' on Beale.* New York: Pharos Books, 1992.

Charters, Samuel. *The Bluesmen.* New York: Oak Publications, 1967.

———. *The Country Blues.* New York and Toronto: Rinehardt Co., 1959.

———. *The Legacy of the Blues.* Da Capo Press, New York, 1975.

———. *Sweet as the Showers of Rain.* New York: Oak Publications, 1977.

Chase, Gilbert. *America's Music: From the Pilgrims to the Present.* (3d ed., revised). Urbana and Chicago: University of Illinois Press, 1987.

Cohen, Norm. *Long Steel Rail: The Railroad in American Folk Song,* Urbana and Chicago: University of Illinois Press, 1981.

Cone, James H. *The Spirituals and the Blues: An Interpretation.* New York: The Seabury Press, 1972.

Cunard, Nancy, ed. *Negro: Anthology.* New York: Frederick Ungar Publishing Co., 1970.

Dance, Helen Oakley. *Stormy Monday: The T-Bone Walker Story.* Baton Rouge: Louisiana State University Press, 1987.

Davis, Gerald L. *I Got the Word in Me and I Can Sing It, You Know: A Study of the Performed African-American Sermon.* Philadelphia: University of Pennsylvania Press. 1986

Dixon, Robert M. W. and John Godrich. *Blues and Gospel Records 1902–43,* 3d ed. Chigwell, Essex, England: Storyville Publications, 1982.

Dixon, Willie (with Don Snowden). *I Am the Blues.* New York: Da Capo Press, 1989.

Epstein, Dena J. *Sinful Tunes and Spirituals: Black Folk Music to the Civil War.* Urbana and Chicago:

University of Illinois Press, 1977.

Escott, Colin with Hawkins, Martin. *Good Rockin' Tonight: Sun Records and the Birth of Rock 'n' Roll.* New York: St Martin's Press, 1991.

Evans, David. *Big Road Blues: Tradition and Creativity in the Folk Blues.* Berkeley: University of California Press, 1982.

———. *Tommy Johnson.* London: Studio Vista, 1971.

Fahey, John. *Charley Patton.* London: Studio Vista 1970.

Garland, Phyl. *The Sound of Soul.* Chicago: Henry Regnery Company, 1969.

Garon, Paul. *The Devil's Son-in-Law: The Story of Peetie Wheatstraw.* London: Studio Vista, 1971.

Garon, Paul and Beth. *Woman With Guitar: Memphis Minnie's Blues.* New York: Da Capo 1992.

George, Nelson. *The Death of Rhythm and Blues.* New York: Pantheon 1988.

Gillett, Charlie. *Making Tracks: Atlantic Records and the Growth of a Multi-Billion-Dollar Industry.* New York: E. P. Dutton, 1983.

———. *The Sound of the City*, new revised edition. New York: Pantheon, 1983.

Groia, Phillip. *They All Sang on the Corner.* Setauket, New York: Edmond Publishing, 1973.

Groom, Bob. *The Blues Revival.* London: Studio Vista, 1971.

Grossman, Stefan. *Rev. Gary Davis: Blues Guitar*, New York: Oak Publications, 1974.

Guralnick, Peter. *Searching for Robert Johnson.* New York: E.P. Dutton, 1989.

Guralnick, Peter. *Feel Like Going Home: Portraits in Blues and Rock and Roll.* New York:HarperCollins, 1989.

———. *The Listener's Guide to the Blues.* New York: Quarto Books, 1982.

———. *Lost Highway: Journeys and Arrivals of American Musicians.* Boston: David R. Godine, 1979.

Handy, W.C. *Father of the Blues.* New York: Collier, 1970.

Harris, Sheldon. *Blues Who's Who.* New Rochelle, New York: Arlington House, 1979.

Harrison, Daphne Duval. *Black Pearls: Blues Queens of the 1920's.* New Brunswick, New Jersey: Rutgers University Press, 1988.

Hayes, Cedric, and Robert Laughton. *Gospel Records 1943–69*, 2 vols. London: Record Information Services, 1993.

Heilbut, Anthony. *The Gospel Sound: Good News and Bad Times.* New York: Simon and Schuster, 1971.

Hemenway, Robert E. *Zora Neale Hurston: A Literary Biography*, Urbana: University of Illinois Press, 1977.

Hurston, Zora Neale. *Mules and Men.* Philadelphia: J. B. Lippincott, 1935.

Jackson, Bruce, ed. *Wake Up Dead Man: Afro-American Worksongs From Texas Prisons.* Cambridge: Harvard University Press, 1972.

Keil, Charles. *Urban Blues.* Chicago: University of Chicago Press, 1966.

Kodish, Debora. *Good Friends and Bad Enemies: Robert Winslow Gordon and the Study of American Folk Song.* Urbana: University of Illinois Press, 1986.

Leadbitter, Mike, and Neil Slaven. *Blues Records 1943–70: A Selective Discography*, vol. 1, A to K. London: Record Information Services, 1987.

Lieb, Sandra. *Mother of the Blues: A Study of Ma Rainey.* Amherst: University of Massachusetts Press, 1981.

Lornell, Kip. *Happy In The Service of the Lord: Afro-American Gospel Quartets in Memphis.* Urbana and Chicago: University of Illinois Press, 1988.

Lornell, Kip, and Charles Wolfe. *The Life and Legend of Leadbelly.* New York: HarperCollins, 1992.

Loman, Alan. *Mister Jelly Roll.* New York: Duell, Sloan & Pearce, 1950.

Lomax, John A. *Adventures of a Ballad Hunter.* New York: Macmillan, 1947.

Lomax, John A. and Alan. *American Ballads and Folk Songs.* New York: Macmillan, 1934.

Lomax, John A. and Alan. *Negro Folk Songs as Sung by Leadbelly.* New York Macmillan, 1936.

Lovell, John, Jr. *The Forge and the Flame: The Story of How the Afro-American Spiritual Was Hammered Out.* New York: Macmillan, 1972.

MacLeod, R. R. *Yazoo: Vol. I (lyrics) 1-20*, Edinburgh, Scotland: Pat Publications, 1988.

———. *Yazoo: Vol. II (lyrics) 21-83.* Edinburgh, Scotland: Pat Publications, 1988.

Malone, Bill C. *Southern Music American Music.* Lexington: University Press of Kentucky, 1979.

Mann, Woody. *Six Black Blues Guitarists.* New York: Oak Publications, 1973.

Oakley, Giles. *The Devil's Music: A History of the Blues.* New York: Taplinger Publishing Co, 1977.

Obrecht, Jas, ed, *Blues Guitar: The Men Who Made the Music.* San Francisco: Miller Freeman Publications, 1990.

Odum, Howard W. and Guy B. Johnson. *The Negro and His Songs.* Chapel Hill: University of North Carolina Press, 1925.

———. *Negro Workaday Songs.* Chapel Hill: University of North Carolina Press, 1926.

Oliver, Paul. *The Blackwell Guide to Blues Records.* Basil Blackwell Press, Oxford (U.K.) 1989.

———. *Blues Fell This Morning,* London: Cassell, 1960.

———. *Blues Off the Record.* Tunbridge Wells, Kent, England: The Baton Press, 1984; New York: Hippocrene Books, Inc., 1984.

———. *Conversations with the Blues.* Horizon Press, New York, 1965.

———. *Screening the Blues: Aspects of the Blues Tradition.* Cassell, 1968.

———. *Songsters & Saints: Vocal Traditions on Race Records.* Cambridge, New York and Melbourne: Cambridge University Press, 1984.

———. *The Story of the Blues.* London: Barrie & Rockliff, 1969.

Olsson, Bengt. *Memphis Blues and Jug Bands.* London: Studio Vista, 1970.

Oster, Harry. *Living Country Blues.* Detroit: Folklore Associates, 1969.

Palmer, Robert. *Deep Blues.* New York: Viking Press, 1981.

Pearson, Barry Lee. *Sounds So Good to Me: The Bluesman's Story.* Philadelphia: University of Pennsylvania Press, 1984.

———. *Virginia Piedmont Blues: The Lives and Art of Two Virginia Bluesmen.* Philadelphia, University of Pennsylvania Press: 1990.

Porterfield, Nolan. *Jimmie Rodgers: The Life and Times of America's Blue Yodeler.* Urbana: University of Illinois Press, 1979.

Ramsey, Frederick, Jr. *Been Here And Gone.* New Brunswick, New Jersey: Rutgers University Press, 1960.

Redd, Lawrence. *Rock Is Rhythm and Blues.* East Lansing, Michigan: Michigan State University Press, 1974.

Rooney, James. *Bossmen: Bill Monroe and Muddy Waters.* New York: Hayden Book Co., Inc., 1971.

Rowe, Mike. *Chicago Blues: The City and the Music.* London: Eddison Press Ltd., 1973; reprint ed, New York, Da Capo Press, 1975.

Russell, Tony. *Blacks, Whites, and Blues.* New York: Stein and Day, 1970.

Sacre, Robert. *The Voice of the Delta.* Liége, Belgium: Presses universitaires de Liége, 1987.

Sawyer, Charles. *The Arrival of B. B. King.* Garden City, New York: Doubleday, 1980.

Scarborough, Dorothy. *On the Trail of Negro Folk Songs.* Hatboro, Pennsylvania: Folklore Associates, 1963.

Scott, Frank, ed. *The Down Home Guide to the Blues.* Chicago: A Capella Press, 1991.

Shaw, Arnold. *Honkers and Shouters: The Golden Years of Rhythm and Blues.* New York: Macmillan, 1978.

Silvester, Peter J. *A Left Hand Like God: A History of Boogie-Woogie Piano.* New York: Da Capo Press, 1989.

Southern, Eileen, ed. *Readings in Black American Music.* New York: W. W. Norton, 1972.

Tilling, Robert, ed. *Oh, What a Beautiful City: A Tribute to Rev. Gary Davis.* Channel Islands: Paul Mill Press, 1992.

Titon, Jeff Todd. *Early Downhome Blues: A Musical and Cultural Analysis.* Urbana: University of Illinois Press, 1977.

Tosches, Nick. *Unsung Heroes of Rock and Roll.* New York: Charles Scribner's & Sons, 1984.

Tribe, Ivan. *Mountaineer Jamboree: Country Music in West Virginia.* Lexington: University Press of Kentucky, 1984.

Welding, Pete, and Toby Byron, eds. *Bluesland: Portraits of Twelve Major American Blues Masters.* New York: Dutton, Penquin Books, 1991.

White, Newman I. *American Negro Folk-Songs.* 1928. Hatboro, Pennsylvania: Folklore Associates, Inc. 1965.

Wiggins, Gene. *Fiddlin' Georgia Crazy: Fiddlin' John Carson.* Urbana and Chicago: University of Illinois Press, 1987.

Wolfe, Charles. *Kentucky Country. Folk and Country Music of Kentucky.* Lexington: University Press of Kentucky, 1982.

———. *Grand Ole Opry: The Early Years, 1925–35.* London: Old Time Music, 1975.

Wolfe, Charles, ed. *Truth Is Stranger Than Publicity. The Autobiography of Alton Delmore.* Nashville: Country Music Foundation Press, 1977.

Zur Heide, Karl Gert. *Deep South Piano: The Story of Little Brother Montgomery.* London: Studio Vista, 1970.

SELECTED PERIODICALS

Blues Access, 1514 North Street, Boulder, CO 80304

Blues and Rhythm: The Gospel Truth, 13 Ingleborough Drive, Morley, Leeds LS27 9DT, England

Juke Blues, P.O. Box 148, London W9 1 DY, England

Living Blues, Sam Hall, Rebel Drive, University of Mississippi, University, MS 38677

INDEX

PHOTOGRAPHY
CREDITS

◆◆◆

*All photographs and memorabilia are from the
Lawrence Cohn Collection unless they are listed
below. The author gratefully acknowledges the
following contributions:*

Mary Katherine Aldin: 339, 395

Mary Katherine Aldin/Manny Greenhill: 322

Russell Barnard, Country Music Magazine:
235, 236 (Robertson), 240 (Hutchison),
241, 257 (Cox)

Bruce Bastin: contents page, 218 (Long),
227 (Moss)

Lawrence Cohn Collection/Lynn Abbott: 120
(newspaper article), 123

Lawrence Cohn Collection/David Evans: 49

Lawrence Cohn Collection/Library of
Congress: 272, 283, 285

Lawrence Cohn Collection/Dick Spottswood:
36

Lawrence Cohn Collection/Kim Whiteside:
47

Tom Copi: 15, 76 (Estes), 83, 129, 170 (bottom), 197, 200, 201, 202 (King), 203, 299,
304, 306, 330 (King), 351, 359, 360 (Crudup), 366, 368, 373, 375, 377, 379, 382,
385, 386, 398, 402

Country Music Foundation: 237, 239, 243,
256

Frank Driggs Collection: jacket front, spine,
back, title page, 9, 16, 17, 19, 20 (sheet
music), 34, 36 (record label), 44, 46 (Mc-
Coy), 50 (record label), 53, 56 (record
label), 61, 62, 63 (advertisement), 65, 68,
70, 75 (Rachell), 76 (record label), 77
(Crudup), 78, 81, 82 (Ross), 86, 88
(Smith), 89, 90 (Smith), 92, 93, 94 (Martin
and Williams), 95, 96, 97 (Thomas), 98, 99
(Spivey), 102, 103, 104, 106, 109, 114
(Gates), 125 (Staple), 135, 136, 137, 138
(Jackson), 139 (Tharpe), 140, 141 (Ward),
144, 150, 157 (Johnson), 159, 160, 161, 162,
164, 166 (Broonzy), 168, 170 (top), 171
(Lewis and Ammons), 173, 175, 177, 178,
181 (Waters), 183 (Jacobs), 185 (Maceo),
186, 188, 192 (James), 196, 198, 207, 217
(White), 225, 238 (Whitter), 244, 246
(Williams), 253, 254, 261 (Arnold), 263,
273 (advertisement), 278, 280, 281, 282,
287, 300, 314, 315, 316, 319 (Brown,
Moore, and Williams), 324 (Mayfield), 326
(Johnson and Davis), 328, 329 (Harris),
331, 332, 334, 335 (Washington), 336, 337,
338, 340, 344, (Green), 345, 349, 352, 354,
355, 357, 363, 364 (Cotton), 366 (Hutto),
369, 371, 392, 403, 404

Frank Driggs Collection/Stephen C. LaVere:
51, 182, 374, 381

Gene Earle: 119, 120 (record label), 242, 262
(bottom)

David Evans: 80 (James), 214 (left), 297

Farm Security Administration/Southern
Historical Collection, University of North
Carolina, Chapel Hill: 230

Bill Ferris: 291

David Fulmer: 296

Ray Funk: 134 (Tindley Singers)

John Goddard: 329

Manny Greenhill: 221

Stefan Grossman, Shanachie Records: copyright page, 60 (advertisement), 85, 127

Edward Guy: 91 (Walker and Williams), 252

Hooks Bros., © Michael Ochs Archives/
Memphis Music and Blues Museum: 18,
32, 37, 79 (Meeting in Memphis), 142, 146,
148, 193 (Louis, King, et al.), 194, 320, 325
(Rushing and Basie), 333, 343

Bruce Iglauer, Alligator Records: 330, 346,
388, 391, 393, 394, 396, 397, 400, 405, 407,
408

© Stephen C. LaVere: 73, 74

Arthur Levy: 40

Library of Congress: 12, 21, 26, 155
(Johnson), 266 (Brown and French), 264,
269, 270, 276, 277, 279, 286

Josephine Harveld Love: 204, 228, 229 (Ezell,
Brown, and Hudson)

Danny McLean: 401

Michael Ochs Archives: 147, 312

Paul Oliver: 208, 307

Hank O'Neal: 133, 358, 361, 362 (James)

John Reynolds: frontispiece, 54, 268 (Lomax)

Chris Strachwitz: 20 (Chenier), 23, 82, 84,
292, 298, 302, 303, 308, 360 (Lipscomb),
364, 365

Gayle Dean Wardlow: 41, 45

Charles Wolfe: 238 (Macon and Macon), 248
(Peer), 250 (Miller), 257 (Ball and Carlisle),
259 (McGee Bros.), 260, 261 (Monroe)

ABOUT THE
AUTHORS

Lawrence Cohn is the creator and producer of Sony Music/Legacy's award-winning Roots 'n' Blues series. He has received four Grammy Award nominations, winning in 1991 for his *Robert Johnson: The Complete Recordings*. In that year he also received the W. C. Handy Award for the Johnson set and was given special recognition by the Blues Foundation for his work in "keeping the blues alive." Sony Music, Inc., presented Cohn with its first President's Award for his work on the Robert Johnson project.

Trained as a lawyer, Cohn has been vice-president at CBS/Epic Records, executive vice-president and chief operating officer of Playboy Records and Music, a blues producer, writer, and music critic. He is also the author of a book on newsreels, *Movietone Presents the Twentieth Century*.

Mary Katherine Aldin, a native of New York City, has lived and worked in Los Angeles since 1962. She was contributing and associate editor for *Living Blues Magazine* for fourteen years, produced and hosted L.A.'s longest-running blues radio show between 1977–88, and has written a regular column for *Blues and Rhythm: The Gospel Truth* since the magazine began in 1985. She has produced and annotated more than thirty reissues of blues, bluegrass, and American folk music for various independent record labels. Her 1990 liner notes for MCA's *Muddy Waters: The Chess Box* were nominated for a Grammy Award.

Bruce Bastin is managing director of Interstate Music, Ltd., and has issued many blues and jazz recordings on an array of labels. He is the author of *Crying for the Carolines* (1971) and the award-winning *Red River*

Blues: The Blues Tradition of the Southeast (1986).

Samuel Charters wrote the first booklength study of the blues, *The Country Blues*, in 1959 and followed it with many more works on the blues and the blues language. His *Roots of the Blues*, product of extensive research in West Africa during the 1970s, won the Deems Taylor Award for 1983. He has produced numerous blues recordings and anthologies for several record companies, including the twelve-volume series, *Legacy of the Blues*, for GNP Crescendo Records. He received a Grammy Award as producer of Clifton Chenier's *I'm Here* and is a poet, translator, and novelist. His novel *Louisiana Black* was made into the 1991 film *White Lie*. His newest novel, *Elvis Presley Talks to His Mother after The Ed Sullivan Show*, was published in 1992. Charters is owner of Gazell Records, which specializes in contemporary jazz and American folk music.

John H. Cowley, whose doctoral thesis is on calypso and Caribbean music, is a contributor to *JEMF Quarterly* and *Black Music in Britain*. He has published many articles for specialist music journals.

Frank Driggs was a major contributor of photographs and memorabilia for the book. His background includes writing, lecturing, producing jazz concerts, running a nightclub, and producing jazz records. For RCA Victor he has produced more than two hundred Bluebird titles, and for Columbia he produced multi-album sets by Fletcher Henderson, Duke Ellington, and Billie Holiday, as well as blues albums by Robert Johnson, Leadbelly, and Leroy Carr. His work has been recognized by

down beat in the U.S. and by *Jazz Journal* in the U.K. He has received awards from the Academie Charles Cros and has earned several Grand Prix du Disque (Montreux) record-of-the-year honors. His collection of jazz and popular music memorabilia is the largest in the world.

David Evans is professor of music at Memphis State University, where he directs a doctorate program in Southern Regional Music Studies. He is the author of *Tommy Johnson* (1971) and *Big Road Blues: Tradition and Creativity in the Folk Blues* (1982). He is a producer for High Water Records.

Mark A. Humphrey is a Los Angeles-based freelance writer. His passion is American roots music, about which he has written for publications as diverse as *Esquire* and *Old Time Music*. He has performed on National Public Radio and throughout Southern California. Humphrey teaches music through the artist-in-residence program sponsored by the State Arts Council of Oklahoma, his native state.

Jim O'Neal, cofounder of *Living Blues: A Journal of the African-American Blues Tradition* and co-owner of Rooster Blues Records, spent most of his early years in Mississippi and Alabama, but didn't get hooked on the blues until he was a college student in Chicago. After graduating from Northwestern University's Medill School of Journalism, O'Neal remained in Chicago for sixteen years, editing and publishing *Living Blues* with Amy van Singel. He returned to Mississippi in 1986 and now operates the Rooster Blues label and Stackhouse Recording Studio with Patty Johnson in Clarksdale.

Barry Pearson, professor of English at the University of Maryland, has written two books and more than forty articles, reviews, and liner notes on the subject of African American traditional and popular music. He has conducted oral history work with hundreds of blues performers and used these in writing *Sounds So Good to Me: The Bluesman's Story.* He is also the author of *Virginia Piedmont Blues: The Lives and Art of Two Virginia Bluesmen.* He is currently at work on *Blues and African American Community Life.* Pearson works extensively with such organizations as the Smithsonian Folklife Festival and the Library of Congress Folklife Center. He is vice president of the National Council for the Traditional Arts and has toured for the Arts America Program of the U.S. Information Agency as a performing musician visiting Africa and South and Central America.

Richard K. Spottswood is the editor of the *Folk Music in America* series produced by the Library of Congress. He has been contributing editor to *Bluegrass Unlimited* since 1966 and is producer and host of "The Dick Spottswood Show" for WAMU-FM radio in Washington, D.C. He is the compiler of the standard seven-volume guidebook, *Ethnic Music on Records.*

Charles Wolfe is the author of nine books and many articles on country music, blues, and folk music, including *Tennessee Strings, Kentucky Country, DeFord Bailey,* and (with Kip Lornell) *The Life and Legend of Leadbelly.* He has been nominated three times for Grammy Awards for his liner notes and work as a producer. A professor at Middle Tennessee State University, Wolfe has worked extensively on historical recording reissues, including several distinguished series for Time-Life Music.